Up from History

Up from History

THE LIFE OF

BOOKER T. WASHINGTON

Robert J. Norrell

—

THE BELKNAP PRESS OF

HARVARD UNIVERSITY PRESS

CAMBRIDGE, MASSACHUSETTS

LONDON, ENGLAND

2009

LIBRARY OF CONGRESS CATALOGING-IN-PUBLICATION DATA

Norrell, Robert J. (Robert Jefferson)

Up from history : the life of Booker T. Washington /
Robert J. Norrell.

p.   cm.

Includes bibliographical references and index.

ISBN 978-0-674-03211-8

1. Washington, Booker T., 1856–1915.

2. African Americans—Biography.

3. Educators—United States—Biography.   I. Title.

E185.97.W4N67 2009

370.92—dc22

[B]   2008032599

FOR KATIE, LEILA, JAY, AND ELIZA

Contents

Illustrations

Up from History

Prologue

The Meaning of the Veil

As the sun rose on October 24, 1905, the air carried an unseasonable chill in Tuskegee, Alabama, a little town filled with visitors atwitter with expectation about the arrival of President Theodore Roosevelt. Wagons and carriages filled the town square and the shaded roads running into the town. Mules, horses, oxen, and people clogged the dirt street heading northwesterly toward the black college, Tuskegee Institute. The crowds included not only many black farm families who came regularly to the school but also whites who had come for the first time to see a president of the United States—and his friend Booker T. Washington, the principal of Tuskegee Institute, the most famous and most powerful black man in America.[1]

At least two visitors, armed white Pinkerton detectives from New York City, had come to the little town not to see the president but to keep an eye out for other white men who had sworn violence against his friend. Threats against the life of Booker Washington had been pouring into Tuskegee for weeks. A white man living not far from the town had vowed to turn his shotgun on the famous black man, in relaxed confidence that any jury in Alabama would rule the murder a justifiable homicide. For the past few days the detectives had been moving around Tuskegee and the nearby villages listening to talk and watching for the assassins who had promised to be there. They had

1. In 1905 Booker T. Washington led both Tuskegee Institute and African Americans in general. Photo by Frances Benjamin Johnston; courtesy of the Library of Congress.

observed some young hotheads talking loosely in train depots, and at a Tuskegee hotel they had heard a man with a German accent condemn Washington as a fraud and a perpetrator of rank immorality. But as they inspected the town and then the Institute campus at first light this morning, no danger was apparent. It was likely to present itself only once the two famous men were together.[2]

Booker T. Washington awaited the president in his big brick house on the campus. A stocky, light brown man of forty-nine years, about five feet nine inches tall, Washington had grown a little heavy over the past decade, years that coincided with constant work, much travel, and incessant worry. His gray eyes, now a little cloudy and marked beneath with dark circles, looked out from a usually placid face with a penetrating intelligence at odds with his genial, slow speech. Perhaps no other man in the United States had a better command of contemporary events and issues—certainly those that pertained to the South—than Washington. He read omnivorously, corresponded voluminously, and listened more intently to a wider variety of perspectives than the best journalists in America, none of whom had been born a slave to an illiterate mother and to a father who never claimed him. Washington personified the power of a man to educate himself.

His abilities were widely appreciated. The most powerful men in the country shared their thoughts with him, and at least three earlier U.S. presidents had sought his opinions. The wealthiest men in America—Andrew Carnegie, John D. Rockefeller, J. Pierpont Morgan, John Wanamaker, Henry H. Rogers, George Eastman, Collis P. Huntington—admired his ability, common with their own, to build a great enterprise as he sought to integrate the aspirations of his beleaguered people into the booming American industrial economy. Carnegie alternately declared Washington the new Moses and the second father of the country after Booker's namesake and fellow Virginian. Mark Twain, William Dean Howells, and other noted men of letters admired his writing. People all over the world had read Washington's autobiography *Up from Slavery* and had taken from it instruction and inspiration about how to improve their own lives. The trustees and presidents of Harvard, Yale, Princeton, and Columbia regularly invited him to their institutions, and both Harvard and Dartmouth had given him honorary degrees—the latter in 1901 having transformed this former slave who had neither a high school nor a college education into "Dr. Washington."

But his appeal extended far beyond the circles of the wealthy, the powerful, and the educated. Over the previous decade, average Americans black and white had been clamoring to hear Washington's inspirational and humorous speeches. Each year he spoke scores of times all over the United States, often to audiences numbering in the thousands, about how African Americans could and would rise in American society and how relations between blacks and whites were becoming more peaceful. His prophecies about a better future for his race, and about a harmonious life among all Americans, won him wide popularity among blacks, who did more than just gather in huge throngs to listen: each year hundreds of African-American mothers named their boy babies "Booker T." Whites who went skeptically to hear the famous Negro usually left amazed and often persuaded by his message of hope.

Washington surely anticipated Theodore Roosevelt's visit with keen appreciation. The two men were close political allies, united in their affection for the Republican Party and in their commitment to bold and virtuous exercise of power. He and Teddy had been close for four years now, almost from the day that the powerful office fell unexpectedly to Roosevelt. The new president had invited the black man to Washington to talk about Republican policies in the South, and one of their meetings, over dinner at the White House, unleashed a racial crisis in the South. A U.S. senator from South Carolina announced that Roosevelt and Washington had committed an act so obnoxious that it would require "lynching a thousand niggers in the South before they will learn their place again." A leading southern newspaper declared that Roosevelt had taught the lesson that any black man who had enough money to pay the perfumer "for scents enough to take away the nigger smell" now had the right to court any white man's daughter. A popular song on minstrel and vaudeville stages went "coon, coon, coon, Booker Washington is his name . . . I think I'd class Mr. Roosevelt with a coon, coon, coon." And the memory of the dinner did not die. Two years later Governor James K. Vardaman of Mississippi insisted that the White House was "so saturated with the odor of the nigger that the rats have taken refuge in the stable."[3]

Even so, Washington and Roosevelt had put forward their political agenda with a determination that had not faltered so far. Booker had found suitable black candidates for federal office, and Teddy had appointed them, in spite of hysterical opposition from the white South. But now, in 1905, Roosevelt was traveling through the South making peace with whites there by reminding them of his mother's Georgia origins and by lauding the heroism of old Confederates in every city from Richmond to New Orleans. He had quietly stopped appointing blacks to office, and he had not invited Booker to dinner again. At the moment, Washington was not quite sure where he stood with the president.

The past year had left Booker in a far less comfortable position than his friend. A litany of slurs flung at him burdened his mind. Exactly a year earlier in the Tuskegee courthouse, his congressman, Tom Heflin, had attacked him as a liar and troublemaker, a fomenter of racial strife, a dangerous Negro. He had threatened to lynch Washington—not a warning to take lightly from a man who only the day before had beaten up his Republican opponent and would later shoot a black man on a streetcar. Not long after that, a book appeared alleging that Tuskegee Institute allowed fraudulent teaching and rampant immorality and criminality on the campus. A few weeks later a man whom Washington knew not at all, Congressman Tom Watson of Georgia, had assailed Washington for teaching blacks that they were better than whites, a patently false accusation but one that caused a stir across the white South. Watson insisted that whites needed to put the arrogant Negro in his place. And in August 1905 yet another stranger, the novelist Thomas Dixon Jr. of North Carolina, had portrayed Booker as a wolf in sheep's clothing, a sneaky conspirator to create racial equality, a Negro trying to raise his race's economic status over whites'. When that happened, Dixon warned, southern whites would start killing blacks, and blame for the violence would rest at Washington's feet.[4]

The assaults by the three Toms did not exhaust Washington's troubles. A small but loud group of northern blacks had intensified their opposition to his nominal leadership of the race. Their hostility had emerged just after Booker had gained national attention as a result of a speech at the Cotton States Exposition in Atlanta in 1895. There he had proposed what he hoped would be a solution to the Negro Problem, the vexing issue about the place of blacks in the United States. At a time when white hatred of blacks was intensifying, manifested in an epidemic of lynchings, Washington had proposed these terms for racial peace: "In all things that are purely social we can be as separate as the fingers, yet one as the hand in all things essential to mutual progress." He went on to say that agitation for social equality was folly and to call for blacks to seek industrial skills as the means to economic improvement. The Atlanta Exposition speech thrust Washington forward as the leader of his race at precisely the moment when African Americans were casting about for someone to replace Frederick Douglass, who had died earlier that year.[5]

To his detractors, Booker Washington seemed a poor replacement. An escaped slave, Douglass had been the most prominent black abolitionist, angrily denouncing the evil of slavery both on the stump and in the newspapers he edited. During the Civil War he had forcefully advocated the rights of black soldiers and of all African Americans to Abraham Lincoln, and for three decades afterward Douglass had championed delivery of the civil rights promised to the freed people. Douglass had consciously projected himself as a heroic figure whose success in American society served as a standard for the potential betterment of all blacks. As a racial leader he had unhesitatingly spoken truth to power about black conditions and the righteousness of blacks' claims to equality. Washington's ascension to leadership as Douglass's anointed successor came at a dark time for African Americans. Between 1895 and 1905 most southern states had disfranchised black voters, instituted segregation in most public places, and tolerated white terrorism against blacks. Among his black critics, each denial of a constitutional right, every indignity against a black railroad patron, and every lynching became a mark against Washington's leadership. His efforts to conciliate the white South in order to reduce racial tensions seemed to some northern blacks only cowardice, when what they wanted was a protest lion like Douglass.[6]

Until 1901 black criticism of Washington had been steady but not sensational. Then began the remorseless verbal violence of William Monroe Trotter, editor of the Boston *Guardian*. Trotter called Washington, among other things, "the Benedict Arnold of the Negro race,"

"the Great Traitor," and a "miserable toady" as he condemned virtually all Booker's actions and many of his statements. In the view of
Trotter and a few like-minded men, he had sold out black political
rights, capitulated to Jim Crow discrimination, and promoted inferior
education for blacks. Trotter's ham-fisted attacks eventually undermined his efforts, but the anti-Booker cause found more effective advocacy in the sophistry of Trotter's comrade W. E. Burghardt Du Bois.
In 1903 Du Bois challenged Washington's leadership with a widely
read critique that put Trotter's complaints in much more palatable
form. He wrote that Washington had willingly accepted disfranchisement, segregation, and inferior education in an unmanly compromise
to achieve peace with the white South. The challenges had pitched
Washington into action against them, with few significant results.
During the summer of 1905 Trotter and Du Bois had formed an organization, the Niagara Movement, to launch a frontal assault against
Washington's leadership of the race. Only a handful had joined their
cause, but they had got a lot of attention that Booker resented.

All these enemies and more had laid siege to Washington in August
1905 in response to a report, at least partly false, that he had entered
the dining room of a resort hotel in Saratoga Springs, New York, with
the daughter of John Wanamaker, the department store magnate, on
his arm. The Wanamaker incident was viewed in the South as a defiant assertion of social equality. Nearly every southern newspaper had
called him a vile corruptor of the social order. It was time, Governor
Vardaman said, that Tuskegee Institute and its principal be removed
once and for all from the South. In the aftermath of that controversy
had come the threats on his life—and therefore the presence of the
Pinkerton agents in the town on the morning of October 24.

Booker was facing all these troubles at a time of personal loss. Since
1895 he had depended on William Baldwin, a successful railroad executive, to advise him on all matters related to the Institute and many
of those concerning his racial leadership. He and Baldwin had established a reciprocal candor that Washington experienced with no other
white person. Baldwin had died of cancer the previous January. Over
the same decade Booker's closest black confidant had been Timothy
Thomas Fortune, the leading black newspaper editor of the day and

the black man most active in promoting Washington as the nominal leader of the race. Washington had hired him to write and edit, and occasionally lent him money, and the two men had become close allies on matters involving Republican politics and divisions among blacks. They typically saw eye to eye on people and politics. But Fortune had a serious drinking problem that worsened over the years. In early 1904 he had attacked Washington for making an allegedly demeaning statement about blacks, and the two men had a bitter argument. Washington withdrew from Fortune, who in turn abandoned his old friend in favor of the whiskey bottle. Thus at a low point in his public life, as he faced the opprobrium of the Toms, Trotter, Du Bois, and innumerable whites screaming for his head after the Wanamaker affair, Booker had few friends to turn to.

On this chilly morning, the president's train first stopped in the town. There the thick-chested, mustachioed Roosevelt peered through his pince-nez and made a brief speech that was politely received, notwithstanding the animus felt toward him by most white southerners for the past four years. When he had finished his remarks the president and his party proceeded by train along a track extending to the Institute, a mile away.[7]

The president witnessed the striking physical achievement that was Tuskegee Institute, which sprawled up and down a series of low hills. In the twenty-four years since its founding, thirty-three buildings had been erected, most of them multistoried structures made from red bricks manufactured on the campus. The students had erected the buildings with materials purchased by captains of American industry. Their names were chiseled above the doors—Carnegie, Rockefeller, and Huntington. Beyond the campus center sprawled almost 2,000 acres of land devoted to vegetable production, livestock husbandry, and cotton cultivation—in the process of being picked, but not today— much of it overseen by the brilliant but eccentric horticulturalist George Washington Carver.

Tuskegee Institute embodied the will of Booker T. Washington. There had been nothing, not one acre of land or one building, when he arrived in 1881, and the only public financial support was a $2,000 annual state appropriation. He had traveled the countryside on foot to recruit his first students, and when a rapidly growing stream of poor Negroes had arrived at the Tuskegee Normal Institute, he had put them to work constructing a campus. After launching the construction, Booker traveled throughout the nation seeking financial support for what he had begun in Alabama. He asked for help so persuasively and so persistently that his school grew rapidly—one new building after another to accommodate the ever-growing enrollment. Now it was one of the largest institutions of higher education in the United States, with an endowment of more than a million dollars. The barons of American capitalism—men who had built railroad networks, integrated steel operations, formed oil monopolies, and perfected huge emporiums for retailing thousands of goods—all admired Washington's capacity for organization and execution of a plan. Like them, he was a builder; unlike them, he had achieved his dream with the considerable handicap of being black.

Once Roosevelt and Washington had greeted each other at Booker's house, the two friends got into a carriage built by the students and rode a short distance to the campus reviewing stand, from which the president could look across the campus to where the horticulture department had planted a large bed of Coleus plants, their deep crimson and auburn still glowing in the Alabama autumn, spelling out "Roosevelt." Over the next hour the Institute's 1,500 students—one of the largest student bodies in the country—paraded before the president. The Institute band led the procession, followed by all the male students marching in military formation in brass-buttoned blue uniforms, white gloves, and cadet caps. Then came the women students in blue dresses with a red braid and blue straw hats, each of them carrying a stalk of sugarcane tipped with a cotton boll. They were followed by sixty-one floats representing all the educational activities of the school. On the millinery department's float, four girls trimmed and draped blue silk on the girdle and collars of what would soon be a hat. On the blacksmiths' rolling demonstration, four boys heated and forged iron to make a wheel. The electrical division's float showed how wire was run from pole to pole. On the floats representing academic subjects, one student was reading President Roosevelt's book *The Winning of the West,* and another was reciting the terms of the Portsmouth Peace

Treaty, which Roosevelt had just negotiated to end the Russo-Japanese War and which would shortly bring him the Nobel Peace Prize.[8]

After the parade Washington, Roosevelt, and as many of the throng as could fit inside moved across to the chapel, where the 150-voice Institute choir sang a program of Negro spirituals. Then Booker Washington introduced the president: "That the Chief Magistrate of our beloved Republic of 80,000,000 people deemed it good and wise to include Tuskegee Institute in his trip through the South, and [to] spend hours in seeing the work we are doing here, brings to the heart of every man and woman of our race in this country, a degree of encouragement and inspiration which it is impossible for any American citizen, not of our race, fully to appreciate." Booker Washington had made it a special mission of his work to point out to his fellow blacks any and all evidence for encouragement and hope.[9]

At the podium, speaking extemporaneously at first, Roosevelt said that his words could not possibly stir anyone there as much as he had been inspired by what he had seen on the Tuskegee campus. "Mr. Washington, it is a liberal education just to come here and see this great focus of civilization." He had read about the achievement at Tuskegee and believed in it heartily, "but I did not realize the extent of your work." He would not have come to Tuskegee on this day if the school only trained its students in intelligence without teaching morality, or if it taught industrial efficiency without training in character. "It is because Tuskegee stands for the moral, as well as the mental and physical side of training, that I will do all I can to help Tuskegee. It is for that reason I have the right to appeal to every white man to stand by this institution." The president was himself a moralist, and he, like most white Americans of the day, believed that blacks especially needed moral education.[10]

Having expressed genuine affection and support for Washington in his impromptu remarks, the president moved on to his prepared speech, which Booker had carefully vetted. Indeed, it might have been a speech that Washington himself delivered, except he would have done it with more style and humor. Roosevelt made a bland, diplomatic appeal for the importance of black education—indeed, the usefulness of black schooling to whites as much as to blacks themselves. "The work of the Tuskegee Normal and Industrial Institute is a matter of the highest practical importance to both the white man and the black man, and well worth the support of both races alike in the South and in the North." Ignorance was the costliest crop raised in America, whether it was the black or white variety, and "merely from the economic standpoint it is of the utmost consequence to all our citizens that institutions such as this at Tuskegee should be a success." Similarly, it was in the interests of whites to provide justice to blacks, "to see that the Negro is protected in property, in life, and in all his legal rights." Roosevelt did not directly condemn white southerners for lynching, even though extralegal executions of blacks had been a blight on the South since the 1880s. He did assert that such calamities did not occur in Tuskegee—a tribute to the salutary effects of the school on the town. To the assembled blacks, the president emphasized the race's progress in recent times, but he immediately moved to their heavy responsibilities in the future: clean living, more education, and thrift were needed. Patience was not only a virtue but a necessity: "The race cannot expect to get everything at once. It must learn to wait and bide its time." And it should remember that "the white man who can be of most use to the black man is that black man's neighbor."[11]

To the relief of the Pinkertons, the Secret Service, and the Institute staff who had seen the threats mailed to Washington, no attack occurred. Even though it was lunchtime when the parades and speeches were over, no repast was offered the president at the Institute, notwithstanding the evident bounty of the Institute truck garden. Such hospitality was just too dangerous at the moment.

As Roosevelt's train pulled away from the Institute, Washington must have been relieved that things had gone so well. The president had honored him at a time when most whites scorned him. Despite four years of unrelenting condemnation for his political alliance with the Tuskegee principal, Roosevelt had come to Tuskegee when the air remained full of angry, ugly denunciations of the black leader. His presence symbolized his loyalty to a political friend, to a man unfairly condemned for doing his job as leader of his race. Washington surely hoped at that moment that the troubles of recent months were past, and that he would reclaim the mastery of events he had usually demonstrated.

His instinct was to believe that the future would be better than the present. He had never failed at any job he had undertaken, and he was hardly willing to accept defeat as the leader of his people. He assumed that history was the story of progress—for Americans, for black people, and for Booker Washington. He intended to rise from the current trouble, and he was counting on his friend Roosevelt to help him. Optimism was in his view the only practical posture, even if the present often made hopefulness about the future seem like folly.

Now in the twenty-fifth year of his tenure at Tuskegee, in the fiftieth year of his life, Booker Washington must have thought that day about his journey. Even the dullest of men in their later years—the average black man's life expectancy in 1905 was thirty-five—feel compelled to assess the meaning of their lives, and Booker was without question one of the most acute men of his time. He was known to sit silently with his family in deep contemplation thinking about things that were a great unknown to those who loved him. He rarely reflected openly on his own experience. He was a busy man, and the natural impulse of his personality was to do and not to talk—and to look forward, not backward. The past was something to overcome, a place from which one moved on. History was a benchmark against which to measure one's progress and that of one's people.

It would take another decade to determine whether Booker Washington would recover his mastery, although the coming year, 1906, would be the turning point for his leadership. Both trouble and triumph lay ahead. He would face the betrayal of men whom he had helped and relied on. He would have to confront the reality that he would not achieve all he intended, and, as for most masterful men, that became one of his greatest challenges.

Virtually everyone who came into contact with Booker Washington during his lifetime was curious about, even fascinated with, his personal story, for indeed it was a remarkable saga of movement up from slavery. But hardly was he gone from the scene when the content and meaning of his life became separated from the realities he had lived. The first lost truth was the ugly opposition of southern whites to Washington's strategy of economic and educational improvement. The violent imaginations of the Vardamans, Tillmans, and Dixons were no longer connected to the black man they hated most during their political activities. Somehow the memory became that Washington was beloved by all whites, mainly because he was friendly to them and gave no offense. He came to be remembered as a great Negro because there were physical reminders of his greatness—the hundreds of segregated schools and other black institutions named for him, the thousands of African-American men who were his namesakes. People assumed that he must have been a great man to have had so many people and things named for him. The fading reality resulted in the common confusion of Washington with the famous horticulturalist on his faculty, George Washington Carver, whose greatness was much easier to explain to subsequent generations. The presence of two famous men from Tuskegee, both bearing the name Washington, often prompted the question about Booker, "Wasn't he the one who used the peanut in so many ways?"

By the 1960s, among Americans engaged in the struggle for civil rights, there would be no confusion about who Booker Washington was. His memory was invoked almost entirely to justify diverse positions in the newly accelerated struggle for racial justice. Tuskegee whites romanticized the race relations of Booker's time as pleasant and uncontested in order to condemn the tensions that accompanied the voting-rights challenges—and so forgot the bitter and dangerous times in the town during Washington's life. Blacks throughout the United States increasingly condemned him as having acquiesced in the racial discrimination that so many were now challenging in restaurants, waiting rooms, and courthouses. They called Washington an Uncle Tom who sold out his own people to secure his power and delay the coming of black freedom. They saw no resemblance between him and the great new leader of American blacks, Martin Luther King Jr., who marched into the face of racial bigotry and then went to jail in protest against injustice. Washington accommodated segregation and discrimination rather than challenged it, they said. Washington's contemporary and rival Du Bois became the paradigm of that earlier time: Du Bois had openly and continuously condemned the wrongs of the Jim Crow era, while Washington had given away everything in a cowardly effort to get along with vicious whites.

This demonization took place even in Tuskegee. In the mid-1960s students at the Institute challenged older local civil-rights leaders because they were advising blacks to share power with whites as the best means to build a truly democratic community, even though blacks now had enough votes to take every office. In 1966 a student who had grown up in Tuskegee dismissed one leader's call for moderation by likening him to the most famous local Uncle Tom. The young man had read *Invisible Man,* the brilliant modernist novel by the former Tuskegee student Ralph Ellison about a young man who goes to a grand, all-black school in the Deep South. Ellison portrays the school's leaders as harsh and indifferent to students, indeed to all blacks beneath them. The protagonist, the Invisible Man, describes a sculpture depicting the school's now-dead founder in front of a kneeling slave. Just such a sculpture, *Lifting the Veil of Ignorance,* has been the focal point of the Tuskegee campus since 1922. The Invisible Man describes the founder's "hands outstretched in the breathtaking gesture of lifting a veil that flutters in hard, metallic folds about the face of a kneeling slave; and I am standing puzzled, unable to decide whether the veil is really being lifted, or lowered more firmly in place; whether I am witnessing a revelation or a more efficient blinding."[12]

In 1966 the very visible Tuskegee Institute student angrily declared: "We got this statue out here of that man who's supposed to be lifting up the veil. Man, he's putting it back on." Other interpreters of Booker Washington would take the same stance for at least a generation. John Lewis, the prominent activist from the 1960s who became a high-profile congressman in the 1980s and 1990s, wrote that in his own time Washington had been "ridiculed and vilified by his own people for working so closely with white America." In fact most of the ridicule and vilification came much later. Either way, the congressman assumed that Washington deserved the opprobrium. The result of the assaults on his reputation during the 1960s, a prominent American historian

2. Some observers believed that the statue *Lifting the Veil of Ignorance* was ambiguous in its meaning. Statue by Charles Keck, erected 1922 on the Tuskegee University campus; photo by Robert J. Norrell.

observed in 2003, was that "the tar brush of Uncle Tomism has stuck to Washington."[13]

A significant portion of those wielding the brush were historians who should have been alert to the fallacy of anachronism, of applying 1960s expectations of protest to a man who had lived two generations earlier. The scholar celebrated as Washington's definitive biographer likened him not just to Uncle Tom but also to a minotaur, an amoral and manipulative wizard, and a bargainer with the devil for momentary earthly power. Since the 1960s nearly all other writers have followed that lead in rendering Washington as a villain in African-American history.[14]

This distortion of Washington contributed to a narrowing of the limits Americans have put on black aspirations and accomplishments. After the 1960s, any understanding of the role of black leaders was cast in the context of Martin Luther King Jr.'s leadership, with the implication that African Americans can rise in American life only through direct-action protest against the political order. To be sure, that confrontational approach accounted for King's great success, but as the sole model for group advancement it has not always worked, because it does not apply to all circumstances. Booker Washington's emphasis on educational, moral, and economic development became a lost artifact for most Americans thinking about how to integrate minorities and any other disadvantaged group in the modern world. This outcome is especially ironic given that in the twentieth century Washington's ideas inspired and instructed struggling people throughout the Third World. Washington's style of interracial engagement has been all but forgotten, and when remembered, usually disparaged: he put a premium on finding consensus and empathizing with other groups, and by his example encouraged dominant groups to do the same. He cautioned that when people protest constantly about their mistreatment, they soon get a reputation as complainers, and others stop listening to their grievances. Blacks needed a reputation for being hardworking, intelligent, and patriotic, Washington taught, and not for being aggrieved. The main lesson that people around the world took from Booker Washington was that hope and optimism were crucial ingredients in overcoming the obstacles of past exploitation and present discrimination. Indeed, the ability to imagine a better future was what African Americans needed most in Washington's time. That may be true at all times, for all people, and yet the dismissal and misapprehensions of Washington's message have obscured it in the society he worked so hard to improve.

Booker Washington's response to his circumstances reflected a sophisticated mind that had contrived a complex means for achieving what, by any standard, were high-minded goals. But his was an awful time that set narrow and unjust limits on what he could do to pursue his ends. In Washington's view, his life was not just a struggle up from slavery but also a great effort to rise above history. Given the fate of his historical reputation, that remains the great challenge of his life, now almost a century after it ended. His story therefore deserves to be told anew.

I

The Force That Wins

On a farm nestled among the rolling hills east of Virginia's Blue Ridge Mountains, not far from the village of Hale's Ford, a slave family heard news in April 1865 that the great war waged for the past four years was coming to an end. None of the slaves on the farm of James Burroughs could read, but they knew about the events of war because one of them was sent to fetch the mail at the post office several miles away, and there he listened to what whites were saying as they read their letters and newspapers to one another. A nine-year-old boy named Booker had heard whispered discussions among the slaves throughout the war. His mother, Jane, had knelt over him and his older brother, John, and his little sister, Amanda, sleeping on a bed of rags on the clay floor of their windowless twelve-by-sixteen-foot log cabin, and prayed that Abraham Lincoln would give them freedom. Jane, the Burroughses' cook, had to whisper about such things because she and the children lived just a few yards down a slope from the master's farmhouse. "Even the most ignorant members of my race in the remote plantations felt in their hearts," Booker remembered, "with a certainty that admitted of no doubt, that the freedom of the slaves would be the one great result of the war, if the Northern armies conquered."[1]

The slaves knew the good news well before they could celebrate it. They heard about the surrender on April 13 at Appomattox Courthouse, which lay only fifty miles to the east of the Burroughs farm. Unsure how their master would respond to losing his slave property, they pretended not to know that anything unusual had happened. The habit of long years of dissembling, of hiding their own thoughts and feelings, still governed their actions. Jane and the other slaves felt certain that James Burroughs was not going to be happy about the prospect of losing valuable property. But a few weeks later they were summoned to the Burroughses' house, where a Union army officer read a declaration of their emancipation. "Now, my children, we are free," Jane said, but still she whispered as they returned to their cabin to contemplate a new life. Soon Jane, her children, and the other slaves—now free people—expressed their feelings about their new condition. "There was great rejoicing, and thanksgiving, and wild scenes of ecstasy," Booker remembered.[2]

His light-brown skin, reddish-brown hair, and gray eyes revealed Booker's white paternity, just as the broad nose and coarse hair marked his African inheritance from Jane. "Who my father was," Booker later wrote, "I have never been able to learn with any degree of certainty." He may well have known who his father was, and this statement may have reflected the old black habit of not telling a white person anything the latter did not want to hear. Jane almost certainly knew the identity of his father, and the evidence was most likely handed down within the family. A century later, Booker's daughter insisted that his father was Ben Hatcher, a hard-drinking blacksmith. According to the family tradition, Jane had run away from the Burroughs place, Hatcher had taken her in, and when Burroughs reclaimed her, Jane was pregnant with Booker. No one but Jane could have been certain, and there were other possibilities among the white men in the area. White men freely had their way with slave women. Jane would have been hard pressed to resist the advances of James Burroughs, his numerous sons, or the near neighbor Josiah Ferguson, who had fathered many children with slave women. She had already yielded to, or had been forced to consort with, another white man: Booker's brother, John, was thought to be the child of one of the master's sons. Although they were slaves and therefore in an inferior position in every way, Jane and her chil-

dren existed in intimate connection—sexually, spatially, and psychologically—with the whites around them.[3]

It surely mattered to Booker more than he later admitted who his
father was. No reality surpasses that one in significance to human beings. It most assuredly made his life seem even more insecure than it
already was, first as a slave and then as an adolescent in the chaotic
world of black emancipation. He must have envied those who had the
love and guiding hand of a father. "Whoever he was, I never heard of
his taking the least interest in me or providing in any way for my rearing," he later said, a statement that came as close as the secretive and
self-protective adult Booker would ever get to expressing justifiable
resentment. That his father was a white man and one who did not acknowledge him only exacerbated the uncertainty of Booker's identity.
But where he might be construed as criticizing a white man, Booker
held on to the slave mask of self-protection even more tightly. "I do
not find especial fault with him," he said of his deadbeat father. Such a
declaration strains credulity: the abandoning father rejected him, he
must have suspected, because his Negro blood canceled out the paternal responsibility for love and nurture and made Booker unworthy. In
a statement of unbelievable humility, Booker later excused the white
man: "He was simply another unfortunate victim of the institution
which the Nation unhappily had engrafted upon it at that time." Perhaps that was true, and perhaps Booker believed it at some level, but it
represented a superhuman generosity that obscured the emotional pain
and insecurity of a fatherless childhood.[4]

Booker came somewhat closer to the truth in remembering his slave
existence. "My life had its beginning in the midst of the most miserable, desolate, and discouraging surroundings," he wrote. Burroughs
owned ten slaves, six of them children. In 1861, when he was five years
old, Booker had been valued at $400, John at $550. In Jane's drafty
cabin—the door did not fill its frame—large pots and kitchen uten-
sils crowded in upon the family. Jane cooked almost constantly over
an open fire that heated the small space ferociously in summer; the
smells of burning oak and smoking meat pervaded the dark structure.
Booker sometimes rose alone and scavenged for his breakfast outside

by picking up kernels of boiled corn intended for the cows and pigs. Never during his childhood did the entire family sit down at the table, ask God's blessing, and enjoy a meal together. Booker's clothing consisted only of uncomfortable wooden-soled shoes and a shirt made of rough flax worn previously by John to soften the bristles. It was the first of many acts of kindness John showed his little brother.[5]

The Burroughs place was a small farm of just over 200 acres where master and slaves lived virtually together. Booker played with the Burroughs children and grandchildren. "We rode together our wooden horses," Booker recalled. "We fished together in the nearby streams; we played marbles, town-ball, 'tag,' and wrestled together on the parlour floor." A Burroughs grandson remembered his childhood the same way but added that Booker was "rather slow" and John was "bright as a dollar"—an interesting misjudgment of Booker and probably a reflection of John's common blood with the Burroughs. Three of James Burroughs's six sons served the Confederacy, and when the body of Marse Billy was brought home, the slaves mourned with the Burroughs family, just as they rejoiced when the other two made it back injured but alive.[6]

Booker worked at small tasks, taking water to workers in the fields and cleaning the yards around the Burroughs house. His most challenging job was to take corn, loaded in sacks onto a horse, three miles to a gristmill for grinding, an assignment fraught with anxiety because he was not large enough at age seven or eight to lift the bags back onto the horse when they inevitably slid off. Another chore awakened in him a great desire. He accompanied the Burroughs children to school to carry their books and food and to return a horse to the farm. This experience sparked an early awareness of the injustice of his condition: although he constantly played and worked with the Burroughs children and grandchildren, activities that undoubtedly fostered a sense of their common interests and equal endowment in abilities, he was forbidden to share in their education. He expressed his resentment to Jane, who explained that it was just a reality of the slave's condition. "From the moment that it was made clear to me that I was not to go to school," he said, "that it was dangerous for me to learn to read, from that moment I resolved that I should never be satisfied until I learned what this dangerous practice was like."[7]

Booker remembered his master as not especially cruel in a system that allowed, even condoned, violence to slaves. Although he must have seen more instances of mistreatment, he later recounted only one episode of physical cruelty that he witnessed during slavery. For some unspecified crime, his uncle Monroe Burroughs was stripped naked, tied to a tree, and struck repeatedly with a leather whip. The scene made a deep impression on the boy Booker. "As each blow touched his back," he wrote, "the cry 'Pray, master! Pray, master!' came from his lips." He told of his uncle's beating without damning commentary, and he did so only for a black audience. Perhaps he thought that the description spoke for itself, or maybe the memory was too painful to say more. And there is the real possibility that, in the intimate living situation of the Burroughs farm, much less cruelty in fact occurred than would have on a large plantation run by overseers. The cruelty of slavery was something Booker acknowledged, but he kept the personal experience of it behind his public mask.[8]

Jane was the figure most responsible for shaping her son's character. She stole eggs to feed her children, an act that Booker later excused as a necessity arising from the conditions of slavery. But once freed, she enforced a strict code of honesty in all things. She instilled the virtues of hard work and thrift, and although she could not read, she had an abundance of common sense that enabled her to meet the many obstacles to the survival of her family. Jane sympathized with Booker's keen desire to learn to read, and she did all she could to help him do so. Her determination, resourcefulness, and ambition were a model for Booker. "If I have done anything in life worth attention," he later wrote, "I feel sure that I inherited the disposition from my mother." His admiration for her may have been amplified because there was no father from whom to learn or to whom he could express filial love. The unnamed white father deserved no credit and got none.[9]

Jane acted on her emancipation as most former slaves did, by leaving the site of her servitude. She took her children to West Virginia to be with Washington Ferguson, her husband and Amanda's father.

Ferguson had fled Hale's Ford during the war years, following the Union Army, and had ended up working in salt mines to the west. Wash Ferguson had been around Jane's cabin enough for Booker to know him, but he apparently never developed any affection for the man. There is no evidence to suggest either that Ferguson wanted to fill the place of a father for all the children or that Booker desired it. Booker may have felt a sense of competition with Ferguson for Jane's affection, and he may have had misgivings about leaving familiar surroundings to live with a man for whom he eventually developed an active dislike. But a nine-year-old did not have veto authority in Jane's household. The journey from Hale's Ford to Malden, near Charleston, West Virginia, was about 200 miles, and it took Jane and the three young children several weeks to hike over the Blue Ridge of Virginia and then through the mountains beyond that shaped most of their path westward. Booker and his siblings walked the distance with Jane, their few possessions piled in a small wagon, usually sleeping in the open air and cooking over a campfire. Once they attempted to sleep in an abandoned cabin, only to be driven out by a snake. Booker remembered the long trip over the mountains as a great adventure.[10]

In Malden the family settled into a small shanty—its windows representing an improvement over their old slave cabin—beneath a railroad embankment in a squalid neighborhood. There the stench of rotting garbage and human waste mingled with the acrid smell of burning coal. Coal soot from railroad engines and chimneys blanketed every surface. Part of the area was populated by poor whites who drank, gambled, and fought. Life in an industrial village contrasted starkly with the quiet days and clean air of Hale's Ford, and the difference appears to have shaped Booker's later preference for the rural life. Close proximity to working-class whites risked conflict, and the unhealthiness of living conditions bothered him.[11]

Ferguson took Booker and John with him to the saltworks, where he received the benefit of the boys' labor. Wash seems to have represented to Booker forced drudgery with no compensating nurture or affection. But Booker demonstrated his practical nature in deferring to Ferguson's wishes. At some point the boy began working in a coal mine that supplied fuel to the saltworks. There he felt a deep dread of

3. Booker's first home as a free person, in Malden, West Virginia. Photo by Frank Beard; from Booker T. Washington, *The Story of My Life and Work* (Atlanta: J. L. Nichols, 1901).

the darkness, a fear of being lost underground, and anxiety about explosions and falling rock. "I do not believe that one ever experiences anywhere else such darkness as he does in a coal-mine," he later wrote. He hated the all-pervading grime and feared the long-lasting effects of mining. He felt certain that boys who worked in such places became mentally and physically dwarfed, unable to do anything else with their lives.[12]

What Booker wanted was education, the desire kindled outside the Burroughs children's school. In this he saw himself as typical of the time. There was great enthusiasm for schooling among blacks in Malden. They had organized their own school, and Booker wanted badly to go. "It was a whole race trying to go to school," he later wrote. "Few were too young, and none too old, to make the attempt to learn." He witnessed a young black man from Ohio read aloud a newspaper to a gathering of illiterate freed people, an achievement that incited both admiration and envy in young Booker. Thereafter newspapers represented knowledge about the world that he wanted desperately to have.[13]

Wash Ferguson saw no purpose in education for Booker or his siblings, and indeed he kept Booker from going to school during the early days in Malden. This decision appears to have been the main source of trouble between Booker and Wash. "My stepfather had discovered that I had a financial value," Booker later reported with chilly detachment, "and so when the school opened, he decided that he could not spare me from my work." At first unwilling to challenge her husband directly, Jane somehow came to her son's rescue when she got him a copy of Webster's blue-back spelling book, from which Booker learned the alphabet on his own with the aid of nighttime tutoring from the teacher at the local school. He sometimes hired another student for a few cents to teach him the day's lessons at night. Finally Jane persuaded Ferguson to let him go to school if Booker worked from four to nine A.M. at the saltworks, and then again after school. So anxious was he to get to school that Booker secretly set the saltworks clock forward a few minutes to enable him to arrive at school sooner.[14]

At school, he discovered that he needed a surname. The lack of one may have reflected his questionable paternity, or perhaps it revealed his disaffection from his stepfather. Booker spontaneously came up with the name Washington, a name that associated him forever with the American nation and its father. He later discovered that his mother considered Taliaferro his surname, and so he took that as his middle name. Thus "Booker T. Washington" was from the outset an adopted, public persona that Booker shaped to his own ends. Booker T. Washington would be ever careful to present a character acceptable to the outside world, especially to dominant whites. As a slave he learned how to dissemble, and he perfected the ability while a nominally free adolescent. He tried to control carefully what people saw of him as a means of gaining approval. With that appreciation secured, he had room to act on his inner desires. The inner Booker was emerging as a personality determined to fulfill ambitions higher than anyone could imagine for a slave boy and to control his fate as much as possible.[15]

He would maintain the separation between the public presentation and the inner person throughout his life. The duality would protect him from occasional later battering of the public Booker T. Washington. The separation also obscured many things about him from the curious, both during his lifetime and afterward.

4. Booker T. Washington as a teenager, ca. 1872. Photographer unknown; from Booker T. Washington, *Up from Slavery* (Garden City, N.Y.: Doubleday, 1901).

Booker's real educational advancement probably began when he went to work for Viola Ruffner, a white woman from New England and the wife of the owner of the saltworks, the former Union general Lewis Ruffner. Ever the advocate and protector, Jane apparently approached Mrs. Ruffner on Booker's behalf when she heard the white woman was looking for a houseboy, having dismissed a string of young men who had not met her high standards of cleanliness and order. At first Booker did not like the duty either. Ruffner required him to cut the grass in her front yard with a scythe, a task that he failed to perform to her satisfaction even after working at length on his hands and knees. Booker ran away to work as a waiter on an Ohio River steamboat but was fired from that position, returned to Mrs. Ruffner, and begged her for a second chance, which she gave him. At this point he learned either to meet her high standards or to appease a difficult white woman—exactly which is not clear, though both could be true. In any case he seems to have acquired two valuable skills: he became an excellent domestic servant, and he learned how to understand what a white person wanted from him and how to deliver it. Ruffner also introduced him to Puritan, Yankee values, which were significantly different from those of southern whites.

As he demonstrated growing competence in his household chores, Mrs. Ruffner entrusted him with marketing the fruits and vegetables she grew. He learned to account meticulously for every peach sold and every penny collected and to appreciate capitalist enterprise at this most basic level. Here again was Yankee enterprise—disciplined, careful, efficient, and intensely acquisitive.[16]

Booker and Mrs. Ruffner began to trust and like each other. He worked for her for four years, and for much of that time he lived with the family. She took up where Jane's nurture of the personality and character of the inner Booker had left off: she helped him become the intelligent, responsible, hard-working, independent young man he wanted to be—one who deserved to rise above his low beginnings. A pattern began to develop in Booker's life: assigned a job, he did it well, and the recognition of his competence brought him new and larger opportunities, which in turn instilled in him more confidence in his abilities. He developed ambitions for himself. One success after another proved that a young black man, regardless of the deprivation in which he began life, could rise. Competent and self-assured, Booker began to believe that if he could rise, so could almost anyone else who tried.

Viola Ruffner instilled in Booker the essence of what the German sociologist Max Weber later called the Protestant ethic, which taught that the values of industry, sobriety, thrift, self-reliance, and piety accounted for success in modern capitalist societies. Hard work Booker knew at the insistence of his slave master and his stepfather, and by Jane's example, but Mrs. Ruffner taught him the virtue of work. Disciplined toil enabled one to be independent and prosperous. Mrs. Ruffner believed that Booker learned her lessons. "He was always in his place and never known to do anything out of the way," she wrote years later. "He seemed peculiarly determined to emerge from his obscurity.

He was ever restless, uneasy, as if knowing that contentment would mean inaction. 'Am I getting on?'—that was his principal question."[17]

Education was the means to self-help, and Mrs. Ruffner promoted Booker's education. She allowed him time off for school and taught him herself. "He was always willing to quit play for study," she remembered. "He never needed correction or the word, 'Hurry!' or 'Come!' for he was always ready for his book." She gave him books, which formed the beginning of a personal library. Formerly the head of a school English department, she was the first teacher accountable for Booker's excellent verbal skills, both written and oral. She undoubtedly provided the first models of pronunciation and syntax that accounted for the removal from the adult Booker's speech of any significant remnant of the African-American slave dialect. By the time he was a young man he had acquired the ability to communicate comfortably with those who had much more formal education than he. His ability to write and speak effectively in conventional American ways would be a key to Booker T. Washington's success.[18]

Booker learned one crucial, nonacademic lesson while serving the Ruffners. In 1869 a payday fight in Malden between two miners, one black and one white, resulted in an assault charge against the black miner and numerous threats against local blacks from the Ku Klux Klan. When blacks armed themselves to defend the accused man from Klan terrorism, a shootout ensued near the Ruffner home. General Ruffner was the leading Republican in town, the local blacks his most loyal followers. The general, with Booker standing nearby, persuaded the local blacks to withdraw, but when he confronted a white mob, Ruffner was struck by a brick, knocked unconscious, and permanently injured. Subsequent Klan night riders attempted to drive all blacks from Malden. They did not succeed, but neither apparently was any official action taken against white terrorism. The purpose of the white violence, Booker Washington later wrote, was "to crush out the political aspirations of the negroes, but they did not confine themselves to this, because school-houses as well as churches were burned by them, and many innocent persons were made to suffer."[19]

Booker saw in Malden that the dominant group in the post–Civil War South regarded black schools and churches, institutions that rep-

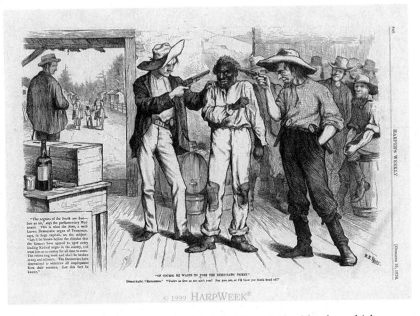

5. Racial conflict between southern whites and free blacks, like that which Booker witnessed in Malden, was the subject of national discussion, as suggested by this cartoon from *Harper's Weekly*, October 21, 1876. Artist unknown.

resented rising black status and independence, as a threat, and as such, they were every bit as vulnerable as the people who filled them. He later remembered thinking at the time that there was no hope for black people in America. Although the thirteen-year-old quickly shed this sense of hopelessness, he assuredly drew a lesson from these events. Racial conflict was so clearly destructive of the interests of black people that it made little sense to engage in it, especially when one saw that the town's most prominent white man could be struck down, apparently without consequence to the attackers, when he tried to thwart other whites who treated blacks as their enemy.[20]

The 1869 conflict served to damp the emerging Republican strength in local politics, but it did not thwart all party activism. In the summer of 1872 the sixteen-year-old secretary of the Malden Republican organization, Booker T. Washington, reported that the membership had resolved that it would not "countenance or support any man who is in any way hostile to the colored people." In fact black Republicans in the postwar South would rarely encounter white politicians who harbored no hostility toward blacks. Booker's youthful participation in the Republican Party suggests an irresistible fascination with the political process, even though he knew from the 1869 Klan riot that politics was a dangerous business for Negroes. Like most recently freed slaves, he believed that democracy should ensure freedom for his people. The need to avoid racial conflict and the desire to engage in the political process were competing instincts that would cause trouble for him all his life.[21]

During the time of his service to the local Republican Party, Booker was planning the most ambitious undertaking of his life so far. While still in the coal mines he had heard two black miners discuss a newly established school for black students at Hampton, on the eastern seaboard of Virginia, a place where poor students could work to earn their tuition and board. Attending Hampton Institute immediately became his ambition, and apparently he viewed his years of work for Mrs. Ruffner as preparation. In September 1872 Booker left Malden with only a vague notion that the school lay far to the east. Wash Ferguson having appropriated most of the wages he had earned, Booker had little cash. His brother John and several older friends had contributed a few coins to his cause, and Jane gave him a small satchel for the clothes he owned.

It took many days to make the 500-mile journey, which was broken into many legs, some on trains, others on stagecoaches. Travel for an almost penniless young Negro was fraught with stress and uncertainty. At least once when his coach stopped at an inn for the night, Booker was refused accommodation and forced to fend for himself outside. After several difficult days he arrived in Richmond, hungry and without money. Unable to beg a night's lodging, he slept under a boardwalk. He worked at a Richmond boat dock for a few days in order to feed himself before undertaking the final 100 miles to Hampton, where he arrived with fifty cents in his pocket.[22]

The campus lay near where Hampton Creek emptied into the Hampton Roads harbor of Chesapeake Bay. To someone who had seen only mountain streams and a few small rivers, the expanse of deep water must have been an astonishing sight. But what most impressed

Booker was the brand-new three-story brick edifice at the center of the campus, Virginia Hall. It struck him as the largest and most beautiful building he had ever seen, and he felt that "a new kind of existence had now begun . . . life would now have a new meaning" in this promised land. Others might have noted that Hampton Institute then consisted of only the one brick building, with dilapidated wooden former army barracks dotting the rest of the low, flat campus. Indeed, Booker would spend one winter living in a tent on the grounds.[23]

Hampton Normal and Agricultural Institute had been established in 1868 on the site where runaway slaves had congregated during the Civil War seeking the protection of the occupying Union Army at Fortress Monroe. The Congregationalists' American Missionary Association (AMA) founded Hampton as one of eight teacher-training schools created for freed people in the South. The concern of northern evangelical Christians for blacks' plight came to the fore as the national government's commitment to uplifting the former slaves began to expire in the late 1860s. The AMA intended to "civilize" the freed people, an undertaking interpreted first to mean the promotion of Christianity consistent with Congregationalist values and morality. The group assumed that many black churches founded at emancipation were places of orgiastic emotion presided over by illiterate and often immoral preachers. Slavery had encouraged wastefulness, unreliability, hedonism, and lack of foresight, all of which had to be unlearned and the Protestant ethic embraced before the freed people could become good Americans and good Christians. Founded to train teachers, Hampton attracted young men and women, many of them older than Booker, who had already acquired a little education and wanted to improve their knowledge and pedagogical skills before returning to the classroom.[24]

The Hampton method for creating a stronger, correctly educated black teacher corps centered upon rigorous discipline in life and work. Students rose at five, marched to class in military style, prayed at appointed hours, and went to bed when a bell rang. Between classes they were required to do extensive manual labor and were expected to recognize the virtue of doing a job well. Unlike most American institutions of higher learning at the time, Hampton was firmly committed to educating men and women on the same campus. The underlying assumption was that both sexes had to acquire the Protestant ethic if freed people were to improve black families and the race in general. Men and women, however, were strictly segregated in their classes, jobs, dormitories, and dining halls. Women students worked mostly as cooks and seamstresses, the men as farm workers, waiters, janitors, carpenters, and painters. Students earned about two dollars per week, which was applied to their monthly board of ten dollars. Their jobs not only enabled students to earn their keep but also gave them a way to support themselves during the months when they were not teaching.[25]

Samuel Chapman Armstrong, who had commanded black troops in Virginia during the Civil War and afterward directed the federal government's Freedmen's Bureau in eastern Virginia, created Hampton and put his unique stamp on it. General Armstrong acted from an unapologetic paternalist posture. The son of a Presbyterian missionary to Hawaii, he believed deeply in his duty to help those who were inferior to him morally and physically, but help was extended strictly on his own terms. The former slaves should look to whites for leadership, at least to those who rejected the exploitation of slavery. He meant to launch the evolutionary progress of blacks by developing their industrial skills and economic independence. To him, teaching industry meant instilling disciplined work habits and strong morality more than teaching specific skills. He rejected the classical curriculum, with its emphasis on reading Latin and appreciating ancient civilizations; courses in English language, mathematics, history, and biology were sufficient for all Hampton students. The education provided at Hampton was about the equivalent of a modern middle-school education, which was deemed sufficient for the training of people expected to teach African Americans in primary schools.[26]

To gain admission to Hampton Institute in the fall of 1872, Booker approached the principal, Mary Mackie, whose embrace of the Protestant ethic was as tight as Viola Ruffner's. His many days of travel had taken a toll on his appearance. Mackie looked over the wiry, five-foot-nine-inch boy in soiled clothes and put him off, although she was admitting other students as Booker waited. Finally she asked him to sweep a recitation room, an assignment he correctly understood as an admissions test. The standard of work he had mastered under Viola Ruffner's tutelage immediately paid off. He swept the room three times and dusted the furnishings four. On inspection, Mackie was satisfied, granted him admission, and gave him a job as janitor. A seventy-dollar scholarship given by a Massachusetts merchant covered Booker's tuition.[27]

One personality dominated Hampton in 1872. Only thirty-three at the time, slender and athletic and blond, Samuel Armstrong represented to the new arrival the most perfect specimen of man. Amateur psychiatrists have speculated that Armstrong might have represented for Booker the white father who had never claimed him. The general certainly acted the part of the authoritarian father, and not just to Booker. He gave students emphatic directions about how to live their lives. "Be thrifty and industrious," he ordered. He never let them lose sight of the white-dominated world in which they lived: "Command the respect of your neighbors by a good record and a good character . . . Cultivate peaceful relations with all." Life would not be easy: "Make the best of your difficulties." Resist falling into bitterness or resentment: "Live down prejudice." Do not be prey to political opportunists: "As a voter act as you think and not as you are told." And they should not be dispirited about the speed of their progress: "Remember you have seen marvellous changes [since 1861]. In view of that be patient—thank God and take courage." Booker grasped each of these admonitions more firmly than most sons would take paternal advice, and indeed he would teach them himself.[28]

The first lessons taught at Hampton focused on personal hygiene and grooming. Students were made regularly to bathe and brush their teeth, to clean their clothes and polish their shoes, and to stand for General Armstrong's inspection of their person. Few if any of the 243 students at Hampton in the fall of 1872 objected to the presumption that their personal habits were subject to scrutiny. Many students lacked basic knowledge of conventional living standards: issued a set of sheets, Booker slept the first night on top of both and the second night under both before discovering the pleasure of rest between the two.[29]

The academic curriculum emphasized language mastery, with specific study of spelling, grammar, composition, rhetoric, elocution, and vocal training. The rhetoric class surely played a significant role in Booker's subsequent prowess as a public speaker. The ability to put forward and defend positions orally was deemed the mark of an educated person and a prerequisite to distinguished citizenship in American democracy in the nineteenth century. Booker studied the speeches of Abraham Lincoln and Frederick Douglass. Nathalie Lord, a Vassar graduate from Maine, taught Booker writing and rhetoric and trained him in public speaking. During chats with Lord while Booker rowed the pretty, precise young teacher on nearby Hampton Creek, he surely acquired more of the New England pronunciation and syntax that he had begun learning from Mrs. Ruffner. The institute's debating societies gave him many opportunities to refine his skills in public speaking, and Booker was soon organizing debates.[30]

A large portion of the Hampton curriculum dwelt on American, English, and world history. Booker acquired a progressive view of history and the presumption of an evolutionary trajectory of civilizations from a strongly triumphalist Anglo-Saxon perspective. Nations and civilizations rose and fell, although the English-speaking Christian people clearly represented the most successful—and perhaps permanently triumphant—group in human history. Races, it was presumed, had distinct and fixed qualities, and some races were decidedly inferior to others, though all peoples could improve themselves if they aspired to rise to the level of the superior northern European races. Although Social Darwinism had not fully infused thinking in the mid-1870s as it would in the next decade, a sense of racial and national competition for survival was taking hold. School texts reinforced the emphasis on comparative civilizations. Booker would later lament the presentation of an inferior and uncivilized nature of Africans when contrasted to Europeans in textbooks. The books he read about Africa, he remembered, "told me of a people who roamed naked through the forest like wild beasts, of a people without houses or laws, without chastity or morality, with no family life and fixed habits of industry." On the other hand, in history classes he studied the lives of the abolitionist Frederick Douglass, Senator Blanche K. Bruce of Mississippi, and Governor P. B. S. Pinchback of Louisiana. Before the emergence of these black exemplars, Booker believed, blacks had had no history of their own; under slavery their experience had been merely an adjunct of whites' history. In his view, free blacks were now moving toward a better future.[31]

As for recent American history, General Armstrong emphasized the evils of slavery and the essential goodness of the American republic, but he did not dwell on the Union triumph of the Civil War, notwithstanding his own contributions to it. African Americans should concentrate on moving beyond the war—indeed, up from that struggle—to address immediate concerns. Booker was surprised that a distinguished Union officer like Armstrong demonstrated no ill will toward white southerners. Instead, "He was as anxious about the prosperity and the happiness of the white race as the black"; such magnanimity taught Booker that great men cultivated love and that only "little men cherish a spirit of hatred." Armstrong admonished his students to cultivate white neighbors when they went out into the larger world. At the same time, he told them not to waste their time and energy on politics. While working for the Freedmen's Bureau in the 1860s, Armstrong had become convinced that blacks' intent focus on politics had been a mistake, a case of putting the cart of civil equality before the horse of education and moral improvement. Booker appears to have heeded the general's lessons, although Armstrong's orders contravened his own fascination with political activity. But he apparently never let the general know about his desire to engage in politics. He still wore the mask of deference to whites, though in the case of Armstrong he believed he was deferring to superior knowledge and higher character.[32]

The science curriculum reinforced the progressive view of history disseminated at Hampton. The study of plant and animal science instilled in Booker a faith in scientific reason, the ability of the human mind to observe, understand, and use the natural world to its own constructive purposes. Perhaps unconsciously, he became a positivist, embracing the common nineteenth-century philosophical presumption that one could observe his environment and make sense of its elements. This positivist faith reinforced the practicality of Hampton's smaller vocational-training curriculum, which included printing and carpentry. Booker, however, aspired to neither trade; he continued to work as a janitor. By far the most extensive vocational study covered the various aspects of scientific agriculture—crop rotation and diversity, soil conservation and drainage, and animal husbandry. Hampton nurtured Booker's deep engagement with agricultural life, but his attachment to farm animals, especially pigs and chickens, dated from earlier in his life.[33]

In 1875 Booker was chosen as one of the graduation speakers. Armstrong made the Hampton commencement a showcase of the school's work to visitors, and a reporter for the New York *Times* was deeply moved by the event: "All in sympathy with the college felt that this was a fore-post of civilization on the old ground of barbarism." He thought the students were about as intelligent as white students would have been but for their limited vocabulary and that the one "who distinguished himself most, bore the name of 'Washington.'" In a debate staged to exhibit student achievement, Booker was assigned the negative response on the question of whether the United States should annex Cuba. The affirmative voice argued for the benefits of slave emancipation and black political rights. "Wouldn't it be wise," Booker T. Washington responded, "before we risk a war for Cuba, to redeem ourselves from the meshes of the last war?" His arguments reflected the anti-imperialist views of General Armstrong. As for the opportunity to educate the four million illiterate Cuban slaves, he answered: "We have enough of that article [ignorance] already. A whole South is stricken with it." Moreover, taking in Cubans would bring into the United States more communicants of the Catholic church, which "was already so degrading to the great masses of white voters." Booker apparently had also acquired religious bigotry at Hampton, in all likelihood from Armstrong. The *Times* reporter was clearly not bothered by his illiberalism. He concluded that Washington's vigorous argument persuaded the whole audience.[34]

Hampton Institute presumed that the tasks ahead for its graduates would be formidable. "All knew that cold and hostile eyes were on every act" of the Hampton students, the *Times* reporter wrote, because their acts would test "the quality and destiny of a race." In the ten years since the end of the war, hundreds of new black schools had been burned across the South, dozens of teachers terrorized and killed. One of Booker's classmates, the reporter wrote, had escaped the Ku Klux Klan only by hiding, and his two fellow teachers had been murdered. Booker Washington rarely acknowledged the harsh realities toward which his education pointed him. If he was to plant another "fore-post of civilization on the old ground of barbarism," he had to go forward with faith and courage.[35]

Hampton reinforced his experience that a job well done resulted in new and larger opportunities. Just as good performance as a houseboy for Mrs. Ruffner had led to the opportunity to be her fruit salesman, and an excellent performance of janitorial work had got him admitted to Hampton, so did diligent schoolwork earn him the opportunity to shine at commencement. His personal experience validated his faith in the Protestant ethic. Hampton proved again that some whites would help a young black to rise in the world. He had a hero in General Armstrong and other role models in white teachers who opened new worlds of knowledge to him and wanted him to succeed.

By the time he graduated, Booker had been asked to conduct the colored school in Malden. This outcome fulfilled the original purpose of his Hampton education—teaching black children. He dutifully returned home, although Malden had been diminished for Booker because his adored Jane had died during the summer of 1874. Amanda was only fifteen at the time and in need of Booker's oversight and encouragement, since Wash Ferguson remained indifferent to his children's well-being. Booker also felt a strong obligation to advance the education of brother John Henry Washington, who had sent him money at Hampton. And there was James Washington, an orphan whom Jane had taken in soon after the family had arrived in Malden. Booker may have returned to Malden out of duty, but he enjoyed conducting the Malden school. He taught ninety students during the day and about the same number of adults in evening classes. True to his Hampton training, he drilled the boys with sticks on their shoulders, tutored students at night, organized a debating society, taught two Sunday schools, and supplemented book learning with lessons on combing hair, brushing teeth, and bathing. "In all my teaching," he would later write, "I have watched carefully the influence of the tooth-brush, and I am convinced that there are few single agencies of civilization that are more far-reaching." Armstrong's and Washington's emphasis on habits of hygiene struck later observers as racially condescending, but eventually others would recognize that good health is a prerequisite to the overall improvement of people in developing societies, regardless of race or place.[36]

Booker's students apparently liked both the lessons and the young man who taught them. Years later one of them wrote about his pride at having a Malden boy return to teach him. "How our hearts swelled with the feeling that some day we would do likewise, and we went about our tasks with greater energy." Booker prepared several of the best students to go to Hampton, including brother John, a young man named Samuel Courtney, and one girl, Fanny Norton Smith. All three would succeed at Hampton. Booker was in love with Fanny, a light-skinned young woman with high cheekbones that revealed her partly Indian heritage. He arranged and financed some of her Hampton education. He also sent his adopted brother James to Hampton. Only Amanda stayed in Malden, where she became a wife and mother and did not progress beyond a bare literacy.[37]

That same Malden student remembered that Booker's intense gray eyes often seemed set on the horizon. "How different you were from the rest of the boys," he wrote years later. "You always appeared to be looking for something in the distant future." Perhaps that faraway look betrayed a restlessness that became apparent in 1877, when Booker campaigned among black voters to locate the West Virginia state capital in Charleston. Apparently his three months of vigorous arguments helped to account for that city's success in the referendum. He made them "in good style, and expressing his idea in a clear manner . . . interspersing his speech with apt anecdotes," one reporter wrote. Certainly this experience honed Booker's skills as a public orator. The campaign stump also nurtured Booker's interest in the law. He had told Nathalie Lord that his people needed lawyers to protect their rights. He began reading Blackstone under the direction of a white Charleston lawyer and political ally. How much study of the law he actually completed is not clear.[38]

Nor is it clear why he abandoned the law. A legal career apparently meant to him a commitment to seeking public office, and he believed he could succeed in political life. But General Armstrong had always insisted that freedmen's enthusiasm for politics was misspent effort, and Booker was not inclined to go against his mentor. He abandoned politics as a potential career, but he by no means lost his absorption with it. Later Booker said that he quit the study of law to answer a higher calling to education, but in fact he immediately pursued a third alternative. In the fall of 1878 Booker went to Wayland Baptist Theological Seminary in Washington, D.C., the denomination's black training school. At Hampton he had had a course on the Bible, and studied it further with Nathalie Lord, and then taught Sunday school in Malden. His oratorical talent made the pulpit a natural home for him. For a young man considering the various paths to serve his people, the ministry was an obvious possibility. But Booker spent only about six months at the seminary. His only explanation for leaving was that the seminary students gave too much attention to "mere outward appearance"—"they did not appear to me to be beginning at the bottom, on a real, solid foundation" as had students at Hampton. Another explanation may lie in the doubts planted at Hampton about the intelligence and morality of the black clergy. He also may have acquired at Hampton more faith in scientific reason than in the scriptures. Although he never revealed any tendency to religious skepticism, his religiosity would be coolly detached rather than warmly evangelical.[39]

Booker was uncomfortable with life in Washington, which had one of the largest urban black communities in the United States. Freed people had migrated there during and after the Civil War, often to seek jobs in the federal government, and the city was home to such distinguished men as Frederick Douglass. But Booker perceived a superficiality in black life there. Young men of small means spent money on carriage rides, while people who earned high salaries from government jobs were constantly in debt. "Among a large class there seemed to be a dependence upon the Government for every conceivable thing," a condition that no follower of General Armstrong could tolerate. He believed they would have been better off in the rural South, there to make their way on the "solid and never deceptive foundation of Mother Nature."[40]

General Armstrong settled Booker's fate in 1879 with an invitation to deliver an address at the Hampton commencement. Booker declaimed on the topic "The Force That Wins," and he predicated his message on the belief that history recorded no moment when there was "a greater demand for work, self-sacrificing work, work that will shape the character of generations yet unborn." His teaching experience in Malden had revealed a way to succeed and another that brought failure. "The force that wins" required "not education merely but also wisdom and common sense, a heart set on the right and a trust in God." After hearing the address, Armstrong asked Booker to return to Hampton as a teacher. He was expanding his faculty to include some black teachers, and he apparently had already tapped Booker for preparation as an educational leader. He sent Booker to study with General J. F. B. Marshall, Hampton's financial manager, to learn about the administration of the institute. Booker was given charge of a new night class for students too poor to muster any money for room and board. They worked all day at the Hampton sawmill or the laundry. After a year under Washington's tutelage, these students, dubbed "the Plucky Class," entered the regular Hampton class, having prepared themselves academically and saved money to pay a year's room and board. Their commitment to learning at night after laboring all day reinforced Booker's optimism about the potential for education to improve his world. If the Plucky Class succeeded in spite of poor backgrounds and having to work all day for the opportunity to go to school at night, then anyone could do it. It confirmed that his calling was to teach.[41]

Booker's success with the night school led Armstrong to make him adviser to a group of Indian students recently arrived from reservations in the West. Many doubted that the Indians, so wild and unruly and condescending to white culture and to Negroes, would take to the Hampton regimen. They did not want to have their hair cut or to give up wearing blankets or smoking. But under the authority of General Armstrong and his disciple, assimilation was not negotiable: no white American, Booker Washington later observed, "ever thinks that any other race is wholly civilized until he wears the white man's clothes, eats the white man's food, speaks the white man's language, and professes the white man's religion." But even while accepting white European chauvinism, he was sympathetic with those who had yet to conform. He liked the Indian boys, became their champion at Hampton, and acquired practical faith in the capacity of non-Europeans to assimilate in American society. He found that the Indian boys were as good as any other students at the industrial arts. After some initial doubts, the black Hampton students generally accepted the Indians and helped them, an attitude of enlightenment that Booker thought white Americans ought to emulate. The Indians taught him a lesson that he carried forward: "The main thing that any oppressed people needed was a chance of the right kind and they would cease to be savages."[42]

In the spring of 1881 General Armstrong told Booker about a request from Tuskegee, Alabama, for a white man to organize and run a normal school. Armstrong had replied that he knew of no good white candidates, but he had "a very competent capable mulatto, clear headed, modest, sensible, polite and thorough teacher and superior man." Booker Washington was, Armstrong concluded, "the best man we ever had here."[43]

Booker probably had not realized that Armstrong thought quite so highly of him, but by this time, when he was twenty-five years old, he knew he had progressed far. He had developed a distinct character, firm personal values, and a clear worldview. He had the inner confidence that is usually found in boys who are certain of their mother's love. The impact of the unknown, or at least unacknowledged, father on Booker's character and personality can only be imagined. The absence of a father's influence appears not to have hampered the development of a strong character and a good mind. Booker's self-confidence was manifest in his loyalty to family, friends, and mentors. He was optimistic that the future held good things for him. His rise from Malden personified the evolutionary progress that all African Americans hoped was their future. He had long since separated the inner Booker, the young man with big ambitions and independent intelligence, from Booker T. Washington, the public person known as a capable mulatto, clear-headed and modest, sensible and polite, a Negro who did not give offense. The division would serve the man well, for Booker Washington would pursue his ambitions in a world that for the most part hated the idea of black men moving upward, while the inner Booker preserved his emotional balance and considered what was possible—and what was not.

Booker had learned a lot about how the world worked. Experience had taught him that one job done well naturally led to a bigger and better assignment. Conflict was best avoided, and Booker was careful about expressing opinions that he knew would be rejected—for instance, his abiding interest in politics in spite of General Armstrong's disapproval of black political engagement. He had learned that although government power had freed the slaves and protected them during Reconstruction, the bitter and unfair terms of the Reconstruction settlement had also made politics an unpromising, indeed dangerous, place for an ambitious young black man to focus his energy. Race informed everything about the society in which he lived. Emancipation had been the main event of his life, but in the decade and a half since the war, he had witnessed the highly circumscribed freedom of black southerners.

Far more than the average person born into slavery in his generation, Booker had benefited from positive relationships with whites. He never romanticized slavery, but he apparently did not suffer much from it physically or psychologically. His early life had been one of intimate connections with whites on the Burroughs farm, and he apparently came away from that experience with a realistic understanding of whites' behavior. They were not a mystery to him, as they might have been had he been born on a large plantation and lived in a bigger slave community more isolated from white masters. Viola Ruffner, General Armstrong, Mary Mackie, and Nathalie Lord—all had nurtured his development with generous, kindly attention. To be sure, they were all northern whites, but Armstrong had led him to believe that some southern whites were capable of helping him. Booker therefore arrived at adulthood believing that whites who knew him well appreciated his abilities and character and would assist his advancement in life. This experience set him well apart from the average black person of his time.

And he now had twenty-five years' experience in dealing with the paradox of his mixed racial heritage. His society so unequivocally categorized anyone with any African heritage as a Negro that the issue seemed to matter little to him—or at least not to occasion much comment. He had at least as much white blood as black and probably more—as did his brother John, his friend Sam Courtney, his girlfriend Fanny Smith, and many of his classmates at Hampton—and yet the Negro blood consigned him to a permanently inferior status. Most whites, even his Hampton sponsors, attributed his success at least partly to his white blood. No person of pure African lineage, whites generally assumed at the end of the nineteenth century, could write, speak, or manage people with Booker T. Washington's acuity. The public Booker accepted the near-total authority of the presumption of white superiority even while the inner Booker quietly recognized it as fiction on many levels. Indeed, racial thinking so infused his world that it was a waste of time to reflect much on the inconsistencies and absurdities of race relations. Eventually he would resist the lie of racial distinction, but for the moment he accepted it and went on.

By 1881 Booker had arrived at the place where most shrewd men of color at the time ended up—at the schoolhouse door. The almost unanimous opinion of all Booker's white friends in the 1870s was that education was the best avenue to black progress. He was an optimist: Booker believed that he had "the force that wins," and Booker T. Washington was ready to leave Hampton to prove it with his deeds.

A few days after his reply to the request from Tuskegee for a white man to start a normal school, General Armstrong received a telegram: "Booker T. Washington will suit us. Send him at once."[44]

2

The Model Community

Booker was pleased to find that Tuskegee's location was healthy and pleasantly high, an ideal place for the new school. The town sits on the last ripple of hills in southeastern Alabama before the land falls into a prairie of dark soil known locally as the Black Belt. The seat of Macon County, Tuskegee was founded not long after the Creek Indians were forced in the early 1830s to cede their remnant of land in eastern Alabama to the mass of encroaching white settlers from Georgia. It was a prosperous market town in the 1850s, with several Greek Revival houses lining the roads leading north and south out of Tuskegee. The most noteworthy structure was Grey Columns, home of the planter William Varner, which replicated the Parthenon with its soaring pillars on all four sides. Although the Civil War and the terrible economic times since had left Tuskegee looking rundown, there remained in its environs in 1881 several local families who planted cotton, practiced law, and retained a usually dominant political influence: the land-rich Varners, Cobbs, and Thompsons, and the mercantile Campbells, who owned the five-mile-long railroad spur that ran northward to connect Tuskegee to the Montgomery and West Point line and the world beyond.[1]

Booker sensed that he would like Tuskegee, but his own happiness mattered less than addressing the numerous tasks at hand. An unhappy surprise was the discovery that there was no building for the school. Having come from the neat Hampton campus, with its impressive main building, Booker felt overwhelmed by the first job, finding a place to have his school. But he did find one. The Tuskegee Normal Institute opened on July 4, 1881, in the only building available to hold classes, the Zion Negro Church, a log-cabin structure a short walk east of the town square. The school also occupied a shanty next door, a two-room house constructed poorly of wood boards with large cracks in the walls and ceiling. Its windows were covered with wooden shutters attached by leather hinges. Through the cracks poured sunlight, cold air, and rain. During wet weather, a student held an umbrella over Booker while he taught.[2]

To recruit students, Booker resolved to travel around the countryside meeting the people of the Alabama Black Belt. He did not have a horse and was obliged to stand in the roads and waylay black travelers. He told them about the school and the good it was going to do for black people. "Now, Uncle," he reportedly told men he stopped, "you can help by bringing your wagon and mule round at nine o'clock Saturday morning for me to go off round the country telling the people about the school." Out in the country, Booker talked about his school on the porches of sharecropper cabins, and on Sundays he recruited from the pulpits of rural churches. Preachers always wanted to know the school's religious affiliation, and when informed that there was none, some warned their parishioners to stay away from the godless school. But when the congregations heard Booker, "they just sent their children as fast as ever they could contrive it," it was later reported. Soon Zion Church and the ramshackle hut beside it were full of students intent on learning what Professor Washington could teach them that would improve their lives.[3]

The professor himself had no doubt learned that Zion Church was a symbol of black political ambitions. He surely had been told that Zion was a central locus of the violent struggle for control of Tuskegee and Macon County in 1870. Booker probably got the story from the black tinsmith Lewis Adams, the town's most prosperous black resident, the person most instrumental in establishing the school. The light-skinned, wiry Adams had lived in Tuskegee all his life and had witnessed two decades of turmoil in the seemingly quiet place. He had seen things that the new principal needed to know if Booker was going to survive there.[4]

Adams might have begun his revelations by telling about the sudden appearance in Tuskegee, within months of the surrender at Appomattox, of the Knights of the White Carnation, a secret vigilante organization that anticipated the more widely known Ku Klux Klan. Adams almost certainly knew the identity of the leader of the White Carnation, Cullen Andrews Battle, who in 1861 had formed the Tuskegee Light Infantry and led his cavalry into conflicts at Richmond, Chancellorsville, and Gettysburg, where he was promoted to general on the battlefield. Only when he was seriously injured did he relinquish his command, but like many former Confederates, the general did not surrender with Robert E. Lee but returned home to engage in a guerrilla struggle against blacks. In 1865, at the same time that he reopened his law practice and was elected to Congress, and as he applied to President Andrew Johnson for pardon for his Confederate service with the promise he would be a "peaceable and loyal citizen in the future," Battle led the Knights on terror campaigns to force black submission to white authority.[5]

Booker could not have been too surprised by revelations about what happened in Tuskegee with the advent of Radical Reconstruction in 1867. With the return of the U.S. army to govern much of the South, a coalition of local Unionists, Yankees, and blacks took control of state government. This new challenge provoked more white terrorism: the Ku Klux Klan rode at night to scare blacks and their few white allies into submission, killing them when necessary. They burned homes and crops, but the special objects of their pitch-pine torches were the newly formed churches and schools that represented the desire for autonomy and opportunity among the freed people. Booker knew that the Klan had torched black churches and schools in Virginia and West Virginia, that it had terrorized and killed teachers, and he would not have been surprised when he learned that schools in dozens of Alabama counties were burned and the first teachers of blacks in Tuskegee run out of the town.[6]

Lewis Adams surely recounted to Booker that the black man elected

6. The home of James Alston, a black Tuskegee state legislator, was shot up in 1870, and he was forced to flee for his life. Artist unknown; from *Harper's Weekly,* February 24, 1872.

to represent Tuskegee in the Alabama legislature in 1868 was James Alston, General Battle's slave and in 1861 his company's drummer on several battlefields. A person he had once owned was now supposed to be Battle's representative in the state legislature. The general and his guerrillas stepped up their terrorist activities when Alston stood for reelection. Returning to his home from a political meeting at Zion Church in June 1870, Alston and his family were hit with a barrage of gunfire. Alston sent word for fellow freedmen to protect him. Battle ordered Alston to send away the armed black men, promising that there would be no further attacks. But the county's probate judge was more honest: "A nigger couldn't hold no office in that county no longer," Alston later reported he was told; "a nigger was fit for nothing else than to drive oxen, and drive the carriage of white folks." Then eight white men, all prominent figures in Tuskegee, called at Alston's door to deliver a message: if he wanted to live, he must leave the county. At that point Alston accepted his fate; he spent the next ten days in outlying swamps on the run from assassins hired by one of those visitors, Robert Abercrombie.[7]

The attack on Alston marked the beginning of months of intimidation and violence leading up to the November 1870 state elections. Battle and his vigilante cavalry patrolled Macon County, looking for any black political gatherings. They may have been responsible for the burning of four black schools. William Bowen, one of Tuskegee's few white Republicans, was burned in effigy and then shot. He later identified his attackers as young men who loitered around the livery stable of Jesse Adams, the white father of Lewis Adams and a man known to be a violent Democrat. Not long before the election, the nightriders attacked Zion Church, where the Reverend John Butler had convened a meeting to discuss the church's finances. "Shoot the damned niggers," Butler heard a white man shout. "Kill them every one." Two Zion members were killed and three wounded, and Butler survived only by hiding under his pulpit.[8]

The antiblack violence in Alabama gained such infamy that in 1871 a U.S. congressional inquiry took testimony about the atrocities, and in response, whites began developing myths about their relations with blacks. Robert Abercrombie, the Tuskegee white who had dispatched men to kill James Alston, reported that the terrible violence of 1870 was a thing of the past: "Perfect quiet, peace, and harmony now prevail between the whites and blacks." General James H. Clanton, then head of the Alabama Democratic Party, flatly denied that any black school had ever been burned in Alabama because of racial animus. "There is not a gentleman in the South, or lady, who would do it . . . There is not a county that would not disgrace a man who would own or acknowledge it." General Battle swore to the congressional committee that there was no prejudice against black education, just as he had sworn to President Johnson in 1865 that he would be peaceable and loyal in the future. One congressman then asked whether there was a Ku Klux Klan in that part of Alabama. General Battle answered that the Klan was a myth. He knew of no man in those parts who was even suspected of "being a Ku-Klux—not a man."[9]

The effort to reclaim white control had established patterns of violence and dishonesty in human relations. Any black person coming into Tuskegee would have to know about that, and accommodate it, if he was to survive. This history certainly was explained to Booker when he arrived, because he needed to know to rise above it. He would hardly have been surprised, because he had long since witnessed the brutality and deceit in southern race relations.

Whites in Tuskegee justified their use of violence and fraud with a new ideological claim, white nationalism. In 1861 white southerners had created their own nation-state, the Confederate States of America, formed in opposition to the U.S. government. After defeat, they replaced Confederate nationalism with a new racial and regional form of nationalism—best understood in this case as southern white nationalism. It was the kind of nationalism that has shaped conflicts throughout the modern world. A group defined itself by several characteristics: identity based on a belief in common blood; myths that nurtured a feeling of their unique historical experience, especially their mistreatment; a long-standing feeling of persecution at the hands of an alien political authority, in white southerners' case the U.S. government; and an abiding hatred of an enemy with whom the group lived in close proximity—the African Americans.[10]

After the Civil War, white southerners insisted on defining themselves by their common Anglo-Saxon blood, ignoring altogether their much more varied genetic inheritance. They fashioned several compelling myths. They imagined a glorious prewar South built on chivalry and Christian virtue. The fulfillment of Old South values was the Confederate States of America, but it was now the Lost Cause whose memory could be honored only by embodying its racial values in the benighted present. Reconstruction became the most powerful myth; it was understood as the postwar atrocity of an occupying foreign nation. The U.S. government was the external oppressor that had defeated white southerners' attempt to create their own nation and then taken over land that southerners believed they had a historic right to control—just as Catholics in Northern Ireland, Serbs in the Balkans, and Palestinians in Israel would later insist had been their fate. Most important in 1881, white southerners were still fighting an internal enemy who had been in league with the occupier. Control of the homeland had been redeemed from the evil Republican coalition, but whites remained intensely insecure about their power to defeat their black enemies and keep out the U.S. government.

White nationalism separated the South ideologically from the rest of the United States, even when the vast majority of white Americans everywhere believed in their superiority to blacks. White nationalists saw northerners as their oppressors, as people who would make them yield to the enemy in their midst in order to guarantee northern control. White nationalists felt more than just an aversion to a people whom they believed to be physically different and culturally inferior; they also viewed blacks as rivals for power and status. Any improvements in blacks' position in society meant a decline of their own status.

General Battle gave voice to southern nationalism in postwar speeches. In embracing the doctrine of secession, Battle said, the white southerner in 1861 had demonstrated that he was a "disciple of the States Rights school . . . of the olden time," and thus a man true to historic southern principles. Battle spoke about the Lost Cause as the time of "common sufferings and common glories," of Confederate comrades "so tried and so true," his partners in a glorious past; but he also warned of a "threatening future." White southerners had become a conquered people who could not "vindicate their right to have been called a nation, and must accept whatever appellation the conqueror bestows." Of course, the southern white nationalist had not capitulated at all, as the general's murderous night riding had clearly demonstrated in and around Tuskegee. The ideology included a license for the white nationalist to lie to his enemies about his real intentions.[11]

The necessity to accommodate white-nationalist thinking conditioned how Booker Washington thought about Tuskegee. In recounting the creation of the Institute, he said only that the black residents of the community had heard of the work of Hampton and wanted a school like it, and they prevailed on local whites to get the state legislature to appropriate money to start a normal school. His account suggests an almost immaculate conception, and he clearly intended to leave the impression that Tuskegee Institute was created with the full consent and active cooperation of whites. Others offered a different explanation: they pointed to the political ambitions of Arthur Brooks and Wilbur Foster, the state senator at the time, who sought black votes in their election campaigns for the legislature in 1880. Lewis Adams reputedly offered to deliver them black votes in exchange for the creation of a black school. In this scenario, Tuskegee Institute was the handiwork of a shrewd black political trader. Yet this explanation, too, has its limits. Black political power had by 1880 been severely compromised by violence and fraud. In 1874 Democrats recaptured control of the state government in a campaign marked by terrorism across the state. In the aftermath of the violence, a Democratic judge oversaw the conviction of the remaining black officials in Tuskegee—some for the crime of adultery—and ordered the removal of the white Republican probate judge for failing to establish an adequate surety bond, now a state requirement for holding office.[12]

Perhaps a more valid explanation is that, more certain of their political dominance, some whites now felt comfortable about accommodating black desires and therefore sustaining a more stable black population in the community. After 1873 the local economy was mired in a depression, which spurred poor farmers to leave the area, mainly for the West. In 1876 scores of blacks were leaving Tuskegee daily, and an emigration agent was recruiting in the area. The white population was also falling. Hundreds of farms were being sold for nonpayment of taxes, and thousands of acres of farmland lay idle. In 1878 Arthur Brooks noted only one truly promising aspect of the local economy, "our magnificent schools and colleges, which have not been in so flourishing a condition at any previous time since the war." Brooks referred to a local boys' academy and the Alabama Methodist Female College. He began campaigning in his newspaper for improved relations with the Tuskegee black community. "Never since freedom has there been in this section a better state of feeling between whites and blacks," he wrote. The new minister of Zion Negro church, Mr. Gomez, was poised to do great good among his people, because local blacks had forsaken the evil teaching of "meddlesome and designing persons" during Reconstruction days. Brooks published a letter from Gomez announcing the creation of an Educational Treasury to benefit the colored youths of Tuskegee and asking for "the aid of our white friends, who are lovers of education and intelligence." A year later another letter, signed by six ministers and Lewis Adams, appeared asking for white aid in the establishment of a colored high school.[13]

White support for Tuskegee Institute grew out of the desire for economic recovery, based on an ample supply of black labor, something that interracial harmony enabled. The feeling of accommodation between blacks and whites was seen in the support Washington received from Tuskegee's white elite. Thomas Dryer, a merchant who had threatened James Alston in 1870, became one of the school's first three trustees. When Dryer died, George W. Campbell, another of the men who had warned Alston out of town, replaced him on the board and became Booker's white confidant in the town. It was fortunate for Booker that General Battle had moved from Tuskegee at some point in the 1870s.[14]

Still, Washington understood that the new school existed only with the consent of whites in Tuskegee. Lewis Adams probably helped Booker imagine what local white men, including Lewis's own white father, would do if the new normal school was perceived as a threat to their control of the town. The new principal surely surmised from recent local history that his success would depend on keeping local whites perpetually assured that there was no such threat. As Booker was en route to his new Alabama home in June 1881, there came a reminder of the jeopardy awaiting any black man in Tuskegee. South of town a Negro flashed a knife while resisting arrest, and, according to the Tuskegee *News,* white deputies were "induced [to believe] that it was necessary to shoot him." Regardless of the current relaxation of racial animosity in Tuskegee, a black person's life remained cheap in the eyes of whites.[15]

Booker had too much to do about his school even to acknowledge white violence. He immediately began to look for land that would be a permanent home for it. He found a hilly, partly eroded 100-acre farm northwest of the town, just beyond the Varners' magisterial Grey Columns. He bought it for $500 from William Bowen, the scalawag. It had no real house, but three small, wood-frame outbuildings could be used if repaired. Because the $2,000 state appropriation could be used only to pay teachers, he had to borrow the $200 down payment for the land purchase from J. F. B. Marshall, the Hampton treasurer, who advised him on all practical matters in organizing the new school. Booker's first decision about the land purchase revealed his instinctive shrewdness about power: he made sure that the land was deeded to the school itself and not to the state of Alabama, which because of its initial appropriation might have been able to make some future claim on Institute property.[16]

Hence Booker manifested a deeply American faith—that landownership was the basis of self-rule, perhaps especially so for a black man living amid anxious whites in the post–Civil War South. Although the land was owned by the Institute, it represented Booker's own opportunity to get what most freed slaves wanted and thought they were due, their forty acres and a mule—except that Washington came to control far more land than that. Within a few years his Tuskegee farming operation would dwarf what his old master James Burroughs had run. Most mornings in Tuskegee, Booker would saddle a horse and ride over the Institute farm and note the conditions of the crops, the livestock, the buildings, and the equipment—just as a successful white planter would have been doing at the time. It appears that in his mind the land, as well as the crops and livestock it yielded, gave him and his institution status—just as they would have done to a comparable white planter. But to him it was crucially important that the land was owned, and the crops and livestock produced, by black people. Tuskegee Institute was an object lesson that blacks could succeed just as well in the agricultural economy as whites if they owned their land.

During his first months of travel to recruit students, Booker stayed in the sharecropper cabins of rural blacks, eating and sleeping with them, investigating the true nature of their existence. He found that in most cases the whole family slept in one room of a tiny cabin similar to the one he had lived in as a slave child. The people were illiterate, but he found few who engaged in the vices that Booker thought were all too common among blacks in large cities. Children were poorly

7. This dilapidated housing was typical for African Americans living in the Alabama Black Belt. Photographer unknown, ca. 1914; courtesy of the Library of Congress.

clothed, in many cases only in a long flax shirt, and the clothes were often filthy. William Holtzclaw, a future Tuskegee student growing up nearby, did not have a pair of shoes until he was fifteen years old. At one rural dwelling two teenaged boys met Booker completely naked.[17]

The people ate a diet composed mostly of pork fat and corn bread. Hunger was common. Holtzclaw and his siblings often went to bed with stomach cramps from lack of food. When his mother returned from her job in a white family's kitchen with a pan of pot liquor, the children gathered around it on the dirt floor of the cabin and ate from it with their hands. "Sometimes in our haste [we] dived foremost into the pan, very much as pigs after swill," Holtzclaw admitted. Booker found that few rural black families raised vegetables; with cotton planted nearly up to the edge of their cabins, their diet lacked most nutrients needed for good health. Booker disapproved of the practice among the rural poor of spending their meager resources on such things as sewing machines that they did not know how to operate and expensive clocks. He dined with a family of five that had only one fork among them but was making installment payments on a sixty-dollar organ. There was far too little attention or money spent on keeping one's hearth—and person—clean and healthy, Booker thought.[18]

Schools for blacks already existed in rural Alabama, but Booker found them miserably equipped and poorly taught. They met in churches and abandoned log cabins; neither state nor local government in Alabama had made any provision for black schoolhouses. There was no equipment other than the occasional blackboard. "With few exceptions, I found the teachers in these county schools to be miserably poor in preparation for their work, and poor in character." Holtzclaw exhausted his teacher's knowledge of arithmetic in a few days and then endured a horrific flogging from the embarrassed teacher. The good teachers had little to work with. At one school Booker witnessed two boys on a bench studying a book. "Behind these were two others peeping over the shoulders of the first two, and behind the four was a fifth little fellow who was peeping over the shoulders of all four."[19]

Thirty students enrolled in Booker's first classes at Tuskegee, all of them from nearby rural areas, but within a month the number had grown to fifty. They were a transient group, frequently dropping out of classes as necessary to earn a living. Some were teaching already, although Washington believed that none was adequately prepared. Some had studied classical languages and memorized long rules of grammar, but they "had little thought or knowledge of applying these rules to the everyday affairs of their life" and only "the merest smattering of the big-sounding things that they had studied." Some professed to know about banking but had no bank accounts and did not know the multiplication table. Booker therefore emphasized basic grammar and composition, history and geography, arithmetic, and hygiene. Most did not have money for school fees, and so he put them to work to earn their way. The work had two purposes—to dignify labor in their minds and to build the school and farm the land. To clear land in order to plant crops, he announced a chopping bee in which students competed in removing trees from a field. Some participants thought that the chopping bee too closely resembled common farm labor—they had not come to school for that—but as one student reported, "they couldn't say they were too good for that kind of work when Mr. Washington himself was at it harder than any of them."[20]

It was clear in his first months in Tuskegee that the young principal, now sporting a mustache to make himself look older, had brought with him from Hampton several important assets: goodwill from his mentors for his new endeavor; empathy for the people he came to serve but also a hard-eyed realism about the deficiencies of their existence; a facility for creating good feeling toward himself among some whites; and a commitment to institutional autonomy. Booker would shamelessly curry the favor of white people, but he quietly arranged his affairs to acquire as much independence as possible.

Later he acknowledged that despite the white goodwill that fostered the Institute's creation, "there were not a few white people in the vicinity of Tuskegee who looked with some disfavour upon the project." Even those who were friendly harbored skepticism. Booker described George W. Campbell, who would be his best white friend in Tuskegee, as "raised up and surrounded by the general popular prejudices against the negro and against the education of negroes." Whites had the image

8. Booker grew a mustache to make him look older when he went to Tuskegee. Photo engraving, artist unknown, ca. 1882; from William J. Simmons, *Men of Mark: Eminent, Progressive and Rising* (Cleveland: George M. Rewell, 1887).

of an educated black man as one wearing "a high hat, imitation gold eye-glasses, a showy walking stick, kid gloves, fancy boots."[21]

In fact Washington never admitted the full extent of continuing white opposition to black education, which rested on a belief that educating blacks undermined the interests of whites. As Ben Tillman, South Carolina's prototype white-nationalist politician, put it, "when you educate a negro you educate a candidate for the penitentiary" or spoiled a good field hand. Many southern congressmen in the 1880s expressed opposition to black education in the ongoing federal debate about the Blair bill, which sought to distribute large amounts of federal funds to educate illiterate people in the South. According to Alabama's preeminent white-nationalist politician, Senator John Tyler Morgan, the amount of money that his county would receive under the bill would double the length of the school term, and having black children in school for six months would ruin the cotton crop. Opposition to the Blair bill inevitably reflected white anxiety about political control. South Carolina's congressmen insisted that with federal money blacks intended to "take advantage of the school houses, get educations and outvote us."[22]

The most powerful argument against black education, and the one that would most vex its proponents in the long run, was that educating black children took the South's limited resources for education from white children. This rationale reflected white nationalists' presumption of a zero-sum racial competition in the South: any black gain automatically meant a loss of status for whites. In the aftermath of relatively liberal spending for education under Republican regimes during Reconstruction, southern Democrats severely limited taxation, and public funding for schools fell. In state after state in the 1880s and 1890s, the remedy pushed for poor white schools was racial separation of tax funds so that money collected from whites went only to educate white children. Blacks and whites understood that this change would beggar black schools because of the low property holdings among blacks. A North Carolina editor was "not willing to be taxed to educate the negro and we don't care who knows it . . . we are desperately opposed to taxing one race to educate another." In 1888 Tuskegee's state representative told the Alabama legislature that white taxpayers of the Black Belt were paying for the education of three black children to every white one. "Did it strike any man's mind as fair for the whites to pay the taxes and negroes [to] get the education?" For the editor commenting on this situation, the question was purely rhetorical.[23]

The whole notion of educating blacks was popularly disparaged. No one did more to stir popular opposition than Bill Arp, the pen name of Charles Henry Smith, a rustic humorist whose weekly column in the Atlanta *Constitution* was reprinted in hundreds of weekly newspapers in the South. Beginning as an opponent of black education during Reconstruction, he became increasingly vitriolic in the 1880s and 1890s about the allegedly pernicious effects of schooling on the black population. "The nigger can't learn," Bill Arp constantly told his readers, and efforts to educate him encouraged idleness and criminality. Not long after the founding of Tuskegee, Bill Arp wrote: "Some of em are right smart and take on considerable schooling, but that don't prove anything, for I saw an educated hog a few years ago that could play cards with his nose and tell the time of day on a watch, but that don't prove we ought to educate hogs and send em to college. The masses of the negro race are never so happy as when in the cornfield or the cotton patch and being dependent upon the white man for protection and advice."[24]

White nationalists always connected their opposition to black education to African Americans' persistent interest in politics. When Booker Washington arrived in Tuskegee, the local blacks told him that they wanted him to vote as they did—that is, they watched the white man and then voted the opposite way. The danger of black political activism was made manifest not long afterward. Independentism, a local version of the new Greenbacker Party, which favored inflation of the national currency, had emerged to challenge Democrats who had captured control of the state in 1874. The possibility of a political alliance between blacks and dissident whites was a continuing worry to the incumbent Democrats. In 1880 in western Alabama's Choctaw County black Republicans had allied themselves with Greenbackers and other independents. The leader of the black Republicans was Jack Turner, a former slave who had become a charismatic political activist during

Reconstruction. Whites called Turner Captain Jack, endowing him with military leadership ability in what they perceived as an incipient race war. At least partly because of Turner's influence, the black vote in Choctaw County remained large and free of white control in 1882, providing a clear majority for the coalition candidate for governor, who lost in most other places. Immediately after the election whites arrested Turner and charged him with crimes associated with an alleged violent plot against whites, the evidence for which seems to have been entirely manufactured. Within hours an extralegal public trial was held. By a vote of 998 to 2, whites in the county convicted Turner, sentenced him to die, and swiftly hanged him.[25]

The so-called Jack Turner rebellion was widely reported in the South, but unlike the violence against blacks in 1870, it elicited no investigation or even sustained condemnation. The message for Alabama blacks could not have been clearer: any political action that was seen as a challenge to white Democratic control risked a swift, unquestioned lynching. Any black leader who had independent influence over blacks was a threat to white interests and thus subject to execution. The Tuskegee *News* reported that in the aftermath of the Turner rebellion blacks in Macon County were holding secret meetings. "Their mysterious gatherings are quite frequent," the editor wrote, and "what their import is, we have not heard, but we do know that the whites do not like the mystery in the movement of the negroes." He did not think that local blacks presented much danger on their own, "but there are ill designing persons, white and black, always ready to stir up strife, and the negroes are so easily influenced and excited."[26]

If the editor's warning was insufficient, Washington and other blacks in Tuskegee received a vivid demonstration of their basic insecurity at precisely the time of the Turner events. A black man named Leonard Coker was charged with the murder of a white woman just north of Tuskegee, near Tallassee. Coker fled Macon County but was captured and returned to the local authorities, whereupon a mob of 200 immediately lynched him on the spot where he had allegedly committed murder. Although Coker's guilt in the woman's death was not proved and the act of rape not even alleged in the first press reports, the editor of the Tuskegee *News* explained that the "virtue and purity of the women of the South was about all that was left by the late war, and when a fiend in human shape attempts to break down this barrier and protection to society—let it be known that they must at once pay the penalty, and that under these circumstances lynch law can be justified."[27]

Having found what he did in Tuskegee during his first year, one wonders why Booker stayed. He probably assumed that every other place in the South posed most of the same problems and concluded that he might as well go forward where he was. The Hampton training had been predicated on the difficulty of the challenge of educating the freed people. If Tuskegee was a particularly harsh environment, it required the most competent Negro available. Booker T. Washington had succeeded at every job he had been given, and perhaps it never occurred to him that he might fail in Tuskegee.

And so he began his work. A sign of his commitment to Tuskegee came in his personal life. In the summer of 1882 Booker returned to Malden and married twenty-four-year-old Fanny Smith. Fanny's face revealed her mixed Indian, white, and black heritage as well as her gentle, kind disposition. She was popular among those who knew her well, but apparently few people beyond Booker had that opportunity. In the fall of 1882 the couple settled into a small frame house on the new campus, one that they shared with the other teachers. Fanny worked at the school, not only teaching but also maintaining the buildings. "Her heart was set on making her home an object lesson for those about her," he later said, noting that from her arrival in Tuskegee, Fanny earnestly devoted her thoughts and time to the work of the school and entirely shared his ambitions for the Institute's success. Like most African-American couples who aspired to rise in status in the late nineteenth century, the partners maintained a strict privacy about their private life together; neither Booker nor Fanny left a record about the emotional content of their marriage. But at one level, it must have been a happy union: the next year, not much more than nine months after the marriage, Fanny gave birth to a girl, Portia.[28]

By the end of his first year in Tuskegee, Booker had learned how diverse and unscrupulous were the means of white oppression. To manage the dangers and dishonesty of whites, Booker created a picture of Tuskegee as a model community of race relations, a place where blacks and whites pretended there were no past conflicts. In the present there were only peace and mutual goodwill. He never spoke of the full context of Tuskegee Institute's founding, and its creation has ever since been obscured in a myth of good feeling that he nurtured. Creating a path up from history at Tuskegee involved ignoring most of the past. The image of the model community, Booker Washington knew, had to be made compatible with southern white nationalists' fictions about the Old South, the Lost Cause, and Black Reconstruction, because those illusions were already fixed in the southern white nationalists' minds. The fiction of a model community encouraged the belief among whites that blacks had no reason to complain about racial conditions, and it prevented blacks from engaging in the dangerous actions of criticizing how they were treated. And so Washington and the leading whites in town promoted the idea that the races respected, helped, and even admired each other. Whites could enjoy the satisfaction that came from living on an island of perfect quiet, peace, and harmony surrounded by the boiling sea of racial conflict that was the reality of life in the South. The myth bought Booker the space and time he needed to do his work. He knew what he was doing, even if he never said it explicitly. He would become a master of indirection, of the hidden hand of action; but he did so because he had to.

3

———

The Self-Made Men

Booker knew from the moment of his arrival that he and the students would have to build Tuskegee Institute themselves. The little frame buildings on the Bowen farm could not hold even thirty students comfortably, and their roofs were no protection when it rained. When the $500 borrowed to buy the land for the campus was paid off, Booker began raising money for a new building. Well before he had the money in hand, construction of the first new building had begun in 1882. Booker saw the commitment to student construction as meeting several purposes: it would require far less money—only what was necessary for building materials; it would enable students to learn the best methods of labor firsthand; and it would help them to "see not only utility in labour, but beauty and dignity; [they] would be taught, in fact, how to lift labour up from mere drudgery and toil, and would learn to love work for its own sake." He accepted that the buildings might not be perfectly crafted, but he was convinced that "in the teaching of civilization, self-help, and self reliance, the erections of the buildings by the students themselves would more than compensate for any lack of comfort or fine finish." He was not just training teachers but enabling those men and women to replicate what they were now doing—to build their own schools. The Institute construction experience would be as valuable as their academic work. And building the school them-

9. The site purchased for the campus had three small buildings. Photographer
unknown; from Booker T. Washington, *My Larger Education: Being Chapters
from My Experience* (Garden City, N.Y.: Doubleday, Page, 1911).

selves would make Tuskegee Institute an exclusively African-American achievement. It would prove to blacks that they could accomplish
a large, complex task, and would demonstrate to whites that blacks
were capable of running a large enterprise without white help or interference. Almost all other black institutions of higher education had
been built and run by whites—including Booker's model, Hampton
Institute. Tuskegee Institute would be different.[1]

The first building project was an all-purpose academic edifice with
an assembly hall and recitation rooms, offices, a library, a dining hall, a
laundry, and dormitory accommodations for women. Booker needed
$3,000 for building materials, and the first significant contribution
came from a New York banker, Alfred Porter. By the fall of 1882
Booker and the students had finished the three-story, wood-frame
Porter Hall. Booker immediately invited rural black people to inspect
the new structure. He later described how they toured the rooms of
Porter Hall, "treading lightly and cautiously, as if they were afraid they
would hurt the floors," stopping to look in amazement. "They would

10. Students built most of the Tuskegee campus. Photographer unknown, 1902; from Emmett J. Scott and Lyman Beecher Stowe, *Booker T. Washington: Builder of a Civilization* (Garden City, N.Y.: Doubleday, Page, 1916).

take hold of the door knobs, put their hands on the glass of the window panes, feel of the blackboards," Booker wrote, "and then stop and gaze wonderingly again at the plastered walls, the desks and the furniture." Booker explained to the rural people that the Institute belonged to them. "It seemed impossible to them that all this could have been brought into existence for the benefit of Negroes."[2]

The enrollment more than doubled in the first year, and in the second year it doubled again. By 1888 there were more than 400 students. The faculty grew rapidly as well, to about twenty-five by the end of the first decade. All the early teachers came from Hampton. Most were people whom Booker knew personally. He was looking for teachers who were as goal-oriented as he was, who would work as long and hard as he would at a variety of tasks. They had to be persons of good character, because, Washington presumed, any failure of morality or honesty might fulfill white expectations of failure. One of the first to come was Warren Logan, a fair-skinned Hampton classmate who taught bookkeeping and music. Samuel Courtney, the Malden boy whom Booker had taught and then sent to Hampton, arrived a while later.[3]

Six weeks into his tenure, Booker welcomed Olivia Davidson, by far the most important early addition to the staff. A delicately beauti-

11. Olivia Davidson served as Tuskegee Institute's first "lady principal" and became Booker's wife in 1886. Photo by Frank Beard; from Booker T. Washington, *The Story of My Life and Work* (Atlanta: J. L. Nichols, 1901).

ful woman born in Virginia, apparently the daughter of her white master, Olivia had fled with her mulatto mother and siblings to Ohio during the Civil War. Olivia was reared there in a colony of recently freed blacks. In the mid-1870s she had taught at a freedmen's school in Hernando, Mississippi, with her brother and sister (or sister-in-law), both of whom were lynched by the Ku Klux Klan. Olivia therefore knew far more personally than Booker Washington the dangers attached to black education in the South. Olivia had then spent a year at Hampton, graduating in the class that heard Booker's commencement address, "The Force That Wins." Like him, she had been a star at Hampton, and was the fellow graduate he most wanted to help him at

Tuskegee. Like him, she wrote and spoke well, had a gift for organization, and got on well with whites. Her skin and features made it easy for her to pass as white but she chose to keep her black identity, a decision that Booker openly lauded. After Hampton she had studied for two years at a Massachusetts teachers' college, so her pedagogical preparation was superior to Booker's. Her academic education was also better than his; the speeches that she wrote and edited for him contained literary and classical allusions. The old abolitionist circles in Boston that had sponsored her education later helped finance her work at Tuskegee.[4]

Davidson's contributions to the success of Tuskegee would be second only to Booker's, so talented and devoted to the cause was she. He insisted that the school owed most of its early success to Olivia. "She was the one to bring order out of every difficulty," he wrote. "When the last effort had apparently been exhausted and it seemed that things must stop, she was the one to find a way out . . . when a campaign for money had ended unsuccessfully, she would hie away North and money was sure to be found." Olivia's only shortcoming was her health: she had a chronic respiratory ailment that sometimes necessitated long periods of rest.[5]

A major goal at Tuskegee was to instill the Protestant ethic of strict morality. In teaching students how to lead chaste, moral lives, this commitment addressed both the lax morality that Booker and others had observed among rural southern blacks and the white stereotype about black sexual behavior. At the same time, the Institute embraced coeducation at a time when most white schools remained single-sex institutions. The men and women attended some classes separately and seldom worked together on campus, but they dined at the same time in separate sections of the hall and went to chapel together. A major imperative for finishing Porter Hall was to provide good housing for female students. The women could not rough it in tents as male students did, nor were they allowed to board in town, because, Washington later explained, "we did not care to expose [the women] in this way." His unspoken implication was that black women would be subject to sexual exploitation by white men, and perhaps black men as well, in the town.[6]

Next to sexual morality, and maybe before it, was cleanliness. Students had to acquire good health practices, which Booker defined as "how to bathe; how to care for their teeth and clothing . . . what to eat, and how to eat it properly, and how to care for their rooms." Booker brought with him from Hampton General Armstrong's "gospel of the toothbrush," which raised this simple tool to the preeminent symbol of an absolute commitment to healthy living. No student was permitted to stay at the school who did not keep and use a toothbrush. "Absolute cleanliness of the body has been insisted upon from the first," Washington later reported.[7]

During his first years at Tuskegee, Booker later wrote, he spent night after sleepless night worrying where to get the money needed for the school. Olivia organized a festival among Tuskegee people at which donated food was sold to pay off the school's initial $500 loan. Having learned from the stories about Reconstruction in Tuskegee the absolute necessity of currying white favor, Booker always took public note of white support for the school—evidence, he claimed, of their approval of his mission. He was equally pleased with the commitment of local blacks. He told of an elderly black woman who came to him with a gift. "God knows I spent de bes' days of my life in slavery," she said. "God knows I's ignorant an' poor; but . . . I knows you is tryin' to make better men an' better women for de coloured race. I ain't got no money, but I wants you to take dese six eggs." At a meeting of local blacks to raise funds for the school's construction, one man announced that he was contributing a hog to the expense of building: "Any nigger that's got any love for his race, or any respect for himself, will bring a hog to the next meeting."[8]

Still, the school depended mainly on raising money outside Tuskegee, mostly in the Northeast. Booker at first sent Olivia there to find donors. She traveled through New England, telling church groups and individuals about the new school in Alabama. Olivia's appeal was powerful, and she found donors, but the work so exhausted her that she was too tired to undress herself at the end of a hard day of fundraising. She simply lacked the stamina to travel for weeks on end. By about 1883 Booker assumed full responsibility for fundraising. As General Armstrong had done, he tapped the old abolitionist network in New

England for the largest portion of financial support. He initially made contacts through the Christian denominations—first the Congregationalists, then the Unitarians, and eventually the Quakers. Once he established a contact and made a friend, he cultivated the donor with letters, reports of Tuskegee's achievements, and subsequent visits. For weeks at a time Booker went from one New England town to another, giving talks night after night about Tuskegee's work and collecting money in five- and ten-dollar increments, which he rushed into the mail to Tuskegee to cover pressing operating costs. He often stayed with individual supporters, who gave him introductions to churches and other individuals. On his first trip he looked all over Northampton, Massachusetts, for a black family with whom to board, finally to discover that the white hotels would accommodate him, something he had never imagined. From then on, Booker understood how different life in the North was from where he lived and worked.[9]

During the first eight days of May 1882, Washington visited six towns in Connecticut and Massachusetts, speaking at churches and calling on thirteen potential donors—including the dictionary publisher Charles Merriam and the Congregationalist preacher Washington Gladden, then emerging as a proponent of a "social gospel" that exhorted Christians to work for reform of society—and collected just over $100. The earnestness of Washington's appeal and his relentless efforts set him apart from other heads of black schools in the South who came North to raise funds. A few supporters were able to be much more generous. Two Boston sisters, Ellen and Ida Mason, contributed several thousand dollars each year for the next several decades. "*Faith* and *hard work* I find will accomplish anything," Booker declared joyfully to General Armstrong at the word of the Masons' first gift.[10]

The people who supported his cause expected Booker to teach their values. The Connecticut industrialist Moses Pierce told him that although it was important to learn to read, write, and cipher, it was equally important to learn to form the *habit* of industry. Southern blacks had been freed "at great cost of life and treasure," the abolitionist Pierce reminded Booker, and admonished him to follow certain guidelines: "Never spend a penny for anything without full consideration of the necessity of doing it. Industry and economy lead to independence. Wealth does not always secure independence. The man with a saw-buck, who saws wood for a living, who owes no man anything . . . who lives and provides for those dependent on him with his daily earnings, is often more independent than many men with more money."[11] Seeing that Booker listened to him and agreed with his attitude about money, Pierce became a large benefactor.

Booker tapped newly emerging educational foundations as well. By 1883 Tuskegee had received $500 from the Peabody Fund, a foundation created in 1867 by the Georgia-born investment banker George Peabody to support southern education. The Peabody Fund was administered by Jabez Lamar Monroe Curry, an educational promoter committed to overcoming southern white opposition to schooling for blacks—and to supporting Tuskegee Institute. A native Alabamian with a keen appreciation for Washington, Curry would favor the school for the next twenty years. Also in 1883, Booker got help from a new fund with a special focus on industrial education created by the textile industrialist Samuel Slater. The Slater Fund's first $1,000 gift purchased various tools, a windmill, and a horse.[12]

Construction on the campus continued steadily. After Porter Hall came the girls' dormitory Alabama Hall in 1884, Armstrong Hall for men in 1886, Teacher's Cottage in 1887, and in 1889 three structures: a foundry and blacksmith shop, Hamilton Cottage for women, and Washington Cottage for teachers. The campus lay along the main road going westward from Tuskegee toward Montgomery, and Booker originally placed the industrial shops on the east end of the campus, nearest the town, to facilitate trade with local whites. A street was graded parallel to the main road along which the academic buildings and dormitories were arranged. A deep cut in the landscape of the original 100 acres made it difficult to build on some of the land, and the school's livestock was pastured there. Nothing was left unused or unimproved.[13]

Booker knew that Tuskegee Institute's buildings would be more permanent and would look more substantial if constructed of brick, but there was no brickworks in Tuskegee. He resolved that the students would make brick. Robert Varner, the Institute's nearest white neighbor, gave the school his unused brickmaking equipment. Booker and the students then went through many trials in finding the right clay and constructing the kiln to fire the bricks. Three successive failures with the kiln left Booker penniless; only by pawning his watch did he get the money for the fourth and finally successful attempt. The story of brickmaking at Tuskegee became an important symbol for Booker: the young men had not only made material essential to building the Institute; in the process they had also learned a trade they would teach across the South. Finally, and perhaps most important, the students' persistence in learning to make the bricks provided Washington with an object lesson in overcoming adversity. Like the Israelites under the oppression of the Pharaoh, the Tuskegeeans had made bricks without straw, thus proving the seriousness of their cause and the inevitability of their triumph.[14]

Just as important to Washington were the benefits to community relations. The successful efforts in brickmaking demonstrated to hostile whites that schooling made blacks valuable, not worthless. In fact the enterprise added wealth and comfort beyond the campus boundaries, because the school sold its surplus brick to whites in the area. "We had something which they wanted; they had something which we wanted," and this economic interdependency, Washington claimed,

12. Students also built the roads on the campus. Photo by Frances Benjamin Johnston; from Booker T. Washington, *Working with the Hands* (Garden City, N.Y.: Doubleday, Page, 1904).

laid the foundation for the more constructive relations that grew between local whites and Tuskegee Institute. The school's thriving trade in carriage- and wagonbuilding also created economic bonds. His white neighbors regarded the black man who supplied these skills as a valuable community asset, and "the people with whom he lives and works are going to think twice before they part with such a man."[15]

Booker thus made racial interdependence a fundamental principle of his materialist strategy for African Americans. "The individual who can do something that the world wants done," he often said, "will, in the end, make his way regardless of his race." He uttered this idea, however, as if it were a settled law rather than a hope. If Washington the pragmatist's first instinct about brickmaking was to see its material benefit in improving race relations, then the psychologist in Booker found deeper and less apparent lessons: "My experience is that there is something in human nature which always makes an individual recognize and reward merit, no matter under what colour of skin merit is found . . . it is the visible, the tangible that goes a long way in softening prejudices."[16] He was correct in his overall psychological theory, but throughout his career Booker Washington would ignore the fact that in practice the visible evidence of black achievement often hardened white prejudice and resentment.

All the while he and the students were putting up buildings, Washington was acquiring land to the west and north, much of it from the Varner family. By 1884 the Institute encompassed almost 600 acres. Some of it was cultivated in cotton, corn, wheat, and vegetables, while the rest remained a forest of yellow pine, post oak, and various other hardwoods. Booker's aggressive accumulation of land undoubtedly pleased some land-poor whites like the Varners, who otherwise lacked buyers in the depressed local economy. But it became a point of contention between him and other whites suspicious of blacks' controlling so much local property. Whites knew that contributions from northerners financed the Institute's land purchases, and therefore Yankee money enabled the black school to get larger. Booker was only practicing what he preached. He exhorted blacks to buy land. He embraced the agrarian ideal popular among nineteenth-century Americans, a faith that landownership was the basis for virtuous citizenship and personal autonomy. It was precisely this implicit desire for citizenship and autonomy that made some whites uncomfortable with the Institute's increasing landholdings.

By the mid-1880s Booker Washington believed he had created a demonstration of what blacks could do on their own. "We were trying an experiment—that of testing whether or not it was possible for Negroes to build up and control the affairs of a large educational institution," he later wrote. "If we failed it would injure the whole race." If whites were running such an institution, he knew, everyone would predict its success, but they would be surprised if blacks succeeded. Blacks themselves needed proof that they could succeed at such an important endeavor. "The Negro is not yet sure of his own ability," Booker would later observe privately. "Nothing helps and encourages a Negro so much as to see one of his own number succeed."[17]

Therefore the success of Tuskegee Institute was regularly celebrated. Booker and Olivia produced commencements modeled on the Hampton ceremonies. They brought to the campus notable black men—the North Carolina educator and orator Joseph C. Price and the nation's leading black lawyer, Richard Greener—to speak at the exercises. Students gave speeches and recitations on such topics as "The Negro as Inventor," "The Negro an Important Factor in American History," and "Is the Proposed Negro Emigration from the South Necessary?" Each year more and more visitors, black and white, came to the Institute for the occasion. In 1887 the commencement attendance rose to 3,000, necessitating the construction of a large open-air pavilion covered with the foliage of mulberry trees. By all reports the visitors went away impressed with the handsome new campus and the rapidly growing student body. The whole enterprise was compelling testimony to what black people could do on their own.[18]

To achieve its full purpose—the education of the black masses— Tuskegee had to extend educational development beyond the campus. The Institute faculty traveled to nearby counties to train teachers already in service. At these in-service sessions, they gave lectures on academic subjects and provided lesson plans complete with simple illustrations. The Tuskegee professors showed, according to one of them, that "useful knowledge, a cultivated mind, and the right way of using it, are the ends to which the Public Schools should direct their attention." Afterward they met with local citizens to emphasize the necessity of generous community support for the schools. Good education, they preached, required skilled teachers, regular school attendance among the children, and well-constructed schoolhouses.[19]

Tuskegee's main outreach came from students who left the Institute and established primary schools of their own. Almost all the graduates in the 1880s built and conducted schools in rural areas or villages within fifty miles of Tuskegee. They reenacted what Booker had done when he took over the Malden school after he first left Hampton. Just as Booker always reported his progress to General Armstrong, Tuskegee graduates told him of the trials and triumphs of their experience. "My school house was not fit to teach winter school in," Hiram Thweatt wrote from Montgomery, "so as I understand something about carpentry, I procured a team of oxens [and] went to the mill and got 300 feet of lumber at my own expense and stripped my little building." "Enemies" burned John T. Hollis's first school in Richland, Georgia, but he and the local people built a bush arbor and then another school, a church, and a house for himself and his family. He had 70 children in the summer and 100 in the winter. Hollis conducted the first Sunday school held in the area for many years, teaching the Bible to children in the morning and to their parents in the afternoon. "Some of the best citizens had planned to leave the neighborhood but now they tell me they are not going any where." Missouri Strong established a school in Pike County with seventy-six dollars of public money and tuition paid quarterly by forty students, which together allowed her to conduct school for five months of the year. She had persuaded the community to build a comfortable schoolhouse that was furnished with a stove, blackboards, a globe, and desks. She also conducted a Sabbath school. "I am trying all I can," she reported to Booker, "to break up some of the bad habits that so many of these people are guilty [of], such as using so much whiskey and tobacco especially . . . very few own land, because these two things take all the cash they make." They learned firsthand what Booker had told them about the difficulty of their task. Iola Gautier found that the local people were not supporting her school thirty miles from Tuskegee. "The future seems dark indeed," she wrote

Booker, who soon found her another assignment. The attendance at her school in Tallassee, Lewis Adams's daughter Virginia reported to Booker, varied greatly according to the time of the year, with heavy enrollment in the winter but low attendance during the spring, when crop cultivation began. "It is one of the most difficult things that I have to contend with to get the people to keep their children in school long enough to do them some good." Still, Adams could see improvement among the people in their habits. "They are very much different from what they were when I came here."[20]

From its beginning, Tuskegee functioned as a kind of informal board of education for black schools—placing teachers, supervising curriculum, listening to complaints, and finding support for the little rural schools. Booker and Olivia Davidson arranged financial support to help construct or outfit a school. Through Olivia's connections, the Woman's Home Missionary Association of Boston supported several primary schools conducted by Tuskegee graduates. When an assignment in a rural community did not succeed, Booker found his graduates another school or else brought them back to work in the Tuskegee Institute training school, a large primary school conducted on the campus for local children. But Washington held no illusions that Tuskegee's efforts were an adequate substitute for publicly supported education. In 1887 he noted that the average black school in Alabama was in session only sixty-five days a year because the state provided only sixty-six cents per year for each black child, and little more for whites. "Is it not very plain that something must be done if the masses are to be educated? At the present rate we are not educating the increase in population." Still, in 1889 he emphasized what blacks themselves had accomplished: "Most Northern and Western States furnish the people with free teachers, free school houses, free apparatus, free furniture and free text-books. The colored people in Alabama who did not own themselves a quarter of a century ago have furnished their own school houses, apparatus, furniture and textbooks, and in most cases, have to pay the teacher themselves if the school remains in session longer than three or four months."[21]

In 1882 Washington organized the first statewide professional group for black teachers, the Alabama State Teachers' Association. In this enterprise his instinct for group psychology was again apparent. Black teachers confronted a daunting challenge in the South of the 1880s, and they needed a communal sense of purpose to bolster them during the inevitable hard times—a feeling that they were not alone, that success was possible. In his address to the teacher association's first meeting, Washington set forward in a prophetic style Tuskegee's ambitions for lifting the entire rural southern black population. He defined industrial training as a combination of mental and manual training that gave the majority of blacks in the South "the only alternative between remaining ignorant and receiving, at least, a common, practical education." Few young blacks could afford education at a residential college, he observed, and even in the rare cases in which it was available, an education provided at no cost to the student often spoiled him for hard work. Self-made people were more likely to succeed. Washington envisioned for every black community two teachers, a man and a woman, committed to uplifting the whole community. "Let them be teachers, not only in the school-house, but on the farm, in the flower-garden, and in the house, and we have a central light whose rays will soon penetrate the house of every family in the community." This new teacher corps would lay the foundation for blacks "so well that the race can stand securely thereon till it has served the great ends of our Creator."[22]

Booker's early public successes were countered by personal tragedy when in April 1884, while fundraising in Philadelphia, he got word that Fanny had suddenly fallen very ill. He rushed home to attend to her. The cause of the twenty-six-year-old's trouble is not clear. One report said she was suffering from "consumption of the bowels," but the explanation handed down within the family was that Fanny had been severely injured when she fell from a farm wagon. Whatever the cause, she died on May 4. She was buried in Tuskegee with a tombstone that read: "Our Lord is risen from the dead Our Jesus is gone up on high." Portia was not quite a year old. Having said little about his relationship with Fanny while she was alive, Booker Washington was equally stoic about her death. His one eulogy was odd in its tribute. "Perhaps the way in which Fanny was able to impress her life upon others most was in her extreme neatness in her housekeeping and general work," he said years later. "Nothing was done loosely or carelessly." Even after her death, Booker apparently felt the need to protect the privacy of their relationship.[23]

Booker hardly had time for grief. Fanny's death left him with sole responsibility for the care of a toddler. And at the very time of Fanny's death, Olivia Davidson was incapacitated by her chronic respiratory weakness and left Tuskegee for convalescence in New England. Her departure deprived him of his second-in-command, the person responsible for discipline among the female students, and an effective fundraiser. The expanding campus needed his attention, but the school would close if fundraising stopped. He had to go north to find money. He began to rely more on his Hampton classmate Warren Logan, who had taken over the school's account books. Booker had learned from General Marshall at Hampton the necessity for strict order in the institution's accounting to maintain the confidence of benefactors, and he had watched Logan to see if he was sufficiently careful. By 1885 Logan had earned Booker's full trust as a financial officer, and in Olivia's absence he left Logan in charge when he was away from the campus. Baby Portia was left in the care of a nurse.[24]

In early 1885 Booker brought his brother, John Henry Washington, to Tuskegee from West Virginia to set up a sawmill operation. The school's expansion required a great deal of lumber, and there was abundant timber available for harvest on the school property. John had worked on dam-construction projects for the U.S. Army Corps of Engineers after leaving Hampton. An effective manager, he soon assumed oversight of the campus building projects and in time took charge of the farming operation and the water supply. Known on campus as "Mr. J. H."—the students called the other Mr. Washington on campus "Mr. B. T."—John also assumed command of the Institute cadet corps. Like Hampton, Tuskegee Institute required male students to participate in military drill to enforce discipline. Not surprisingly, the head of the corps also carried the title of "disciplinarian" of students. Booker had a strong bond with his older brother. They had shared the love of their beloved Jane and Amanda and endured together the indifference and exploitation of their stepfather. John had helped finance Booker's education, and in turn Booker had given John his surname and helped him get through Hampton. John was independent-minded, less in awe of his little brother's authority and certainly less wary of his disapproval than others at Tuskegee. As irascible as he was capable, John never spared his brother his opinion about Institute affairs. As the campus grew and its management became more complex, John resisted the assignment of some of his original responsibilities to others; yet he remained loyal to Booker and Tuskegee at all times. Soon after coming to Tuskegee, John married and fathered eight children. John and his brood filled the vacuum of family for Booker and Portia.[25]

Booker's family extended even further in ensuing years with the arrival of James, the orphan boy whom Jane had taken into the family soon after their arrival in Malden. James, too, had adopted Booker's surname. In the 1880s James married, had a son whom he called Booker Jr., and struggled to make a living as a coal miner in Malden. No doubt remembering his own aversion to coal mining, Booker sent for James to come to Tuskegee. He served as baseball and football coach and later as the postmaster for the Institute. Only Amanda, now married with four children, stayed in Malden. Barely literate, Amanda may not have imagined that there would be a comfortable place for her at the school. Amanda's son Albert Johnston eventually came to Tuskegee for an education and spent his career working for the Institute. Booker and Albert would become close in later years, sharing an interest in politics.[26]

The incessant work of building the school inevitably took its toll on Washington, as it had done on Olivia Davidson in 1884. In the fall of 1885 he became ill and went to Montgomery for several weeks of treatment and rest. In the months before this illness, he had dealt with two incidents of racial conflict between Tuskegee students and employees and local whites, one of which is described below; the other Booker alluded to but never explained. He recovered in a few weeks from what in all likelihood was exhaustion from overwork and from stress induced by the threatening racial environment in which he had to operate. The possibility of physical breakdown from overwork loomed over Washington from then on. For the rest of his life he manifested a pattern: he would labor to the point of exhaustion and then experience some intensely stressful racial situation, after which he had to step away entirely from his duties for a few weeks at a time. As with the emotional content of his marriage or his grief over Fanny's death, Booker never spoke openly about the effects of work and worry on him, but others saw it. In 1887, at the behest of General Armstrong, who had just had a heart attack at age forty-seven, Booker attended a course on health improvement at Harvard. Extended rest improved his health, but in his normal routine he was never able to reduce his workload.[27]

By early 1886 Olivia had returned to Tuskegee and resumed her central role at the school. She apparently saw the effects of heavy responsibilities on Booker, because she took a special interest in his well-being. A romantic relationship developed between them. Olivia was a beautiful woman. Otherwise unwilling to comment on female beauty, Booker called hers a "rare face." They clearly had always admired each other, and he fully appreciated Olivia's talents. By then they had been full partners in the building of Tuskegee Institute for the better part of four years. She was by all reports a refined woman who could not only teach English, personal hygiene, homemaking, and chastity to poor farm girls but also solve vexing administrative problems on campus and then board a train to coax money from New England's elite. Beyond her appearance and brains, he admired her devotion to the Tuskegee cause. She had contributed more than anyone else to the realization of his goals. Booker left few clues about his emotional self, but he obviously felt deep affection for Olivia. Although he apparently appreciated the talents and virtues of all his wives, he commented openly far more on Olivia's. She was probably his most intimate companion.

In August 1886 Booker and Olivia traveled to her home in Ohio and were married. Despite her recent poor health, she was pregnant within a few weeks. Carrying a child taxed her health severely, and she went to Boston in the spring of 1887 to receive extensive care for the final weeks of her pregnancy. In late May 1887 she gave birth to a boy whom she named Baker T. Washington, in honor of both the father and the white Baker family in Boston who had long supported her work. When he was older, Baker changed his name to Booker T. Washington Jr., although the family continued to call him by his birth name. Less than a year after the first child's birth, Olivia was pregnant again. Ernest Davidson Washington arrived in February 1889. Booker's immediate family suddenly numbered five, with three children under six years old.[28]

Olivia created a happy home for the serious-minded principal of Tuskegee. By the time he was thirty in 1886, Booker had married two women who were much like himself: of mixed blood and probably more white than black, inner-directed, goal-oriented, race-conscious, and hard-working. Each shared qualities with his beloved mother. He was attracted to partners who embraced his mission and could help achieve it. Sadly for him, once he found those mates, frail health brought their lives to an early end.

Booker's success at Tuskegee was always predicated on assuaging white fears, but the impossibility of stifling white hostility was made clear by a single event in 1885. Several Institute staff members, including Washington's old Malden friend Samuel Courtney, were traveling between Tuskegee and Montgomery to celebrate a wedding. Courtney reported that the party—"all of us were mulattoes, and would pass for white people"—were seated in the first-class compartment of a train as it made a refueling stop northwest of Tuskegee, near the place where Leonard Coker had been lynched three years before. A mob of whites encircled the train. "There are three coons on the first class car," Courtney reported one of the whites saying. Twelve white men approached the blacks, each with revolver drawn, and addressed Courtney because he looked like "an intelligent nigger." One of them said: "Don't you know better than to ride in a first-class car? Before we'll let you ride any further in that car we'll take you out there in the field and fill you with bullets." Courtney and the others moved to the second-class smoking car. The trip resumed, but farther down the line the bride and groom were arrested and fined on a spurious charge. At that point the party abandoned train travel. To avoid the vigilantes, they found horses for a thirty-five-mile ride back to Tuskegee.[29]

The incident spurred Washington to complain to the Montgomery *Advertiser* that blacks could buy a first-class ticket but were often re-

fused first-class service. Blacks were typically given filthy accommodations that were not even segregated: "Whenever a poorly dressed,
slovenly white man boards the train he is shown into the colored half
coach. When a white man gets drunk or wants to lounge around in an
indecent position he finds his way into the colored department." As
a result, blacks approached rail travel with trepidation. "The mere
thought of a trip on a railroad brings to me a feeling of intense dread
and I never enter a railroad coach unless compelled to do so," Washington told the *Advertiser.* This was not a matter of "social equality or
anything bordering on it," he wrote. "To the negro it is a matter of dollars and cents." If the railroads would not allow blacks to share first-
class accommodation with whites, they should give blacks separate cars
with equal amenities or sell tickets to them only at reduced rates. But
he made clear the expectation for equal treatment: if he was buying a
yard of calico at a Tuskegee dry-goods store or a newspaper from the
Advertiser, Washington said, he expected and received the same quality
item as the white man. Having made his protest, he couched his objections in a respectful context. "I have written thus plainly because I love
the South, had rather live here than in the North, and expect to remain
here." He had faith that southern whites would correct this wrong: additional federal laws to protect blacks' civil rights would do little good.
He thus deferred to white southern nationalists' extreme sensitivity—
which easily became a violent hysteria—about northern interference
in southern race relations, at the same time that he reminded whites
implicitly of the promised equal protections of the U.S. Constitution
and the continuing possibility of outside help for black rights. The protest had the desired effect. The *Advertiser* printed an editorial that identified Booker as "a man who stands well in the community where he
lives," meaning that he was well regarded by whites. The letter was "not
only conservative in tone, but has justice on its side in what it asks."[30]
The editor called on the railroads to heed Washington's requests.

By the time he wrote this letter, Booker was already at work organizing other blacks to complain to railroad companies about discriminatory treatment. He advised them to approach railroads, privately
and respectfully, and demand equal treatment for the service they purchased. Such a strategy was consistent with his belief that economic

interdependence was the means to peace between the races. Where the dollar was involved, equality and fairness should prevail. If no relief was forthcoming from the railroads, he counseled a more public appeal like the one he made in the *Advertiser*. It was a style of protest he would advocate and practice in the years ahead. In 1885 he could not see how hard and fast racial segregation was going to become.[31]

His railroad diplomacy reflected Booker's keen awareness that a black man in his position had to step lightly. Southern whites enforced a conformism of thought that brooked no criticism of current practices by whites or blacks. In 1884 the Louisiana novelist George Washington Cable, recognized as the South's leading writer at the time, gave a speech in Tuscaloosa, Alabama, in which he decried at length the white South's moral failure in its treatment of blacks. Cable followed this speech with magazine articles that reiterated his thoughts on the South's systemic racial injustice. White editorialists across the region condemned the writer for his apostasy. In 1885 Cable abandoned the South for the peace and safety of New England, never to return to the region to live, though he remained engaged with southern race issues from afar and maintained a friendly acquaintance with Booker Washington. "If a few more Southern people would come out boldly as Mr. Cable has," Booker wrote privately, "it would help matters much." There were many whites in the South "who *think* as Mr. Cable does but have not the moral courage to express their sentiments."[32]

Booker could control his own tongue but not others'. During the summer of 1885 a Tuskegee graduate made a speech that angered local whites, although what exactly he said is not known. In response, whites made threats against the Institute. In light of the railroad trouble, Washington was worried. The anger died down, but for Booker there was always the possibility that someone associated with the school might spark white anger. A surge in lynchings increased the sense of active danger. Beginning at the time of the Jack Turner and Leonard Coker executions in 1882, white southerners practiced lynch law with impunity. About five lynchings were reported each year in Alabama, several of them in counties near Tuskegee. No doubt other ritual executions were not reported in the public press. In time Washington would speak out against lynching, but in the 1880s his position was too precarious to allow him to issue any public criticism. In 1886 he made a brief statement that foreshadowed the position he later took to wide public note: "There is nothing truer than that the whites and blacks are to occupy this south-land together for all time. This being a fact that no man can change, there is nothing more absurd than for any man, white or black, to strive to keep up strife between the races. Socially we can be as separate as the fingers yet united as the hand for every good purpose. The Negro needs the white man and the white man needs the Negro."[33]

The experience of blacks who did condemn lynching showed Washington the dangers of doing so. Jesse Duke, editor of a black newspaper in Montgomery, was an ally of Washington in the capital city. In 1887 Duke denounced lynching and said that ritual executions typically resulted not from rape but from "the growing appreciation of the white Juliet for the colored Romeo as he becomes more intelligent and refined." Fury arose in white Montgomery over Duke's claim. The editor of the *Advertiser* called on "the boys" in Montgomery to warn Duke out of town. The departure occurred swiftly, but white anger spilled over onto other Montgomery blacks who had said nothing about lynching publicly. Cornelius N. Dorsette, Booker's physician and closest confidant in Montgomery, came under attack for having what whites labeled a "big head"—a conclusion reached because Dorsette had defended black interests.[34]

In 1888 the perils of speaking out against lynching became even clearer in Tuskegee when an employee of the school, George W. Lovejoy, wrote to a Mississippi newspaper about an attempted lynching in the town. "The white people of our county have caught the spirit of the lynch-law," Lovejoy wrote. A black man had allegedly been caught in the room of a white girl. Lovejoy pointed to the hypocrisy of a lynching under those circumstances, when nothing would happen to a white man found in a black servant girl's quarters. "This is a wide contrast between the two rascals both guilty of the same offense," Lovejoy wrote. Unfortunately for Booker, Lovejoy ended his letter with an appeal for black Mississippians to enroll at Tuskegee Institute.[35]

The Tuskegee *Weekly News* responded to Lovejoy's criticism with a lengthy and poetic headline:

> Lying Lovejoy is His Name,
> Of Ginger Cake Color,
> The Third Dusky Romeo Turned Out to Roam
> From the Tuskegee Normal School
> That has Ventilated his Spleen and Hate of the White Race.
> Is it the Purpose of this School to Breed Such Whelps.

The editor did not reveal the identity of the two previous black critics, although one was probably the unnamed graduate who had drawn fire in the summer of 1885. The article did reveal that some Tuskegee whites were suspicious of the Institute's impact on white authority in the town. Booker was away from Tuskegee when the letter became known, but other Institute employees sent Lovejoy packing. On his return, Washington wrote apologetically to the editor of the *Weekly News* that it had "always been and is now the policy of the Normal School to remain free from politics and the discussions of race questions that tend to stir up strife between the races." Rarely had Institute blacks given offense to whites. He insisted that the feeling between the races had always been "as pleasant as it well could be." His apology must have been accepted, because the controversy subsided. But the Lovejoy incident revealed the fragility of racial peace in Tuskegee. An ill-considered phrase exposed the lie of the model community. Booker wanted to preserve the illusion so that his work could continue, but he could never be secure in the vaunted harmony in Tuskegee, because it never really existed.[36]

During the years of building his school and starting his family, Washington was becoming a public man who took positions on important issues. Since his adolescence in Malden he had engaged racial matters. But as with his complaint about railroad discrimination in 1885, he stepped into the public light only as part of the execution of his Tuskegee responsibilities. During fundraising trips, Washington sometimes made reports on racial conditions that were published in northern newspapers. These talks were more candid than any he could make in the South. His observations about circumstances in the South were realistic and often plainly dismal. In 1882 he told a group in Springfield, Massachusetts, that blacks in Alabama had largely withdrawn from politics. Less than half of the eligible men were voting, a response to both the futility of challenging white political domination and the recognition that educational and economic uplift held more promise for blacks. Teachers in Alabama's black schools were in desperate need of more training. Still, he could not leave white northerners, potential donors to Tuskegee, with the idea that the situation was futile: Washington was confident, the Springfield *Daily Republican* reported, that blacks had their best chance for advancement in the South, because competition for jobs was greater in the North.[37]

Booker strongly condemned the sharecropping system, saying in 1886 that the crop lien system robbed black farmers of nearly half their earnings. Blacks were tired of working hard all year and getting nothing for it. It was impossible under the sharecropping system to escape debt and gain independence. Many had reached the conclusion that their only option was to move west. Too many indebted black farmers landed in the convict lease system, in which prisoners were leased to private contractors to work on railroads, mines, or farms. The system resulted in appalling inhumanity, as in the case of the Georgia prisoner whose feet rotted off when he was forced to work without shoes on a chain gang during winter. Convict leasing, Washington declared, failed to make "a better man when released, but rather a worse one."[38]

Anything Booker Washington said publicly in the 1880s about lifting his race came in the context of whites' belief that blacks would not be able to survive in freedom—that ultimately they would die out in the absence of the care and concern of white masters. Some of this represented the wishful thinking of white nationalists that their black enemies were disappearing. A large undercount of blacks in the 1870 census suggested blacks' imminent demographic demise, but the more accurate count in the 1880 census indicated the opposite: the black population was booming. An outpouring of speculation about race competition ensued, much of it based on applications of Charles Darwin's ideas. "At some future period, not very distant as measured by centuries," Darwin wrote in 1871, "the civilized races of man will almost certainly exterminate and replace the savage races throughout the world." In 1884 Alabama's white-nationalist Senator John Tyler Morgan predicted that as the growing black population gained status, it would compete with whites, and blacks' increasing prestige and wealth would be checked by "the jealousy of caste." Education of the Negro, Morgan warned, raised expectations and desires among blacks that would inevitably intensify racial competition. For Morgan and other white nationalists, the only solution to this competition was an old one: removal of blacks to Africa. Another southerner wrote that, as a growing black population gained education and wealth and sought opportunities, "then disastrous social disorders are threatened, and colonization—enforced, if necessary—is the remedy."[39]

Washington tried to defuse whites' anxiety about black competition. In 1884 he spoke to a gathering of 4,000 at the National Education Association, his first truly national address. His overriding message was optimism about southern race relations. He began by reporting that whereas the first northerners who came to Tuskegee in 1870 to teach the freed people were run out of town, whites in recent years had taken the lead in establishing Tuskegee Institute. He drew the lesson that interracial harmony was a necessity for black advancement: any successful movement "for the elevation of the Southern Negro must have a certain extent the cooperation of Southern whites." He advanced his materialist strategy: good race relations would grow out of economic interdependence and better education opportunities for blacks. "Harmony will come in proportion as the black man gets something that the white man wants, whether it be of brains or material," he said. "Good school teachers and plenty of money to pay them will be more potent in settling the race question than many civil rights bills and investigating committees." He asserted that the Negro's home was permanently in the South, and therefore it was in the interest of all for blacks and whites to learn how to get along. In advancing a kindly view of southern blacks, he was both rejecting the white nationalists who saw blacks as their racial enemies and exploiting the tension between them and other whites, mostly planters and industrialists, who wanted to keep blacks in their midst and benefit from their cheap labor. By saying that blacks would remain permanently in the South, he expressed what he thought was best for blacks, but he also subtly warned whites of the continuing possibility of black migration if conditions in the South were bad.[40]

In this speech, Washington manifested a prophetic instinct. He offered both warnings and affirmative prophecies. He promised that there would be progress in race relations and that education and hard work would pay off. This vision of deliverance from the troubled present has been characteristic of African-American leadership. Although many black leaders would be far more emphatic in their warnings to whites about future punishment for wrongs done to blacks, few would be more insistent than Washington to fellow blacks that the future would be better if they worked faithfully now.

As for what blacks should do, Washington recommended exactly what most black leaders of the day did—a turn inward and an emphasis on race consciousness, self-help, and group solidarity rather than political action. The Reconstruction commitment to politics and protest now seemed like a lost cause as antiblack Democrats regained power in the national government and dominated every southern state. Most of the black heroes of Reconstruction politics like Blanche K. Bruce and P. B. S. Pinchback no longer held elective office. Nearly all black spokesmen in the 1880s advised their followers to reorient their strategies away from politics toward the economy. Even so fierce a protest lion as Frederick Douglass voiced this view in 1880 when he declared that "neither we, nor any other people will ever be respected till we respect ourselves, and we will never respect ourselves till we have the means to live respectably." Only when blacks developed a group of wealthy men, Douglass said, would they get their full due of political rights. In his most famous lecture, delivered more than fifty times, Douglass called for the creation of a large class of black "Self-made Men," which he defined as "the men who owe little or nothing to birth, relationship, friendly surroundings; to wealth inherited or to early approved means of education; who are what they are, without the aid of any of the favoring conditions by which other men usually rise in the world and achieve great results." Self-made men were simply men of work. "Honest labor faithfully, steadily and persistently pursued, is the best, if not the only, explanation of their success." Booker Washington believed what Douglass said and often preached the same message.[41]

When pressed in the mid-1880s about black political rights, Washington said he believed that a literacy test for voting would cause political parties to commit more resources to education. Requiring literacy would encourage illiterate blacks and whites to get an education. In turn, an educated black population would undermine whites' opposition to blacks' voting on the basis of ignorance. This represented, at best, hopeful thinking, for Washington knew all too well the intense opposition to any black political influence. He presumed that a literacy test for voting would be applied equally to blacks and whites. That supposition would prove to be wrong.[42]

Booker publicly challenged the worsening depictions of black character. In 1886 he criticized an unnamed U.S. senator, probably John Tyler Morgan, who had said that despite the public and private aid lavished on blacks since the Civil War, the Negro had made no progress. Washington said he was sure the man had never spent an hour in a black school or visited the home of an educated Negro. Too many whites knew blacks only as servants or miscreants, he told the National Unitarian Conference. "If a colored man gets into a fight, or steals a chicken," he said, "it appears in the papers in glaring head-lines." But if he "buys a hundred acres of land or builds a home, or his son graduates from a school, it is not mentioned."[43] Washington had begun a lifelong preoccupation with the way blacks were portrayed in the media.

Washington resisted the antiblack message by embracing whites who expressed positive views of blacks. He praised Jabez Lamar Monroe Curry, the philanthropist-educator who insisted that it was "eternally right to Christianize and to educate the Negro." Washington often cited Atticus Haygood, the Methodist minister who administered the Slater Fund, who had asserted that "the progress of the negro in the United States during the last twenty years is one of the marvels of history." He extolled the benevolent paternalism of Henry Grady after the Atlanta editor told a New York audience that "relations of the southern people with the negro are close and cordial" because of the "fidelity [with which] for four years [during the Civil War] he guarded our defenseless women and children." He appreciated George Cable's sympathy for blacks, although after the writer was exiled for criticizing the white South he was no longer a useful exemplar. Washington liked the symbolic message of wisdom and kindness about blacks in Joel Chandler Harris's Uncle Remus stories in the *Constitution*. Curry, Haygood, Grady, Harris, and a few more like them were proof that not all southern whites opposed black education or wanted to remove blacks from the South. They stood for reconciliation with the North, dismissed the fears of another federal invasion, and believed that blacks were worthy of affection and support.[44]

Such men justified Washington's positive emphasis on white southerners in his predictions of progress. He treated them as representative of the white South—indeed, the truest to southern tradition and the most powerful men in the region. But in fact the white nationalists like Ben Tillman, Bill Arp, and John Tyler Morgan were becoming more numerous and more influential. Washington must have seen this, but he refused to acknowledge it openly.

The rapid building of Tuskegee Institute aroused envy in the leaders of two emerging black public colleges in Alabama—themselves also remarkable, self-made men. Far to the north of Tuskegee, in Huntsville, Alabama Agricultural and Mechanical College, the first black public college in the state, was headed by William Hooper Councill. Born a slave in North Carolina and brought to Huntsville by slave traders, Councill acquired an education in the early years of emancipation and became a teacher, lawyer, newspaper editor, and, during Reconstruction, an active Republican who held appointive office. With the Democratic takeover of the state in 1874, Councill suddenly changed his political affiliation. To prove his Democratic bona fides, he now embraced the white-nationalist ideology, saying that "the love and attachment between the races of the South are more than wonderful when we consider the untiring efforts of busy and meddlesome enemies—the politicians, the newspapers, the magazines and even the pulpit seeking to scatter seeds of discord and break up our peace." But even an opportunist like Councill was subject to white-supremacist discipline. He was charged with rape and assault in 1885 but was acquitted, because, some thought, his Democratic Party friends quashed the criminal charges. In 1886 he sued a railroad over its mistreatment of black passengers, similar to the Tuskegee faculty members' experience the previous year. A federal tribunal upheld the justice of his claim, but Councill quickly learned the meaning of a pyrrhic victory. His success in court earned him the enmity of the conservative Democratic establishment, including the editor of the Montgomery *Advertiser,* who wrote that Councill was behaving "in a fair way to get his head cracked." The white fury was so great that it forced Councill's resignation from the Huntsville school.[45]

Washington distrusted Councill as an opportunist, but his demise was nonetheless clear warning of what could happen to a black who challenged white authority: he risked losing his job, his freedom, and possibly his life. It had to be a threatening lesson to Booker, given the close parallels between his own ambitions and Councill's.

Councill certainly learned the lesson of his undoing. A peerless political operator, within a year he ousted his replacement at the Huntsville college and regained the support of powerful Democrats. Thereafter he yielded to no black man in sycophancy to white power. He became without question the preferred black leader among white nationalists, in part by pandering to whites' obsessions with sex and race: "Were it not for white ladies in this country, hell would have broken loose long ago. God bless the white woman! I know she wants me hung when I assault or insult her and she is right! I tell you negro men you had better let that white lady alone for she is the goddess of all virtue and purity." But by taking public positions that ratified white-nationalist thinking about black criminality and moral degeneracy, Councill limited Washington's room for maneuver. Any position for civil rights taken by a black leader in the South, however carefully muted, looked radical next to Councill's. He was clearly jealous of Booker's greater success with white philanthropists. When influential whites connected with Hampton Institute opposed Councill's fundraising efforts on the basis of the morals charge, he blamed Washington. His potential to hurt Booker was great: he was a persuasive orator who understood as well as Booker the use of newspapers to advance his own cause, and apparently there were no lengths to which Councill would not go.[46]

He and Washington competed for the state's resources, and while Booker sometimes held his own, he lost out to Councill on the biggest prize available to black colleges: designation as the black land-grant agricultural college under the Morrill Act of 1890. Washington had hoped to get all or a portion of the fund, and Tuskegee clearly had the best record of agricultural education among black colleges in the state. But during legislative discussions, Tuskegee's financial support by northerners and the fact that the state did not control the school's property were used as reasons to place the land grant elsewhere. Councill got it. The fact of Washington's relatively autonomous authority over his institution made the unctuous Councill the safe choice for federal largesse.[47]

Washington also engaged in a long-running competition with the head of the other black public institution in the state, Alabama State University for Colored Youths, run by Councill's only real rival for unprincipled opportunism, the Scottish immigrant William Burns Paterson. After a fight between his students and those at a local white college in 1887, Paterson's school had to flee the Black Belt town of Marion, proof that a black school existed only at the sufferance of whites. Paterson decided that Montgomery was the best place to relocate. Booker considered the capital city part of Tuskegee's natural territory. He recruited students there, traded for goods and services, and developed strong black and white supporters in the city. Avoiding direct involvement, Booker enlisted his friends and hired a lobbyist to pull political wires to keep Paterson out. It was a bitter conflict but one characteristic of the political infighting that occurred at the time in the placement and funding of public institutions of higher education. Booker was overmatched in political machination by the wily Paterson, who persuaded Montgomery town boosters that his college would invigorate the local economy. From then on, Washington had to cope with Paterson's hostility to Tuskegee. Paterson had barely arrived in Montgomery when he began a campaign for the Morrill Act money, despite having no agricultural program at all, and his aggressive efforts helped to undermine Tuskegee's.[48]

13. By 1889 Booker had achieved a lot but had also suffered serious personal setbacks. Photo possibly by Harry Shepherd, late 1880s; courtesy of the Library of Congress.

Paterson and Councill set limits on what the head of a black college could say and do in Alabama, and they effectively eliminated prospects of more public support for Tuskegee. They stirred up white suspicions about Washington's close ties to northern philanthropy and the obvious fruits it yielded in Tuskegee. Already a man who instinctively played his cards close to his vest, Booker acted carefully and often secretively because it was necessary to do so in the face of unscrupulous rivals and competitors for funds nearby.

Whatever trouble might arise from external threats must have seemed insignificant in comparison with a new tragedy in Booker Washington's personal life. New joy had entered it on February 6, 1889, with the birth of little Ernest, just twenty months after Olivia had delivered Baker. Her second pregnancy must have gone more easily, because Ernest was born in Tuskegee. But on the night of February 8 the Washingtons' house at Tuskegee burned to the ground, the cause of the fire reportedly a defective flue. Booker was in the North raising money when it happened. The convalescent Olivia ran from the flames with the children in her arms. The exposure worsened Olivia's already weak condition, and when she did not recover from the shock, Booker took her to Boston. Her friends there arranged the best care available for her, and Booker sat at her hospital bedside for most of two months, leaving only to make short fundraising trips. He sent brief, hopeful letters about her health back to Tuskegee, but to General Armstrong he was more honest on April 21: "As hard as it is I guess it is best for me to look the matter in the face and say that at present she is not gaining and without a change soon can not last much longer." Olivia died on May 9, apparently of her long-standing respiratory illness, possibly tuberculosis. Booker had barely enough money to take her body back to Tuskegee. She was buried beneath a tombstone with the simple epitaph "She lived to the truth." Booker revealed more of his feelings to Armstrong than perhaps to anyone else, although that amounted to little. "Few will ever know just what she was to Tuskegee and me," he wrote, without actually describing his feelings of grief. "But I can not trust myself to write more now."[49]

In the summer of 1889 Tuskegee Institute teetered on the verge of closing, so precarious was its financial condition as a result of the grieving principal's neglect of fundraising. Booker finally appealed to General Armstrong. "I know no one else to apply to," he wrote to his mentor a few months later.[50] The general sent enough money for his star student and Tuskegee Institute to survive.

4

The Survival of the Race

Olivia's long illness and her death had surely raised doubts in Booker as to whether he and his mission could survive so much personal tragedy. Having married two good women, both models of Christian womanhood and excellent helpmates, he had not managed to sustain a happy, settled home life. Now he was widowed a second time, lonely and distraught with three little children to care for. His work was challenging enough in itself; his personal tragedy left him with little emotional energy to face the monumental task of keeping Tuskegee Institute alive. Nearing the end of his first decade in Tuskegee, he was unable to enjoy the remarkable achievements of his time there. He had established his school with precious little and expanded it beyond the most ambitious hopes. Tuskegee had 400 students, almost twice as many as were enrolled at the University of Alabama in 1890 and a third more than at the white Agricultural and Mechanical College at Auburn. Tuskegee was producing about as many black teachers as all the white normal schools in Alabama together. The Institute had a physically impressive campus, with seven new buildings sitting on several hundred acres of land. It showed what blacks were capable of doing; no other institution of learning for blacks had developed nearly so far under the direction of a black man.[1]

But the deep economic depression of the early 1890s endangered this success. Money became harder to raise in the North. In April 1893 merchants in Montgomery, who supplied most of the goods purchased at the school, refused to fill orders without payment in hard currency. In August the Tuskegee banks refused to pay out currency from the Institute's deposits, and only the merchant and trustee George W. Campbell would cash an Institute check. Times were so hard that the school had to borrow money from students and faculty to open that fall.[2]

It was a tribute to the determination of Booker Washington that from this low point he began an ascent that in a few years would make him the most famous and respected black man in America. His survival and success derived from his acute sensitivity about racial attitudes, his will not to be defeated by whites who saw all blacks as their enemies, and his ability to circumvent opposition through skillful indirection. His agility and resolve personified blacks' endurance at an awful moment in history. The great symbol of Washington's purpose was Tuskegee Institute; its visible success became for him an emblem for the eventual triumph of the race as a whole.

Tuskegee Institute survived simply because Washington raised more and more money. He engaged fundraisers to help him, but they were sometimes more trouble than they were worth, and in the end he did most of it himself. During his northern trips he continued to speak night after night and then during the day went door to door, collecting individual contributions that came mostly in checks for $10 and $25. His appeal was a simple and straightforward promise: $50 would educate one Tuskegee student for an entire school year. "How can $50 be made to do more good? It provides a chance for a student to remain in school a year, working out what he cannot pay, and at the same time learning some useful industry, developing the highest form of self help." He plotted constantly to find new support. In 1889 he received his first $1,000 from Collis P. Huntington, the railroad magnate, and perhaps the first gift from those deriving huge wealth from America's burgeoning industrial development—the men Mark Twain called the Robber Barons. In 1890 he received the first of many significant gifts from Caroline and Olivia Phelps Stokes of New York City, heirs to a commercial and mining fortune. Like the Mason sisters of Boston, the

14. By 1890 students at Tuskegee could learn a wide variety of industrial skills, including woodworking. Photo by Frances Benjamin Johnston, 1902; courtesy of the Library of Congress.

Phelps Stokeses shared their abundant inherited wealth with the cause of black education, especially as embodied in Tuskegee.[3]

The successful fundraising paid for an even greater expansion of Tuskegee Institute. In 1890 the more than 400 students could choose to learn, in addition to academic subjects and farming, one or more of fourteen trades: brickmaking, plastering, painting, carpentry, blacksmithing, wheelwrighting, sawmill work, printing, tinsmithing, shoemaking, harnessmaking, sewing, laundering, and cooking. That year the school's operating budget was just under $30,000, fully $25,000 of which was covered by donations. The remainder came from the $3,000 state appropriation and $1,500 from the Slater and Peabody Funds. The school owned 680 acres of land, and Booker put its value, including the many buildings erected since 1881, at $100,000.

Then the Institute experienced a five-year boom. In that time the first science hall, the first big building for teaching trades, a religion hall, and a chapel went up. Now eighteen buildings were sprinkled across the rolling campus. By 1893 the school's budget had doubled, and the student population exceeded 500. Landholdings had risen to 1,100 acres, 400 of which were in cultivation. By 1895 there were almost 800 students. At that point Tuskegee Institute had the largest enrollment among institutions of higher education in Alabama and perhaps the largest in the South.[4]

By 1895 the school owned 1,810 acres. This large holding was more than was needed for the campus and even for "the farm"—the school's agricultural operations. The acquisition of so much land perhaps indicated Washington's faith that the school's growth would continue at the current rapid rate, or he might have seen it as an investment hedge against future hard times. Large landholding was a compelling measure of Tuskegee's success, proof of substantial black accomplishment. But it also fed Washington's ego. Land represented autonomy and status, the values of the dominant white society, and Booker had embraced both. He had acquired a large stretch of property, and he managed his large holdings just as wealthy planters did. He never acknowledged the similarity, but whites noted it, and many did not like it. Whites objected for the same reason that Booker acquired so much land: it represented black achievement and independence measured in the material form most widely valued by nineteenth-century Americans.

Tuskegee's growth was enabled by Washington's response to a major reorientation of northern support for southern education in the early 1890s. When the Institute was founded as a school to train teachers, industrial education had essentially meant the teaching of good work habits. In the late nineteenth century, curricula in higher education in the United States shifted away from classical education to a more hands-on, applied commitment to practical knowledge. Colleges and universities moved to an elective curriculum in which students could choose to master a particular discipline at the expense of a unified liberal-arts curriculum. This sort of focus was especially encouraged in technological and business fields. Colleges like Oberlin, Berea,

15. Mattressmaking was a skill taught to female students. Photo by Frances Benjamin Johnston, 1902; courtesy of the Library of Congress.

and even Wellesley embraced an approach to hands-on, experiential learning that integrated practical knowledge with academic study. In the 1880s philanthropists supporting black education began to insist on instruction in particular trades and much less on academic subjects. This trend reflected the spread of white opposition to any classical education for blacks as well as the growing influence of large industrialists in educational philanthropy. The captains of industry wanted a black workforce trained for their shops and mills, not a people educated to believe that working with their hands was demeaning.[5]

The Slater Fund tied its support for institutions of higher learning to those whose curricula emphasized education in the trades. To enforce implementation of this orientation, J. L. M. Curry, now the administrator of the fund, began to concentrate its donations among fewer schools. Hampton and Tuskegee were among the main beneficiaries. Washington accepted this change not just to get the Slater money but because it was necessary to maintain the confidence of the most influential white philanthropists. "I am quite convinced that donations from the North in the future are going to be more largely than ever devoted to industrial education," he told Warren Logan in 1893. "I meet this sentiment on every hand." Once imposed on Booker, the change created new problems even as it ensured philanthropic support. In the years ahead the Tuskegee curriculum became more bifurcated, its academic and trades teaching more difficult to reconcile. And Tuskegee's continued receipt of funds generated resentment among schools that were losing financial support. Atlanta University suffered, and its administrators and faculty would blame Washington for their hard times and the skepticism among wealthy northerners about their work. The trades emphasis also encouraged an identification of Tuskegee as a trade school rather than a teacher-training institution. Although it still mostly produced teachers, Washington allowed the false impression to persist to ensure continued success in his fundraising.[6]

Washington tried to put the change in the best light. He argued that industrial training would reduce white hostility to black education. He was convinced that teaching specific skills was appropriate to the evolving economic conditions that blacks faced. For the first decade of Tuskegee Institute's existence, he had worked mainly to prepare teachers to educate rural blacks in how to become independent, landowning farmers. No doubt in response to severe depression in the agricultural economy in the early 1890s, Booker began to envision blacks as proprietors of small businesses based on the craft skills they acquired at industrial schools. Having seen the rapid industrialization and urbanization occurring in the United States, he perceived a burgeoning demand for skilled workers in the generations ahead. He assumed that the nation's dynamic capitalism would need and accept black entrepreneurs. He had confidence in the market economy to reward black businessmen who met an economic need.

But at the same time he warned blacks about an intensifying racial competition for jobs. Washington presumed that economic opportunity was a zero-sum game in which every white gain meant a black loss, and vice versa. At least by 1893, and probably earlier, Booker believed that blacks in the United States were losing their jobs in skilled crafts. He noted the displacement of black barbers, who had dominated that trade after the Civil War. At a meeting of Hampton alumni in 1893, Booker polled his fellow graduates, virtually all of whom were teaching in industrial schools, and found that most thought that blacks were not holding their own in industries. By 1895 he was telling his students that blacks' loss of positions in skilled crafts like barbering, painting, and cooking resulted from poor preparation and weak job performance. He also acknowledged that the loss of skilled jobs owed much to increased competition from southern- and eastern-European immigrants, who in the 1880s had started to flood into the United States. Growing strength in the labor movement threatened black opportunity, because nearly all unions discriminated against blacks and many denied them membership altogether. Such discrimination hardened Booker's already existing suspicion of organized labor. At some point during his youth, he had witnessed a strike at a Malden coal mine. The lesson he extracted from that event was that conflict between labor and management resulted in unnecessary suffering among workers and no lasting gains.[7]

Booker's fears about the impact of immigrants on demand for black labor and his opposition to unions reinforced the practical fundraising imperatives at Tuskegee. He realized he could not expect white workers or white immigrants to support his efforts on behalf of blacks. He further understood that the industrialists who might be willing to help him were adamantly opposed to unions. His appeal to them was strengthened by the suggestion that blacks were instinctively suspicious of unions and less likely to join them than were white immigrants. Washington's embrace of industrial education was entirely motivated by economic thinking, but it presumed the impossibility of interracial working-class unity.

At the same time Washington declared that petit-bourgeois blacks would settle American race problems. "Nothing else so soon brings about right relations between the two races in the South as the industrial progress of the negro," he wrote later. "Friction between the races will pass away in proportion as the black man, by reason of his skill, intelligence, and character, can produce something that the white man wants or respects in the commercial world." Every black operator of a sawmill, brickyard, printing press, or tin shop made whites dependent on a black man rather than vice versa. Economic success led to property ownership, which would result in black landlords and black moneylenders. The white man whose mortgage was held by a black would not prevent that Negro from voting, and therefore through commercial life the Negro would realize all his rights in the South. Booker promised that "a white man respects a negro who owns a two-story brick house."[8]

Washington's materialist strategy for racial uplift was a bold promise—and a new one in African-American life. Although other blacks had emphasized economic independence and self-help, no one else had ventured so far in imagining an economic basis for racial harmony. It marked a sharp departure from the tradition of ideological and constitutional appeals to racial justice made by, and on behalf of, African Americans. It seemed appropriate to the times, coming as it did not long after Andrew Carnegie had advanced a "Gospel of Wealth" to Americans; but it remained to be seen if American materialist values could in fact overcome racial bigotry, especially the virulent form of it found among white nationalists.

If Booker's survival instinct—and his ambition—kept him going in the aftermath of Olivia's death, his practical nature dictated the need for someone to replace her in his life. Her death not only took his wife and the mother to his three children; it also left him without his best female teacher and administrator. The responsibility for teaching morality and monitoring the sexual behavior of the growing student population—and the growing faculty, for that matter—demanded a strong "lady principal." He met Olivia's replacement the month after she died when he spoke at the Fisk University graduation. At the commencement dinner he was seated across the table from Margaret James Murray, one of the new graduates. The daughter of a black washerwoman and an Irish railroad worker in northern Mississippi, Maggie Murray had been reared from age seven by Quaker teachers and at fourteen became a teacher herself. In 1881, at age twenty, she made her way to Fisk University and began slowly working her way through the school. At lunch eight years later, she asked the young widower for a

16. Margaret Murray became the third Mrs. Booker T. Washington in 1892. Photo originally published by the Bain News Service; courtesy of the Library of Congress.

job at Tuskegee, even though she had already accepted one elsewhere. Several months earlier a friend at Fisk had advised Booker to hire Maggie, and so he did that day, perhaps with no thought other than that he always had room for a good teacher.

She proved to be just that, and in 1890 he appointed her lady principal. Like Fanny Smith and Olivia Davidson, Maggie Murray was a highly competent woman of mixed race, although she lacked Olivia's literary sophistication. Unlike Olivia, Maggie was robust—in time somewhat overweight—as well as handsome. A few years later a white New Yorker described her: "Lighter than [Booker] and has beautiful features, arched brows, blue (?) eyes, a Grecian nose, and a poise of the head like a Gibson girl. Her hands are white as mine and beautifully shaped. But her hair is kinky." An Englishman thought she looked like a "Spanish woman of distinguished presence." Maggie had a hearty physical constitution to go with her strong personality. She turned out to be a good administrator, one to whom Booker assigned many curricular responsibilities and also the crucial task of overseeing the moral behavior of students and faculty. She kept a close eye out for male students and faculty who loitered around the women's residences and workplaces.[9]

By the fall of 1891, two years later, any Victorian formality between Booker and Maggie had evaporated. "I called you Booker because I knew that it would make you happier," she wrote to him. She was closing her letters with the demure valediction "Take lots of love for yourself." The green eye of jealousy emerged when Maggie realized that Mary Moore, an old friend of Olivia's, also had designs on Booker. "Has she written you any more love letters?" Maggie asked Booker about Moore. "Her letters are more like love letters than are mine?" She worried about the difference in religious enthusiasm between herself and Booker: his was a cool, detached faith, hers emotional—in her word, old-fashioned. She was realistic about the challenges of mothering the three children. In 1891 she was already helping to tend to them, with ease toward the two little boys but not so with eight-year-old Portia, for whom she admitted her lack of affection. "I can not feel toward Portia as I should," she confessed to Booker. "I somehow dread being thrown with her for a life time . . . She kinder understands it too and I hate it." The unease between Maggie and Portia may have reflected the inevitable distrust of two females vying for the affections of the same man. Whatever its root, the tension apparently continued through Portia's teenage years.[10]

Booker must not have shared Maggie's various worries, because in October 1892 she became the third Mrs. Booker T. Washington. Theirs was apparently a conventional Victorian marriage, with clear boundaries about their separate spheres but a strong commitment to their common purposes—the rearing of three children, the success of Tuskegee Institute, and in time mastery of his much larger public role. Although little remains to substantiate the existence of intimacy and affection, neither is there evidence that it was anything but a happy union. Respectable black couples in the 1890s—perhaps even more than Victorian whites—closely guarded their privacy. If the marriage was unhappy or in any way less than proper, the Washingtons successfully kept any imperfections hidden.

Booker was a tolerant and loving father, indeed often indulgent, probably out of guilt for being away from his children so much. In 1893 ten-year-old Portia wrote to him that "we are very sorry that you have to go a way so much," but she went on to confide in him her worries, including her discomfort with Maggie's stern rule over her.[11] Booker apparently offered little comfort to Portia, no doubt because he needed Maggie to provide the parental care he could not. Within a few years he would arrange to send Portia away to boarding school in Boston, to advance his daughter's musical education but perhaps also to alleviate conflict between his daughter and his wife. For the two little boys, Maggie would have been the only mother they remembered, and she adored and indulged them in much the way Booker did.

Even though he was away from the school about half the year, Booker still managed Tuskegee Institute closely, monitoring essentially the performance of every school employee, if not the progress of every student. Every morning he was at Tuskegee he inspected all activities on horseback, noting problems to be addressed in a little book. Booker knew that the school's rapid growth had come at the expense of "neatness and tidiness indoors and outdoors, that help constitute an education." He assumed that the school was always subject to the critical scrutiny of outsiders, and the best way to make the right impression was to run a tight ship. When in 1892 he realized that the Institute's farming operation was not up to snuff, he insisted to the farm manager that it must be a model for students to emulate. "Our farm work should be the best that our surroundings will allow, and we must be satisfied with nothing less." A while later he found no one at the barn at milking time. The cows were not being fed properly. "It is evident that there is little if any system of work at the barn." He reminded the man that he had already been fired from managing the brickyard. "The school is growing and every man and every department in connection with it must grow, and if this is not the case some one must suffer." When, during an inspection tour of the Institute, J. L. M. Curry of the Slater Fund found "an air of untidiness, bordering on a want of neatness," he provoked Booker to action. He found Alice J. Kaine, a white home economist from Wisconsin, and gave her full authority to make necessary changes. For a few months, Kaine's word was law, and

17. Some academic classes like chemistry were coeducational. Photo by Frances Benjamin Johnston, 1902; courtesy of the Library of Congress.

although the teachers resented her, she did indeed transform the campus's appearance and achieve orderliness.[12]

Booker monitored the academic program with the same rigor. In September 1893, soon after the fall term had begun, Booker informed the faculty committee on instruction that the fall class schedule was in bad disarray and told its members to rearrange the schedule so that students went to class at optimum times and teachers offered classes they were fit to teach and no more. "I beg the committee to give at once this matter IMMEDIATE, but careful attention as the school has now been in session two weeks at an expense of $2500 with the programme not right." In 1894 he informed the head of the music department that his program lacked quality. "It is with music as with anything else, it must either go backward or forward."[13]

By the early 1890s Booker had relatively little direct contact with students, but he remained a teacher with his Sunday evening talks. Delivered in the chapel, the talks were sober homilies on the Protestant ethic, given in the manner of a father's directions to adolescent children. They lacked the funny anecdotes he used with white audiences and were instead intensely didactic, replete with admonitions—"*I* want *you to do*" a particular thing, he often said. He spoke on such topics as "Self Denial," "Sowing and Reaping Good Habits," "What to Read," and "Mastery of Self." His talks presumed that students would be teachers in the Black Belt. "Go to work where you can do the most good," he instructed, and then he told them how to proceed in that work. They should read books on practical morality and self-help. They must be alert to opportunities and teach skills that were needed. They should study the example of Abraham Lincoln. Good health followed good habits, and vice versa. They must practice Christianity faithfully and work with ministers, even the illiterate, immoral ones. Start building a schoolhouse and extend the school term, he commanded.[14]

In his last Sunday evening talk for the 1894–95 school term, titled "Growth," he warned students that they would sometimes find themselves discouraged. "There is nothing so discouraging to teachers . . . [as] young men and women on whom much time and money have been spent, who are going downward instead of upward." The antidote to discouragement was for teachers to hold on to their ambition, "that animal spirit . . . that spirit of satisfaction" that came from being better prepared for the work tomorrow than they were today. But they should not draw comparisons with those who had had many more advantages, he warned; only "if you measure yourself by yourself" could a Tuskegee graduate judge whether he or she was progressing. Progress for the race began with the progress of the individual, Booker taught, but blacks should reserve for themselves the judgment about whether they were in fact moving up. The outside world, he knew too well in the early 1890s, told African Americans they were going down, not up. The students should look inside for the affirmation they needed to keep faith amid hard circumstances. Progress was a slow, evolutionary process, one that moved in fits and starts. Blacks began the evolutionary journey far behind whites, but being in that rear position was far less important than seeing that they were ahead of where they had been a while earlier.[15]

Booker's teaching about the evolutionary progress of the darker races was reinforced powerfully by his own life: he and Tuskegee Institute were the embodiment of black people's upward movement. Oppressed people needed to have a sense of success, of rising status, in order to sustain themselves during their frequent hard times. Washington understood that blacks needed to develop this sense of honor, even if whites persisted in degrading them at virtually every turn. Every day that he labored for Tuskegee Institute, every year that Tuskegee survived, everything that he and his students achieved—all nurtured a sense of honor among blacks and demonstrated to a skeptical and hostile world that they would rise by their own efforts.[16]

Washington continued to extend the school's mission beyond Tuskegee. The Institute staff conducted more summer teacher institutes in rural communities. The steady proliferation of Tuskegee outposts leveraged Booker's work to ever more extensive effect. William James Edwards took his 1893 Tuskegee degree home to Wilcox County, Alabama, and built Snow Hill Industrial Institute on the Tuskegee model. Edwards intended to offer practical rather than theoretical education, to teach men and women "to be good workers, good leaders, good husbands, good wives, and finally train them to be fit citizens of the State and proper subjects for the Kingdom of God." Starting with three students in a log cabin, Edwards was given land and other assistance by a local white man, but his success owed most to his determination to emulate Tuskegee's success. He did just that, acquiring hundreds of acres of land, building many buildings, and teaching several hundred students each year. Edwards also created the Black-Belt Improvement Society to promote agricultural cooperatives, scientific farming, and better domestic living. He believed, as did Booker, that to elevate one's status, a person had to acquire more and more property. Even black schools not established by Tuskegee students looked to Booker for help and guidance: In 1891 two northern women were inspired by a talk Booker had given at Hampton to solicit his guidance in creating a school at some needy place. He directed them to Lowndes

County, Alabama, sixty miles west of Tuskegee, where they founded
Calhoun Industrial School. But it was Booker who vouched for the
two Yankee women with local whites and then negotiated the purchase of land for the Calhoun School. He served on its board for many
years.[17]

In 1892 Booker initiated the Tuskegee Negro Conference, a gathering of black farmers and their families to discuss their problems and
hear solutions from the Institute staff. "The aim of Principal Washington," read the circular announcing the meeting, "is to bring together
for a quiet conference, not the politicians and those usually termed the
'leading colored people,' but representatives of the masses—the bone
and sinew of the race—the common, hard working farmers with a
few of the best ministers and teachers." Booker had long been impressed by "the unusual amount of common sense displayed . . . [by]
the uneducated black man in the South, especially the one living in the
country district." People with such natural sense "could be led to do
a great deal towards their own elevation," but the isolation of rural
existence and the hopelessness that often accompanied the difficult life
had to be addressed. Booker invited 75 farmers, but more than 400
showed up. He asked them questions about conditions, eliciting both
complaints and solutions to problems. Farmers recounted the trials of
the crop-lien system and the obstacles to their efforts to educate their
children. They described the trouble that came from trying to operate
schools in churches, broken-down cabins, or bush arbors. Washington summarized the views and sometimes engaged individual farmers
in debate about issues. A good-humored repartee often resulted. After
the conversation, the conference agreed on a set of self-improvement
measures: to buy land and raise their own food, to learn a trade, to
demand that ministers and teachers instruct people in domestic economy and morality, to build their own school buildings and extend their
school terms. The farmers rejected the current fascination among some
blacks with emigration to Africa, asserting that they could become
"prosperous, intelligent, and independent where we are."[18]

The prophetic language of this first declaration embodied Booker's
larger goal to raise the morale of African Americans in the South. He
reported to Samuel Chapman Armstrong that the common sense of

the 400 farmers would have warmed the general's heart because, while they realized their miserable condition, they knew that education was their only salvation. Booker believed that the Negro Conference transformed communities. One participant reported that since he and his neighbors had begun attending the conference, eleven people had bought homes, fourteen had got out of debt, and others had stopped mortgaging their crops. Together the people had built a school and extended the school term from three to six months. "We is done stopped libin' in the de ashes!" the man reported proudly to the one who set the changes in motion.[19]

The Tuskegee Negro Conference became a yearly reunion of black farmers and teachers that worked to bolster the knowledge and morale of those who embraced the Hampton-Tuskegee faith in black progress. More than 800 attended the second conference, and in 1898 they numbered 2,000. The agenda became more ambitious and comprehensive. During subsequent conferences, Margaret Washington set up a model-home demonstration in a Tuskegee building and sent emissaries out to lure black farm women inside for Maggie's lessons in nutritious cooking, sanitary housekeeping, and proper morality in the home. These Mothers' Meetings became a main feature of the conferences. "We talked it all over," Margaret recalled of the first meeting, "the needs of our women of the country, the best way of helping each other." Within a few years a second day was added to the Negro Conference—called the Workers' Conference—at which teachers advised rural people on how to improve their schools.[20]

The Negro Conference nurtured a network of connection among those trying to lift the race in the Black Belt—to be sure, a seemingly small effort in the larger context of their grinding existence, except that it was the only such opportunity for most of those who came. Its purpose mirrored all the efforts emanating from Tuskegee Institute, beginning with the sending out of teachers but also including the teacher institutes and the creation of the Alabama State Teachers Association. Washington intended to help black farm families sustain good morale in the discouraging circumstances of the rural South by promoting a stronger communal sense and a belief that they were making progress. Newspapers, especially black-owned ones, covered the Negro Conference every year, but Booker carefully controlled what information was disseminated from the gathering. He wanted it to remain largely a confidential conversation among blacks. Published proceedings, he wrote privately, might chill discussion or, worse, subject an honest person to punishment. "We have not yet gotten to the point in the South, I fear, where we can discuss the interests of the race along all the lines with perfect freedom." Criticisms about whites made during the honest discussions at the conference represented potential danger for the Institute and for Booker himself. For blacks to advance, he believed, they needed a realistic understanding of their world, but they could not afford to incur more wrath from whites than they already received. It was a tightrope between candor and survival that Booker had already mounted and one that he stayed on for the remainder of his life.[21]

He did more than talk about the evils of the crop-lien system. At the time of the first Negro Conference, he arranged for a Boston benefactor, Silas Dizer, to establish a revolving fund at the Institute to lend money to black farmers to build a house. The Dizer Fund was meant to create examples of the "model Christian home" for other black farmers to emulate. The effort was relatively small, but it marked the beginning of more ambitious home- and farm-ownership projects that Booker would organize and for which he would find financing in the years ahead.[22]

Model Christian homes, Booker had long assumed, would be nurtured by model Christian churches. At Hampton he was persuaded of the intellectual and moral shortcomings of many black preachers, and nothing he had seen since alleviated his doubts about the overall impact of the black clergy. He favored practical religion, which he defined as a faith focused on improving the earthly experience of Christian living and not on imagining the joys of the hereafter. Washington found a natural affinity with what was coming to be called the Social Gospel movement. In his fundraising efforts, he was already friendly with such proponents of the Social Gospel as Washington Gladden and Lyman Abbott, both Congregationalist ministers broadly engaged in public life. To Gladden, black preachers were "emotional rather than ethical" and cared "nothing for righteousness." Washington was not so blunt, but he believed that too many black ministers neglected social and moral reform—and work in general. They lacked the Protestant ethic that Booker had embraced—hard work, strict morality, and self-improvement—and therefore the right application of Christian values. In 1888 Washington spoke of a Tuskegee church that had 200 members and 18 preachers, and he illustrated the alleged indolence of the black clergy with the story of the farm worker who stopped chopping cotton, looked heavenward, and said: "De cotton is so grassy, de work is so hard and de sun am so hot, I believe this darkey am called to preach." He later told a story about a black parishioner who confessed that he had broken every one of the Ten Commandments since the previous Sunday and thanked God that even amid so much sinning he had not lost his religion yet.[23]

Washington decided to address the problem of inadequate preachers with the creation of a Bible training school at Tuskegee. In early 1890 he contacted a black Congregationalist minister from Georgia, Edgar D. Penney, about heading such a school. He believed he could raise the money needed for a building. A few months later, in Lyman Abbott's magazine *Christian Union,* he boldly declared that three-fourths of the black Baptist ministers and two-thirds of the Methodist preachers were "unfit, either mentally or morally, or both, to preach the Gospel to any one or to attempt to lead any one." Their emotional preaching was intended to start the congregation "groaning, uttering wild screams, and jumping." The poor character of the black clergy meant that many black church members were as lacking in true Christianity as people in Africa or Japan, and just as much in need of missionary work. The seminaries of the leading Protestant denominations produced a mere handful of educated black ministers, and those served only churches in the big cities. He called for the establishment of a nonsectarian Christian seminary to train rural black ministers. Almost immediately the Phelps Stokes sisters underwrote the costs of the new religion building because, as one of them explained, "in listening to colored preachers I have felt their lack of Bible knowledge in their sermons, and of definite practical Christian instruction." The Phelps Hall

Bible School was not a full-blown seminary but a smaller effort to teach the Bible to students and to conduct short courses for preachers at the Tuskegee Summer Assembly.[24]

The article brought scorn down on him for what one Methodist bishop called Washington's "wild, random thoughtless . . . slanderous statement." Another minister questioned Booker about which race he belonged to, "for the whites as a rule say better things than these about us as a race." Critics insisted that Booker was "selling his opinions for ill-gotten gains, of slandering his race to curry favor with white men" who could give money to Tuskegee Institute. The criticism of the black clergy, it was alleged, amounted to a cynical effort to elicit financial support for the Bible school. Yet it was a commonly held belief of educated blacks that many southern preachers lacked the knowledge and skills of a useful minister.[25]

Other prominent figures believed that Washington was sincere in his concern and correct in his assessment of the black clergy. The venerable African Methodist Episcopal bishop Daniel Payne, long an advocate for an educated ministry, declared "emphatically, in the presence of the great Head of the Church, that not more than one-third of the ministers, Baptist and Methodist, in the South are morally and intellectually qualified." Ida Wells, the fiery young Memphis editor, wrote to Booker that she had long believed that someone with standing *amongst ourselves,* must call a halt and be the Martin Luther of our times in condemning the practices of our ministers, and I know no one more fitted for the task than yourself." Francis J. Grimké, a prominent black Presbyterian minister in Washington, D.C., seconded Booker's criticism and encouraged him to go ahead with the building of a full-blown seminary in Tuskegee.[26]

Washington did not retract the criticism or cease making it, but after 1890 he muted it. Although he remained convinced that many in the black clergy were unworthy, he apparently concluded that such broad-brush disapproval, even if warranted, created controversies that undermined his other goals. He surely recognized that his remarks unintentionally reinforced the caricature of the immoral and illiterate black preacher popular on the minstrel stage in the 1890s. He appears to have drawn the lesson that open criticism of blacks' behavior fed white animosity toward blacks and created divisions among blacks when a united front was needed to advance the race's progress. He could either be a sharp internal critic of black behavior or he could be a booster of black morale and the black image, but he could not be both effectively. He soon chose the latter.

His criticism of the black clergy did elevate his profile outside Tuskegee, and more notice was taken of what he said. He was offered more opportunities to speak around the country on racial issues. His speeches helped the Institute fundraising, for they often put him in the company of whites who could support the school. Outside the South he was realistic about southern black problems. He told a gathering of Congregationalists in New York that although slavery was dead, blacks remained in economic bondage. He described how the crop-lien system beggared most blacks in the South. It was hard to make a Christian of a hungry man, he often said. The lasting injury from slavery had been the deprivation of "self-dependence and executive power," Booker said, the only remedy for which was the education of the freed people. In the Congregationalists' magazine, he observed that the current epidemic of lynching blunted whites' moral sense, but "all this has been said and more, and still the evil does not cease."[27]

At the same time, he sharpened a message of black progress. To a mass meeting of blacks in the nation's capital in 1891, he reiterated a favorite point: racial problems would be solved "in proportion as the black gets hold of something that the white man *wants* or *respects*." Whereas in his early years at Tuskegee he had heard complaints from whites, even threats to get rid of the school, such talk had subsided as more buildings went up on campus. Now blacks in the South could build a school and expect it to flourish, often with the help of whites. A better future, he prophesied, awaited blacks who pursued a materialist strategy even through discouraging times. Blacks could and should acquire a skill, purchase property, and accumulate wealth. It was a message of hope, made increasingly in defiance of reality.[28]

In the 1890s white nationalists intensified the demonization of their black and northern enemies. The decade began with what they viewed as a new assault from the U.S. government on their domination of blacks. Answering the call of President Benjamin Harrison to save the black vote in the South, Senator Henry Cabot Lodge of Massachusetts put forward a bill authorizing federal oversight of elections in the South to protect black voting rights. Southern whites were enraged. George W. Campbell, Booker's best white friend in Tuskegee, wrote to him that the Lodge "force" bill would humiliate and degrade all southerners. "*Class* legislation ought not to be tolerated . . . *Just let us alone.*" If the federal government did not interfere in the South, Campbell told Booker, then "there is no question but what the whites and blacks will harmonize." When the Lodge bill was defeated in Congress, whites in the South felt freer to get blacks all the way out of politics. In a constitutional convention in 1890, Mississippi disfranchised blacks by requiring that voters be able to read, pay an annual poll tax, and demonstrate to a white board of registrars that they understood the state constitution. In fact South Carolina, Tennessee, and other southern states had already removed most blacks from the voter rolls with secret-ballot procedures that made it impossible for illiterate blacks to cast a ballot. Disfranchisement was proposed in Alabama in 1890, but implementation was thwarted by conflict between the entrenched conservative Democrats, who favored literacy and property requirements for voting, and Populists, who knew that such restrictions would also exclude poor whites. Alabama did pass a secret-ballot law in 1893.[29]

White hostility to black education gained momentum rapidly in the 1890s. In 1891 an act was proposed to give Alabama school boards the discretion to spend their funds as they saw fit, in defiance of the equal spending on schools mandated in the state constitution. For the past decade whites all over the South had been agitating for segregation of school taxes, and the growing Populist movement was adding support to the cause of racial separation of tax receipts as angry white farmers demanded better schools without paying any more taxes. Washington instantly saw that the Alabama Apportionment Act was a ruse to allow school boards to spend funds disproportionately on white children. He denounced it at a convention of black Democrats in Montgomery, a group convened by the likes of William Hooper Councill—that is, blacks who had allied themselves with the controlling Democrats in the hope of getting patronage favor. One of the black Democrats chastised Washington for his condemnation of the legislation, saying that such attacks from blacks never helped their cause because it made them look like complainers. The opprobrium of a black sycophant bothered Washington far less than criticism from the editor of the Montgomery *Advertiser,* who had written approvingly of Booker's letter about railroad discrimination in 1885 but now characterized his remarks against the apportionment act as "a bitter speech." Realizing that the black Democrats and the newspaper were collaborating to portray him as a Negro agitator, Booker complained to the *Advertiser* that its report misrepresented him. His work at Tuskegee demonstrated that education cemented good relations between the races. But his response sounded defensive and did little to mend fences.

From this episode Booker learned that however justified his opposition might be to unfair action, he could incur the wrath of powerful whites by speaking out. Public life was a minefield for anyone attempting to protect black interests. Regardless of how careful he was in phrasing his dissent, some whites responded hysterically to any expression of displeasure with the current racial situation. The Alabama Apportionment Act of 1891 did pass, and white-controlled school boards began spending far more on whites than on blacks. The emerging malapportionment of funds was felt most acutely in the Black Belt, where the schooling of the black majority was beggared in order to educate the white children adequately. The legislation signaled the beginning of a drastic decline of public support for black education in Alabama.[30]

The threats to black education sometimes appeared more immediate and ominous, as they became in Tuskegee on a Saturday night in June 1895. The events of this single evening reminded Washington of how precarious race relations in his hometown were at any moment. Thomas Harris, a black lawyer in Tuskegee, sponsored a visiting white preacher in the town. Whites alleged that Harris was advocating social equality between blacks and whites, because the white preacher had been seen around town in the company of Harris's two young daughters. A white mob went to order Harris out of Tuskegee, a shootout ensued, and a white man and Harris were injured. Now incensed, the mob began chasing Harris to lynch him. Harris fled to the Institute campus, to Booker's door, and begged for sanctuary. Booker quickly arranged to hide Harris off campus and then got him transported secretly to Montgomery. When the mob came to his home, Booker told them that he had turned Harris away and did not know his whereabouts. Both statements were only partially true, but Booker apparently dissembled so effectively that the mob went away satisfied that he had no involvement in Harris's escape. Harris did not return to Tuskegee, and whites in the town apparently never learned of Booker's duplicity in protecting Harris. Several months later, now exiled to a distant Alabama town, Harris wrote to Booker expressing gratitude for Washington's crucial help.[31]

When the Tom Harris incident was reported, some black editors criticized Washington for not providing Harris asylum. "We shall await to hear the explanation of Prof. Washington with reference to his refusal to admit a wounded man," wrote John Mitchell Jr., editor of the Richmond *Planet*. Much louder criticism about how he had treated Tom Harris would come a few months later, after Booker's rise to national prominence. No explanation was ever made, of course, because Booker simply could not afford for local whites to know that he had interfered with their vigilantism. Public knowledge of the actual events would not only have enraged local whites but would also have exposed as a lie the myth that both he and whites maintained about Tuskegee as a model community. If blacks far from Tuskegee chose to condemn his actions, Booker nevertheless had to live with the criticism, because it was simply too dangerous to tell the truth. His was a precarious existence, and his survival depended on never forgetting that white men could end it on a whim.[32]

5

The Settlement of the Negro Problem

The deteriorating racial environment in the 1890s created doubts about whether African Americans, much less any black educational institution, could survive. An awful surge of violence threatened all black people and every black institution. Two hundred blacks were lynched in the South each year. In Alabama alone in 1891 and 1892, twenty-four blacks were reported lynched each year. The months of April and May in 1892 brought multiple public executions of black men: five in Lithonia, Georgia; four in Fishville, Louisiana; four in Citrus, Florida; three in Childersburg, Alabama; and three in Clarksville, Georgia. "The lynching habit has gotten to the point," Booker Washington wrote in the summer of 1893, that "white men lynch black men for rape, attempted rape, murder, attempted murder, incendiarism, stealing and for murdering black men, and for the same class of offenses we now and then hear of white men lynching white men and black men lynching black men." Economic competition also lay at the root of a form of racial terrorism known as whitecapping that emerged in Mississippi in 1892 and spread to other southern states. Terrorists wearing white caps—they could now expose their faces in the way that Klansmen wearing hoods had believed they could not during Reconstruction—burned the homes and crops of black families, and sometimes killed the farmers, in order to cleanse whole neighborhoods of

black inhabitants and remove competitors for the diminishing agricultural opportunities in that depressed time. In 1894 and 1895 whitecaps
disrupted blacks' lives in several Alabama counties. At Tallassee, just
northwest of Tuskegee, long a center of white vigilantism, whitecaps
whipped several black farmers and then killed the white man who tes-
tified about their violence. Beyond the threats to life, whites blocked
black economic opportunities, undermined legal protections, and demeaned black social and cultural life.[1]

The causes of rising racial antipathy can only be suggested, not established, but the 1890s were a time of rapidly accelerating change
resulting from urbanization, industrialization, and immigration—and
of economic depression and dislocation. Perhaps the insecurity of whites
caused them to persecute more viciously the perceived enemy in their
midst. But there is little question that underlying the attack was a
deepening negativism in whites' thinking about blacks.

By the 1890s Darwinian thought fostered the widespread belief that
competition among races would inevitably bring the demise of blacks.
Most white intellectuals were certain that the black population was on
the road to extinction. Joseph Le Conte, a nationally respected scientist, insisted that blacks' fate was either disappearance or mixture, and
he quickly added that mixing races yielded offspring who were weak
physically and mentally and therefore doomed demographically. The
Virginia novelist Thomas Nelson Page added literary conviction to the
scientific view when he wrote that "the Negro race in America will
eventually disappear, not in a generation or a century, it may take
several centuries." But the voice most widely heard belonged to an in-
surance actuary, Frederick Ludwig Hoffman, who, in justifying his
company's refusal to write policies on blacks, declared that blacks' high
mortality rates made them a vanishing race. The leading government
demographer echoed Hoffman that blacks would die en masse from
disease and that even those capable of "the white man's civilization will
ultimately be merged and lost in the lower classes of whites, leaving
almost no trace to mark their former existence."[2]

The predictions of disappearance were bolstered by the widespread
belief that blacks were degenerating into beasts. "The Negro has not
progressed," Page wrote in 1892, "not because he was a slave, but be-

cause he does not possess the faculties to raise himself above slavery." The historian Philip Alexander Bruce, pointing to the alleged surge in rapes of white women, declared that crime and sexual immorality had risen since African Americans were freed from white governance under slavery. Even the South's few white progressives, those who assumed that blacks would not disappear and could be improved, were pessimistic about their present behavior. Booker's friend J. L. M. Curry justified black education as the antidote to the current Negro bestiality: "When the interest and authority of owners was removed and former religious instruction was crippled or withdrawn, the negroes fell rapidly from what had been attained in slavery to a state of original fetishism."[3]

White nationalists insisted that if their black enemies did not disappear, they would have to be deported forcibly. In 1890 John Tyler Morgan, Alabama's white-nationalist U.S. senator, exhorted the Senate to underwrite a massive removal of blacks from the South, marking for particular attention the best-educated blacks on the grounds that the "most cultivated Negro is constantly armed with inveterate suspicions toward the white race." Another southern senator proposed a five-million-dollar fund to transport blacks to Africa; the bill did not pass but gathered much attention and support in the South. In 1892 the editor of the Charleston News & Courier said "it would be better for the South if [blacks] should go, not all at the same time or in a hurry, but gradually and surely, until, by the end of the next quarter of a century, the South will be relieved from the black cloud which hangs over it." Two high-profile blacks, the Liberian theologian and race-nationalist Edward Blyden and the Methodist bishop Henry McNeal Turner, seemed to second the white nationalists' call with plans to move American blacks to Liberia. The worsening race conditions in the 1890s gained the emigrationists a greater hearing among blacks than they would otherwise have got.[4]

Black demographic demise and removal were answers to the Negro Problem, a term used to encompass the whole issue of blacks' place in American life. Frederick Douglass had noted in 1889 that when he was a slave, the Negro was largely outside of the nation's thought, but now his freedom made him discussed at every turn. "The platform, the pulpit, the press, and the legislative hall regard him, and struggle with him, as a great and difficult problem, one that requires almost divine wisdom to solve." Until total erasure of the black presence could settle the Negro Problem, white nationalists wanted to impose racial separation, soon to be called segregation. One imperative of the Negro Problem was to remove blacks from politics. John Tyler Morgan claimed that blacks had "uniformly used the ballot as a means of inflicting the penalties of resentment and race animosity upon southern people." Senator Wade Hampton of South Carolina asserted that blacks were "incapable of self government, they are not fitted to govern that great race before which all others have gone down, the masterful, the conquering, and the unconquerable Caucasians."5

As he traversed the country raising funds for Tuskegee, Washington constantly read newspapers and popular magazines that reinforced pessimism about the Negro Problem with illustrations and humor that demeaned black character. *Harper's Weekly,* the *Atlantic Monthly,* and *Century* ran short stories, poetry, and cartoons that depicted blacks speaking outlandishly, acting crudely, and looking grotesque. The authors and cartoonists, most of them northerners, referred to African Americans as "niggers," "darkies," and "coons," and regularly described them as savage, uncouth, bestial-looking, dishonest, and idle. The plots of the short fiction usually turned on blacks' petty criminal behavior, especially watermelon and chicken thievery; the dishonesty of black preachers and lawyers; or the immorality of black men and women. Southern newspapers projected the negative images even more forcefully. As newspapers became better illustrated because of improvements in printing in the 1890s, their editorial cartoons and new comic sections often featured stereotypical caricatures of blacks. Washington considered the Atlanta *Constitution* the most influential newspaper in the South. Whereas it had earned a reputation for sectional and racial enlightenment under Henry Grady in the 1880s, it reflected the typical bigotry of white-owned southern newspapers in the 1890s. In a story on Washington, D.C., a *Constitution* reporter wrote: "Here are gathered the most insolent and worthless representatives of their race who could possibly be found in searching the country over. Here we have the political 'nigger' in his most virulent and useless and nauseating form."[6]

Booker certainly knew that for southerners in rural areas and small towns, the main sources of information and opinion were weeklies committed entirely to white-nationalist ideas. Editors typically depicted blacks as uncivilized animals and sexual fiends who hated whites and would attack them when least expected—a dangerous enemy in their midst. Black men were portrayed as predatory, black women as promiscuous, and black marriages as devoid of fidelity. The weeklies commonly disparaged blacks physically, referring to unpleasant smell, kinky hair, and thick skulls. Northern people did not know blacks and thus were unqualified to offer opinions on race relations. The country press was jubilant when disfranchising efforts emerged, and it generally opposed any black education. And hundreds of weeklies carried the white-nationalist views of Bill Arp on the Negro Problem. Bill Arp had long since decided that there was no place for African Americans in politics. "The universal sentiment of the south is that the negro shall not rule us," he declared in 1890. "The sentiment of the north is that the he shall not rule up there, but shall have a fair chance to do it here." He insisted that the South was suffering under an explosion of black crime. "There are 30 per cent more whites than Negroes in this state, and yet the Negroes commit nine times more crime . . . What is the matter with the Negroes?" Most of the black convicts were young, had never experienced slavery, and had attended school. "The old-time negroes are not in the chaingang. They had no schooling but they had moral training . . . Crime among the Negroes increases with their education." Black criminality made lynching a necessity, not a reflection of "depraved and lawless public sentiment" but "evidence of minds charged, perhaps overcharged, with love and respect for wives and daughters." Bill Arp maintained that whites all agreed that they could no longer live together in peace with blacks. They had been forced to share the region for twenty-five years, but the experiment had failed, and now both were ready for the exodus. It would be a great relief, he wrote, "if this restless, trifling, insolent, crime-loving class would go somewhere."[7]

Popular culture in the 1890s reinforced the antiblack propaganda. The main trends in entertainment were a powerful vehicle for the demonization of the Negro. Since its emergence in the 1830s, the minstrel show had exploited pernicious black stereotypes as the basis for its appeal, using white male actors whose faces were corked black to play the African-American stereotypes Jim Crow and Zip Coon. The Jim Crow character was stupid, superstitious, and slow-moving, and Zip Coon the criminal dandy, overdressed in a long-tailed coat, who spoke in a nonsensical way. In the 1890s Jim Crow and Zip Coon became more dangerous characters, wielding razors and stealing without conscience. The main musical feature of the minstrel show became the "coon song," which featured a bright melody and relentlessly racist lyrics. Popular titles included the perennial favorite "All Coons Look Alike to Me." In the South, any town with a performance hall received a touring minstrel company. The arrival of a minstrel troupe in Atlanta or Nashville was reported in the newspapers with much fanfare, including photos of actors in blackface, this at a time when real blacks were depicted only if they were notorious criminals. Booker may have seen the announcement in Union Springs, a small market town just south of Tuskegee, that local boys had performed a minstrel show in blackface to a full house, about which the local newspaper commented that "there were some good 'niggers' on the stage." A few years later the girls of Union Springs did a minstrel show in blackface to benefit the Confederate Ladies' Memorial Association, which also drew favorable newspaper comment. "The children were at their best and the coons in splendid humor."[8]

Coon imagery was everywhere. The Zip Coon and Jim Crow characters made the transition to both burlesque and vaudeville. Coon songs became the main offerings of the emerging sheet-music industry known popularly as Tin Pan Alley. A million copies of "All Coons Look Alike to Me" were sold within a few years of its appearance in 1896. Virtually all of the dozens of newspapers that Booker examined each week carried coon illustrations in advertisements for a wide array of products. Cigar packages contained coon trading cards. Popular culture and mass communications incessantly presented blacks as lazy, stupid, immoral, and criminal. The distortion was so universal that it

18. In the 1890s the minstrel character Jim Crow became a menacing character. Color lithograph, 73 × 50 cm, Calvert Lithograph Company, Detroit, 1892; courtesy of the Library of Congress.

went essentially unquestioned among whites, something that Bishop Turner of Atlanta, the black emigrationist, acknowledged in 1893 to Bill Arp: "I fully recognize the fact that a white man in this section of the country must respect the popular prejudices that exist against my race, or forfeit his influence among the whites. No white man dares to speak in defense of the negro and command the respect of the whites."[9]

But perhaps a black man could defend the Negro and still gain whites' respect. In 1895 Washington attempted to challenge the demonization of blacks. His opportunity to do so originated in a committee hearing of the U.S. House of Representatives in May 1894, at which funding was requested for the Cotton States and International Exposition, to take place in Atlanta in 1895. At the 1893 Columbian Exposition in Chicago, blacks had been excluded, and there had been loud criticisms about the slight. The twenty-five prominent white men planning the Atlanta exposition—among them Clark Howell, editor of the Atlanta *Constitution,* and the former governor of Georgia Rufus Bullock—resolved to forestall any such criticism by having black advocates for the Atlanta exposition speak to the House committee. They brought Booker to help argue their case. In brief but incisive remarks, Booker told the congressmen that he had urged the Negro to own his land, keep out of debt, and become part of the "conservative body of the government," and as a result blacks had made progress that they were ready to display. His appeal was heard sympathetically, and the Congress appropriated the money for the Cotton States Exposition.

In recognition of his effectiveness before Congress, the exposition's planners asked him to oversee the preparation of a Negro building for the event. Booker declined but arranged the appointment of a friendly acquaintance to represent black interests in the exposition. Some blacks objected to the segregated black exhibition space, but Booker accepted it as an opportunity to showcase black achievements—Tuskegee Institute in particular—rather than have blacks simply disappear in a sea of white exhibits. Atlanta's elite decided that it would be a good public-relations gesture to have a black speaker at the opening ceremony. Washington's effectiveness before the Congress instilled confidence among the Atlanta boosters. His emphasis on economic goals among blacks and his conciliatory posture toward southern whites made him a perfect complement to the "New South" boosterism that underlay the Atlanta enterprise. Indeed, Washington seemed to mimic the rhetoric of the late Henry Grady. The exposition's planners asked Booker to speak at the opening event.[10]

In the summer of 1895 Booker contemplated what he would say at the Cotton States Exposition. Perhaps the frightening events of the Tom Harris incident in June shaped the careful tone he eventually adopted, although ultimately what he said echoed themes he had long since embraced. If he did not already know he had accepted a daunting task, a white farmer in Tuskegee reminded him on his way to the train to Atlanta: "Washington, you have spoken with success before Northern white audiences, and before Negroes in the South, but in Atlanta you will have to speak before Northern white people, Southern white people and Negroes altogether. I fear they have got you into a pretty tight place."[11]

September 18, 1895, turned out to be a blistering hot day in Atlanta, but the heat apparently inhibited no one from attending the parade to celebrate the opening of the Cotton States Exposition. Some Atlanta homes were draped with Old Glory, a decoration not displayed much in recent decades. Peachtree Street, lined with thousands of citizens black and white, was crowded with military units and carriages filled with governors, diplomats, and wealthy Americans. Booker Washington sat with other dignitaries to observe the procession that the reporter for the New York *World* described as "a picture beyond words to express—waves of dark blue bodies with light blue legs, gleaming gold lace, jingling spurs, rumbling cannon wheels, clattering horses, white helmets, acres of Georgia colonels, scarlet, yellow, gray, every color under heaven, sparkling, blazing, glowing and dancing with the liltings of music." After three hours the official party finally moved inside the exposition's main hall for the opening ceremony. Booker waited for his opportunity to speak, sitting in the front row of podium seats. A nervous Atlanta dowager, her face covered in a white veil, welcomed the crowd, but she read her greeting in a voice so low that few could hear her. Then the band played "The Star Spangled Banner," eliciting cheers that mounted into a roar when it picked up "Dixie" and that dwindled to near silence with "Yankee Doodle."[12] Sectional reconciliation was by no means complete in the Atlanta of 1895.

Finally Washington was introduced. He walked to the edge of the stage and turned his head to avoid the glare of a late-afternoon sun that also bathed him in bright light. "There was a remarkable figure," a New York reporter later wrote, "tall, bony, straight as a Sioux chief, high forehead, straight nose, heavy jaws and strong, determined mouth, with big white teeth, piercing eyes and a commanding manner." As he spoke, "his muscular right arm swung high in the air with a lead pencil grasped in the clenched brown fist." According to the reporter, Booker's voice rang out clear and he paused effectively as he made each point. He knew how to make his voice heard in the far corners of the building.[13]

Washington began by thanking the exposition's organizers for recognizing the value and manhood of the American Negro—this when many white southerners dismissed blacks as worthless and bestial. He thus suggested that leading southerners, indeed the organizers of this great exposition, did not see blacks in such negative ways. He then conceded what virtually every white southerner presumed about blacks in politics: it had been a mistake to enfranchise them, and the days of blacks' political activism were over. Reconstruction had been a misguided experiment that misled blacks to believe they could begin their freedom at the top, that a seat in Congress was more valuable than owning land or having a skill. Washington was in effect conceding what was already lost—independent black political power—in order to reduce white hostility. Although blacks deserved all privileges guaranteed them by law, it was "vastly more important that we be prepared for the exercise of these privileges," which meant achieving economic independence.[14]

It was in this context of putting economic goals first that he said: "the wisest among my race understand that the agitation of questions of social equality is the extremest folly, and that progress in the enjoyment of all the privileges that will come to us must be the result of severe and constant struggle rather than of artificial forcing." By disavowing any claim to social equality—by which he meant integration in social institutions—Washington hoped to soothe the anxieties of whites.

Then Washington insisted that blacks had learned from the past that "the masses of us are to live by the productions of our hands." He told a story about people on a lost ship who had run out of fresh water and were unaware that they had drifted into a river. "Cast down your buckets where you are," their rescuers called. The cast-down-your-buckets story was Washington's rejection of colonization proposals for African Americans, but he directed it not to the southern nationalists but to "those of my race who depend on bettering their condition in a foreign land"—like Atlanta's Bishop Turner, who was still campaigning among blacks for emigration to Africa. Regardless of the ugly feelings of many whites and the pipe dreams of a few blacks, Booker suggested without saying so explicitly that blacks were in the South to stay. Nor did he say what else he believed—that black prospects were worsening in the North all the time. He then applied the metaphor to whites, imploring them to cast their buckets among black southerners and not to rely on foreign labor, which some white nationalists hoped would replace blacks. "Cast down your bucket among these people who have, without strikes and labour wars, tilled your fields, cleared your forests, built your railroads and cities, and brought forth treasure from the bowels of the earth, and helped make possible this magnificent representation of the progress of the South." He thus reminded white capitalists of the threats to their control posed by organized labor, something still fresh in their minds in the aftermath of the nationwide railroad and coal strikes of 1894, and promised the greater loyalty of black labor. Just as blacks needed to get and hold onto industrial jobs, whites needed black workers. Such economic interdependence, Booker believed, was the best long-term hope for his people.

Booker described blacks as faithful, law-abiding, and unresentful, all traits that contradicted the widening contemporary opinion that they were idle, criminal, immoral, and hostile to whites. He even invoked the southern nationalists' own myths of the Old South and the Lost Cause to challenge the current image of blacks: "As we have proved our loyalty to you in the past, in nursing your children, watching by the sick-bed of your mothers and fathers, and often following them with tear-dimmed eyes to their graves, so in the future, in our humble way, we shall stand by you with a devotion that no foreigner can approach, ready to lay down our lives, if need be, in defence of yours." Blacks would do this, he immediately added, while remaining socially apart—at which point he raised his large right hand. About black and white southerners, he said: "In all things that are purely social we can be as separate as the fingers, yet one as the hand in all things essential to mutual progress." It was the most-quoted statement of the speech.

In its larger thrust, the Atlanta exposition speech represented Washington's attempt to counter the belief that free blacks had declined in character and morality from the time of slavery. He was, after all, speaking at an exhibition of progress. He said that blacks took pride in showing their achievements of the past thirty years, having begun with only a few quilts, pumpkins, and chickens "gathered from miscellaneous sources"—the one point at which he deferred to the common Negro stereotype. His message was progress, black movement forward and upward, to counter the overwhelming message of black degeneration that seemed to come from every other direction.

Washington suggested his ultimate goal near the end of the address when he pledged to help "work out the great and intricate problem which God has laid at the doors of the South." He wanted to achieve a solution to the Negro Problem, indeed to end whites' discussion about erasing their enemies from their presence, to secure the survival of his race. He was redefining the Negro Problem, away from the doomsday talk and toward a discussion of how to make the Negro useful and accepted in a peaceful, biracial society. Booker aimed to freeze the downward spiral of black conditions and white discrimination where they were, before they got worse. He wanted to ease sectional differences and racial animosities so that blacks would be granted some space to work and improve. If he could halt the erosion of black rights, and the corollary degeneration of blacks' image in whites' minds, black progress remained possible. He did not acknowledge the converse: if the downward spiral continued, the pressure for a violent solution to the Negro Problem would only build to more dangerous levels. The survival of African Americans in the United States would be in real jeopardy.

That day Booker T. Washington began trying to turn the momentum of history in a different direction—indeed, upward—and to give whites a new way of viewing blacks, a task that had become the main purpose of his life. The continued existence of his people depended on acceptance of his proposed settlement, and he started to work for it.

At the conclusion of Washington's speech, Governor Bullock hurried across the platform, took his hand, and shook it enthusiastically. The former slaveholder and Confederate officer held on to Booker's hand, and the two men faced each other for a long moment as the crowd let go a roar of approval, handkerchiefs and canes waving, hats flying in the air. One writer said that the fairest women in Georgia tossed flowers on the stage for an orator who had bewitched them. Clark Howell went to the podium and announced that the speech was "the beginning of a moral revolution in America." Within hours, Howell reported to a New York newspaper that Booker Washington's Atlanta exposition address represented a platform on which "whites and blacks can stand with full justice to each other." After the speech, hundreds surrounded Booker in the lecture hall to congratulate him, and on the streets of downtown Atlanta the next morning, he was constantly hailed by well-wishers.[15]

Washington moved quickly to amplify the speech's significance, an indication of his remarkable instincts for shaping public opinion. He declared in the next day's New York *World* that the opening of the Atlanta exposition constituted the "brightest, most hopeful day in the history of the negro race," one for which William Lloyd Garrison, Frederick Douglass, and Henry Grady all had prayed. He thus paid homage to the beliefs in black liberation and intersectional harmony that many northerners held. But he also bowed to southern beliefs. He hailed Atlanta as the place where American nationalism in the person of the attacking Yankee general William Tecumseh Sherman had clashed with the southern nationalism of the Georgia Confederates Robert Toombs, Alexander Stephens, and Joseph Brown. Having honored both nationalist myths, he declared their conflict ended, a necessary prelude to the settlement of the Negro Problem. He invoked Henry Grady, a symbol of the white South's acceptance of blacks as well as the North's acceptance of white authority over southern race relations, a reminder that some whites rejected the nationalists' racial antipathy. Washington advanced his own creed to encourage support for his proposed settlement of the Negro Problem. "Let us as a race throw aside complaints and useless criticism," Booker wrote, "and enter with hand and mind as we have never done before the industrial field." The Negro of the future would seek equality of industrial opportunity rather than waste time over questions of social equality. The rising Negro would become indispensable to the economy. "No one cares much for a man with empty hand, pocket and head no matter what his color is."[16]

The speech made Washington an instant national celebrity. A Chicago newspaper was typical in calling him "the colored man whose address at the opening of the Atlanta exposition made him famous and installed him as the recognized leader of his race in the United States." Extravagant praise came from powerful men who probably had never heard of him. "Your words cannot fail to delight and encourage all who wish well for your race," wrote President Grover Cleveland. The president had chosen his own words carefully, surely knowing that most of his fellow Democrats in the South wished nothing well for Booker's race. Longtime white supporters delighted in his new fame. You have "struck the keynote of *Twentieth* century civilllization [*sic*] in America!" wrote an old friend from the abolitionist circle in Boston; the speech was "worthy to rank with Lincoln's 'Gettysburg' in eloquence, elevation, and far-reaching influence." Ellen Collins, a Tuskegee benefactor from New York, offered the only note of reservation among his white northern supporters: "Perhaps you might have been a little more independent; in view of the long, long, suffering of your people a little irritation would have been pardonable," but Collins was glad he had left it unsaid in order to gain a "general advance in public sentiment toward recognition of the rights of the colored people as men."[17]

African Americans from around the country sent joyous praise. "The weeping among the colored people reached my eyes," wrote the underground railroad hero William Still from Philadelphia, so great was the "rejoicing it had awakened in the breasts of people" who heard "such grand truths under such grand circumstances." A black lawyer in Chicago offered that "no word uttered by a colored man during the past 20 years will go farther and do more to set us right in public opinion." The pan-Africanist Edward Blyden wrote that the speech was greater than George Washington's Farewell Address in the way it freed "two races from prejudices and false views of life and of their mutual relations which hamper the growth of one and entirely cripple the other." A young sociologist at Wilberforce College declared the speech "a word fitly spoken" and "the basis of a real settlement between whites and blacks in the South." The perspicacious William Edward Burghardt Du Bois had seen clearly Washington's goal in the Atlanta speech.[18]

Blacks were looking for a new leader, because Frederick Douglass had died earlier in 1895. Most assumed that the race should have a single person to lead it. Douglass's precedent was compelling. He had articulated the desire for freedom and the demand for equal citizenship in a public manner so that every white American had a clear idea of blacks' goals. He had lobbied Abraham Lincoln for equal treatment of black soldiers and then for a complete emancipation. After the war, blacks had looked to Douglass for guidance on dealing with the new problems of freedom and citizenship. His success encouraged the assumption among both blacks and whites that a new racial leader should be found.

The sudden fame that Washington gained in Atlanta thrust him forward as that person, and he was a logical choice in several ways. He was in step with the general shift in the orientation of black uplift away from politics toward economic and educational progress, a change that had begun among black leaders in the early 1880s. Booker was not the architect of this reorientation of black goals but its latest and most articulate spokesman. His only critics were preachers upset over his earlier criticism of them. Later critics would say that he was a weak

19. Frederick Douglass had been the leader of African Americans for more than a generation when he died in early 1895. Photographer unknown, ca. 1895; courtesy of the Library of Congress.

substitute for Douglass. In the last decade of his life Douglass had become more insistent in his demands for political and civil rights than he had been in the 1870s and early 1880s, when he had turned to economic advancement and away from the political preoccupations of Reconstruction. Douglass's final militancy may have been partly a response to criticism he received for marrying a white woman in 1884. He clearly was swimming against the main current of thought among other black men of influence in the 1880s and early 1890s. But he and Washington agreed on most issues: they shared strong commitments to the Protestant ethic and the Republican Party, objections to emigration to Africa, suspicions of the labor movement, an emphasis on industrial education, and optimism about blacks' future in America. Each understood the prophetic role: a black leader had to identify the wrongs of the day and then describe a better future. To be sure, Douglass was more likely than Washington to blame whites for blacks' circumstances, but he did not live in the South. Washington understood the need for the jeremiad—the sermon denouncing current evil—which he would preach mostly, but not exclusively, to blacks.[19]

Washington's ascent to national racial leadership was a result of the timing of the Atlanta speech, Douglass's death, and the fact that there were few other good candidates. A more likely successor to Douglass might have been Joseph Charles Price, a preacher and the founder of Livingstone College in Salisbury, North Carolina, which like Tuskegee was staffed entirely with black faculty. A great orator, Price was nationally known among blacks in the 1880s and had led such civil-rights efforts as the Afro-American League and the National Equal Rights Convention, which Booker had not joined, probably because of his economic orientation for black uplift. But Price's death in 1894 prevented him from taking Douglass's mantle. Another prospect might have been Ida Wells, who had fled her native Memphis in 1892 after her condemnations of lynchings provoked white threats on her life. From the safety of Chicago she had become the nation's leading public crusader against lynching. An emerging feminist, Wells would in all likelihood have embraced the leadership role, but her gender apparently disqualified her in the eyes of most influential men.[20]

A few blacks later dismissed Washington as a leader selected by whites, and to some extent he was indeed chosen by northern white businessmen, philanthropists, and newspaper editors, who wanted a single black with whom to deal about the Negro Problem. More conservative and approachable than Douglass, and less critical of white society, Washington was an easy choice for whites. His emphasis on economic progress, and the corollary acceptance of less involvement in politics, better reflected the prevailing mood of whites. Like them, Washington wanted a settlement of the Negro Problem, and he offered terms that seemed reasonable to some. He had remarkable skills as a speaker and writer, and whites found it easy and interesting to communicate with him. He was a mulatto. In an age when whites took as given the physical and mental superiority of Anglo-Saxons, Booker Washington had a half measure of the genetic content that defined high status. A great many whites assumed that it accounted for his obvious gifts of intelligence and wisdom.

Beyond the boosters like Clark Howell and Governor Bullock, the white South remained mostly quiet about Washington and his Atlanta address. Bill Arp did not comment, and the rural press said little about the speech. White nationalists were suspicious of any black man given such a prominent role as Washington had been at the Atlanta exposition. In their view no black deserved such status in the South, regardless of how careful he had been not to give offense. Washington could have earned their approval only by consenting to their drastic solution of the Negro Problem. He would not do that, but neither would he willingly antagonize them.

Booker apparently accepted the leadership role and responsibility without much hesitation. He said later that events simply thrust him into the position, and he never offered any more penetrating analysis of his own motives. Before the speech in Atlanta, Booker had rarely sought the public limelight or taken steps to gain popularity or fame among blacks, but he had shown great ambitions for his institution. Many of his goals had been achieved by 1895: Tuskegee was thriving and running efficiently, and it already represented a remarkable personal success for him. In Booker's life, one job well done had led naturally to a larger challenge. Becoming the leader of blacks in America may have seemed to him simply the next demanding job. He had left

Hampton with a strong missionary sense to help his people, and it must have seemed that fate was handing him his next mission to raise African Americans nationally. Indeed, as he grew into his role as leader, he manifested more and more the zeal of a man called to a high purpose.

Important people thrust the role on him. Timothy Thomas Fortune, the most influential black journalist of the day, believed that events had conspired to usher Booker onto the national stage. "It looks as if you are our Douglass," Fortune wrote to Booker soon after the Atlanta speech. "You are the best equipped of the lot of us to be the single figure ahead of the procession." Fortune was emphatic that blacks needed one leader. *"We must have a head,"* he wrote, and that man should come from the South, and "every one of us should hold up his hands." In an article for a white New York newspaper titled "Is He the Negro Moses?" Fortune declared that the Atlanta address had reversed the belief in the South that blacks were not capable of the "mental grasp and development of the Anglo-Saxon." As false as it was bold, Fortune's assertion did show the enthusiasm generated among blacks by Booker's instant fame.[21]

20. Timothy Thomas Fortune, editor of the New York *Age*, thrust Washington forward as the new leader and became his chief black confidant for a decade. Photo engraving from William J. Simmons, *Men of Mark: Eminent, Progressive and Rising* (Cleveland: George M. Rewell, 1887).

Fortune relished the role of kingmaker. Tall, thin, light-skinned enough to pass for white, and emotionally erratic, Tim Fortune was in many ways Booker's opposite in character. The two became acquainted in the 1880s as Washington traveled to raise funds and Fortune's newspaper emerged as the most influential among African Americans. After Atlanta they became intimate friends, writing to each other frequently. The son of a free black tanner who became prominent in Reconstruction politics in Florida, Fortune had started as a printer's devil and risen to become publisher of the New York *Age* in the 1880s. Early in his career as a publisher, he advocated interracial labor activism, but as white labor's hostility to working alongside blacks proved intransigent in the 1880s and early 1890s, he became more devoted to self-help and education as the means to black betterment. He voiced the widespread despair at how little political participation had yielded blacks, saying that they had been born into political responsibility before they had acquired the economic power necessary for political independence. "The moral, mental and material condition of the race must be properly looked after before we can hope to establish any sort of status in the politics of this country." Fortune never wavered, however, in his crusade for black civil rights. In 1887 he had founded the Afro-American League to organize blacks against the mounting assaults on their rights, and he apparently never spared any words in condemning white mistreatment of blacks anywhere in the United States.[22]

Washington surely understood at the outset that the times were troubled enough to make the job difficult, but he could not have known how physically and emotionally grinding the role and responsibility would be. He was accustomed to extensive travel, but the new job required even more as he was asked constantly to represent blacks to white assemblies, to express black opinion and interests in councils of power, and to appear at noteworthy public occasions for blacks in America. He spent more and more of his life on trains, and when not sleeping in a bumpy Pullman car, he stayed night after night in hotels. Suddenly requests for his views on issues and his advice on all manner of concerns filled his daily mail. It must have seemed that every black person in the United States now turned to him to solve problems and settle disputes. Newspaper reporters and editors constantly sought his opinions, and Washington, an astute consumer of news, felt the inevitable stress that came from having to guard every word. At the same time, every news article and editorial presented an opportunity to put forward his message and to counteract the vicious views of white nationalists.

From the beginning of this period of national celebrity, some blacks openly rejected Washington as their leader. Amid the praise of the Atlanta exposition speech came sharp criticism as well, most of it emanating from the nation's capital. Bishop Henry Turner correctly predicted that whites would use Washington's statement against agitation for social equality as evidence that blacks willingly accepted inequality, adding that he would "have to live a long time to undo the harm he has done our race." Calvin Chase, editor of the Washington *Bee,* asserted that Booker took positions that were death to blacks and elevating to whites. "What fool wouldn't applaud the downfall of his aspiring competitor?" he said of whites' alleged celebration of Washington. The Atlanta address, Chase wrote, was an apology for southern outrages and Booker a "trimmer, pure and simple" who was interested mostly in gathering money for Tuskegee. At a meeting of Washington's Bethel Literary and Historical Association, several black critics insisted that Booker was playing into the hands of the southern whites. One man called him the cat's-paw of the white directors of the exposition and objected to the "chickens from miscellaneous sources" joke. "To compare Mr. Booker T. Washington with Frederick Douglass," another said, "is as unseemly as comparing a pigmy to a giant—a mountain brook leaping over a boulder to great . . . Niagara."[23]

The Tom Harris incident was recounted and Booker denounced for not providing protection and medical aid to the fleeing Negro. Washington confidentially gave a full account of his actions in the incident to a prominent minister in the District of Columbia, with the understanding that his moves to protect Harris could not be revealed further. His detractors considered him vulnerable on the matter of manliness—whether he stood up courageously to whites—and mostly ignored the dangerous environment in which he lived. People could say patently false things about him and get a public hearing because anything said about a person as famous as Booker T. Washington was newsworthy. A letter to the Washington *Post* in March 1896 claimed that Booker had said that "the colored man's lack of inventive genius accounts for his non-recognition by the whites" and that "the negro is incapable of utilizing his brain to pecuniary advantage." Both statements were virtually the opposite of Booker's clearly articulated positions, and yet they appeared uncontradicted in an influential national newspaper. All Booker could do about such misrepresentations was smolder—a public response only brought his detractors more attention—and recognize that one price of fame was loss of control over one's reputation. Still, it was clear from the outset of Washington's leadership that some northern black leaders did not like his positions or his words.[24]

The burdens of leading his race began to weigh heavily almost from the beginning. Washington's every utterance was subject to criticism and to lies, or the careless removal from the context in which it was said. Whites began immediately to interpret his Atlanta remarks as a total and final rejection of black political participation and an acceptance of permanent second-class status. Some blacks chose to accept the white misinterpretation and to blame Washington for what he had not in fact said. They assigned him responsibility for allowing himself to be misunderstood. Objecting to his sudden prominence as leader of the race, various black spokesmen began to challenge the validity of his positions. A dozen black men could look at Booker's previous obscurity and imagine that the baton could just as easily have passed into their hands. Booker Washington would spend much time in the years ahead fencing with those who opposed him from the start, but he would never become reconciled to doing so.

Despite the dissent, praise and even exaltation of Booker T. Washington dominated the comments about him in the aftermath of the Atlanta speech. He received a strong vote of public confidence to go forward in implementing his proposed settlement of the Negro Problem. If he could get blacks and whites thinking in new ways, moving in new directions, then his leadership would be successful. And so he plunged ahead.

6

———

The Rising People

Although his strategy for settling the Negro Problem was mainly economic, Booker Washington's method for achieving the plan was ideological. He had to change what blacks and whites believed about their future together in America. He understood that his real power as a racial leader resided in the bully pulpit, the place from which he could teach Americans, black and white, how to think about race. He had little authority to shape public policy directly; blacks' political power was already minor, and they were rapidly losing what little electoral influence they had acquired. But his newfound national celebrity brought many speaking invitations. The 1890s were the heyday of the large lecture hall, the lyceum, and the Chautauqua, where well-known personalities drew large crowds seeking to be entertained, inspired, or enlightened. It was the age of the traveling evangelist Sam Jones and the humorist Mark Twain and the Democratic orator William Jennings Bryan, men who spoke to great throngs and whose arrival in a town stirred excitement like that sparked by a national minstrel troupe or a circus. After the Atlanta exposition, Booker's speeches in public forums were events of similar magnitude, drawing big crowds and much newspaper coverage.

Washington was a different kind of speaker from Frederick Douglass, whose orations were usually formal and serious discourses, akin to

21. Much of Booker Washington's influence as leader of his race came from his prowess on the speaking platform. Photographer unknown, ca. 1910; from Emmett J. Scott and Lyman Beecher Stowe, *Booker T. Washington: Builder of a Civilization* (Garden City, N.Y.: Doubleday, Page, 1916).

sermons. Douglass spoke in the manner that Americans admired when they had listened to Daniel Webster and Edward Everett Hale in the mid-nineteenth century and when they would hear Martin Luther King Jr. in the mid-twentieth. Washington carefully attuned his speeches to the moment. He delivered them conversationally, near the edge of the platform, usually with no podium (and if there was one he stood beside it) and only a note card in a pocket. His unpretentious dress reinforced the common style of his speech: he typically wore a business suit with no vest and a small black bow tie. He usually had a pencil in his right hand, and he habitually hooked his left thumb in the pocket of his trousers. He gestured only occasionally but often bent his whole body toward the audience to emphasize a point. William Dean Howells, America's preeminent man of letters in the 1890s, described Booker's coming onto the platform, where he "stood for a moment, with his hands in his pockets, and with downcast eyes, and then began to *talk* at his hearers the clearest, soundest sense." Howells said that Washington made him forget all the distinguished white speakers he had heard. Booker's voice did not sound loud to his listeners, but it was

easily heard in big halls in the days before amplification. His pronoun-
ciations were characterized as those of the educated American with
southern inflections. "Shutting one's eyes," an Englishman said on
hearing Booker, "it would be impossible to know that a Negro was
speaking." For many of his listeners, black and white, Booker would
have been the first black man they had heard who revealed none of the
expected Negro inflection in his speech.[1]

Booker's audiences usually remembered his aphorisms. For example, a listener in Indianapolis in 1897 recalled his saying, "It's a mighty
hard thing to make a good Christian out of a hungry man." He offered
ethical maxims that he applied to race relations: "I would permit no
man to drag down my soul by making me hate him" and "One man
can't keep another man in the ditch without being in the ditch himself." He frequently said that in every community in the South "every
Negro has a white friend and every white a Negro friend." About
blacks, he claimed many times that "in slavery or freedom, we have
always been loyal to the Stars and Stripes," and that "no schoolhouse
has been opened for us that has not been filled."[2]

Washington offered his problack perspective in an unassuming
manner. In speeches attended by both blacks and whites, as were most
of his large public addresses, he devised contrasts and balances, ex-
pressly pointing some remarks at blacks and others at whites. He mod-
estly asserted opinions, prefacing them with "I believe," "It seems to
me," or "Were I permitted to say." He referred to himself as "a humble
representative" of his race. His humility was reminiscent of that of
Abraham Lincoln on the stump, and the presentation was undoubtedly deliberate. A student of rhetoric who observed Booker closely
characterized it as having "the quality of the sinking self . . . [which]
takes attention away from the speaker and turns it to what he is saying." Booker convinced his listeners that he was "not thinking of his
own glory but of the cause for which he pleads." His down-to-earth
manner was sincere: blacks frequently noted that that they were surprised at how ordinary he was in appearance, demeanor, and address.
There were reports of the famous Tuskegeean arriving at train stations
in a new towns and left stranded because the party assembled to receive him had expected a larger man wearing a high hat and gold spec-

tacles, not the ordinary-looking, hatless fellow in the plain sack suit. His unprepossessing manner led rural southern blacks to call him not Dr. Washington or Professor Washington but "Booker" and sometimes "Uncle Booker."[3]

Booker's listeners always relished his humor. James Hardy Dillard, the southern classics professor and race reformer, thought Booker's was the best sense of humor, used most effectively, of any man he ever saw. "He could not only tell a good joke well, but tell what was only the shadow of a joke so well that his audience would be shaken with laughter. The story might be a simple one. The effectiveness lay in the artistic way of telling it." In his storytelling, there was again a strong similarity to Lincoln, with a rustic character always delivering the punch line. But much of Booker's humor came from the subtle social comment, the kind of deadpan irony in which Mark Twain specialized. It was no accident that Twain and Booker became friends. Although he told some stories over and over, Booker constantly gathered new material, like the story a white Episcopal priest told him on a train headed to Richmond. When his family occupied the rectory at a new assignment, they inherited an old black man who had long tended its yard. The new rector's wife told the yardman that she wanted a certain shrub moved to a new location. The old man agreed but failed to move the plant and agreed a second time when she reminded, but still the shrub stayed put. When she angrily issued the order for the third time, the old man faced his new mistress, removed his hat to reveal tears rolling down his cheek, and said: "My old missis, what's dead now, planted that bush right there. I can't dig it up."[4] Booker often used this story to illustrate the affection of blacks for whites whom they had historically served in the South. He invoked it to counter the ugly images of blacks prevalent in the 1890s.

Washington's humor depended in part on "darky" stories. Some of the humor of these stories came from the contrast between the black dialect in them and Washington's uninflected speech. To most listeners, he sounded like a white man mocking a black person. In this regard his assumption of dialect amounted to pandering to white prejudices, because it won him laughs and approval from white audiences. Dialect humor was an old tradition in the United States, which by the

1890s was finding new expressions among comedians imitating European immigrants on the vaudeville stage. Other noteworthy blacks of the time mimicked dialect when quoting African Americans, and black-owned newspapers and magazines included dialect humor— and would for another generation at least. Frederick Douglass, the novelist Charles Chesnutt, and the poet Paul Laurence Dunbar did so for realistic political or artistic purpose. Booker did it to warm up his audiences, both black and white, with popular and familiar humor.[5]

But such jokes brought down on Washington severe criticism from some blacks for playing to white bigotry. Although he was guilty as charged, Washington's racial humor had a strategic purpose. The literary critic William Dean Howells probably captured some of Booker's objective when he observed that the darky stories allowed Booker "to place himself outside his race, when he wishes to see it as others see it, and to report its exterior effect from his interior knowledge." To influence whites' thinking, Washington adapted to their conventions of humor, just as he acknowledged and addressed whites' myths about the past. Bishop Henry Turner, the black emigrationist and a critic of Washington, observed to Bill Arp that whites had to respect popular prejudice against blacks in order to be influential among whites. Demeaning as it was to some, Washington recognized that a black man had to engage those same prejudices if he hoped to shape whites' views. Booker's darky stories were intended not to raise himself by disparaging blacks but to appeal to the remnants of sentimentality that some whites had for blacks. A white Philadelphia benefactor advised Booker privately in 1897 that his approaches to whites "must aim at the heart," because helping the Negro rise to the point of competing successfully with whites, which was Booker's true goal, was a "pill that needs a *little* coating of sentiment."[6]

Much of his racial humor involved ironic criticism of whites. On social conditions in the South: "The colored men down south are very fond of an old song entitled 'Give me Jesus and you take all the rest.' The white man has taken him at his word." Concerning blacks' reputation for stupidity, he told the story of a white man who asked a black fellow to lend him three cents to take a ferry to cross a river, but the black man refused, saying, "Boss I knows yous got moah sense dan dis yeah niggah," but "a man whats got no money is as well off on one side of the river as on de other." On the issue of the removal of blacks from the United States: blacks came to the United States "by special invitation" and "at great cost and inconvenience," he told his overwhelmingly white audience in Indianapolis, and "it would be very ungrateful for us not to oblige you by staying here."[7]

As he accepted the role of racial leader, Washington began to exercise the power that had suddenly accrued to him. His main influence lay in the opportunity to throw light on problems, and he began to speak out on the many issues. Notwithstanding how some interpreted the Atlanta address, he had by no means relinquished the black claim to equal rights. Indeed, he pursued all the rights due blacks, though in his own way.

The first public position he took after Atlanta involved the defense of black education. Attacks on it were building during the 1890s. The writings of Bill Arp and other white nationalists continually stoked opposition to black education, and the threat increased as poor white farmers, in their Populist challenges to Democratic control, had demanded more money for the education of white children. Many Populists opted for the panacea of racial separation of school funds. During South Carolina's disfranchising constitutional convention in 1895, convening as the Atlanta exposition began, Governor Ben Tillman supported segregating school funds. Tillman had claimed in the 1880s that education of a Negro either made a criminal or spoiled a field hand, and in 1892 he refused Morrill Act funds for South Carolina's black industrial college rather than allow a black school to have large sums of federal money. Washington knew that disfranchisement was a foregone conclusion, but he thought that stopping school-fund separation might be a winnable battle in South Carolina. In his new role, he wrote a public letter to Tillman, flattering him as a member of the "great, intelligent Caucasian race" and pleading on behalf of 650,000 black South Carolinians who were "supplicants at your feet, and whose destiny and progress for the next century you hold largely in your hands." The true test of the civilization of a race, he declared, was its desire to help the unfortunate—a reminder doomed in this case to fall on stony ground: as the New York *World* reported, Tillman knew that segregating the school funds would mean "the end of negro education and negro progress," and that result was fine with him—indeed, it was the measure's real purpose. Washington was actually appealing more to Pitchfork Ben's political enemies, South Carolina's white paternalists, who felt more kindly toward blacks and were generally hostile to Tillman's appeal to the lower classes. Washington also played on white nationalists' obsessive fears about northern interference. If the state ceased to support black schools, Washington warned, enough northern money would flow in to "keep the light of the school-house burning on every hill and in every valley in South Carolina." Blacks in South Carolina *would* be educated, Booker wrote; "Shall South Carolina do it, or shall it be left to others?"[8]

Tillman's opponents did prevent the separation of the school funds, and the cause of black education was saved for the moment. But black schools had a permanent enemy in the one-eyed white-nationalist demagogue. From 1895 on, Tillman regularly argued that it was stupid to disfranchise the Negro on the basis of illiteracy and then compel him to go to school. Those who had helped establish black education in the South were to him the biggest fools alive, and the ones who failed to see that black education threatened white political control were besotted with ignorance. He marked down Booker Washington as an enemy to the interests of white men. The Populist–white nationalist alliance failed to separate South Carolina's school funds, but the political merger of the two groups into an intensely anti-black-education coalition was under way.[9]

Washington decried the continuing humiliations of railroad travel for blacks. Just days after the Atlanta address, Robert W. Taylor, an Institute fundraiser, was traveling from Atlanta to Boston on the Southern Railroad when a conductor physically attacked him after a disagreement over which direction Taylor's seat was to be turned. Portia Washington, age twelve, was traveling with Taylor and witnessed the beating. Booker complained privately to the line, and apparently the conductor was dismissed, but the incident brought closer to home the persistent indignities that blacks suffered. Washington warned publicly that forcing blacks to ride in an inferior Jim Crow car would not "stand much longer against the increasing intelligence and prosperity of the colored people." In 1896 he expressed bitter disappointment in the U.S. Supreme Court's decision in *Plessy v. Ferguson,* which validated segregation in public accommodations with a doctrine of "separate but equal." His experience of fifteen years as a frequent railroad passenger had taught him that "separate" never was and never would be "equal." If the Supreme Court allowed whites and blacks to be separated, he wrote, then why not "put all yellow people in one car and all white people, whose skin is sun burnt, in another car . . . [or] all men with bald heads must ride in one car and all with red hair still in another"? Laying aside the sarcasm, Washington returned to his more usual tone of sober moralism. Such an unjust law only inconvenienced the Negro, but it actually injured the white man, because "no race can wrong another race simply because it has the power to do so, without being permanently injured in morals."[10]

Washington spoke often about black job opportunities, saying that blacks had to acquire industrial education to make economic progress in modern America. Noting that blacks had lost jobs in the building trades and in service skills like barbering, he attributed the decline to blacks' indolence and their preoccupation with unattainable higher-status callings. But he also discussed job discrimination. Let the Negro who grew the cotton in the South ask for a job at a textile mill in the North or the South, he declared in a widely reported speech in Washington, D.C., in early 1896, "and the door will be shut in his face." He wrote that many white men in the North earnestly hoped for the end of racial problems in the South but never thought of letting the "colored boy who sweeps the office or runs errands in a bank or factory feel that one day he may become a clerk or a cashier in the bank or a partner in the factory." In 1897 he criticized the American Federation of Labor for protecting white monopolies in many trades. His effort elicited only the personal rancor of union leaders, one of whom condemned Booker for portraying blacks as "the victims of gross injustice and himself as the Moses of the race." The Negro, Washington answered, was committed to the United States and "not here to grab a few dollars and then return to some foreign country." Blacks were not prone to strike but believed in "letting each individual be free to work where and for who he pleases." Booker privately expressed urgency about blacks' getting a share of industrial opportunities. "If we do not, through the instrumentality of the stronger brain in the race, lay hold of the business and industrial openings in the South during the next ten years," he wrote to Fortune, "these opportunities will pass beyond our recall."[11]

Washington tried to change how the media reported about blacks. The press left the impression of constant friction between whites and blacks in the South, he said, because evidence of friendly race relations was rarely noted. Newspaper coverage constantly promoted the image of the Negro as criminal beast. With Fortune's advice, Booker mounted a campaign of positive publicity, and in 1897 he hired the Texas newspaperman Emmett J. Scott as his assistant and gave him responsibility for issuing press releases that noted black achievements—including, but not limited to, Booker's own good works. He and Scott assumed that positive news about himself and other African Americans would help blacks show "the narrow white people that their prejudices are not shared by other parts of the world, and at the same time such news would encourage the colored people."[12]

Of first importance in the campaign was a challenge to whites' hope for a permanent solution to the Negro Problem, namely the disappearance of all blacks. Washington indirectly rejected Frederick Hoffman's widely accepted assertions that high African-American mortality would bring the extinction of the race. To a black audience in the South, Washington acknowledged high black mortality, attributed it to bad whiskey, poor food, and inadequate houses, and called for close attention to home sanitation and better infant care. But to mostly white audiences in New York and Boston and an integrated group in Nashville two years later, he gently rebuked experts' wild estimates that blacks were either about to overrun the white population or would soon disappear. Because a man who was 99 percent white and one percent black was counted a Negro in America, Washington said with his tongue in cheek, it was more likely that blacks would absorb the white population. So-called experts had proved both that black crime was on the increase and that it was declining, that education helped the Negro and that it hurt him, and that the Negro "is our greatest criminal and that he is our most law-abiding citizen." Amid such confusion,

Washington could only assert what *he* knew: "that whether in slavery or freedom, we have always been loyal to the Stars and Stripes, that no schoolhouse has been opened for us that has not been filled; that 1,500,000 ballots that we have the right to cast are as potent for weal and woe as the ballot cast by the whitest and most influential man in the commonwealth." Then he added tartly that "almost every other race that tried to look the white man in the face has disappeared." His unspoken but clear implication was that blacks would be the one race to survive white hostility in America. In response to the insistent call for blacks to be removed from the South, he said that a plan to resettle all blacks in the West, currently being trumpeted by the Atlanta newspaper editor John Temple Graves, was impractical: "In the first place you would have to build a wall about that territory to keep the black men in; in the second place you would have to build a much higher wall to keep the white man out."[13]

A major responsibility of racial leadership was representing black interests in politics, a role that Frederick Douglass had created with Abraham Lincoln and then fulfilled periodically after the war, especially during times of Republican control. Washington had mostly avoided politics since he left West Virginia in 1878. In 1896, under Tim Fortune's influence, he had supported the Iowa senator William Allison for president, but when that candidacy failed to gain traction he transferred his allegiance to William McKinley. He liked McKinley but shared the suspicions of many black Republicans about the influence of Senator Mark Hanna of Ohio, McKinley's campaign manager. Hanna encouraged what would become known as the Lily White movement: a white takeover and a corollary exclusion of blacks from power and patronage among southern Republicans. Washington thought that blacks should benefit from the party of Lincoln: beyond simple fairness and reward for loyalty, black officeholding had symbolic importance for the race's morale. He lobbied the McKinley administration to appoint former senator Blanche K. Bruce register of the Treasury, traditionally the highest federal position held by a black. A black appointee, Washington announced publicly, would demonstrate that the Negro still had a place in national affairs. If a poor black saw a Negro's name on every dollar that came into his possession, it

would show him that "this is not a white man's government, as demagogues tell him, but is a people's government . . . that the Negro can
rise here just as well as the white man if he has the energy and ambition to do it." He exaggerated the significance of the appointment,
which did go to Bruce, but for Booker black officeholding remained
symbolically important.[14]

Politics might engender hope in the black masses, but it also generated intense hostility to a black man in the South, something that
Booker saw when the press claimed that he would direct patronage
appointments in the South and might himself be appointed to McKinley's cabinet. Those were ridiculous lies, Washington quickly answered, although Fortune insisted privately to him that the talk enhanced his influence. The truth was that both men relished political
life, and Booker began to see that with Fortune's counsel he could indeed affect Republican decisions. Still, political action was a very dangerous path to follow in the South.[15]

State and local politics in Alabama were almost as perilous in the
1890s as they had been in the early 1870s. From 1890 on, the state was
embroiled in a tense and corrupt conflict for control between the Democrats and the Populists. The Democrats were generally thought to
have stolen the 1892 and 1894 elections for governor from the Populists
by stuffing ballot boxes in the Black Belt. Both factions were well represented in the Tuskegee area: Populists dominated the area north of
Tuskegee, and the Democrats were powerful in the town and to the
south, where they stole and stuffed heavily black voting boxes. James
E. Cobb, a Democratic circuit judge responsible for removing black
officeholders in Tuskegee in the mid-1870s, was elected to Congress
three times in the early 1890s, only to have congressional investigating committees overturn the election and seat the Populist. Booker
could not afford to engage in the struggle, but his best white friends in
Tuskegee were Democrats, and the Populists came from the areas of
Alabama known for terrorism against blacks. He could do nothing
to stop it, and he stood to incur the wrath of both sides if he said
anything. The situation was volatile: in the summer of 1896, while he
was away from home, Booker got a report from Tuskegee: "A White
man was lynched near Tallassee last night for stuffing ballot boxes,"

his nephew Albert Johnston wrote, referring to the nearby town noted for its white vigilantism. "The populites have threatened to kill several others, among the number are two prominent whites in [Tuskegee]."[16]

The political tensions of 1896 increased the threats to black education. William Benson, a Tuskegee graduate, had built a school thirty miles to the northwest, not far from Tallassee, and northern support had enabled him to erect several substantial buildings. In late 1896 white vigilantes torched some of the campus. The arson was the result of envy and jealousy, Benson wrote to Booker. "You know how much help we are to this community and how hard we have labored to help our people here but it seems that there is an element here that is determined to keep us from succeeding." Indeed, Booker already knew well that success begot envy, which often turned to violence and destruction. The second reality was one that Booker had difficulty acknowledging, but the time was approaching when he could no longer avoid the truth.[17]

Although he felt more comfortable with paternalistic Democrats, Booker knew that they also posed a danger when angry. This fact was made clear at the Institute's 1896 commencement, when one of the speakers was the empty-sleeved Democrat and former Confederate William C. Oates, who had been put in the governor's office with fraudulent votes in 1894. John Dancy, a prominent black Republican in North Carolina, preceded Governor Oates at the podium and at some length lauded the New England whites so helpful in building Tuskegee Institute. Apparently Dancy's speech and the enthusiastic response from the audience brought to Oates the sudden revelation that the ultimate goal of a Tuskegee education was full black equality. Now furious, the governor advanced to the podium waving a sheaf of papers containing the speech that he now said he would not deliver. "I want to give you niggers a few words of plain talk," he began. There followed a diatribe that condemned any and all hope for black equality, regardless of what might happen on this impressive campus. Blacks should understand that the South was a white man's country, Oates shouted angrily, and "we are going to make you keep your place." When the governor resumed his seat, Booker ignored Tim Fortune, the next scheduled speaker and a man quick to meet a threat with a threat. Washington declared that the gathering had heard enough eloquence for one occasion and pronounced the benediction.[18]

He enjoyed far more another commencement a few days later. Harvard University affirmed Washington's rise to fame by conferring on him an honorary master's degree. At the alumni dinner after the commencement, Booker stood before a body of the richest and most powerful. "I feel like a huckleberry in a bowl of milk," he began. Turning serious, he declared that one of the most pressing needs in American life was a means of keeping America's wealthy and learned in touch with its poor and humble people and a way to "make the one appreciate the vitalizing, strengthening influence of the other." If the conscience of any of the Harvard men was not already aroused, Washington made it so with a simple question: "How shall we make the mansions on yon Beacon street feel and see the need of the spirits in the lowliest cabin in Alabama cotton fields or Louisiana sugar bottoms?" He then made a bold assertion of black progress, something that would be the hallmark of his rhetoric in the years ahead, just as it had been a central message of his Atlanta address. He appropriated the statement made by a young black student in postwar Atlanta when the head of the Freedmen's Bureau had asked what message he wanted delivered to the North. "Tell 'em we're rising!" the boy had shouted, a line that the abolitionist poet John Greenleaf Whittier later memorialized in "The Black Boy of Atlanta":

> The slave's chain and the master's alike are broken;
> The one curse of the race held both in tether;
> They are rising, all are rising—
> The black and the white together.

"We are coming," Washington told the Harvard dignitaries, by means of hard work in industrial shops and on farms, study in colleges and industrial schools, and habits of thrift and economy. "We are crawling up, working up, yea, bursting up." In spite of discrimination and prejudice, blacks were rising, and there was "no power on earth that can permanently stay our progress."[19]

Booker's fame and his prowess at the podium brought him endless invitations to speak, including another a year later in Boston at the unveiling of the monument honoring Robert Gould Shaw, the young white colonel who had commanded the Fifty-fourth Massachusetts Volunteers, an all-black regiment formed in Boston. Shaw and many of his men had died during an attack on Fort Wagner in Charleston Harbor in 1863. Thirty-four years later, Boston's Music Hall was full of flags and martial music and, according to a local newspaper, "the old abolition spirit of Massachusetts . . . the crown and glory of the old war days of suffering and strife." After the singing of the "Battle Hymn of the Republic," Washington went to the podium, offered his praise for the Christ-like Shaw, and turned to surviving members of the regiment on the platform behind him. "With empty sleeve and wanting leg," he declared to the old soldiers, they had honored the occasion with their presence, and "in you and the loyal race which you represent, Robert Gould Shaw would have a monument which time could not wear away."[20] At that point the regiment's old flagbearer, reputed never to have let the flag fall at Fort Wagner, rose and waved Old Glory back and forth, causing the audience to explode into a sustained roar of patriotic shouting.

Washington embodied the faith among neoabolitionist whites that the sacrifices made for freedom and equality during the Civil War were warranted, that in fact black people were rising from slavery. He was a slave who in freedom had proved he could become a useful citizen, one who embraced their most cherished values. No black person, not even Frederick Douglass, was any better at demonstrating obeisance to their exalted meaning of the Union victory or more committed to living up to that legacy.

A group of black Bostonians, however, rejected Booker as firmly as the local white elite embraced him. By 1896 Booker's detractors, led by a local minister and two lawyers, had gathered in the Massachusetts Racial Protective League. They no doubt resented the status afforded him at Harvard and at the Shaw monument. The opponents objected most strongly to his conciliation of the white South and his rising influence in Republican politics. In early 1897 the Harvard-educated lawyer William H. Lewis reportedly told Booker that he should tend to his educational work in the South and "leave to us the matters political affecting the race." In the North, Booker honored myths of Union triumph and other symbols of American nationalism. In the South, he apparently offered fealty to competing myths: the Old South, the Lost Cause, and Black Reconstruction. He tried to have it both ways because he needed the support—or at least the toleration—of each for blacks to rise. The people close to Booker accepted this duality as shrewd strategy. Some blacks in the North, however, viewed his homage to southern myths as treachery to the race. Those suspicious of him, both black critics in the North and white nationalists in the South, recognized that he often succeeded in having it both ways.[21]

Washington considered his black critics to be insulated from the real world of most American blacks. The most outspoken were northern-born, prosperous products of Ivy League colleges. William Lewis had been an undergraduate at Dartmouth before going to Harvard Law School. Washington believed that such men knew little about conditions in the South—or cared; otherwise they would have gone there and worked for change. He thought that they were embarrassed by the ignorance—the lack of respectability and "civilization," in the vernacular of the day—of southern blacks. They had adopted the common nineteenth-century understanding that people of culture lived in cities in close proximity to universities, museums, and libraries. Washington, on the other hand, had an emotional connection to the unlettered freed people of the rural South and a deep appreciation of their speech, music, humor, and religiosity. He thought his critics' insularity in the more racially tolerant northern cities left them poorly informed and smug. They viewed Booker from the elevation of Harvard, looking down on a fellow with a middle-school education from a trade school. Booker knew how much he had learned from intense engagement in the real world of the South—and how much he had achieved in it—and he resented their condescension. Now that circumstances had thrust him into this position at the head of the parade, he felt that these relatively privileged northerners should fall into step behind him as he tried to reverse the worsening trend in black conditions.

Washington's critics usually condemned him for rejecting the classical curriculum in favor of industrial education. Some blacks who had heard reports of the Atlanta address jumped to the conclusion that he wanted to keep the Negro "a hewer of wood and drawer of water." Alexander Crummell, a black minister educated at Cambridge University, was convinced that his race would advance only when it achieved higher culture, and to that end in 1897 he founded the American Negro Academy, a group of forty black intellectuals and artists whom he envisioned as the vanguard of black cultural advancement. Crummell and his followers viewed cultural achievement as the way to acceptance in American life, now that political equality seemed a remote possibility, whereas Washington was offering economic progress as the path to full integration into the nation. Crummell's cultural elite would show blacks the way to civilization, and only through broad liberal education could cultural distinction be realized. Crummell argued that the emphasis on industrial training was therefore misguided.[22]

According to Washington's instrumentalist perspective, education without a real-world application was out of place among a developing people, the vast majority of whom needed primary schools and some training in skills to prepare for either agriculture or industry. Higher education was entirely appropriate for blacks who became professors, doctors, lawyers, and ministers. "Understand me," he told Tuskegee students in early 1895, "I am not now, nor have I ever been, opposed to any man or woman getting all the education they can." It mattered not where or how they got it, but "what are they going to do with it." At the current stage of black development, all education should advance the race's material conditions; it should work "in the direction of filling up our stomachs . . . in supplying food, shelter, raiment—something that we can lay by for a rainy day." In response to Crummell's criticism, Washington reiterated the argument for black education based on a realistic assessment of the current situation of black people in the South. Industrial education had been misrepresented as an obstacle to the Negro's higher mental development. "I would say to the black boy what I would say to the white boy, get all the mental development that your time and pocketbook will afford—the more the better; but the

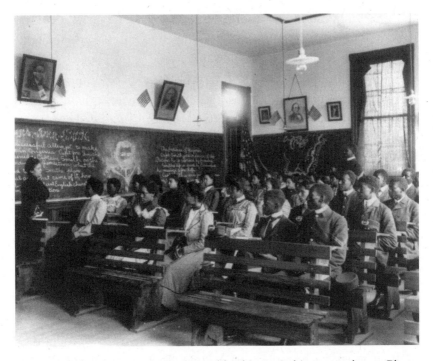

22. As Tuskegee grew, academic classes, like this one in history, got larger. Photo by Frances Benjamin Johnston, 1902; courtesy of the Library of Congress.

time has come when a larger proportion—not all, for we need professional men and women—of the educated colored men and women should give themselves to industrial or business life."[23]

But just after Booker answered Crummell, the poet Paul Laurence Dunbar wrote that too many people were "in the throes of feverish delight over industrial education." Washington's promotion of industrial education was doing blacks an injustice because "the world quotes him . . . as saying that we must not have anything else."[24] Booker never said that blacks should have only industrial education, but he was unable to prevent people from misrepresenting his views. The higher his profile became as the leader of African Americans, the more willing were both blacks and whites who opposed his point of view to ignore what he did say and condemn him for what he did not.

Even as new leadership responsibilities additionally complicated his life, Washington retained general authority over Tuskegee Institute.

The school was continuing to grow; by 1898 there would be 1,000 students, and the increasing numbers increased the scale and complexity of the Institute's problems. In 1896 Booker told a faculty committee that the curriculum overburdened students with too many subjects. Simplify it and emphasize the core subjects, he ordered, especially for the younger students. He instructed the school's choir director to redesign the performance repertoire so that one-third of it would consist of Negro spirituals, which Booker loved and which would also benefit fundraising for the Institute. In 1898, backed by the advice of a faculty investigating committee, Booker summarily fired a senior teacher, a longtime colleague and friend, for having made advances to two female students. He expressed his pain at having to take such action, but when the teacher rallied students to his defense, Booker ignored them, angry that the man had encouraged the students' meddling in such affairs. The Institute's outreach to black farmers was expanding. With new federal and state funding in 1897, the Institute organized an agricultural college and an experiment station. The Slater Fund underwrote a new two-story agricultural building, which Booker said inspired hope that the 85 percent of southern blacks who were farmers would not be left "to forever endure the serfdom and moral slavery of present farming conditions." Tuskegee-trained scientific farmers would, he predicted, liberate those farmers who still clung to "the broken down plow and the half-fed mule and the little patch of half cultivated cotton." To lead the expanded effort, Booker recruited George Washington Carver, a horticulturalist who as a slave child had been abducted from his Missouri home by thieves but overcame the trauma to excel as a natural scientist at Iowa State College.[25]

Fundraising continued to be Booker's main preoccupation, and he complained as early as 1896 about the misperception that his and the Institute's growing national fame had translated into a flood of money. Tuskegee Institute still lived a hand-to-mouth financial existence, but the mouth was now much larger. Booker continued to travel half the year seeking the $100,000 needed annually to cover operating expenses. He complained that the growing number of black schools seeking financial help from northern philanthropists was making the task harder. But his national fame enabled fundraising success with the new industrial magnates. He now spent extended periods in New York City, usually lodging at the Manhattan Hotel and often dining in the homes of white business leaders. During the summers he often visited Bar Harbor, Maine, and Saratoga Springs, New York, to meet the wealthy as they vacationed, and in those places he was usually entertained as the rich would host any other American celebrity. By 1898 he had received money from John D. Rockefeller of Standard Oil. That year the railroad magnate Collis P. Huntington and his Alabama-born wife, Arabella, contributed $10,000 for a girls' dormitory. They made the gift, Collis Huntington said, because Tuskegee was "doing much for the negro race, and the credit for it is due to the practical sense and ability of its guiding spirit—yourself." A few more "well-organized training schools" were needed, he thought, but "where shall we get another Booker T. Washington for these other schools?"[26]

The next year the Institute trustees organized a special meeting at Madison Square Garden to launch a Tuskegee endowment. The event attracted an impressive array of the wealthy and influential, including Rockefeller, Huntington, the investment banker J. P. Morgan, and Henry H. Rogers, Rockefeller's partner in Standard Oil. The following morning Rogers summoned Booker to his office, lauded the speech, and said that he had expected to contribute the previous night, but since no collection had been taken, he wanted to chip in now; whereupon Rogers handed the astonished Booker $10,000 in thousand-dollar bills. This represented a marked departure from his long years of collecting money in ten- and twenty-five-dollar increments. From 1899 on, Booker enjoyed the benefits of fundraising among industrial barons, including time relaxing with chum Mark Twain on Rogers's yacht.[27]

Support from the industrialists came with strings attached. The Slater Fund's emphasis on trades education put pressure on Tuskegee to reshape its curriculum. Even with the full commitment made to teaching industrial trades in the early 1890s, Tuskegee required at least half of each student's courses to be in academic subjects, on the assumption that most graduates were going to be rural schoolteachers responsible for the whole curriculum in one- or two-room schoolhouses. In 1897 the railroad tycoon Henry Villard gave Tuskegee $100 in the be-

23. Botany classes at Tuskegee attracted both men and women, who planned to teach their own students how to grow plants. Photo originally published by the Bain News Service, ca. 1905; courtesy of the Library of Congress.

lief that unlike Atlanta University, which was giving blacks a liberal education that he felt they were not prepared to receive, the Alabama school provided no academic training beyond an elementary level. But when a Tuskegee student wrote Villard a letter of thanks for his gift, she revealed that she had studied natural philosophy, ancient history, and algebra. Villard fired off an angry letter to Booker accusing him of a bait-and-switch fraud and expressed his outrage to a Slater trustee, President Daniel Coit Gilman of Johns Hopkins, who also disapproved of "the travesty of higher education" at Tuskegee and gave Villard other examples of "mental confusion produced [at Tuskegee] by the pursuit of classical studies on immature minds." Booker had resolved to get the support of powerful men like Villard and Gilman, but keeping them happy was a hard job.[28]

Not all whites were so overbearing in their views, and one would be singularly important in advising Booker for the next few years. William H. Baldwin Jr., an executive with the Southern Railway, visited Tuskegee, examined the school closely, and enthusiastically accepted an appointment to the Institute board of trustees. Baldwin brought with him the sharp managerial habits of the modern railroad corporation. He had, Booker later said, "an astonishing gift to get instantly at the weakness of the situation." His questions penetrated the school's operation: "How were they keeping their accounts? Where are your funds? How are your investments made?" Baldwin's close oversight of the school's finances gave benefactors confidence that their money was being well spent. And with his hard-nosed managerial approach came a powerful moral commitment to black uplift. The scion of a Boston abolitionist family that had supported Tuskegee, Baldwin bridged the gap between Booker's original neoabolitionist supporters and the new industrial elite that would provide most of Tuskegee's support in the future. Through his railroad business, Baldwin was connected to Wall Street investment capital and was friendly with, and respected by, the Rockefellers, Andrew Carnegie, and other magnates who would soon be drawn into the cause of black education. By 1898 Baldwin was soliciting large gifts for Tuskegee from America's wealthiest men. An active Republican, Baldwin knew the rising New York politician Theodore Roosevelt. A man with such broad and varied connections was invaluable to Washington, because Baldwin not only appreciated his talents but also was capable of entertaining Booker's honest opinions about whites. When General Armstrong died in 1892, Booker had lost his mentor and white confidant, but Baldwin began to fill that role just as Washington stepped into the national limelight and most needed a trustworthy white point of view.[29]

All the while he was working on Tuskegee's finances, Washington was advancing his message of black progress. In 1898 he embarked on what would become a regular part of his annual agenda when he made a long speaking tour of South Carolina, sponsored by the Slater Fund for the announced purpose of promoting black industrial education. The unspoken motive was to challenge the influence of Ben Tillman, who now as a U.S. senator continued to condemn black education. In Charleston many whites opposed Tillman, and those thousands of whites who came to hear Booker were exposed to a message that flatly contradicted Pitchfork Ben's insistence that blacks were the enemy within. Booker rejected the popular demographic predictions of blacks' disappearance but tackled head-on the bad living conditions of the growing black urban population. He addressed the terrible health consequences of bad whiskey, poor food, and decrepit houses. Improving health conditions would strengthen home life. To make sure that a positive message to women came through clearly, Margaret Washington followed her husband to the podium to give instructions to women on maintaining cleanliness and morality. At this point, Maggie was emerging as a forceful reform voice in the National Association of Colored Women. Settlement of the Negro Problem would require improvements in black family life and changes in black women's household habits.[30]

Washington applied his expanding influence to teaching African Americans specific lessons about how to rise in society. *Black Belt Diamonds,* an 1898 collection of quotations from Booker's speeches and writing, addressed this goal. It may have been Tim Fortune's idea to have a great black man dispense wisdom acquired during his rise to the top, in the way Benjamin Franklin had done in *Poor Richard's Almanac.* The 400 quotations in *Black Belt Diamonds* constituted less a book of inspiration than an instructional manual about how to settle the Negro Problem. Booker analyzed the black experience, instructed blacks on how to succeed in the future, and told whites some hard truths about their behavior. The selections portrayed blacks as the rising people—a hardworking, patient, faithful group who had made great progress in the United States, first as slaves and now as freed people. "We are a new race, as it were, and the time, attention, and activity of any race are taken up during the first fifty or one hundred years in getting a start." Once emancipated, blacks had erred at times: "We began at the top. We made mistakes, not because we were black people, but because we were ignorant and inexperienced." They were, after all, heavily burdened with the legacy of slavery: "Slavery taught both the white man and the Negro to dread labor,—to look upon it as something to be escaped, something fit only for poor people." Now blacks were truly rising: "Though the line of progress may seem at times to waver, now advancing, now retreating, now on the mountains, now in the valley, now in the sunshine, now in the shadow, the aim has ever been forward, and we have gained more than we have lost." Progress was the law of God, he insisted in the last entry in the book, and "under Him it is going to be the Negro's guiding star in this country."[31]

About half of *Black Belt Diamonds* taught blacks how to lift themselves. They should stay in the South, adapt to their environment and opportunities, and not fiddle around with politics, drinking, or card-playing. And they should work! "You cannot afford to do a thing poorly. You are more injured in shirking your work or half-doing a job than the person for whom you are working." They should practice scientific agriculture and learn how to use the latest machinery: "Ignorant labor can no more produce the finest Berkshire and Jersey red hogs than ignorant labor can operate the finest machinery." Material wealth would bring independence and respect to black people: "Two nations or races are good friends in proportion as the one has something by way of trade that the other wants." Prosperity would stop terrorist violence: "With the masses of the white people and the colored people in the country and towns well educated, the black man owning stores, operating factories, owning bank stocks, loaning white people money, manufacturing goods that the white man needs, interlacing his business interests with those of the white man, there will be no more lynchings in the South than in the North."[32]

But if he made promises to blacks that he surely could not keep, Booker devoted much of his book to instructing whites on how to treat blacks better. "The slavery of ante-bellum times has passed away, but there is moral slavery existing in the South," the crop-lien system, a curse to the Negro that "blinds him, robs him of independence, allures him, and winds him deeper and deeper in its meshes each year till he is lost and bewildered." Many whites did not want blacks to advance: "As long as the Negro will be about the streets drunk, lazy, and shiftless, there is no resistance to him. The resistance comes when he begins to move forward." Whites let the worst sort rule the South: "The rights of the Negroes in the South are too closely bound up with those of their white fellow-citizens to be sacrificed at the dictation of demagogues and political despots." Class divisions among whites caused many black problems: "So long as the poor whites are ignorant, so long will there be crime against the Negro and civilization." The persistent hope of black removal to Africa deserved scorn, even offered in Booker's gentle way: "Some say, 'Send the Negro to Africa, the land of his fathers.' But the white man is fast getting about as much control of Africa as he has of the South. And such advisers forget, too, in speaking of our 'father's land,' that, while Africa is the land of our mothers, the fathers of about a million and a half of us are to be found among the blue-blooded Anglo-Saxons."[33]

Washington's occasionally ironic tone suggested that he was gaining confidence in his role as a racial leader. By 1898 he had begun to set aside the appeal to white-nationalist mythology used in the Atlanta address. *Black Belt Diamonds* contained none of the remarks he had made over the years about the gallantry of the Old South and the courage of the Confederates. He included only one disavowal of social equality, the famous Atlanta statement about separate fingers. It did reflect Washington's certainty that a rising people had to attend to their moral education. But the book also made clear his belief that, for his people to rise, whites would have to be taught how to treat them better. Three years of racial leadership had persuaded him that whites needed less flattery and more direct reproach. He was taking a chance, as he would soon find out.

7

The Lion and the Fox

A six-month spasm of violence looked as if it might wreck Washington's leadership just three years after he rose to national prominence. Scenes of intense brutality undermined his efforts to persuade whites that blacks were improving themselves and to convince blacks to be hopeful about their future. The trouble started in the fall of 1898, and the climactic event took place in Palmetto, Georgia, just ninety miles up the railroad line from Tuskegee. There five black men who had been accused of arson were lynched in a mass murder which was little noted outside the Georgia village but which formed the background for the most sensational act of violence the South had seen since Reconstruction. A month later in Palmetto, a young farm worker named Sam Hose flung an ax at his employer during an argument over a work assignment, killing Alfred Cranford. A manhunt ensued, and day after day for two weeks the Georgia newspapers, led by the Atlanta *Constitution*, reported on little else but the pursuit of Sam Hose. One false and lurid story was outdone by the next day's. Every report insisted that Hose had raped Cranford's wife. Eventually, when it no longer mattered, Mrs. Cranford would contradict the allegation. The *Constitution*'s headlines were far less a report of events than a plan of action: "Determined Mob after Hose; He Will Be Lynched If Caught; Assailant of Mrs. Cranford May Be Brought to Palmetto and Burned at the

Stake." When Hose was finally captured and returned to Palmetto, railroads put on excursion cars to take Atlantans to the village. A mob wrested Hose from authorities, chained him naked to a pine tree, and, while thousands of spectators cheered, a succession of white men stepped forward to cut off first his ears, then his fingers, and finally his genitals. They doused Hose's bloody body with kerosene and burned him alive. They cut up his burnt corpse and distributed the parts as souvenirs. His knuckles were put up for sale in the window of an Atlanta grocery store.[1]

The Sam Hose atrocity took place in April 1899. Awful as it was, its impact on Americans would not have been nearly so great except that it came at the end of a succession of violent acts that shocked many whites and terrified African Americans. Each event demonstrated in deadly ways the great dangers of being black in the United States at the end of the nineteenth century. Together they raised hard questions about those charged with improving the plight of blacks. Progress for the race seemed a futile hope.

The first link in this chain of violence was forged in the town of Virden, in the Illinois coalfields, in October 1898. There union miners attacked a train bringing black strikebreakers from Alabama. Armed company guards arriving with the blacks fired back, and the gunfight left ten black strikebreakers dead. The governor of Illinois did nothing more than outlaw the importation of strikebreakers. To African Americans, the Virden massacre amounted to casual acceptance of the mass murder of men simply looking for work.[2]

Just then a political campaign in North Carolina was coming to a heated conclusion. Conservative Democrats there had lost power in the mid-1890s to a Populist-Republican coalition. North Carolina had not enacted disfranchising mechanisms, and 120,000 blacks still voted. In Wilmington, blacks sat on the city council and served as policemen. To defeat their opponents, Democrats mounted a fierce campaign demanding that all white men stand together. They made an explicit psychosexual appeal based on an editorial written by Alex Manly, the black editor of the Wilmington *Record*. Manly had replied to a statement on lynching made by Rebecca Felton, a Georgia white nationalist. "If it needs lynching to protect woman's dearest possession from the ravening human beasts," Felton had said, "then I say lynch; a thousand times a week if necessary." Manly responded that many of the black men lynched were good-looking enough for "white girls of culture and refinement to fall in love with them, as is well known to all." White girls were no "more particular in the matter of clandestine meetings with colored men than are the white men with colored women." Discoveries of these trysts, Manly wrote, were the usual cause of lynchings. It was the same allegation that had got the Montgomery editor Jesse Duke banished from Alabama in 1887.[3]

Manly lit the Democrats' political fire, and they called in Ben Tillman from South Carolina to fan the flames. "Why didn't you kill that damn nigger editor who wrote that?" he shouted in late October. "Send him to South Carolina and let him publish any such offensive stuff, and he will be killed."[4]

Alfred Waddell, an out-of-favor politician remaking himself as a white-nationalist leader, became the most vitriolic nativist firebrand. "You are Anglo-Saxons," Waddell told a crowd. "Go to the polls tomorrow, and if you find the negro out voting tell him to leave the polls, and if he refuses, kill him, shoot him down in his tracks." In early November tens of thousands of black men were too frightened to vote, and the Democrats regained control of North Carolina. Two days after

24. This cartoon stirred white North Carolinians to riot against black political power. Artist unknown; from the Raleigh *News and Observer,* September 27, 1898.

the election, Waddell led a mob in destroying Manly's newspaper office. They gathered the resignations of all Republican city officials at gunpoint, and Waddell was named mayor.[5]

Waddell's mob swelled to 2,000 men, including whites from all classes and vocations. When a shot hit one of them, the mob raged throughout Wilmington, with whites hunting down blacks in running gun battles through the city's streets. The gunfire alerted militias and vigilante groups from outside the city to join the attack. Literally thousands of blacks ran for their lives. As many as 300 African Americans may have been killed. Eyewitnesses later recalled seeing wagon carts piled high with dead black bodies being removed from the city. The mob focused especially on Wilmington's prosperous blacks. One eyewitness later reported to Booker about seeing wealthy black men drummed out of Wilmington. "In that unfortunate trouble, it was not the insignificant negroes that were disturbed, it was the well-to-do and prosperous ones." The riot depopulated Wilmington of its large black majority.[6]

The shooting had scarcely stopped in North Carolina when a similar bloodletting ensued in Phoenix, South Carolina, where another circumstance of black political alliance with white Republicans provoked vigilantes to visit enough violence on blacks to drive them from that part of the state. The deaths in South Carolina combined with those in Wilmington and Virden to render undeniable the reality that in the fall of 1898 blacks in the United States lived only at the sufferance of white terrorists.[7]

As he read reports of what was unfolding in the Carolinas, Washington was stunned but powerless to do anything helpful. The authority to maintain order—in constitutional terms, the police power—rested with the states, and in Illinois, North Carolina, and South Carolina, state officials showed indifference to wholesale violence against blacks. Since the end of Reconstruction, the federal government had not interfered in states when atrocities against blacks occurred—and indeed it had very rarely done so during Reconstruction. In the aftermath of Wilmington, many blacks made demands for federal intervention to President McKinley, but no action resulted. Federal officials treated such events as state matters beyond their reach, and the least expression of concern from Republicans elicited howls from the white South.

At the moment of the Wilmington riot, Washington was preoccupied with white attacks on himself. In a particularly bitter irony, they arose from his efforts to celebrate the patriotism of African Americans. When the United States went to war with Spain in the spring of 1898, Washington had offered to help raise black troops. He wanted the current generation of young black men to have the opportunity to gain the same national honor he had celebrated at the Shaw monument in 1897. His offer was declined, but four black regiments did serve in Cuba, and when the war ended, Washington moved quickly to assign meaning to the experience. "No nation can disregard the interests of any part of its members without that nation growing weak and corrupt," he told a large interracial gathering of Christians. "For every one of her subjects that she has left in poverty, ignorance and crime, the price must be paid." In October 1898 he spoke to 16,000 people in Chicago at a Peace Jubilee. With President McKinley and a stage full of dignitaries behind him, he recounted the heroism of blacks fighting for the American nation, starting with Crispus Attucks at the Boston Massacre, continuing with the Fifty-fourth Massachusetts at Fort Wagner, and ending with the valor demonstrated at San Juan Hill. In all places, he said, "we find the Negro forgetting his own wrongs, forgetting the laws and customs that discriminate against him in his own country, and again we find our black citizen choosing the better part." The United States had won all its battles but one, "the blotting out of racial prejudices." Americans should celebrate peace by making the trench dug by black and white soldiers around Santiago "the eternal burial place of all that which separates us in our business and civil relations." Then came his boldest assertion: "I make no empty statement when I say that we shall have, especially in the Southern part of our country, a cancer gnawing at the heart of the Republic, that shall one day prove as dangerous as an attack from an army without or within."[8]

Washington thus took a chance that surging national honor after the Spanish-American War might propel blacks up the next rung of acceptance. He had reason to hope that the demand for equality in American life would work. At the end of the speech, when he said "whether in war or in peace, whether in slavery or in freedom, we have always been loyal to the Stars and Stripes," the crowd let go a mounting roar that caused the building to tremble.[9]

Why did Washington, having assumed such a careful posture in Atlanta in 1895, now offer criticism that was sure to incense southern nationalists? Perhaps it was a temporary lapse in judgment, a moment in which he forgot the limits on his action. Given his typical presence of mind, however, such an explanation seems unlikely. Or he might have thought that he was at a safe remove from the white South's ire, but such an explanation would discount Booker's astute sense of modern mass communications. Or maybe he thought he had persuaded enough people in Atlanta that a settlement of the Negro Problem had been reached, and now new rules applied. But although he was an optimist at heart, Booker probably had not come to so sanguine a judgment amid so many persistent signs of antiblack hostility. The most logical explanation was that he had not yet realized how dangerous it was for him to play the lion of protest. The Chicago speech was a demand for justice toward which he had been moving for three years. No whites in South Carolina wanted his counsel at their disfranchising conventions, but he still offered it. Only a few whites cared to know his views on railroad segregation, job discrimination, or lynching, but he gave his opinions anyway. The Chicago speech reiterated his earlier criticism in broad strokes before a huge and influential audience.

But if he had got away with his earlier criticisms because of the obscure places in which they were offered or because of the indirect way in which he couched them, the Peace Jubilee speech had gone way over the line of the white South's tolerance. He had uttered the kind of direct censure that got blacks run out of the South. Clark Howell, editor of the Atlanta *Constitution,* had been in Chicago. His newspaper dismissed Washington's assertion of racial prejudice as the demand of "colored agitators" for social equality. Washington was "talking to the grand stand, and when he escapes from the enthusiasm of Chicago and returns to the regular performance of routine duty in Tuskegee, he will take a more practical view of the situation." Washington's secretary Emmett Scott, his chief adviser on dealing with the press, advised him that his detractors wanted a disavowal of the statement, but that anything he said would weaken the courageous plea. A great public character like Booker Washington could not afford to engage "every spiteful sensitive soul that attacks you." Booker stayed silent.[10]

Others were venting. Thomas Fortune organized a large meeting at Cooper Union in New York City, where he decried white mobocracy and where every suggestion of retaliatory black violence was cheered. At a meeting in Washington, D.C., a few days later, Fortune declared that he was so angry at William McKinley for not coming to the aid of blacks that he felt like stabbing the president. Fortune demanded an eye for an eye: "There [should] have been no thirty colored men killed in Wilmington unless there were also thirty white men killed. If the colored people did not have Winchester rifles, they had pitch and pine, and while the whites were killing the blacks should have been burning [white sections of Wilmington]." The season of violence spurred the revival of Fortune's Afro-American League, defunct since 1893, which met to register outrage at McKinley's inaction.[11]

People began to ask about Washington's position on the terrorism. He had been in New York during the Cooper Union protest meeting but had not attended. Fortune asserted that the subject of the gathering was "altogether foreign to Prof. Washington's work." He was attempting to insulate Washington from the protest movement—and from the harsh condemnations he himself was making of the white South. But criticism of Washington surfaced anyway. A black minister in the District of Columbia claimed that the Wilmington violence had resulted directly from the Atlanta exposition speech. Others said, irrefutably, that Booker had done nothing to keep the atrocity from happening. A dynamic of Washington's tenure as a racial leader was emerging: he was blamed when terrible things befell his people, whether or not he could have done anything to prevent them from happening.[12]

The violence in the Carolinas may have been what finally impelled him to answer the criticism of his Chicago speech. As Emmett Scott had predicted it would, his response sounded defensive, and in it he also distorted the truth. In a letter widely printed, he denied that he had changed his attitude toward the South. He insisted that he said the same thing in the North that he did in the South, when in fact he always tailored his remarks to his audience, which meant he said things in the North that he knew would anger white southerners. He did so as a matter of survival, and he would continue the practice.[13]

Washington's self-serving and partly untruthful response showed that he had yet to learn how to cope with a crisis. His unsteadiness had led him to lie publicly, always a dangerous strategy in the emerging modern age of mass communications. But his self-defense also revealed how little freedom of expression existed for a black who lived in the South. Southern whites did not tolerate criticism of racial practices at any time, at any place, from any black. That fact applied regardless of how sensitive the person had been to white feelings in the past. Booker only had to remember the editors Jesse Duke and Alex Manly, or George Lovejoy, who had been banished from Tuskegee for condemning lynching. So, rather than admit that he had offered criticism, he lied that he had not.

Events in the fall of 1898 showed Washington that the only role open to him was that of the fox. To play the lion was to invite disaster. It was a bitter lesson that showed the limits on his ability to lead his race. A black leader who could not speak freely was not able to pursue equal economic and educational advancement. But if he owned up to that fact, he would be accepting that blacks' hopes for improvement were futile, and he knew that progress would not grow from despair.

The tensions of late 1898 exposed sharp divisions among those on whom Booker relied most. William Baldwin told him that Fortune and his kind were on a wrong course: "No matter what artistic phrases they use, they hide only a bitter resentment against their enemies, and if they are allowed to go on as they have been, will cause a bad setback to their people." Though descended from an abolitionist family, Baldwin insisted that blacks now needed not a firebrand like William Lloyd Garrison or Wendell Phillips but a leader who mediated racial and sectional hostility. Confrontation served the aims of Tillman and his ilk. Conflict spurred whites to oppress blacks even further: Baldwin attributed the Wilmington violence to a sudden push from the railroad brotherhoods to fire black workers. Whatever the cost, it was in blacks' interest at that moment to avoid conflict.

If Washington shared Baldwin's disapproval of Fortune, he also understood the frustration the latter felt. Fortune was a respected voice among blacks, one that Booker could not control, and the two men seemed to understand and accept their differences. Fortune insisted that Washington's residence in the South severely limited his freedom to speak, whereas Fortune himself, as a northerner, could refuse to sacrifice "anything that justly belongs to the race of manhood or constitutional rights." Furthermore, Fortune condemned Baldwin's public renunciation of black social equality and his acceptance of disfranchisement. It was a pity, Fortune told Booker, that their few white friends felt compelled *"to give away so much in discussion to gain so little."* But Fortune's friendship came at a cost. He was reportedly drunk when he declared that blacks in Wilmington should kill whites in retribution. In the end, Booker kept both Fortune and Baldwin close and sorted out their differences in his own mind.[14]

President McKinley's visit to Tuskegee in December 1898 diverted Booker from racial tension and promised to help him recover some lost prestige. Virtually the entire state government of Alabama met the president and nearly all his cabinet, and they all sat together on a platform of cotton bales for an hour and a half as the 1,000 Institute students paraded by. On floats students offered demonstrations of the old and new ways of dairying, tilling soil, cooking, and housekeeping. In welcoming McKinley, Washington declared that Tuskegee was a place "where without racial bitterness, but with sympathy and friendship, with the aid of the state, with the aid of black men and white men, with southern help and northern help, we are trying to assist the nation in working out one of the greatest problems ever given to men to solve." The president complimented the Institute for uplifting the Negro race and Booker Washington for his genius, perseverance, enthusiasm, and enterprise.[15]

The compliments of a president who had done nothing to protect blacks from white terrorism hardly reconciled disaffected northern blacks to Washington's leadership. McKinley and Washington were guilty by association with each other, and a few days later Washington's name elicited hisses at a meeting of blacks in Boston. In early January Booker addressed the criticism openly for the first time there, but

25. William McKinley's visit to Tuskegee in December 1898 honored Booker
Washington at a time when his standing had fallen among Americans. Here
McKinley appears between Washington and Alabama governor Joseph E.
Johnston. Photo copyright Underwood and Underwood, 1902; courtesy of the
Library of Congress.

with the images of death in Illinois and the Carolinas still so fresh, it
was a hard sell, and he apparently persuaded few.

Washington was sensitive to all criticism, but the northern black
critics bothered him particularly, because they refused to understand
the intractable racial hostility in the South. He despised their tendency
to condemn as a traitor any black who cultivated good relations with

southern whites. He cast around for something to relieve racial tension. He told Fortune that blacks needed to avoid all conflict with whites in politics. "Is not this the source of nearly all our trouble? Unconsciously we seem to have gotten the idea into our blood and bones that we are only acting in a manly way when we oppose Southern white men." By then Booker apparently agreed with Baldwin's view that blacks were inevitably the losers in racial conflict and should avoid it. He now believed that constant, bitter protests—however justified by atrocity—hurt more constructive strategies and tainted all blacks as complainers.[16]

Washington did not, however, oppose all direct protests. At just this time, blacks in many southern cities were confronting efforts to segregate seating in streetcars by mounting black boycotts of trolleys. Washington approved of these protests, because the withdrawal of patronage and the lodging of complaints with traction companies represented businesslike, careful responses that he thought might yield benefits. The boycotts were typically led by the black business and professional class, generally Booker's staunchest supporters and political allies in these cities. A boycott was an exercise of economic power designed to elicit a specific change in future behavior, whereas protests against white violence came to be perceived as after-the-fact ranting. Washington wrote that no street railway company could survive if its black patrons boycotted it. The white man would see that "the Negro's nickel is necessary to keep the street railway corporation alive," Booker predicted, and would accordingly act against Jim Crow's enforcement. His prediction was wrong: the streetcar boycotts that took place in many southern cities between 1895 and 1906 failed everywhere in the end, in spite of Washington's support.[17]

Washington was still trying to cope with the fallout from the Wilmington riot when the horrors of the Sam Hose lynching received national attention. When the news reached a group of black Bostonians, they condemned both President McKinley and Booker Washington. "We can no longer, with safety, allow men, however honest and earnest they may be," one man said about Washington, "to lead us along danger paths." The Bostonians blamed Washington without waiting for his response. Never mind that he was powerless to stop the injustice and that he had registered his objections to the lynching. But he was the leader of the race, the man in charge when something terrible happened to a black person, and to his northern critics his refusal to condemn the white South immediately and firmly made him appear unmanly.[18]

Their alienation led them to denounce every aspect of his leadership. Booker's critics typically reduced his educational philosophy to an exclusive acceptance of industrial education, which they typically defined as teaching manual labor—cooking, cleaning, and farm labor—rather than the skilled crafts emphasized at Tuskegee. Washington regularly maintained that a liberal education was appropriate for those who could afford it and put it to use. In a speech in February 1899 he said: "I do not want to be misunderstood. I favor the highest and most thorough development of the Negro's mind. No race can accomplish anything until its mind is awakened. But the weak point in the past has been, in too many cases, that there has been no connection between the Negro's educated brain and the opportunity or manner of earning his daily living." At exactly this time, Booker's thinking was finding a firmer basis in the relationship between black education and his overall strategy for racial improvement. He was reading Henry Thomas Buckle's *History of Civilization in England.* A highly influential public intellectual in Victorian England, Buckle extrapolated from the English experience a larger theory about societal evolution. "For although the progress of knowledge accelerates the increase of wealth, it is nevertheless certain that, in the first formation of society, the wealth must accumulate before the knowledge can begin." Buckle was sure that "without wealth there can be no leisure, and without leisure there can be no knowledge." Typical of the kind of immutable laws of human behavior promulgated by Victorian intellectuals, this view was widely accepted in the United States at the time and formed part of the rationale for the growing popularity of practical education. In early 1899, on the basis of his growing certainty about racial competition in the economic sphere, Booker felt a special urgency about the need to apply Buckle's principle. He felt that blacks had to gain a foothold in the industrial economy in the next decade, or they risked falling into worse poverty.[19]

The Hose lynching prompted Washington to write to a Birmingham newspaper that he opposed mob violence under all circumstances. Those guilty of crimes should be surely, swiftly, and terribly punished but by legal methods. He prepared a statement of complaint to send to the governor of Georgia, but Fortune destroyed it, saying to Booker that "you are the only man that now stands between the whites and the colored man as a bond of sympathy." Tuskegee was little more than ninety miles from Palmetto on a main railroad line, and Fortune surely imagined possible jeopardy to the Institute from enraged mobs if Washington condemned the lynching too strongly or too soon. Fortune was right to worry about white southern anger at the black criticism of the Hose lynching. Bill Arp registered it when he read the condemnations in an Atlanta black newspaper, reprinted from Fortune's New York *Age*. "The truth is that the north is responsible for every outrage and every lynching at the south," Bill Arp wrote. "New York niggers come out in their papers and advise the shotgun and the torch in retaliation, and those things are copied in the nigger papers in the south." Black violence was thus incited, and lynching naturally followed.[20]

Washington waited a month and then issued an open letter that appeared in many southern newspapers. He had waited to speak out, he explained, because previously the public had been too agitated to listen calmly to a discussion of lynching. He declared his love for the South and his hurt about the condemnations of the region that came in the aftermath of the Hose lynching. He acknowledged that lynching was not just a southern phenomenon: "No one can excuse such a crime as the shooting of innocent black men in Illinois who were guilty of no crime except that of seeking labor." He reminded white southerners that northerners and the federal government for the last decade at least had left the white South alone to work out its treatment of blacks, a sacred trust that lynching put in severe jeopardy. He set forth the facts that lynchings were in most instances white executions of southern blacks for a wide variety of alleged crimes, and in only in a few instances for rape. Contrary to whites' belief, lynching did not deter crime; it led only to more extralegal executions, which caused areas of the South to lose black labor and advertised southerners to the world as a lawless people. Too few southern whites realized how profoundly lynching was damaging their moral sense. A blue-eyed blond nine-year-old had told his mother that, having seen a man hanged, "now I wish I could see one burned." Washington insisted that lynching blacks was entirely unnecessary to ensure their punishment for crime, because all southern sheriffs, judges, lawyers, and juries were white. Negroes condemned criminal activity just as strongly as whites did. He ended with a call for black industrial opportunity and a declaration that many southern whites were sincere friends to the Negro.[21]

Washington's exposition of the facts about lynching was characteristic of the kind of argument he would make to white southerners throughout his years as a racial leader. In his careful statement of reality and his cautions about its effects he appealed to both whites and blacks. Few southerners, black or white, were publicly discussing the facts of lynching at the time. His comments apparently did not raise the ire of many southern whites. But neither did they appease whites who believed that blacks were their enemies, nor did they convince Booker's northern black critics that southern whites were not beyond reason or redemption. By then both groups had decided that Washington was a man who could not be trusted.

By the spring of 1899 the stress of the past few months was evident in Booker's health. His white friends in Boston had noted that he seemed exhausted. They believed that a physical breakdown was inevitable. Booker was complaining privately at this time about headaches. The cause of the headaches apparently was not established. The intense stress since the Chicago Peace Jubilee could have set off migraines, but in all likelihood he was already suffering from the high blood pressure that would debilitate him in the future. The past few years had aged him. He had gained weight, which showed in his face, and his visage at rest now appeared not so much placid as tired. He bemoaned the burden of constant fundraising, but he was far more beleaguered by the racial tensions he was unsuccessfully trying to manage.

The job of leading his race absorbed the best part of Booker's time.

26. The Washingtons were a handsome family in 1899. From left to right: Ernest
Davidson, Booker T. Jr. (Baker), Margaret, Booker, and Portia. Photo by Frank
Beard; from Booker T. Washington, *The Story of My Life and Work* (Atlanta:
J. L. Nichols, 1901).

It took a toll on how he attended to his family. The children, now between the ages of ten and sixteen, noted how the stress affected his behavior. He engaged them less than he might have and surely less than
they desired. Portia told a newspaper that the family joked about her
father's silence at home. "I suppose he is thinking always of the work
when he is at home," she said. "The public sees him at his best. When
he loses himself in his subject, he is much more animated than in the
family circle." Portia was devoted to, and protective of, her father and
perhaps more at ease with him than either of her brothers. The letters
between them reveal affection and honesty. A thin, bespectacled teenager who pulled her hair back in a loose bun, Portia looked the part of
the studious musician who taught music and aspired to be a classical
pianist. Perhaps because of discomfort with her stepmother, she studied for three years in her early teens at a Massachusetts prep school be-

fore returning to Tuskegee Institute, graduating in 1900. The next year she enrolled at Wellesley College to further her musical education.[22]

It was probably even harder being the male offspring of the most famous and powerful black man in the United States. Booker T. Washington Jr. often tried his father's patience with his indifference to academics and his enthusiasm for play of all kinds. "Baker" bore a strong physical resemblance to his father but lacked his diligence in pursuit of learning. Baker acquired an education through fits and starts at several New England prep schools. Ernest Davidson "Dave" Washington inherited Olivia's delicate looks and health, if not her capacity for work. Dave was slow to leave Tuskegee and not successful at the Ohio prep school he attended at age sixteen. Confessing his own indulgence of the boy, Booker told the headmaster that Dave had never been made to study and liked above all things to have a good time. "He has been made a pet and a baby of by every one in our family and on the school grounds," where he ingratiated himself to teachers so that they, too, pampered him. Dave eventually developed a severe eye problem that required six months of rest, which brought him home to Tuskegee for the remainder of his education and young adulthood. An old family friend put her finger on the predicament of Baker and Dave in a letter to Maggie. "So few sons of famous men have ambition to do anything more than be sons of their fathers, and I feared that the unnatural life which they have had at Tuskegee—among the masses and yet not of them, a class alone to themselves—would make them less ambitious than boys who were not so situated." She had landed very close to the truth about Booker Washington's sons.[23]

Margaret Washington proved to be a steadying influence both in Booker's private life and in his administration of Tuskegee Institute, but she occupied no more than half his personal time. The emotional content of the marriage remains a mystery. She rarely traveled with him on his fundraising tours and apparently had relatively little part in his political activities, but after 1900 they began to spend several weeks together each summer in rented homes at northern vacation spots. There is evidence of neither alienation nor intimacy, although the absence of any children raises questions about the latter. Margaret was thirty-one when they married, and she may have thought herself too

old to have children of her own, especially given the heavy childrear-
ing responsibilities already facing her. On the other hand, her letters to
Booker reveal intense romantic feelings during their courtship, and
they were married almost three years before he stepped on the merry-
go-round of racial leadership. And the couple were real partners in the
success of Tuskegee Institute. She functioned as dean of women students and exerted a powerful influence on the school's executive council. Her dignified demeanor—accented by pince-nez—belied her tolerant and humane approach to students and faculty. Her increasingly
Rubenesque presence seemed always to please and impress the many
visitors who called at "The Oaks," the family's fourteen-room Victorian house near the center of the campus.

And there is no question that she shared Booker's commitment to
Tuskegee's success and the uplift of the race. Cultivating virtuous
motherhood and efficient domestic life was the main means of Margaret's work, a complement to the economic prosperity that Booker
was promoting among black men. She founded the Tuskegee Woman's Club, which addressed the living habits of blacks inhabiting ramshackle houses on a plantation outside Tuskegee. Margaret set up
mothers' meetings at which she and other Tuskegee women taught
sewing, home management, and childcare. They created a school on
the plantation, hired a teacher, and eventually built a church. Margaret's activism reached far beyond Tuskegee. In 1895 she became the
first president of what later would be named the National Association
of Colored Women (NACW), the leading reform organization among
black women for the next generation at least, which through various
activities promoted women's rights, black racial pride, and civil rights.
In 1899 she led in the creation of the Alabama Federation of Colored
Women's Clubs, which organized orphanages and libraries and supported the state home for delinquent boys. The state federation sponsored the first recognition of black history in Alabama with celebra-
tions of Frederick Douglass's birthday and essay contests about famous
African Americans. Margaret's rising profile emboldened her to speak
out on matters that her husband avoided in public. In 1899 she condemned the apparent toleration of cohabitation among male and female prisoners in southern prisons. In 1904 she would insist that the

NACW move its meeting from the grounds of the St. Louis World's Fair because of the fair's refusal to hire black women and otherwise treat blacks equally.[24]

In the spring of 1899 Margaret shared the fears of Booker's white friends in Boston that he was near collapse. Francis Jackson Garrison, son of the abolitionist, and Ellen Mason, the generous Tuskegee supporter, resolved to force a vacation on him. He responded, as he had to similar suggestions in the past, that he could not stop work, because the Institute was kept afloat only by his constant fundraising. A Boston investment banker promised to raise enough money to operate Tuskegee for three months while Booker and Maggie were sent to Europe. Garrison planned the trip, and after several tries he found a steamship line that promised to treat the travelers exactly as it would whites. In May 1899, with the nation still buzzing about the Hose lynching, the couple left. On board ship for ten days, Booker slept for fifteen hours each day. Even after they arrived on the continent, he slept for most of many days.[25]

One of their first excursions was a tour of Dutch farms, which impressed Booker with the large amount produced on a few acres and for the great beauty of Holstein cows grazing on deep green fields. Dutch farmers had much to teach black farmers in the South, he surmised, with their careful husbandry and tidiness. A farmer did not need a vast acreage to prosper, Booker thought, just a commitment to care and order.

They were soon off to Paris, where they met former president Benjamin Harrison, Supreme Court Justice John Marshall Harlan, and other lesser-known American dignitaries; but the American exile who made the largest impression on Booker was the black painter Henry Ossawa Tanner. Booker had previously known Tanner and his father, a prominent Methodist bishop who had taught in the Phelps Bible School at Tuskegee. Henry Tanner had gained some fame as the creator of *The Banjo Lesson,* an 1893 rendering of a black music teacher that challenged the ugly stereotypes current in popular visual depictions of blacks. In Paris Tanner had turned to biblical subjects and in 1896 had produced the first of several noteworthy sacred paintings, *Daniel in the Lion's Den.* Booker went to the Luxembourg palace to view Tanner's *The Raising of Lazarus*. He liked to write and talk about Tanner as a black exemplar, one who proved that "any man, regardless of colour, will be recognized and rewarded just in proportion as he learns to do something well—learns to do it better than someone else—however humble the thing may be." Booker did not, however, acknowledge that Tanner's life was otherwise all too representative of the black experience of the time: he lived in Paris because he had found it difficult to make a living as an artist in the United States despite his extraordinary talent and because he feared harassment of his white wife. From Paris, Booker wrote to a black newspaper exhorting readers to purchase prints of Tanner's paintings directly from the artist. In the years ahead Booker would successfully promote patronage for Tanner among wealthy Americans.[26]

The Parisians fascinated Booker. He found them similar to American blacks in their love of pleasure and excitement but more advanced in the economic realm. On the other hand, he thought that blacks were their moral equals and decidedly their superiors in "so far as mercy and kindness to dumb animals go."[27] The French encounter encouraged him about blacks' relative achievements in the great competition of the races.

In England many of the old abolitionist families, through connections of Francis Garrison, feted the Washingtons. In place after place, Booker was struck by the warm feelings between the servants and their aristocratic masters, a condition that he hoped could be restored between the races and classes in the United States. In London he met Mark Twain, who would become a friend, and Lord James Bryce, the British expert on all things American. He talked with Sir Henry Stanley, the explorer of Africa and collaborator with King Leopold II of Belgium on the brutal exploitation of the Congo Free State, which convinced Booker even more that American blacks should not emigrate to Africa. He and Maggie had tea with Queen Victoria at Windsor Castle, along with Susan B. Anthony, the great American advocate of women's rights. On several occasions in England, Booker was asked to speak to groups, a task ordinarily easy for him but one that proved to be a formidable challenge in the new environment. "The average Englishman is so serious, and is so tremendously in earnest about everything," he later wrote, "that when I told a story that would have made an American audience roar with laughter, the Englishmen simply looked me straight in the face without even cracking a smile."[28] Unfailing in their hospitality, politeness, and curiosity toward Booker, the British apparently missed much of the basis of his appeal to his countrymen.

Booker and Maggie returned to the United States in August 1899 with his health restored and his spirits lifted. He had enjoyed being away from the intense racial environment of the United States, but in his preoccupations with comparing Europe and Europeans with American conditions, in some ways he had never left the country. His job was leader of his race, and he performed it every waking moment, wherever he was.

While the Washingtons were in Europe, little had changed for the better in the South. During the summer of 1899 thirty-eight blacks were reported lynched, twelve of them in Georgia, five in one mass execution in the village of Safford in July—all of which lent credence to Washington's suggestion that the Sam Hose atrocity would beget other such violence. That summer in Mississippi, where disfranchisement had long since occurred, James K. Vardaman, publisher of a newspaper in the Delta town of Greenwood, based a campaign for governor on the next step in assuring white-nationalist domination, abolishing black education. He pronounced that education was treacherous to the African American: "It simply renders him unfit for the work which the white man has prescribed, and which he will be forced to perform." Vardaman stated that the Negro was a curse to the nation, "a lazy, lying, lustful animal which no conceivable amount of training can transform into a tolerable citizen." Vardaman lost the 1899 election, but his particularly virulent opposition to black education was just beginning. Education did not help blacks, Bill Arp still maintained; "Booker Washington says it does, but observation and the statistics of the prison commission prove the reverse." When Maggie alleged that black women convicts were being housed with men, Bill Arp railed that it was impossible to keep up with the lies circulated by black educators trying to raise money. He demanded that Washington answer the allegedly false claims. "He had better say something about it, for he has had the support and encouragement of the southern people and he will be held responsible for such malignant claims." But Booker made no response, knowing better than to engage such hostility openly, especially with a man who enjoyed such wide support among southern whites.[29]

Through the summer of 1899, northern blacks increased their criticism of Washington's racial leadership. The extensive violence in the Carolinas and the Sam Hose lynching still weighed heavily. Fresh condemnations came from Cleveland, Washington, D.C., and Chicago. Calvin Chase, editor of the Washington *Bee*, pronounced Booker an inauthentic racial leader put in power by white men. The Afro-American Council was to meet in Chicago in mid-August, and Fortune, the organizer and main influence in the group, was unable to attend for health reasons. He advised Booker not to go either lest he be held accountable for the condemnations of whites that would certainly be made there. Booker did stay away. This decision was probably a mistake, because his absence from the meeting prompted unchecked criticism. The Chicago minister Reverdy Ransom was reported to have used the words "traitor," "trimmer," and "coward" to condemn Booker. Several participants came to Booker's defense, among them the sociologist W. E. B. Du Bois. White newspapers around the country reported on the apparent rift among black leaders. Washington told the New York *Times* that some blacks thought he should engage in politics, but that he intended instead to devote himself to blacks' moral, educational, and industrial development, and that he did so with the knowledge that he enjoyed the "confidence, the sympathy, and respect of the most thoughtful and forceful members of the Afro-American race." The response was disingenuous: he had not forsaken politics, and the criticism came because he refrained from open, angry condemnations of the white South. And the attacks prompted him in August 1899 to pay John Bruce, second only to Fortune in influence among black journalists of the day, to write letters to newspapers defending Booker Washington.[30]

Between the Peace Jubilee in Chicago in October 1898 and the Afro-American Council meeting there ten months later, Washington's leadership had been subjected to intense criticism both from whites for his muted disapproval of southern race practices and from blacks for his failure to condemn the same thing more vociferously. Booker's instincts were to ignore the most vocal criticisms of whites, who viewed all blacks as their enemies. But he took the black criticism as a betrayal from people who should support him against the real enemy. In his view, northern black critics indulged themselves out of ignorance and jealousy. His perception of their disloyalty provoked him to go to such lengths as hiring a prominent journalist to plump for him to prove that they were an insignificant minority.

The criticism made Booker ever more self-conscious and protective about his public image. In September 1899 the New York *Evening Post,* owned by the railroad magnate and Tuskegee supporter Henry Villard, reported that northern contributors to black education were concerned about the South's racial violence, and that some believed that the black population was growing faster than their financial aid could sustain. The paper said that Washington had returned from Europe discouraged about black conditions and his ability to shape events. Fortune wrote to him: *"you can't afford to get discouraged,"* because that response would do *"more than anything else to discourage the friends of your work and to lessen the financial support of your work."* Booker disavowed any discouragement and privately attributed the article to jealousy of Tuskegee's fundraising success, particularly at Atlanta University. People might speak falsely—and anonymously—about Booker Washington, and he could either respond defensively or keep silent, but either way his position was weakened.[31]

The criticisms and misrepresentations made Booker wary of situations that in the past he might have seen simply as opportunities to get out his message. He worried about a request that he speak on the same Atlanta program with Clark Howell of the *Constitution,* who had pounced on him after the Chicago Peace Jubilee, and Georgia's white-nationalist Governor Allen Candler, whom he suspected of wanting to use him to blot out the public's memory of the Hose atrocity. An invitation to speak on the same day that William Hooper Councill addressed the Huntsville Industrial Convention to promote southern industry also worried him. Booker was no doubt thinking of a recent discussion of Councill in the *Constitution*. "That negro's head and heart are both right," Bill Arp had said after quoting a speech in which Councill pronounced that no black should forget that slavery was "the blessed ante-room in which four millions of miserable, ignorant savages," fetish worshippers, were made into Christians. Councill pled all blacks guilty of criminality: "Our women and children are left unprotected by fathers; mother and sisters are deserted by sons and brothers and often leave home to increase the army of idlers and criminals." Earlier that year in the national journal *Forum,* Councill had written that racial antagonism was permanent, black education exacerbated racial tensions, and John Tyler Morgan's plan for removal of blacks from the United States remained the best solution. He attacked Booker without mentioning his name: "One orator declares that when a Negro gets what the white man wants—when a Negro gets a mortgage on a white man's farm—no one will bother him about voting. Now all this is just what I fear—the *battle over the loaf.*" Councill's sycophancy, as always, gave succor to the white nationalists and undercut Booker's message of progress and hope.[32]

At the Huntsville convention, Councill declared that "the cruel, costly experiment with negro voters, without the exercise of their will, has hurt the negro more than it has injured the white south," and he begged only for blacks to have the opportunity to get a job. Following Councill to the podium, Washington first reminded the assembly that the Negro, "though forced from his native land into residence of a country that was not of his choosing," had earned his American citizenship "by obedience to the law, by patriotism and fidelity." Having offered this corrective, Washington turned to the economic questions under consideration at the industrial convention. In response to the constant calls for immigrant labor in the South, Washington reiterated his themes about the abundance and worthiness of black labor—again noting blacks' aversion to strikes and anarchy and their similarities in language and religion to southern whites. With good education, blacks could meet every labor need of southern industry. But if the South was to realize its industrial promise, it had to stop advertising to the world with brutal lynchings that it had a race problem. "Capital and lawlessness will not dwell together," Booker declared. "The white man who learns to disregard law when the negro is concerned will soon disregard it when a white man is concerned." At his behest, the convention resolved that industrial growth in the South would depend on "an intelligent standard of citizenship THAT WILL EQUALLY APPLY TO BLACK AND WHITE ALIKE."[33]

By late 1899 black morale was flagging badly. The violence in the Carolinas in the fall of 1898, the Hose lynching in April 1899, and the drumbeat for disfranchisement throughout 1898 and 1899 inevitably took their toll on black communities. In Huntsville a black editor wrote that there was "nothing in politics for us, it makes no difference which side wins none of them want the Negro." Blacks had got accustomed to being mistreated and had stopped fighting back. "What's the use?" An editor in Mobile observed that even though the Negro was "as docile as can be" he was continually reminded in the white newspapers that "some additional project is on foot, or is about to be promulgated to stand as a menace to his development, or a curb to his ambitious manhood."[34]

In response to such expressions of discouragement, Washington insisted that conditions for blacks were improving. He used what had become one of his main means of advancing his positions, the newspaper interview, in which he gave lengthy, mostly unchallenged answers to questions about race relations. In an interview in the Memphis *Commercial Appeal* that was widely reprinted in other newspapers in late 1899, Washington was emphatic that blacks would not be disappearing, that the black population was growing despite higher mortality rates, but that blacks would never outnumber whites. He believed that blacks in time would earn and receive full equality in American life and that the average black child and white child had equal intellectual ability. He even predicted that a black man would one day become president of the United States. Black people often did not receive justice in the South, but neither did they get it in the North in the economic realm. Lynching was a calamity in every way—and he detailed them—but he noted that leading whites were now publicly disavowing it. Blacks in the South should stay hopeful. "I do not think we have

8

The Train of Disfranchisement

No amount of positive thinking could overcome the reality that disfranchising movements were gaining momentum across the South in 1899. They had already succeeded in Mississippi and South Carolina. Now, flush with their victory in 1898, a cadre of white-nationalist leaders was putting in place mechanisms to exclude nearly all black voters in North Carolina. With the national defeat of the Populists, Alabama Populists and Democrats were overcoming some of their deep mutual suspicions and, led by John Tyler Morgan, were finding common ground in the desire for total removal of black voters. "It is good bye with poor white folks and niggers now," a multimetaphorical black editor in Alabama would soon write, "for the train of disfranchisement is on the rail and will come thundering upon us like an avalanche, there is no use crying, we have got to shute the shute."[1]

Booker Washington would not throw himself in front of that train as his northern black opponents would have liked, but like an underground resistance operative, he tried to sidetrack it and at least keep it from delivering the full measure of antiblack cargo that many southern whites wanted. He had objected to South Carolina's 1895 disfranchising effort in the hope of preventing the separation of the school funds, and he had successfully discouraged the constitutional degradation of black education. In contradiction to his perceived disavowal of politics in the Atlanta exposition speech, Washington had determined to fight disfranchisement. But whites' hostility to black voting rights had grown so strong that he simply misled them to believe he accepted disfranchisement, when in fact he intended to do what he could surreptitiously to thwart it. He understood that blacks were probably going to face limits on their access to the vote in the future, but he fought that battle in the hope of winning again the one over black education. It amounted to the same studied dishonesty that caused him to lie about whether he had criticized southern racial practices at the Chicago Peace Jubilee. Agents in a resistance movement usually lie to the enemy.

Some of his opposition to disfranchisement was open. In early 1898 Louisiana had convened a disfranchising convention that considered property and literacy requirements, a grandfather clause to exempt white voters from those requirements, and a poll tax. As Booker no doubt knew, the state's recently enacted secret-ballot provision had already disfranchised most blacks—and about half of white voters as well. Still, in an open letter to the Louisiana convention, he warned that no southern state could enact laws that let an ignorant white man vote but denied the same right to an unlettered black man "without dwarfing for all times the morals of the white man." Vote fraud would inevitably follow, and from it, loss of respect for all government. The plea made, he moved to defend what he hoped was a more salvageable right, black education. He insisted that it would cost Louisiana more not to educate blacks than it would to provide good schools. He pleaded with the convention not to do anything that would prevent blacks from becoming intelligent producers in the Louisiana economy. Once again, the separation of school funds was kept out of the constitution, but the degradation of black schools moved relentlessly ahead. In 1900 the city of New Orleans canceled academic study for blacks above the fourth grade.[2]

The tension about disfranchisement increased in late 1899 when an Indiana Republican congressman, Edgar D. Crumpacker, proposed legislation to enforce the punitive provisions of the Fourteenth Amendment. Southern states that had disfranchised blacks would have their congressional representation reduced proportionately with the decline in black voters. He was soon vilified in the South in the same angry tones that Henry Cabot Lodge had been with the 1890 "force" bill. The white South's response to Crumpackerism was a campaign for the repeal of the Fifteenth Amendment, which would end all federal authority over voting and allow southern states to disfranchise without fear of intervention. By 1900 some southern whites were advancing repeal of the Fifteenth Amendment as the panacea for racial tensions.[3]

Crumpacker asked for Booker's support for his plan at the same time that a Louisiana congressman demanded that he condemn it, claiming that Crumpackerism would remove from Congress the southern whites who protected blacks. "For, as you know, the Negroes as a race are like children and need a quieting and protecting hand." Other whites demanded that Washington endorse repeal of the Fifteenth Amendment. Booker avoided making public statements about either proposal, but he opposed both. He agreed with Tim Fortune, who was "very sure that it will be bad *for us* to have the United States recognize the right of any State to disfranchise a part of its citizenship for failure to live up to the requirements of the 14th and 15th amendments." In other words, the Crumpacker bill would remove the potential for constitutional pressure on southern states to give blacks the franchise. States would accept the punishment for disfranchisement—the loss of a seat or two in Congress—and then argue that the case for black voting rights was closed once and for all. Washington wanted to keep alive the promise of voting rights, hoping that the current movement for disfranchisement might be turned back or, if successful now, that it might eventually be reversed on the basis of Fourteenth- or Fifteenth-Amendment claims. He believed Crumpackerism provided an incentive for border states that had not yet disfranchised to move in that direction, because their black populations were so small that they would not lose any congressional representation. But as with everything else about black voting, controversy roiled around both Crumpackerism and repeal of the Fifteenth Amendment, and Booker suffered the fallout.[4]

In the fall of 1899 Washington entered a fight to stop disfranchisement in Georgia. He went to Atlanta to organize black efforts against a proposed disfranchising law, the Hardwick bill, being pushed by

Populist remnants in the state. This bill created a board of registrars to ascertain whether a voting applicant understood the state's laws—an autonomous, quasi-judicial panel of local whites in every county who would ensure white political control. Washington told the *Constitution* that the understanding clause was "meant to leave a loophole so that the ignorant white man can vote or to prevent the educated negro from voting." Mississippi had instituted such a clause for just this purpose. No state, he declared, should make a law "to mean one thing when applied to a black man and another thing when applied to white man without disregarding the constitution of the United States." At first Booker found the Atlanta black community indifferent to the assault on their voting rights, but soon he was able to get the city's leading black men to collaborate on a petition against the Hardwick bill that reiterated Booker's assertions to the *Constitution* about fairness to blacks. A chief ally in plotting a black response was W. E. B. Du Bois, now teaching at Atlanta University, with whom he met often during the fall of 1899. "If we do not win we have certainly shown them that we were not cowards sleeping over our rights," Booker confided to Fortune. In the end the Georgia legislature, under the influence of the Populists' more powerful Democratic enemies, rejected the Hardwick bill. Thrilled finally to be getting some good news, Booker told his Boston friend Francis Garrison that the defeat in Georgia marked a turning of the tide against the disfranchisement movement—a triumph of Booker's hope over his reason, it would turn out.[5]

If Washington was a lion against disfranchisement in Georgia, he had to be a fox to fight it in Louisiana. Despite his opposition, the 1898 Louisiana convention had imposed a grandfather clause to exempt whites from the new suffrage limits. In 1899 members of the Afro-American Council asked for his help in organizing a constitutional challenge. Booker put together a network of supporters to fund the litigation, including whites in Boston, and he became a main contributor. It was understood by all that Booker's role would be kept secret to protect him from southern whites' condemnation. In early 1900 he began quietly bringing together the council with New Orleans leaders, but the effort soon became a classic case of too many chefs with too many recipes for how to make a challenge. Finally Booker instructed

Emmett Scott to sound out a Texas attorney, Wilford Smith, and in due course Smith instituted a court case that Booker secretly managed and financed for the next several years. The Louisiana case began a pattern of behind-the-scenes civil-rights activism that would characterize Washington's leadership for the next decade.[6]

The growing preoccupation with disfranchisement in Alabama created a vexing situation for Washington in early 1900, when Edgar Gardner Murphy, an Episcopal priest in Montgomery, scheduled a conference of racial experts in the Alabama capital ostensibly to find solutions to the Negro Problem. Booker cooperated in the planning in the hope that the conference would showcase whites who were sympathetic to black education and black progress in general. On the assumption that the continuing threat of black influence in politics was the cause of white racial hysteria, Murphy advocated repeal of the Fifteenth Amendment. Although he disagreed with Murphy about that course, Washington tried to accommodate the young priest because he personified the sympathetic white southerner whom Booker needed to counter the far more abundant white-nationalist hatred of blacks. As the conference approached, Murphy became skittish about including speakers who he thought might antagonize white nationalists. Booker put forward the names of several liberal-minded whites, but Murphy rejected nearly all of them. Finally he even rejected Booker as a speaker on the grounds that the safest course was to make the discussion of the Negro Problem exclusively a deliberation among white men. He loaded the program with some of the most vociferous antiblack voices in the South.

At this point Washington faced a decision about whether to withdraw from participation as an observer of the Montgomery conference and perhaps alienate his white friends who would be there, or to attend and take a chance that he would be associated with the antiblack bigots who would be there. He did not know what the white nationalists would say, but he surely could guess that their remarks about African Americans would not be flattering. He decided to keep quiet about Murphy's poor judgment and attend the gathering in the hope it would turn out well. It would prove to be a bad decision—and not the last time he would make such a mistake.

At the conference, only four men among the dozen speakers had anything good to say about blacks in general; these four at least supported black education. The Alabama congressman Hilary Herbert, a paternalist on racial matters, declared that an era of good feeling had emerged between the North and the South because the white South now had the sympathy of thoughtful northerners. The Lodge force bill had been set aside forever, President McKinley had done nothing for black political rights, and the U.S. Supreme Court had recently upheld the constitutionality of Mississippi's disfranchising constitution. Total white political control was virtually secured, Herbert suggested, and therefore the conferees could move on to other aspects of the Negro Problem. Walter F. Willcox of Cornell University, a nominally pro-black northern speaker who was the chief statistician of the U.S. Census, reported that blacks' idleness, criminality, and poor health were resulting in such low birth rates and high mortality figures that that they were, like the American Indian, on the road to extinction. In fact Willcox's own 1900 census would show just the opposite, an increase in the black population at about the same rate as the native white population.

The conference turned into a deluge of white-nationalist propaganda against the Negro. Alfred Waddell, Wilmington's murderous mayor, described the horrors of black voting that had ended only with the Wilmington riot. Waddell asserted that the Fifteenth Amendment had to be repealed and that black education, on which white southerners had spent $100 million in the last generation—a gross exaggeration—ought to be severely limited, because with each year of education blacks had become "less fitted for the duties of citizenship, and more and more a menace to civilization and good government." For every speaker like Hilary Herbert or J. L. M. Curry who identified Washington as the answer to the Negro Problem, there were others who manipulated Booker's message to demonstrate a danger he represented. Paul Barringer, the physician who chaired the faculty at the University of Virginia, and thus was the head of one of the South's most prestigious institutions, denounced industrial education for teaching "too little industry and too much education." Barringer pronounced black education a waste of money because blacks were on the road to extinction. Industrial education amounted to the worst squander of all. "We might as well, moreover, be frank, and confess that the trades union[s], fast coming into the South, will not let a Negro work at a trade."[7]

John Temple Graves, the Atlanta newspaper editor, pitched his plan to deposit all blacks in the far West, his answer to the question: "Will the white man permit the Negro to have an equal part in the industrial, political, social and civil advantages of the United States?" That question had been posed by William Hooper Councill of Huntsville, who Graves thought was "the wisest, the most thoughtful and the most eloquent Negro of his time—as discreet as Washington, a deeper thinker and a much more eloquent man." The answer to the question was in the heart of every white man, Graves said, although it came out in different ways: it might be expressed diplomatically or indirectly or even softened by philanthropy and restrained by conservatism or timidity, but however it came, "it rings like a martial bugle in the single syllable—NO!" Industrial education was a dangerous notion. "Carry every theory of Booker Washington to its full and perfect consummation, and you only make a new and deadlier competition between antagonistic races. The conflict heretofore has been social and political . . . The battle of the loaf will be the deadliest battle of the races." Graves drove home the point that Washington's work ultimately raised the issue of social equality. "Take Booker Washington. He is the type and embodiment of all worth and of all achievement in his race. His linen is as clean as yours. His fame is broader than the repute of any statesman in this hall. His character, stainless and unimpeachable . . . His patriotism is clear, his courtesy unfailing."[8]

Sitting the balcony of the hall among 100 other Alabama blacks, including Councill, Booker must have been steaming at the attention of so shameless a Negrophobe. "And yet I challenge this Conference," Graves said, "with a proposition: What man of you, gentlemen, philosophers, statesmen, metaphysicians, problem-solvers that you are— what man of you would install this great and blameless Negro in your guest chamber tonight? If he were unmarried, what man of you would receive with equanimity his addresses to your daughter?"[9]

The national press focused on the antiblack statements that gushed forth in the Montgomery conference and, to Booker's annoyance, made no mention of the few positive statements about black potential. The negative reaction to the conference among northern blacks rubbed off on Washington, because he had attended it, he was the leader of the race, and he had not condemned the dominant sentiment expressed there. His silence no doubt stemmed from a belief that any condemnation from him would have prolonged attention to the miserable affair. It reflected Booker's instinct to avoid conflict and even to minimize public discussion. Open discourse invited the worst bigots to grab the limelight. The conference exposed the poor judgment of Murphy; with friends like him, Booker hardly needed enemies.[10]

Although Washington never reacted publicly to the indignities he suffered in Montgomery, he did not forget them. Six months later he confided to Ellen Collins, a New York benefactor of Tuskegee to whom he gave his honest views about southern whites. During the two days he sat listening to speeches at the Montgomery conference, he told Collins, there was not one white speaker "who did not lay special stress upon the superiority of his own race and the weaknesses of other races." Why was that not as much in bad taste as it would be for an individual to be continually praising himself over some other individual? This "unconscious egotism of the average Anglo-Saxon" plagued Washington at every turn.[11]

Spurred by the rhetoric at the Montgomery conference, opposition to industrial education mushroomed. Barringer and Graves had succeeded in directing antiblack thought against industrial education. Washington pointedly challenged Barringer in a *Century* magazine article and invited the Virginian to Tuskegee in the hope of changing his mind about industrial education, but Barringer predictably ignored the gesture. Immediately after the conference, Bill Arp wrote that a black industrial-school professor had reported that, of 1,243 blacks given industrial education at his school, only 3 were practicing the trades they had studied. These results, Bill Arp said, proved that industrial education was a fraud. "Of course, we can't stop Booker Washington from teaching, nor the north from giving him money." Soon a well-known white sociology professor, John Roach Staton of Mercer College in Georgia, asked in an article in *North American Review:* "Will

Education Solve the Race Problem?" Staton could not prove positively that education made crime rise, but he could show that blacks with the least education were the least criminal. They had committed few criminal acts as slaves but many in freedom. Like most white social scientists of the day, Staton ignored the fact that the criminal justice system functioned as the legal arm of the ruthless white-nationalist war against blacks.

Booker answered the claim as soon as possible. To say that the Negro had been at his moral best during slavery, Booker wrote, was the same as saying that the 2,000 prisoners in Boston jails were the most righteous 2,000 people in Boston. Slavery had prevented family life, stifling the development of stable homes that nurtured a healthy, moral existence. High crime rates in the South reflected the failure of states to provide any juvenile reformatories, and black boys were made hardened criminals in prisons. In the North, prejudice kept blacks out of factory jobs, making criminals of people who would otherwise have become law-abiding breadwinners. On the matter of rape, Washington pointed out that a lynching drew the whole nation's attention to an alleged black rapist, whereas white rapists were rarely lynched and therefore usually not known outside their own communities—"To say nothing of the cases where the victim of lynch law could prove his innocence, if he were given a hearing before a cool, level-headed set of jurors." Washington clearly did not want any debate cast in such a negative context, and he moved it to higher ground. "As other men are judged, so should the Negro be judged, by the best that the race can produce, rather than by the worst."[12]

The campaign against black education accelerated in the summer of 1900. Ben Tillman kept pushing his point about the stupidity of educating blacks when states had disfranchised them because they were illiterate, and he frequently peddled his appeal in the North. At the University of Michigan he pointed to a black student in the audience: "You scratch one of these colored graduates under the skin and you will find the savage. His education is only like a coat of paint." Tillman attacked industrial education: "Booker T. Washington simply equips the negro for more deadly competition with the white man, a hundred more colleges like his would only arouse more race antagonism. If you establish them you will have to take the graduates up here and put them to work, and your trades unions will not permit it." Paul Barringer was leading an anti-black-education charge with propaganda support from the Richmond *Times-Dispatch*. "Any education will be used by the Negro politically," Barringer declared, and thus black education promoted racial warfare. In North Carolina, as Democrats solidified their recently won control by introducing property and literacy requirements for voting, they imposed sharp limits on the ability of counties to fund education, an indirect way of attacking black schools. A Democratic politician provided a litany of reasons for using local taxes just for whites: educating a Negro ruined a good field hand; poor whites hated blacks for competing in the labor market; any dollar that went to educate blacks was one that did not help poor white children. In the states where disfranchisement had not yet occurred, opinion ran high against black education. A newspaper editor in Alabama wrote in an open letter to the governor that the danger to whites was not the illiterate Negro but "the upper branches of Negro society, the educated, the man who, after ascertaining his political rights, forced the way to assert them." Southern whites, the editor insisted, held no prejudice against the ignorant Negro, but "our blood boils" each time the educated Negro encroached "upon our native superior rights" and made himself "a dare-devil menace to our control of the affairs of the state." A Georgia physician wrote to the *Constitution* that industrial education was deemed the best schooling for blacks, and that as a result Booker Washington had risen, but training blacks for industry increased racial competition that would cause blacks to suffer. In such contests, the doctor said, the inferior race inevitably lost.[13]

The mounting hostility to black education cowed the people who should have provided some comfort and hope to southern blacks. In early 1901 a group of reform-minded men in the North began to connect with a few southerners to address the problems of southern education. Robert Ogden, a New York department store executive who had been working on behalf of black education in the South since the founding of Hampton Institute in the late 1860s, organized a fact-finding trip of northern philanthropists and southern educators through the South. Named the Southern Education Board (SEB) but known informally as the Ogden Movement, the group included some of Tuskegee Institute's strongest supporters: the banker George Peabody, William Baldwin, the publisher Walter Hines Page, the Social Gospel preacher and magazine editor Lyman Abbott, and J. L. M. Curry. Edgar Gardner Murphy and several college presidents represented the South. But no black person, not even Washington, was invited to share in the inquiry, even though Booker counted most of the travelers as old friends and notwithstanding that he had taught many members of the Ogden Movement what they knew about southern education. His exclusion reflected less disrespect to Booker than the participants' nervousness about the times. Murphy regarded the temper of the white populace as so ruthlessly destructive that the SEB could not afford to include blacks. The president of the University of Tennessee imposed on the Ogden Movement his certainty that any expression of concern for the Negro would further incite white opposition to black education. Tulane University's president believed that the education of one ignorant white man was worth more to the black man than the education of ten Negroes. Such specious logic often prevailed within the Ogden Movement.[14]

The effort actually did real harm to black education by fueling white-nationalist opposition. The Ogden Movement's visit to Atlanta prompted Governor Allen Candler to announce his opposition to higher education for "the darky" and to all the Yankee money going to that cause. "Do you know that you can stand on the dome of the capitol of Georgia and see more negro colleges with endowments than you can white schools?" Industrial education encouraged the desire of blacks to work in factories and offices, the governor said, which in turn created racial competition for jobs and white dissatisfaction that might lead to a race war. In fact most education was bad for the Negro, because "when he is taught the fine arts he gets educated above his caste and it makes him unhappy."[15]

The Ogden Movement damaged black education indirectly with its propaganda campaign to increase local taxes for education. Its success in fostering whites' desire for better schools resulted in the further beggaring of black schools. Booker complained to Ogden members that they were ignoring the needs of black education, but to no avail. He could afford to do no more than complain privately. Because they and their industrialist friends provided most of the operating funds for Tuskegee Institute, he could not alienate the philanthropists. Through interlocking boards, the movement's leaders had enormous influence with the General Education Board, John D. Rockefeller's fifty-million-dollar foundation created in 1902 to improve southern schools. Soon the Peabody and Slater Funds were integrated into the board. A monopolistic trust of philanthropy and reform policy for southern education now existed, and black opinion had been excluded, at least formally, from its deliberations. They made a token gesture toward black interests when they gave Washington a stipend to deliver speeches on behalf of school improvement around the South. Otherwise Booker had no direct influence with the Ogden Movement. He was not even invited to its meetings outside the South.[16]

The policies of the Ogden Movement presented Washington with the same kind of dilemma he had faced about the Montgomery race conference. Confronted with white bigotry and racial callousness, did he publicly disavow the efforts of white men who thought they were working for betterment of the South, including blacks? Again Booker chose to maintain a public silence about the injustice of the Ogden Movement in the hope that an opportunity for constructive influence might emerge in the future. He did not have many white friends, and many of those had proved not to be constant, but he clearly felt that he could not afford to lose the remaining few. He assumed, probably correctly, that open condemnation of Ogden's policies would not change their minds. Instead he exerted what influence he could through Baldwin and Ogden. In 1903 Baldwin threatened to quit the board if Washington was not brought on, but he found the southerners so cowed from living "amongst their insane people" that his threat had no effect, and he chose to stay.[17]

Some northern friends of black education felt that their concern gave them the right to tell Washington what to think. In the mid-1890s Booker had served on the board of the little Tuskegee school at Kowaliga, Alabama, the school partly torched by arsonists in 1896. At some later point he resigned from the board and withdrew his support. William Benson, Kowaliga's founder, had refused to maintain financial records in the manner that Washington thought proper. Washington's alienation also was based on Benson's slur that Booker had "married three of his teachers, & would marry another in a fortnight if this one should die." When his lack of support became apparent, Booker earned the ire of the Garrison family, who strongly supported Benson's school and who saw that Booker's failure to endorse it undermined Benson's ability to raise funds. Francis Garrison exhorted Booker to endorse Benson and criticized him when help was not forthcoming, even though Garrison knew from Benson's own admission about the latter's crude remark. Garrison still expected Booker to set aside his own feelings and do what the righteous of Boston wanted. Thus even while he publicly ignored white insults of blacks, Washington showed little tolerance for personal insults from other blacks. Despite Garrison's entreaties, he left Benson on his own.[18]

It surely vexed Washington that opposition to industrial education was rising at the very time that Tuskegee Institute's success was becoming ever more apparent. The school had well over 1,000 students in twenty-two industrial departments. Its enrollment was almost twice the combined student population of the two leading white Alabama universities at Tuscaloosa and Auburn, and it surpassed that of nearly all institutions of higher education in the South. By then perhaps 4,000 African Americans had attended the school, although not all had earned degrees. The Institute owned 2,000 acres of land, of which 700 were under crop cultivation. The campus had become an architectural showplace. In the past decade, ten new buildings had been completed, including a chapel and a fourteen-room home for the Washingtons, "The Oaks." Day-to-day operations at the Institute usually ran smoothly under the direction of Warren Logan, John Washington, Emmett Scott, and Margaret Washington.

Such rapid growth and so many students still required exhaustive fundraising, which Booker carried out through constant travel. His fundraising trips were combined with ceremonial appearances and inspirational speeches expected from the leader of the race. On the road, he typically traveled with a stenographer who helped him attend to personal and political matters and to write magazine pieces and books.

27. George Washington Carver brought fame to the Tuskegee faculty with his lessons on the practical uses of southern plants, especially the sweet potato and the peanut. Photo by Frances Benjamin Johnston, 1906; courtesy of the Library of Congress.

He moved at an exhausting pace. In a thirty-three-day period starting on October 23, 1900, he went from Tuskegee to New York City, where he was putting the finishing touches on his autobiography with the editors of *Outlook* magazine, who were serializing the work. Then he went to Springfield, Massachusetts, where he gave two speeches to the American Missionary Association; back to New York for meetings on October 25; the next day to Great Barrington, Massachusetts, to speak at the local high school; from there on October 27 to Lenox, Pittsfield, and Adams, Massachusetts, for fundraising and speeches at Congregational churches; back to New York on October 29 and then to Norristown, Pennsylvania, for a speech the following day; back to New York for a meeting on October 31 with Tuskegee graduates on their way to Africa; and the next day to Charleston, South Carolina, to meet with planners of that state's forthcoming industrial exposition. From there he went home to Tuskegee, but on November 7 he traveled back to New York City to speak at a dinner at the Waldorf Astoria honoring General Oliver O. Howard, head of the Freedmen's Bureau, where he shared the podium with presidents, generals, and senators. His speech was so well received that he was asked to speak two nights later at a dinner honoring Mark Twain. Then he made a quick trip to West Virginia to see his sister, Amanda, who was worried about health and money matters. He returned to New York and on November 15 went to Boston to speak to a Catholic literary society. On November 17 he was back in New York to speak to the Congregational Club on the evils of lynching. He gave an interview on the same subject to the New York *Times*. Four days later he was again in Boston for fundraising. While in Boston, he sent directions to Emmett Scott to lobby against a proposed railroad segregation bill in the Alabama legislature and wrote letters to southern newspapers on prison reform and equal funding for black schools.[19]

Booker always managed to be in Tuskegee to receive the ever-larger crowds coming to the annual Negro Conference. Those attending heard practical instruction for making better farms and homes and pep talks exhorting them to keep trying even amid the many discouraging signs of the times. In 1898 the Institute's agricultural department had begun issuing pamphlets for farmers on how to improve their production and living conditions. George Washington Carver wrote many of them in an elementary style, covering such topics as restoring worn-out soil, using fertilizer and rotating crops, and maintaining a good vegetable garden. Instruction in practical farming was Carver's most distinguished contribution to the Tuskegee enterprise. In 1900 Wash-

28. Farmers at the annual Tuskegee Negro Conference, ca. 1900. Photographer unknown; from Emmett J. Scott and Lyman Beecher Stowe, *Booker T. Washington: Builder of a Civilization* (Garden City, N.Y.: Doubleday, Page, 1916).

29. Annie Davis's school near Tuskegee was one of many spawned by the Institute. Photo by Frances Benjamin Johnston, ca. 1902; courtesy of the Library of Congress.

ington was planning a program to help Institute graduates overcome the obstacles to becoming farm owners. This was a way of following up on the Dizer Fund, a credit program for farmers that he had established in 1895. In 1901 William Baldwin and Robert Ogden provided funds to help Washington launch the Southern Improvement Company, which sold graduates small farms in Macon County and provided both credit and advice about how to become successful through scientific agriculture.[20]

Tuskegee's chief focus and impact remained the educational work of its students, most of whom, despite the industrial training, became not craftsmen but teachers. Little Tuskegees existed across the Deep South, and new ones emerged each year. William Henry Holtzclaw, an 1898 Institute graduate, established the Utica Normal and Industrial Institute in a farm village in southwestern Mississippi. In his school and his life Holtzclaw emulated Booker Washington in many ways: he started his school with twenty students under a brush arbor and then held it in a log cabin before buying 2,000 acres of land and building an impressive campus with money raised mostly in the North. His curriculum was pure Tuskegee, in part because he hired mostly Tuskegee graduates to teach, and he developed a farmers' conference and a program to help local farmers buy their farms. He would even write an inspirational autobiography, *The Black Man's Burden,* at about the same age that his mentor had written his, for the same didactic and fundraising purposes.[21]

The work of Tuskegee Institute was also gaining influence in Africa. Throughout his life, Booker had heard Africa discussed from a Eurocentric perspective that denigrated any African claim to civilization. Washington had sometimes deferred to the softer representations of African cultural inferiority among his white paternalist friends. By 1899 he was getting opportunities to demonstrate whether he truly believed in that inferiority. Black leaders in several African countries embraced his work for its emphasis on self-help and racial solidarity. They admired Tuskegee Institute as a model of black achievement without necessarily subscribing to its curriculum. Perhaps his most noteworthy follower on the continent was John Lagalabalele Dube, the Congregationalist minister and graduate of Oberlin College who visited Tuskegee in 1899 and embraced the gospel of industrial education. Often called "the Booker T. Washington of South Africa," Dube returned to Natal and in 1901 built the Zulu Christian Industrial School. He also established the Bantu Business League, modeled on Washington's National Negro Business League. Dube had many of his hero's gifts for political indirection and compromise, but like Washington, his long-term goal was freedom for his people. He became a founder of the African National Congress, the organization that eventually brought the downfall of the apartheid system.[22]

Tuskegee's first involvement on the African continent came through its partnership with a German company attempting to develop a farming operation in the German colony of Togo, on the Coast of Guinea in West Africa. In 1899 a group of Germans had visited Tuskegee and left with an understanding that Institute graduates might be hired to oversee the development of a cotton operation in Togo. For Washington, the Togo experiment offered an opportunity to export the Tuskegee idea to a new environment and test its validity. In 1900 three graduates, one faculty member, and a large array of supplies were deposited on the coast of Togo. The Africans receiving them had no draft animals to pull the wagons the Tuskegeeans had brought, but they

30. These four men were the first Institute graduates to go to Togo in 1900. Some of them died there. Photo by Frank Beard; from Booker T. Washington, *The Story of My Life and Work* (Atlanta: J. L. Nichols, 1901).

readily hoisted them—and all the other supplies—on their heads and hiked forty miles inland to the place designated for farming. The experiment turned into a great trial for the Americans, because neither they nor the oxen they secured to pull farm equipment could withstand the insect-borne diseases. In the end, the Africans themselves drew the plows, planters, and cultivators to produce twenty-five bales of cotton during the first season. Over the next few years, nine Tuskegee graduates worked in Togo, and four of them died there. The one who stayed established an agricultural school that trained 200 Togo men in farming and would have doubtless done more except that he, too, died in 1909.[23]

Washington may have given German colonialism more credit than it deserved for its influence on Togo—no doubt because his own people were engaged there—but he held no illusions about the Congo Free State, where King Leopold II had imposed a horrific rule over the

native peoples. Booker had met Sir Henry Stanley, Leopold's adviser
on suppressing the Africans, during his 1899 visit to England, and he
probably knew then the Europeans were up to no good in the big colony along West Africa's great river. When reports of forced labor and
police brutality surfaced in the United States in 1904, Booker took the
lead in protesting the inhumanity. He wrote articles for the Congo
Reform Association, took a party of black Baptists with him when he
called on President Roosevelt to pressure Belgium to change its policies, and joined his friend Mark Twain in protests around the country.
The Reform Association first brought Washington in touch with the
sociologist Robert Ezra Park, the organization's secretary, who advised
Booker about Leopold's invitation to visit him. "The King of Belgium
hopes to win you over to his theory of dealing with the Blackman,"
Park told Booker. He did not go.[24]

Washington's concerns about the future of black education intensified
when Alabama convened its long-awaited constitutional convention to
disfranchise blacks in May 1901. Booker must have had a sense of *déjà
vu:* exactly a year earlier, he had been in the state capital hearing successive speakers at the Montgomery race conference disparage blacks
and demand repeal of the Fifteenth Amendment. The current deliberation carried great implications for Booker: if he could not prevent
Alabama law from becoming more hostile to blacks than it already
was, his leadership would come under more criticism. Yet by the time
the convention finally started, disfranchisement had been virtually a
foregone conclusion for a decade. In 1899 the state superintendent of
education had decried black voting rights: "What a fearful mistake!
What a stupendous error! What a crime against civilization!" One editor wrote on the eve of the convention that the ballot box in Alabama
had been "afflicted with negro smallpox for thirty years," but he promised that it would "go to the pest house next Tuesday." In the convention, the powerful chairman of the suffrage committee would say that
"not one of our fair women has ever been assaulted in this land but that
the infamous act may be traced to the fifteenth amendment."[25]

Washington led a group that considered how to respond to the convention, which had no black member despite the fact that African

Americans accounted for 45 percent of Alabama's population. Washington wrote a declaration, signed by the state's leading black men, that Negroes were not stirrers of racial strife but hard-working, tax-paying, law-abiding citizens with a keen interest in the convention's work. "It requires little thought, effort or strength to degrade and pull down a weak race," the statement said, "but it is a sign of great statesmanship to encourage and lift up a weak and unfortunate race—destruction is easy; construction is difficult." Alarm was being spread among blacks by "emigration agents and exodus associations, who are telling them that under the new constitution the Negro's citizenship will be taken from him and that his schools will virtually be blotted out." Booker concluded that any new law that could be "interpreted as meaning one thing when applied to one race and something else when applied to another race, will not in our opinion improve our present condition, but may unsettle the peace and interfere with the thrift of our people and decrease the wealth and prosperity of Alabama." It was classic Washington style—full of flattery and indirection and ending with a velvet-gloved warning of bad consequences for the wrong decision. It was a bad omen for black Alabamians that many in the convention objected even to having the petition read, though finally it was.[26]

Beyond that, there was little for blacks to do but watch the machinations of white men divided on how—not whether—to remove them from politics. The main concerns of convention delegates were how many whites would be disfranchised in the effort to remove the black voters, how to remove the blacks without causing federal intervention, and whether school funds would be segregated. Conservative Democrats from the Black Belt wanted only property and literacy requirements and a poll tax, while a small contingent of Populists and Republicans opposed all suffrage limits because they would also disfranchise poor whites. A large majority of the convention wanted to create loopholes ensuring that illiterate and propertyless whites would remain voters, while removing every single black voter. The antiblack feeling ran highest among the younger delegates: "We of the younger generation," declared one speaker, "have known but one slavery, and that— slaves to the negro vote." No Negro was the equal of the "least, poorest, lowest-down white man I ever knew." Another said he opposed the enfranchisement of any Negro in Alabama, "let it be Booker Washington or any one else."[27]

Washington's political ties in the convention were mainly with the Black Belt Democrats. Booker stayed in close touch during the convention with the former governor Thomas Goode Jones. A Confederate officer who had carried his regiment's flag at Appomattox, Jones was described by one writer as "the very apotheosis of the suave temperament and philosophy of the Conservative wing of the party." Understood to have beaten his Populist opponent for governor in 1892 with stolen black votes, Jones had got religion about fraud and now took a strong stand against unfair voting laws: "Any scheme, no matter how fair on its face, which is administered so as to discriminate in favor of the white man and against the negro as such, is vicious, and sooner or later liable to bring the State in collision with Federal corrective measures, both by the courts and Congress." Another point of contact for Washington was William C. Oates, the man who had become so angry at the 1896 Institute commencement. He had been Jones's successor, likewise elected with stolen votes, equally repentant about fraud: "We have gone on from bad to worse until it has become a great evil." Oates declared that disfranchisement of all blacks was unwise and unjust: "They constitute a large minority of our state's population—over 800,000. Among them are many honest, industrious, and good citizens, capable of fairly understanding the issues of a campaign."[28]

All the white men whom he trusted advised Booker to stay aloof from the proceedings. George W. Campbell said that Booker had done everything he could for black interests. *"Don't be too persistent* in this matter," he warned. Booker did meet privately with the head of the convention's suffrage committee and argued for a property requirement as the only suffrage limit. He quietly asked several influential whites to speak up for fair treatment. His low public profile soon came under attack from two black newspapers, one of which condemned as humble and unnecessary the conciliatory statement made at the convention's outset. Negroes should not *ask* for fair play but *demand* it, wrote the editor of the Mobile *Weekly Press.* "The negro submits now, but that submission is by force and with discontent, a cancerous sore, which will come to the surface in an eruption in a few years." Thomas Goode Jones was sure that Booker's refusal to respond was the best course. "Fools with pens who assail your fidelity," Jones said, made it harder for white friends to help the black cause.[29]

The convention's suffrage committee produced a plan that used all known disfranchising mechanisms. The most oppressive measures required prospective voters to understand the constitution, established a state-appointed board of registrars in each county to interpret that understanding and assess good character, and exempted a prospective voter from the qualifications if his grandfather had fought in a war. In several weeks of debate before the full convention, Jones and Oates put up a fierce fight against the grandfather clause, saying that it was so flagrantly discriminatory against blacks that it invited a court to overturn the constitution. At one point in the grandfather-clause debate, Governor Jones, standing only with the help of crutches, became so angry that he pulled a knife on another delegate. Everyone in the convention was aware that Louisiana's grandfather clause was currently being challenged, though none knew that Washington was directing and financing the lawsuit. In the end, all the mechanisms were included in the constitution submitted to the people.[30]

Booker did get directly involved in the proceedings when a threat to Tuskegee Institute arose. James Edward Cobb, the delegate from Tuskegee, advocated the removal of tax-exempt status for land owned by private colleges. "There are private institutions chartered in this State that have vast amounts of money coming to them year after year," Cobb had declared, "and they are buying every acre of land they can put their hands on." Cobb and other whites in Tuskegee saw the Institute's 2,000 acres as emblematic of the school's success and autonomy, precisely the same meaning of prosperity and independence that Booker attached to it. The land remained a matter of controversy among whites. Cobb eventually backed off the proposal after delegates with allegiance to landowning white colleges objected, no doubt at the encouragement of Washington and Tuskegee's many white friends.[31]

The racial separation of school funds loomed as the biggest threat to black education, and that looked like a probable outcome of the convention. In 1893 the Alabama legislature had passed a constitutional amendment providing for just such separation, and only an insufficient turnout of voters in the ratification election prevented its implementation. As the 1901 convention approached, a Mobile newspaper announced that "Negroes in Alabama pay three per cent of the taxes and receive fifty percent of the educational advantages"—a gross falsehood but the kind of statement that many whites believed. Separation of school funds fired the convention's most vociferous white nationalists. J. Thomas Heflin, a young state senator from a county near Tuskegee, said that it was folly to educate blacks, because it encouraged them to compete with whites. "The negroes are being educated very rapidly," Heflin told the convention, "and I say in the light of all the history of the past, some day when the two separate and distinct races are thrown together, some day the clash will come." It would be the survival of the fittest, he said, "and I do not believe it is incumbent upon us to lift him up and educate him on an equal footing [so that the Negro] may be armed and equipped when the combat comes."[32]

Jones and Oates warned that such overt discrimination might result in widespread condemnation from the North and perhaps an unfavorable court ruling on the constitutionality of the suffrage changes. "We must not disfranchise the Negro on account of his ignorance," a Mobile editor also cautioned, "and then refuse him help to escape from his ignorance." Delegates surely knew that separation was unnecessary to discriminate in school spending, since with the Apportionment Act of 1891 school boards had already awarded grossly disproportionate funding to white schools. In the decade since its enactment, black and white teachers' salaries had gone from near equality to a statewide disparity in which white teachers made at least 50 percent more than blacks for teaching about half as many students. Separation was kept out of the constitution approved in the convention.[33]

Washington's thoughts now turned to how to keep the constitution from finally becoming law. It still had to be approved by the people, and he heard from blacks who wanted him to fight it. A black editor convened a group that resolved to appeal the new constitution to the

U.S. Supreme Court. Washington did not attend the protest meeting, perhaps out of fear of the fallout that might come from any demonstration of his dissent. But he was certainly contemplating a court challenge of his own. Thomas Goode Jones warned him that whites would try to destroy Booker if he campaigned against the new constitution—especially if he succeeded. More stringent disfranchising measures would be put in its place, Jones predicted, and school funds might yet be segregated. Booker responded that the new constitution would tempt the white man "to perjure and degrade his own soul" by applying the voting laws differently to blacks. Perhaps no man in Alabama politics had benefited more from voting corruption than Jones, and Booker's sermon was intended to induce Jones somehow to pay penance for his past wrongs. The former governor had already declared himself as a friend to the Negro. He had written Booker that he remembered his "good old black mammy well, and my body servant during the war, who risked his life for me." In Booker's mind, such paternalist sentiment made Jones a potentially valuable ally, and he had all too few of those among white Alabamians in 1901.[34]

In the end, Washington stayed out of the ratification campaign, accepting the futility of trying to defeat it. The constitution was ratified by a lopsided vote in the Black Belt, probably the result of fraudulent black votes. When the new requirements were implemented, the number of black voters in Alabama fell from 180,000 to about 3,000. The main culprits in the removal of black voters were the boards of registrars and the poll tax, and the latter also significantly reduced white voter participation. All the discussion about protecting the democratic rights of poor white men proved to be mere blather.

The constitutional deliberations in Alabama had been a long, humiliating ordeal for Washington, one for which even so determined an optimist as he had difficulty finding a silver lining. As with other examples of white degradation of blacks—the Montgomery race conference and the Ogden Movement—Booker maintained a studied silence in the aftermath of shameful mistreatment. He believed that there was nothing he could say that would change what had been done, but still his silence came at the cost of his being viewed as weak or even as tacitly condoning the injustice. In fact he had schemed and fought in various secret guises; but still the train of disfranchisement moved forward. It was an experience that would have driven many a man from political engagement, but in the end it did not defeat Booker Washington.

9

The Leopard's Spots

Washington saw that his political engagement, even in so worthy a cause as preserving black participation in the democratic process, could undermine his leadership almost as surely as had the atrocities in Wilmington and the Hose lynching. Black despair spread as white hostility grew relentlessly. Washington had begun his tenure as the leader of his race with the resolve to change the way Americans, black and white, thought about racial matters. So far he had failed to reverse the main currents of thought. But, determined man that he was, Washington redoubled his efforts. If he rendered enough positive judgments about his race, and if he expressed sufficient optimism about the future, he might influence as many minds as needed to reverse the downward course of black morale—and at the same time stop the swell of white antipathy to blacks. In 1900 and 1901 he worked toward those ends, writing newspaper editorials, magazine articles, and books to show Americans that blacks were rising. By that time, he knew as much as anyone else in the United States about the nature of modern mass communications. He was a skilled, if not always successful, propagandist.

Newspapers left an unavoidable impression of continuous racial friction in the South. Any instance of black crime or white violence against blacks was widely reported, but examples of friendly relations were seldom noted. "In most sections of the South," Booker insisted, "there is little, if any trouble between the races." To get more good news into circulation, he assigned his secretary Emmett Scott, the former Texas newspaperman, to send out frequent press releases to both black and white newspapers. These releases highlighted black achievements—including, but not limited to, those of Booker Washington and Tuskegee Institute. Positive news about himself and other African Americans, Washington thought, helped all blacks by showing "the narrow white people that their prejudices are not shared by other parts of the world, and at the same time such news would encourage the colored people." Booker also used his informal news bureau to encourage certain actions. For example, in 1900 he called for all blacks to prepare a full account of their property for the 1900 census. The census was a racially sensitive document used to prove that blacks were dying out or degenerating, and he was convinced that if blacks cooperated fully their census numbers would demonstrate the progress of the race as propertyholders. Scott also disseminated protests against discrimination, but they went as clippings from newspapers published far from Tuskegee. He sent out an editorial in the Boston *Transcript* denouncing the Georgia Railroad for refusing a sleeping berth to the gravely ill Bishop Henry Turner. "A very pitiable spectacle," the editorial declared, that "could have taken place nowhere in the civilized world but in the United States." Booker had ghostwritten the editorial to expose the shameful treatment without bringing the wrath of whites on himself. Tim Fortune wrote appreciatively of Booker the fox: "There are more ways to kill a cat than one."[1]

By 1900 the task of shaping public thinking toward a more benevolent view of blacks had got more difficult, because better photoengraving enabled the larger urban dailies to present more racially inflammatory visual material. The *Constitution* rarely depicted a black person like Booker of whom it sometimes approved, but in 1901 it ran realistic illustrations of three black men thought to have attacked an Atlanta woman. The *Constitution,* the Birmingham *Age-Herald,* and the Memphis *Commercial Appeal* all featured illustrated police-court columns. The *Constitution*'s daily "Police Matinee" recounted the stupidity and criminality of blacks—its text always had them speaking in heavy, awkward dialect while white Atlantans used correct, unaccented English—and accompanied it with outlandish caricatures of black men and women. It was a daily visual reminder of black deviance.[2]

Some whites saw clearly the true purpose of Washington's newspaper campaign and did not like it. A white weekly near Tuskegee criticized Washington for writing newspaper articles, asserting that he was "too much infatuated with the idea that he is a great writer" and that he was "trespassing on dangerous ground." A reader of the New Orleans *Times-Democrat,* angered by an account of a speech that Booker had given, said that Washington's "smooth and fallacious philosophy he so glibly dispenses to credulous ears" promoted the delusion among both whites in the North and the blacks in the South that "education and property will solve the problem by elevating the negro to be the equal of the white man." Washington told northerners that blacks were improving while "the census says it is degenerating from its character in slavery." Washington was leading blacks to a precipice with "the false ideals he inculcates, the impossible hopes he excites, the utterly misleading sympathy he enlists in behalf of the negro."[3]

Washington made it general policy not to respond publicly to criticism. He knew what public-relations experts tell anyone captured in a critical spotlight: answering criticism can fuel a crisis. "If a charge is made to-day and I deny it," he explained privately, "and another false one is made tomorrow and I fail to deny it, people will reason that because I denied the first and failed to deny the second, that the second is true, and so I should be in continual controversy and hot water." He quoted Oliver Wendell Holmes: "Controversy equalizes wise men and fools, and the fools know it." That must have been a hard resolve to maintain in the face of some attacks. The socialist Eugene Debs, head of a railway union that did not accept black members, excoriated him in 1900 for accepting aid from the nation's "plutocrats." If Tuskegee Institute was "conducted with a view to opening the negro's eyes and emancipating him from the system of wage slavery which robs him while it fattens his masters, not another dollar would be subscribed for the negro's industrial education." Somehow Washington maintained silence in the face of this hypocrisy.[4]

Booker's own writing was a major part of his strategy. Throughout the 1890s he had written magazine articles to shape public opinion. In the *Atlantic Monthly* in 1896 he offered a positive account of Tuskegee's achievements under the title "The Awakening of the Negro," and in another long article in the same publication in 1899, "The Case of the Negro," he presented his arguments for industrial education and against disfranchisement. In about 1900 Booker began to adapt his style to that of the new mass-market popular magazines—*McClure's,* the *Ladies' Home Journal, Cosmopolitan:* texts were shorter, more suggestive than explicit about setting and narration, more anecdotal, and less didactic in communicating a message. Readers had to extract meaning, although good articles left little doubt about the moral of the story. Illustrations accompanied the text and helped to carry the narrative. Booker himself would not write often for those magazines, but his style in other magazines—particularly two older journals, *Century* and *Outlook,* which started to use more illustrations—began to reflect the new trends. Walter Hines Page, editor of the magazine *World's Work,* liked an article that Booker had published in *Century* titled "Signs of Progress among the Negroes," in which Washington told seven stories, including one about William Edwards's creation of Snow Hill Institute with the aid of his white landlord and another about a black woman whose garden was admired by a passing white lady. Each story carried a message of black progress and interracial friendship, and each made a deep impression on Page. "These are the things, I tell you, that strike home in print just as they do in life; & these are the things that will make a most interesting book."[5]

In 1899 Washington published *The Future of the American Negro,* an assertion of black progress pieced together from his writing and speeches and presented in passages of conversational, first-person narration, rather than the pithy quotations of *Black Belt Diamonds.* The earlier book was still in circulation, but apparently it had had less of an impact than Fortune and Washington had hoped. *The Future of the American Negro* was Washington's most complete statement of his racial views to that point. He addressed the most common negative assumptions of whites about blacks. There would be no final solution to the Negro Problem: the black population was growing, would survive, and was not going anywhere. Blacks had not declined since slavery;

31. Booker Washington tried to address the vicious images of blacks with an outpouring of his own positive views. Photographer unknown, ca. 1900; courtesy of the Library of Congress.

they had built on the language, religion, and skills acquired during slavery to move steadily forward to a firm embrace of American civilization. He conceded that blacks had made mistakes in the past in their overemphasis on politics, but since then their focus had been on equipping themselves morally, educationally, and economically to fit into the larger society. Some blacks committed crimes, but as a group they were no more given to criminality than was any other disadvantaged group, and the incidence of crime had declined as blacks acquired education and prosperity. Because of poor schools, blacks had suffered from inadequate education, especially in the form of practical schooling. But Washington insisted that education benefited blacks, and that good black schools would redound to the benefit of all whites, who, he claimed, were accepting black education more readily.

To blacks, Booker emphasized the importance of demonstrating their progress at every opportunity. Whites needed object lessons in black achievement, and he presented Tuskegee Institute as one of them.

"Having been fortified at Tuskegee by education of mind, skill of hand, Christian character, ideas of thrift, economy, and push, and a spirit of independence, the student is sent out to become a centre of influence and light in showing the masses of our people in the Black Belt of the South how to lift themselves up." Blacks should at all times work to achieve and maintain a good reputation; doing so would cause many of the discouraging aspects of black life to disappear. "You cannot keep back very long a race that has the reputation for doing perfect work in everything that it undertakes." Once that reputation was established, blacks would inevitably prosper. "Nothing else so soon brings about right relations between the two races in the South as the commercial progress of the Negro." On this issue, as on the continuing opposition to black education, Booker ignored evidence of white hostility to black economic improvement.[6]

Though mainly a work of propaganda to promote the morale of blacks and the support of whites, *The Future of the American Negro* described candidly how discrimination made blacks suspicious of whites. "At the present moment, in many cases, when one attempts to get the Negro to co-operate with the Southern white man, he asks the question, 'Can the people who force me to ride in a Jim Crow car, and pay first-class fare, be my best friends?'" Near the end of the book he identified six dangers that imperiled the Negro's future. The first was black radicalism, born of the frustrations arising from discrimination, promoted mostly from outside the South and encouraged by incendiary newspaper reporting. The other dangers included white mob action, disfranchisement, and inadequate black education. Not surprisingly, a major worry was the decline of black hope. "We should not, as a race, become discouraged. We are making progress. No race has ever gotten upon its feet without discouragements and struggles."[7]

In 1900 Booker's life story became part of his effort to improve the black image. He believed that his example might inspire other blacks to have hope for a better future and whites to be more optimistic about black potential. His effort at autobiography occurred within several traditions of American narrative. Benjamin Franklin's *Autobiography* perhaps began the genre in America, with its bemused account of a young man's rise to a position of high status amid difficult circumstances, overcoming numerous trials along the way. Slave narratives, and in particular the autobiographies of Frederick Douglass, told of the triumph of blacks over the many inhumanities of slavery. In popular fiction, the novels of Horatio Alger typically tracked the rise of a poor but lucky young man to middle-class respectability. In 1899, with one or more of these models to serve as a background, Booker had begun work on an autobiography at the encouragement of a publisher of books sold door-to-door among blacks. He hired a black journalist, Edgar Webber, to ghostwrite the book, but the young man proved to be incompetent and lazy and the draft he produced a calamity of bad writing and miserable editing. Booker fired him but only after a shoddy work, *The Story of My Life and Work*, appeared in mid-1900. Booker immediately revised the book, and a competent edition appeared in 1901. By then he had engaged a new ghostwriter, Max Bennett Thrasher, a white journalist from New England who traveled with Booker through much of 1900 and worked with his dictation to revise the earlier version.

The Story of My Life and Work told of Booker's own rise from humble beginnings to become the leader of his race. The implicit message was that if African Americans followed his path and embraced his attitudes and behavior, they, too, would rise. He scattered through the text evidence of his own elevation. He remembered his family's arduous trek on foot from Hale's Ford over the mountains to West Virginia, but "since I have grown to manhood it has been my privilege to pass over much the same road . . . in well-appointed steam cars." Booker's personification of black success was most evident in Tuskegee Institute, which he expounded by describing the buildings built, the land acquired, the wealthy whites who gave money, and the visits of famous Americans. His description of slavery was brief but realistic: he recounted the beating of his uncle, including Monroe Burroughs's plaintive cries of "Pray, master! Pray, master!" But notably absent from *The Story of My Life* was any discussion of Reconstruction or black political action after the Civil War, or the white violence it sparked. One could hardly tell from this book that blacks had engaged in political life.[8]

Soon after publication of his *Story*, Booker was at work on another autobiography. It is not surprising that a man who had exploited two competing national myths—the northern commitment to racial equality and the southern honor of the Old South and the Lost Cause—should write a separate autobiography to appeal to whites. Both Walter Hines Page, now a publisher, and Lyman Abbott, the Congregationalist preacher and editor of the magazine *Outlook,* encouraged the new work, with the understanding that Abbott would serialize it before Page brought it out as a book. Booker's motives for writing *Up from Slavery* were largely financial: his children were growing up and attending expensive Eastern prep schools, and he needed to earn extra money for his family. Just as important, Abbott thought that whites might read the book and be awakened to support the cause of black education. Tuskegee needed new donors. In 1899 it had run a deficit of $40,000, a financial catastrophe for the fiscally conscientious Washington. The $100,000 he had been raising each year had become inadequate to support the continually rising number of students. William Baldwin had determined that an endowment of two million dollars would free Washington from constant fundraising, and to acquire so much money they needed to tap the large fortunes based in New York. Baldwin had just organized a meeting of wealthy people in the city when Abbott suggested that Booker write another autobiography.[9]

Up from Slavery is a revised version of *The Story of My Life,* with many passages from the earlier work included verbatim; but the differences are important. Parts of *Up from Slavery* mimic *Narrative of the Life of Frederick Douglass,* the most important African-American biography up to that time and one well known to white readers. Booker had read a Douglass autobiography during his European trip, and he perhaps borrowed language consciously. "I have no accurate knowledge of my age, never having seen any authentic record containing it," Douglass wrote, whereas Booker said: "I am not quite sure of the exact place or exact date of my birth, but at any rate I suspect I must have been born somewhere at some time." Of his paternity, Douglass wrote: "My father was a white man. He was admitted to be such by all I ever heard speak of my parentage. The opinion was also whispered that my master was my father; but of the correctness of this opinion, I know nothing; the means of knowing was withheld from me." Booker wrote that he did not know his father, not even his name: "I have heard reports to the effect that he was a white man who lived on one of the near-by plantations. Whoever he was, I never heard of his taking the least interest in me or providing in any way for my rearing. But I do not find especial fault with him. He was simply another unfortunate victim of the institution which the Nation unhappily had engrafted upon it at that time."[10]

As the pardon of his unknown father suggests, *Up from Slavery* dealt carefully with the subject announced in the title. The book is not in fact a slave narrative at all. Whereas the narrative arc of Douglass's autobiography and dozens of other slave memoirs encompasses an escape from bondage, *Up from Slavery* is about coping with freedom. Still, Washington had to address slavery, because it was necessary to describe the depths from which he rose to account for his remarkable rise. In *Up from Slavery* he presented slavery as more benign than he had in *The Story of My Life*. He left out the account of his uncle Monroe's beating, and he was generous in his judgment of his master's character. Slavery had given blacks an opportunity to learn skills and acquire the English language and Christianity, things that most white Americans in 1900 insisted had been benefits of the slave system and that Booker readily agreed were valuable acquisitions. Here Booker was trying to establish a common historical understanding with whites so that they would be open to the overall thrust of his message. Had he begun with the diatribe against the moral evil of slavery that many slave narratives typically offered, he might have lost white readers from the outset. His softer view of slavery also offered blacks a useful understanding, because it made the past less than horrific and the residual resentments about slavery perhaps less intense. He did not say that slavery was good for blacks—as, for example, William Councill claimed—and he emphasized its legacy of dysfunction: it undermined family life, degraded work, prevented education, and stunted blacks' capacity for self-rule. Slavery had deprived blacks of many of the ingredients necessary for success and left them behind whites, although since gaining freedom they had been rapidly catching up.

Emancipation was an even trickier challenge. To achieve legitimacy with white audiences, he had to address Reconstruction. He wrote that the emphasis on political participation and officeholding had put the cart before the horse of black progress. He thus acquiesced in the over-whelmingly popular view in 1900, North and South, that Reconstruc-tion, and black voting in particular, had been a mistake. Blacks' shift to a pursuit of economic goals represented a more viable path to progress. Still, *Up from Slavery* told hard truths about Reconstruction. About the Ku Klux Klan, Booker wrote that "their objects, in the main, were to crush out the political aspirations of the Negroes, but they did not confine themselves to this, because schoolhouses as well as churches were burned by them, and many innocent persons were made to suf-fer." He noted that many blacks had died during Reconstruction. Al-though some black officeholders in Reconstruction had not been quali-fied, others had been "strong, upright, useful men." Nor, he said, were "all the class designated as carpetbaggers dishonourable men."[11]

Despite the overwhelming and often hysterical white southern op-position to blacks' voting at the time, and the acceptance of disfran-chisement by most northerners, *Up from Slavery* emphatically sup-ported black voting rights. Washington denounced the idea that any state should make a law that "permits an ignorant and poverty-stricken white man to vote, and prevents a black man in the same condition from voting." Disfranchisement was a short-sighted, immoral policy, because "the white man who begins by cheating a Negro out of his bal-lot soon learns to cheat a white man out of his." In asserting that the South would eventually encourage all to vote, he expressed an opti-mism that few Americans black or white embraced at the time. He qualified his call for universal suffrage, writing that current conditions justified "the protection of the ballot in many of the states, for a while at least, either by educational test, a property test, or by both combined; but whatever tests are required, they should be made to apply with equal and exact justice to both races."[12]

Up from Slavery's overriding theme implied a positive historical tra-jectory. "One might as well try to stop the progress of a mighty railroad train by throwing his body across the track, as to try to stop the growth of the world in the direction of giving mankind more intelligence, more culture, more skill, more liberty, and in the direction of extend-ing more sympathy and more brotherly kindness." Blacks marched in step with other Americans. "No one can come into contact with the race for twenty years as I have done in the heart of the South," he wrote, "without being convinced that the race is constantly making slow but sure progress materially, educationally, and morally." African Americans were improving their lives in every successive generation: a farmer who produced the best sweet potatoes laid "the foundations upon which his children and grandchildren could grow to higher and more important things in life." Washington's life served as an example of the progress that he wanted whites to believe was possible for blacks in general. If he had been "a member of a more popular race, I should have been inclined to yield to the temptation of depending upon my ancestry and my colour to do that for me which I should do for my-self." The achievement of any black person who rose meant more be-cause of the obstacles surmounted: "When a white boy undertakes a task, it is taken for granted that he will succeed. On the other hand, people are usually surprised if the Negro boy does not fail. In a word, the Negro youth starts out with the presumption against him." *Up from Slavery*'s proof of progress was blacks' emerging self-mastery. Unsani-tary living habits, poor morality, and bad schools had been overcome with good educational opportunities. The Tuskegee campus demon-strated that blacks had learned how to work.[13]

Booker's emphasis on progress led him to claim that there was no Klan activity in 1901, when in fact forms of white terrorism existed for generations after the Civil War. Perhaps his faith in justice and prog-ress overrode an acknowledgment of such realities. "Every persecuted individual and race should get much consolation out of the great hu-man law, which is universal and eternal, that merit, no matter under what skin found, is, in the long run, recognized and rewarded." Like-wise, "The individual who can do something that the world wants done will, in the end, make his way regardless of his race." And again: "My experience is that there is something in human nature which al-ways makes an individual recognize and reward merit, no matter un-der what colour of skin merit is found." He paid special tribute to the powerful influence of object lessons: "I have found, too, that it is the visible, the tangible, that goes a long way in softening prejudices."[14]

The spare, unadorned prose of *Up from Slavery* rendered it inert rather than energetic. The language lacked metaphor, drama, or rich description. Nor did it suggest the fun in the telling that imbues Franklin's *Autobiography* or that characterized many of Booker's speeches to white audiences. "Washington's principles are themselves his only pleasure," surmised one insightful critic. "He hardly knows how to play." But at one point Washington did pander to "darky" humor. When the Institute was moving into a henhouse in its early days, he recounted, an old man asked: "What you mean, boss? You sholy ain't gwine clean out de hen-house in de *day-time?*" The joke may well have resonated with white audiences in 1901, but it reinforced the ugly minstrel stereotypes and undermined the higher purpose of his book. In other places, though, Washington used Negro dialect to show that rural blacks could make serious and admirable statements while using it.[15]

Up from Slavery was an instant success. It riveted the 100,000 readers who followed the progress of Booker's life through seventeen installments of *Outlook*. Barrett Wendell, the Harvard English professor who then taught virtually the only college course on American literature and who had written a widely used text on English composition, had grown impatient with writing that lacked "simple, manly distinctness." No book satisfied more on that account than *Up from Slavery*. "Yet few styles which I know seem to me more laden—as distinguished from overburdened—with meaning." The U.S. commissioner of education wrote that *Uncle Tom's Cabin* had produced the Civil War, and *Up from Slavery* would "guide us to the true road on which we may successfully solve the problems left us by that civil war." Walter Hines Page delighted in the book and its reception, although the firm of Doubleday, Page published several works that did better than the 30,000 copies of *Up from Slavery* sold in the first year. Few titles would, however, match its sustained sales in the decades ahead.[16]

The book's influence reached far beyond the United States. A teacher at a Methodist school in northern India wrote of *Up from Slavery* that "it dealt with so many of the problems that face us native Converts that I took the liberty to translate it into Urdu." A teacher in southern India wrote that all 700 students at a local high school were reading his own Malayalam translation. "I hope they will learn some lessons of self-help therefrom, and learn to recognize the dignity of manual labour and training." The book drew students and visitors from all over the world to Tuskegee. Cubans and Puerto Ricans had in fact enrolled just after the Spanish-American War, but others came from Latin America for years afterward. From his experience as house-father to the Indian boys at Hampton, Booker had been open to diversity of colors and cultures at his school. There were West Indians from both the British and the French islands, and a few Japanese and Chinese students. Booker readily accepted the Asian students when the heads of other black schools worried that it would be dangerous to take people whom some would consider white.[17]

The book had the desired effects on the Institute's fundraising. George Eastman, inventor of the Kodak camera, wrote that, having read *Up from Slavery,* he had "come to the conclusion that I cannot dispose of five thousand dollars to any better advantage than to send to you for your institute." Belton Gilreath, a Birmingham coal operator, said that *Up from Slavery* was "more interesting than any book I have ever read with the single exception of part of the life of Abraham Lincoln," and he declared his intention to distribute copies among the men at his three mines in order "to get them interested in your institution, *and* to take pride in it & look on it as our own." Gilreath did as he said and was soon appointed to the Tuskegee board of trustees. The book pricked the conscience of Julia Emery, a wealthy American living in London, who wrote to Booker: "Oh! How wondrously has God appeared on your behalf! Over-ruling all the sadness and bitterness and disadvantages of your early life! And has in the end recompensed you a thousand fold, in blessing you to others. And in causing your own heart to sing for joy that such a useful life, as is your present, sh'd have been the outcome of all yr early sufferings." Emery soon underwrote new Tuskegee dormitories. Washington had never achieved a meeting with Andrew Carnegie, but when a golf partner recounted to the steel magnate anecdotes from the book, Carnegie read it. Washington embodied much of the spirit that Carnegie had advanced in *The Gospel of Wealth* in 1890. "Give the man a library," the little Scotsman told his assistant. The neoclassical Carnegie Library soon rose into being, marking only the start of his largesse to Tuskegee.[18]

32. The Carnegie Library at Tuskegee Institute was the first of the steel magnate's gifts to the school. Photographer unknown, ca. 1906; courtesy of the
Library of Congress.

Up from Slavery functioned ever after as a fundraising tool for
Tuskegee Institute, a book-length grant proposal to anyone with philanthropic instincts and ability. It detailed the institution's successes and
its future needs, and its very essence declared the good character of
Washington, the steward of any gift made, not to mention the Protestant, capitalist values he espoused on every page. In the years ahead a
number of wealthy men and women would put down *Up from Slavery*
and immediately pick up a checkbook. The financial circumstances
would never be easy at Tuskegee, but they would have been much
worse in the absence of that book.

Most of the published reviews of *Up from Slavery* praised the man first
and the book second. In *North American Review,* William Dean Howells, the preeminent literary critic of the day, admired the writing,

which reminded him of the clear reasoning of Othello in the Venetian senate. "Interfused with the sweet, brave humor which qualifies his writing," the narrative tended to place Booker "outside his race, when he wishes to see it as others see it, and to report its exterior effect from his interior knowledge." *Up from Slavery* made "assurance doubly sure that the negro is not going to do anything dynamitic to the structure of society." Howells appreciated Washington's shrewdness: "He seems to hold in his strong grasp the key to the situation; for if his notion of reconciling the Anglo-American to the Afro-American, by a civilization which shall not seem to threaten the Anglo-American supremacy, is not the key, what is it?"[19]

The only negative review came from W. E. Burghardt Du Bois, and like Howells's it focused far more on the man than on the book; indeed, it was a critique of Washington's leadership. Du Bois wrote that Washington had come to power "at a time when the nation was a little ashamed of having bestowed so much sentiment on Negroes and was concentrating its energies on dollars," and that Booker's influence derived from his having taken the idea of industrial training for blacks and "broadened it from a by-path into a veritable Way of Life." Washington had embraced "so thoroughly the speech and thought of triumphant commercialism and the ideals of material prosperity" that he had disparaged a black boy's studying French grammar, demonstrating a crassness that insulted the values of both St. Francis and Socrates. He implied that Washington viewed the first black colleges—Atlanta, Howard, and Fisk Universities—as "wholly failures, or worthy of ridicule." Washington's positions elicited deep suspicion from blacks but admiration from southern whites. "Among the Negroes, Mr. Washington is still far from a popular leader."[20]

Du Bois knew that Washington thought well of Fisk and supported it. He surely also knew of Washington's careful comments in support of higher education for those blacks who could put it to practical use. As for Booker's not being a popular leader, Du Bois had to know of the great admiration for Washington among the rank and file of blacks; the evidence of his popularity was too apparent not to see. To be sure, Washington had his detractors, but curiously Du Bois mentioned none of those who by then had firmly rejected Washington: William Lewis,

33. William Edward Burghardt Du Bois had a complex and increasingly troubled relationship with Booker Washington. Photo by J. E. Purdy, 1904; courtesy of the Library of Congress.

Calvin Chase, Reverdy Ransom, and Ida Wells. The men whom Du Bois mentioned as Washington's challengers were ones who had supported Booker but sometimes disagreed with him: the poet Paul Dunbar, the painter Henry Tanner, the writer Charles Chesnutt, the academic Kelly Miller, and the lawyer Archibald Grimké. Du Bois may have hoped to detach them entirely by claiming them as leaders of an anti-Booker party.

Until recently Booker would have been surprised by such a negative assessment from Burghardt Du Bois. They had known each other since 1894, when Booker first offered him a teaching job, which he had turned down in favor of a position at Wilberforce College. Du Bois had written to Booker approvingly about the Atlanta address, and they had corresponded periodically after 1895 about an appointment at Tuskegee. Du Bois had defended Booker's leadership from attacks at the Afro-American Council meeting in the summer of 1899. Before

1900 there apparently had not been a cross word spoken between the two, or a negative opinion voiced by one about the other.

Du Bois had visited Tuskegee and studied its work, including the impact of the annual Negro Conference for black farmers. In 1900 he surveyed 200 participants at the conference, discovered that about 30 percent of them were landowners with an average holding of 124 acres, and concluded that the ten Negro Conferences had resulted in real progress among rural blacks. "Here is a school planted in the midst of the rural black belt which has sought to raise the standard of living, and especially to change the three things that hold the Negro still in serfdom—the crop lien system, the one-room cabin, and the poor and short public school."[21]

But they were very different men. Du Bois had been born a decade later in western Massachusetts into a poor but respectable black family. He was keenly aware of his mixed racial and national heritage, including Dutch, French, and African ancestry. He had associated extensively with whites in the strongly abolitionist town of Great Barrington, where he was viewed as the smartest black student around. Disappointed that he did not get to attend one of the well-known New England colleges, Du Bois went to Fisk for undergraduate school but then returned to Massachusetts to get a second baccalaureate degree from Harvard. He studied at the University of Berlin before becoming the first African American to receive a doctorate of philosophy from Harvard. His dissertation on the slave trade was well respected. He had done a sophisticated study of black urban life in Philadelphia, and after moving to Atlanta University in 1899, he had begun an ambitious series of inquiries into black social and economic life. By 1900 the most distinguished black scholar in the United States, Du Bois was vastly better educated than Booker Washington. Du Bois admired European culture, whereas Washington assumed that the American way of life was inherently better. Du Bois appreciated cities and universities as the places that fostered thought and culture. Washington was suspicious of urban life and assumed that the best places in America, especially for blacks, were rural. The educational and cultural differences carried over to their personal styles: Washington often wore overalls at home in Tuskegee and always the standard sack suit when at work or traveling, while Du Bois often dressed the part of the European professor, including the accessories of kid gloves and a cane.[22]

Still, in the fall of 1899 Booker invited Du Bois to come to Tuskegee to lead research on all aspects of black life, work that he envisioned would facilitate his campaign to improve the black image in the white mind. In February 1900 Du Bois expressed his reservations about coming to Tuskegee. "Would not my department be regarded by the public as a sort of superfluous addition not quite in consonance with the fundamental Tuskegee idea?" he asked. It had probably occurred to Du Bois that there might be room at Tuskegee for only one opinion, Washington's. Booker was so invested in industrial education that critical research on the black experience might take a back seat. Both would have been legitimate concerns. Du Bois declined the offer, claiming that he thought he could do more good in Atlanta working to reconcile the Tuskegee approach with Atlanta University's purely academic model. By 1900 the suspicions between Tuskegee and Atlanta University, arising from conflict over foundation support, were entrenched.

A third option had emerged, and Du Bois liked it best. The Washington, D.C., school system was searching for an assistant superintendent for colored schools. "Could I not serve both your cause & the general cause of the Negro at the National capital better than elsewhere?" he asked Booker. He wanted Washington's endorsement for the position, though he quickly added that he had not decided conclusively to reject the Tuskegee offer. The District of Columbia job paid much more than Tuskegee, and his wife preferred the big capital city to a small Alabama town. Booker sent the letter of endorsement but immediately heard objections from allies in the capital, who were supporting Robert Terrell, a strong Booker ally, for the position. One of them told Booker that he should not have pushed Du Bois for the job. "Your friends almost to a man are against him," he said. "We fight to make you and you must sometimes listen to us." Fortune also objected to Booker's support of Du Bois, probably because he associated Du Bois with the criticism of Booker emanating from Atlanta University. Still, Washington had already written a letter of recommendation, and he told Du Bois that he followed up on his initial blessing with another letter to the selection committee. When another candidate, not Terrell, was appointed, Du Bois was deeply disappointed, suspected that Booker had betrayed him, and blamed him for the outcome. Nothing in the surviving record provides evidence of betrayal, but Du Bois rejected the Tuskegee offer and stayed in Atlanta. For several years, however, he continued to pursue a school job in Washington, always failing to get an appointment.[23]

At precisely the time that Du Bois was first seeking the job in the District of Columbia, he was denied a sleeping berth on a Pullman car in Atlanta. He complained bitterly and, after sitting up all night in the Jim Crow car, filed a formal complaint. He asked for Booker's help, and Washington took up the matter with William Baldwin, who counseled against a lawsuit. But Booker knew all too well the indignities inflicted on blacks on trains, and he pursued the matter on Du Bois's behalf with several years of persistent complaints to the Pullman Company and its chief executive, one Robert Todd Lincoln. The son of the Great Emancipator proved to be wholly indifferent to the injustice. Finally Booker offered financial support for a court case, although none materialized. The coincidence of Du Bois's disappointment about the job in Washington and his anger about his mistreatment by the railroad appears to have alienated him from Booker. Still, he had not yet written a negative word, nor had he indicated any of the ideological opposition for which he would soon become so famous. The estrangement between the two was personal before it became ideological.[24]

Du Bois's alienation apparently jelled in the summer of 1900. Some part no doubt reflected the anger that American blacks were then feeling about racial conditions. Washington had been the nominal leader of blacks for five years, and for the past two years events had defeated his efforts to reduce racial conflict. Du Bois had observed the Sam Hose atrocity from the frightening perspective of Atlanta. Washington's complaints against that and other racial violence were measured, never expressing the outrage that blacks felt. Nor were things improving at the moment. In July in New Orleans, a police hunt for an alleged black criminal, a gunman named Robert Charles, had turned into a violent assault by whites on black neighborhoods after Charles killed several policemen. In August a police killing in New York City's Tenderloin district similarly evolved into surges of white rioting against black residents.[25]

Developments at the Afro-American Council meeting in August probably nursed Du Bois's hostility. Conflict arose over the council's Negro business bureau, established in response to Du Bois's recent study of black businessmen. Booker had come to the council meeting from Boston, where he had overseen the creation of the National Negro Business League (NNBL), a kind of black chamber of commerce created to nurture entrepreneurship. Washington's motive in creating the National Negro Business League had little to do with Du Bois. The Afro-American Council had been founded as a vehicle for protest, and Booker assumed that it would remain that. An organization of businessmen was not likely to achieve a strong, independent identity under the council's aegis. Washington wanted a national black organization that gave priority to an economic approach to uplifting the race. He envisioned a group that would provide an institutional framework for black businessmen to share ideas and build morale—essentially what the Tuskegee Negro Conference was to farmers. The NNBL would hold a convention each summer at which speakers discussed ways for a black person to succeed in a capitalist society. Booker's yearly address elaborating on this vision showed him at his prophetic best, and NNBL members were his most devoted supporters.[26]

Ida Wells-Barnett, the Chicago newspaper editor, asserted that Booker had usurped Du Bois's project by creating a new group for which he could be president and dictator. Washington, she claimed, would not "go anywhere or do anything unless he is 'the whole thing.'"[27] Originally friendly to Washington when he had criticized black preachers in the early 1890s, Wells-Barnett had settled in Chicago just ahead of a Memphis lynch mob and married the lawyer Ferdinand Barnett, editor of the Chicago *Conservator* and a critic of Washington. An emerging feminist, Wells-Barnett resisted the dominance of men in the circles of racial leadership, and in time she would similarly censure Du Bois. By 1901 Washington and his allies regarded her as one of the northern critics who, because of her own Memphis experience, should have had a better understanding of the limits on his ability to protest.

Du Bois needed an ideological rationale for challenging Washington. The two men shared a remarkably similar viewpoint. Du Bois had been reared in the Calvinist environment of New England, where he had embraced a Protestant ethic similar to what Booker acquired from Mrs. Ruffner and the teachers at Hampton. While training in sociology at the University of Berlin he had adopted the positivist commitment to scientific observation of the social world taught by August Comte. Under this approach a scholar sought to study existing problems objectively to find solutions to them. Booker had acquired the same outlook at Hampton, and it had been reinforced intuitively as he contemplated how to overcome the misrepresentations of black character. Du Bois's study of blacks in Philadelphia focused on a problem that Booker often emphasized: economic discrimination in northern cities that resulted in high crime rates and family breakdown. And he echoed Washington in his admonition about black responsibility: *"Unless we conquer our present vices they will conquer us; we are diseased, we are developing criminal tendencies, and an alarmingly large percentage of our men and women are sexually impure."* Like Booker, Du Bois saw the low esteem that the racial environment forced upon the black psyche, and he agreed that self-confidence was a fundamental need among blacks. Not surprisingly, Du Bois had consistently supported Washington's public positions through 1899.[28]

But Du Bois had a romantic racialism at odds with Booker's practical assimilationism. Perhaps his exposure to Goethe's romanticism and European nationalism in Germany made Du Bois believe more firmly in racial characteristics. In 1890 he wrote an essay describing the Confederate leader Jefferson Davis as conforming to the Teutonic ideal of manhood and heroic character but also to its "moral obtuseness and refined brutality." Davis's racial aggression, Du Bois argued, required another race—African Americans—to oppress. He essentially characterized Davis as the prototype for the white nationalists who by 1890 were dominating southern life and demonizing their black enemies. In 1897 Du Bois argued that every race made a distinctive contribution to the civilized world: the English gave it commercial freedom and constitutional liberty, the Germans advancement in science and philosophy. African Americans had a racial spirit entirely different from the Anglo-Saxons'. They constituted a "a nation stored with wonderful possibilities of culture . . . whose subtle sense of song has given America its only American music, its only American fairy tales, its only touch of pathos and humor amid its mad money-getting plutocracy."[29]

Washington accepted the reality of racial thought but saw race as socially constructed, often merely contrived, and he believed that racial distinctions would disappear over time. Through the 1890s he promoted appreciation of the cultural achievements of blacks, especially the painting of Henry Tanner, the poetry of Paul Dunbar, and what he called plantation melodies, the Negro spirituals. But he never associated black cultural achievement with racial nationalism. Rather he saw it as blacks' contribution to American exceptionalism. He acknowledged racial differences when whites demanded to know his opinions, but his acceptance sounded like acquiescence in—perhaps even pandering to—insistent white racial preoccupations, as when in 1896 he told a white assembly that blacks as a race were rather emotional: "We have a good deal of feeling about us, and we feel our religion in a way that you do not. I believe the average black man can feel more religion in ten minutes than the average white man can in a day." Booker himself was apparently never subject to religiously provoked emotion. When asked several years later by an Alabama congressman for his private views about the content of racial differences, Washington was somewhat more definite, though still keenly aware of whom he was addressing. Asserting his belief that dark-skinned blacks were just as smart and capable of success as whites, he offered as examples the poet Dunbar, the preacher-educator J. C. Price, and the horticulturalist George Washington Carver, among others. "In those matters where the feeling or imagination plays a large part I do not believe that there is any difference," Booker told the congressman. "In the application, however, of education or mind development . . . I have the feeling that there is a difference." Given the high incidence of mixed-race people in positions of leadership in black America at the moment, Booker may have been speaking his mind. But he also knew what the white man wanted to hear and that he could not afford to advocate perfect equality when talking to white men.[30]

Du Bois, on the other hand, believed that Africans possessed a keener religious feeling, not just a proclivity for enthusiastic expression; this capacity had originated in the forests of Africa and carried over into their unique understanding of Christianity in America. He understood blacks' religious capacity as based in their instinctive moral superiority to whites. He adopted the mantra, expressed by older black intellectuals and preachers, of the "Christ-like Negro," who had suffered so extensively in America that he provided moral authority and an object lesson to sinful and exploitative whites. Washington was keenly aware of the moral shortcomings of white Americans, but he did not see blacks as their redeemers.[31]

In 1900 Du Bois evidenced a duality in his thinking—the sociologist's positivism and the mystic's faith in a superior racial soul—that created internal tensions and conflicts in how he understood the world he inhabited. Indeed, the two ideals would, to use his own phrase from another context, war within him. By 1899 at Atlanta University, he was embarking on a series of sociological studies. Although these began as empirical research on black artisans and business, his efforts gradually became less systematic and detailed and more impressionistic in connecting social behavior to the Negro soul. The mystic increasingly won the battle within, and his social and racial attitudes reflected more of his racial nationalism and less of the empirical sociologist committed to this-world reform. Du Bois the black nationalist grew progressively more hostile to whites over time. That antipathy no doubt arose from being beleaguered by white bigotry, but it was also a manifestation of his growing alienation from Washington. After 1900 the main expression of, and motivation for, his racial nationalism became his opposition to Washington's racial leadership.

Some of Du Bois's subsequent behavior belied his pen. He accepted an invitation from Booker to camp with him in West Virginia at precisely the time that his negative review of *Up from Slavery* appeared. He continued to solicit and accept Booker's help in challenging his mistreatment on the railroad. He accepted payment for teaching at Tuskegee and invited Booker to lecture at Atlanta University. This state of affairs may have reflected two enemies' deciding that it was safer to keep the other close than at a distance. But it is more likely that the subsequent meetings were Washington's attempt to keep Du Bois in his fold. Du Bois may have been unsure for a while about whether to break with Washington once and for all. But soon the break would be permanent, the feelings intensely bitter and getting worse all the time.

Completely apart from Du Bois's criticism, a new surge of intellectual racism at the turn of the century limited the positive impact of *Up from Slavery* on the image of African Americans. In a 1900 book Paul Barringer promised to prove that the Negro's "return to barbarism is as natural as the return of the sow that is washed to her wallowing in the mire." It was not the former slaves but "the negro under thirty, which crowds our jails and penitentiaries throughout the land," Barringer declared. "The term 'worthless' is so universally applied to this class that I think it must be the proper one." Also in 1900, Charles Carroll published to wide notice *The Negro a Beast,* which resurrected the old claim that African peoples were of a different biological species from whites. The next year William P. Calhoun of South Carolina published his analysis of the Negro Problem, giving away his thesis in the title: *The Caucasian and the Negro in the United States. They Must Separate. If Not, Then Extermination. A Proposed Solution: Colonization.*[32]

The most direct challenge to Washington's influence came from the pen of another black man, William Hannibal Thomas, who in January 1901, at the very time that *Up from Slavery* was being serialized, published a book called *The American Negro: What He Was, What He Is, and What He May Become.* A free-born mulatto from Ohio who had lost his right arm while serving in the Union army, Thomas had been a Republican lawyer and legislator in Reconstruction South Carolina and then a Methodist minister and teacher at two seminaries and a college, from each of which he apparently stole money. He had moved in black intellectual and religious circles in the 1880s and 1890s and was well known, if not admired, when the prestigious transatlantic publishing house McMillan produced his massive analysis of the Negro. Whereas Booker Washington strained always to discover reasons for optimism about blacks, William Hannibal Thomas saw only evidence for pessimism. The Negro, Thomas wrote, was "an intrinsically inferior type of humanity," his history "a record of lawless existence, led by every impulse and every passion." Thomas embraced the white nationalists' explanation of the past: slavery had partly civilized the savage African, but the good effect had been lost in freedom, a decline accelerated by black educators who bilked northern philanthropists to create fraudulent schools. To Thomas, the future posed huge challenges: "The negro is immoral; he must be endowed with morality. He is lazy, and therefore needs to be made industrious. He is a coward; he must acquire courage. His conscience is dead, his intellect dense; one must be resurrected, and the other set aflame by the light of heaven." Black social life was "an open page of execrable weakness, of unblushing shame, of inconceivable mendacity, of indurated folly and ephemeral contrition." His answer to the Negro Problem was the white nationalists' final solution: whites should "exterminate at all hazards and at any cost the savage despoilers of maiden virtue or wifely honor." But degenerate people, Thomas said, could be saved by "an infusion of virile blood," and the best Negroes were the ones, like himself, whose white ancestors went back three or four generations. He called for the "utter extermination, root and branch, of all Negroid beliefs and practices."[33]

Reviews of Thomas's book in the leading American newspapers were mostly positive, including those in the liberal New York *Evening Post* and the Boston *Evening Transcript* and the more conservative Washington *Post,* New York *Times,* and Chicago *Daily Tribune.* All said that Thomas's criticisms had an authority that any white man's necessarily lacked. White nationalists seconded the praise. Paul Barringer instructed whites to "go read the work of the one negro who has thus far dared sacrifice himself on the altar of truth." Bill Arp saw Thomas's portrayal of blacks' degenerate character as symptomatic of a decline in northern sympathy for the Negro. "Is the north about to abandon the Negro and turn him over to the mercy of his former masters? If so, the Negro will be the gainer, and so will the south." A Maryland white man declared that philanthropists in the North who were showering money on Tuskegee Institute should instead cover the country with Thomas's writing. "One thousand dollars so spent would go further than $10,000 given to Tuskegee."[34]

Washington mounted a drive to undermine Thomas. To avoid being drawn into a public debate, he reviewed the book anonymously and politely in *Outlook*. Although Thomas himself was not proud of being a Negro, Washington wrote, "he is making the most of the fact that he has enough blood connection with the race to enable him to speak from the inside" to claim knowledge of the material, moral, and mental failures of blacks. "The remedy for such an extreme case of the blues as Mr. Thomas evidently has is to be found in going right into the field among the people and entering into hard, earnest work for their uplifting." The journalist John Bruce and the novelist Charles Chesnutt mounted the main black counterattack on Thomas, with evidence of Thomas's criminality and abuse of women dug up by investigators working for Booker. Extensive exposure of his bad character did not persuade McMillan to withdraw the book from the market. *The American Negro* sold well for at least four years, a testament to the huge appetite among Americans for scurrilous allegations against blacks' "character" at precisely the time that others were admiring the life of Booker Washington.[35]

But the most damaging piece of counterpropaganda to Washington's public-relations campaign was still to come. The publishing world was astonished in 1902 at the phenomenal success of Thomas Dixon Jr.'s novel, *The Leopard's Spots: A Romance of the White Man's Burden*, which, published within months of *Up from Slavery* by the same house, sold many more copies in the ensuing years. Dixon's life had been almost as varied and circuitous as William Hannibal Thomas's, although he always stayed on the right side of the law. Born to a family of North Carolina Baptist ministers, Dixon went to graduate school in history at Johns Hopkins just long enough to become friends with an older student, Woodrow Wilson. He tried acting, but after failing again he returned to North Carolina, studied law, and was elected to the state legislature. Perhaps inevitably he wound his way back to the family path and became a much-celebrated Baptist minister, first in Raleigh and then in Boston and finally in New York. Tall, gaunt, with a mop of black hair and dark eyes, Dixon in the 1890s was mesmerizing audiences in lecture halls, speaking to big crowds on secular as well as religious topics. He became such a star on the lecture circuit that he quit preaching. His most popular lectures warned of the peril of the Negro to the nation. In 1901 he happened to see a stage production of *Uncle Tom's Cabin,* the message of which incensed Dixon, and in sixty days he wrote *The Leopard's Spots* and sent it to his old Raleigh friend Walter Hines Page, Booker's publisher, who immediately brought it out.[36]

The Leopard's Spots makes a loud statement on race with a melodramatic plot about the South after the Civil War. A loyal slave brings home from the Civil War the dead father of eight-year-old Charles Gaston of North Carolina. The boy's distraught mother neglects him, and a Baptist preacher, John Durham, an all-knowing authority on racial matters, oversees Charles's education and rise to manhood. After the war, the local freedmen become viciously antiwhite and uncontrollably lustful after white women. An educated black man from the North tells white aristocrats that their Desdemonas desire an Othello. The preacher warns the mature but racially naïve Gaston against allowing blacks to have the vote: "One drop of negro blood makes a negro. It kinks the hair, flattens the nose, thickens the lip, puts out the light of intellect, and lights the fires of brutal passions. The beginning of Negro equality as a vital fact is the beginning of the end of this nation's life. There is enough negro blood here to make mulatto the whole Republic." The racial imperative is then inevitably political, as Durham-Dixon finally shouts: *"Can you build, in a Democracy, a nation inside a nation of two hostile races?"* *The Leopard's Spots* reprises the 1898 events in North Carolina: Gaston leads a violent overthrow of the Black Republican government, restores white control, and as governor advocates disfranchisement but also industrial education for blacks overseen by leaders who resemble Booker Washington. But preacher Durham insists that even industrial education is a terrible mistake. "If the Negro is made master of the industries of the South he will become the master of the South. Sooner than allow him to take the bread from their mouths, the white men will kill him here as they do in the North ... The Negro must ultimately leave this continent." Gaston argues for agricultural education for blacks, but Durham is insistent: "Make the Negro a scientific and successful farmer, and let him plant his feet deep in your soil, and it will mean a race war . . . The Ethiopian can not change his skin, or the leopard his spots."[37]

The success of *The Leopard's Spots* made clear who was winning the war to shape the racial thinking of Americans: it would sell a million copies. Booker Washington worked tirelessly with his speeches and writing to promote the idea that blacks were going up, not down. But he could not make people listen, nor could he stop those whose propaganda insisted that blacks were dangerous beasts, unworthy of sympathy, incapable of improvement. As more Americans acquired the art and craft of shaping public opinion, the harder it became to reverse the deep pessimism about the Negro.[38]

10

―――

The Violence of Their Imagination

In the fall of 1901, at the time he was trying to minimize the damage done by William Hannibal Thomas, Booker Washington was coping with blacks' depressing loss of democratic rights. He had not lost hope that the train of disfranchisement might somehow be hijacked, but the prospects looked bad. The ratification campaign for Alabama's constitution was gaining speed, fueled by loud, incessant declarations about the black threat to good government—at least some of them made by white men preparing to use fraudulent black votes to disfranchise black men. Then, in a moment, fate altered these miserable circumstances and gave Washington an unforeseen opportunity to recover some semblance of democratic participation for blacks. On September 7, 1901, an anarchist named Leon Czolgosz shot William McKinley. The popular president died of the wounds a week later. The assassination permanently changed the course of Washington's leadership.

He had supported McKinley in two elections and was heartened by his praise at Tuskegee, but Washington had objected to McKinley's acquiescence in southern white Republicans' efforts to push all blacks out of the party. McKinley's chief political adviser, the Republican national chairman Senator Marcus A. Hanna, had dispensed federal patronage in the South mainly to the so-called Lily Whites, who were challenged in most states by a faction of black Republicans and the few whites willing to ally with them—the Black-and-Tans. When he suddenly became president on September 14, Theodore Roosevelt sent word within hours that he wanted to meet with Washington. He had known Booker casually for several years and thought of him as most wealthy eastern Republicans did—as a remarkable Negro of high character and sound judgment. Roosevelt had made overtures for political discussions with Booker even before the president was shot, because he already had begun looking toward the 1904 presidential race. He assumed that his chief Republican rival would be Hanna, who had opposed his selection as vice president. Roosevelt knew that black voters could help him get nominated and might hold the balance of power in the election in several states. But as a political reformer, he opposed the appointment of professional jobseekers, and he assumed that in the past Republicans had given federal jobs in the South to unqualified blacks. But neither did he want to appoint white party hacks. The men he put in would have to be of high character, even if they were not Republicans. Rather than appoint a southern Republican who owed Hanna loyalty, Roosevelt said he would consider "Gold Democrats"— men of the other party who had rejected the inflationary monetary policies advocated by William Jennings Bryan, the Democratic nominee for president in the last two elections—for important jobs.[1]

Washington saw Roosevelt's ambitions as means to several of his own ends. He could get support for the Black-and-Tans in the South and thus check the Lily White movement. He could influence the president on which white southerners to appoint—and perhaps direct him away from the antiblack Republicans and white nationalists and toward other men more sympathetic to black concerns. And, most important, he could get some blacks appointed to federal jobs and thus have tangible evidence of a continuing black presence in the democratic process, even as black voters were being systematically removed from southern politics. Washington had good reason to believe that Hanna would not appoint black men.

Like most Americans who came into Teddy's company, Washington was enamored of Roosevelt's energy, intelligence, and willingness to challenge the status quo. Washington also had personal reasons to like Roosevelt. They had known each other for some time, and

34. As soon as he became president, Theodore Roosevelt sent for Booker Washington to ask his advice about federal appointments in the South. Photo by Rockwood Photo Company, copyright February 24, 1903; courtesy of the Library of Congress.

Roosevelt had been friendly and hospitable. Booker had stayed at the Roosevelt home at Oyster Bay on Long Island. He knew that Teddy was friendly with at least one other black man, the Boston lawyer William H. Lewis. Lewis had been a football star at Harvard, later coached the team there, and demonstrated the kind of physical prowess that Roosevelt admired. Although Lewis was no friend of his, Booker had surely noted that Roosevelt treated his classmate as virtually an equal, having hosted Lewis in the New York governor's mansion. During the 1900 election Roosevelt had sought the advice of both Lewis and Washington. He no doubt had already expressed to Washington his disapproval of southern racial obsessions. He condemned lynching, thought white southerners were entirely hypocritical in their preoccupations with interracial sex, and objected to the political exploitation of race by the likes of Ben Tillman. In contrast to white nationalists, Roosevelt believed that blacks were improving morally and culturally, that education improved blacks in every way, and that the educated, respectable blacks should vote. All this surely augured well for greater presidential sympathy for black rights.[2]

But Washington had surely heard negative views of Roosevelt's character from white friends. Staunch Republicans considered him an unreliable party man, so devoted was Teddy to cleansing politics of corruption. Businessmen liked his conventional views on hard money and fiscal responsibility but were suspicious of his occasional sympathy with organized labor. After his exploits with the Rough Riders in the Spanish-American War in 1898, and then his use of his military celebrity to advance his political career, some accused him as a jingoist and mindless expansionist. The Garrisons of Boston held such a view. But perhaps the most persistent critique was that he was impetuous, that he acted without first thinking carefully. "Mind in the technical sense, he has not," said the writer Henry Adams, because "his mind is impulse." Booker's closest white adviser, the New York railroad executive William Baldwin, essentially subscribed to that view, calling Roosevelt a "sophomore"—immature, unpredictable, and inconsistent in his actions.[3]

Washington resisted such opinions, later defending Roosevelt as thoughtful and farsighted in his planning, but he certainly had ample warning about the limits of Roosevelt's racial thinking. Teddy viewed blacks as a naturally inferior people who had been held back by the slave experience. As a group they did not deserve full enfranchisement, although some individuals like Washington and Lewis were worthy of equal treatment. Roosevelt's racial bigotry had been exposed in 1899 when, in his self-congratulatory book *The Rough Riders,* he asserted that black soldiers in Cuba performed adequately only under white command, and even then they panicked in battle and fled the front lines. "I attributed the trouble to the superstition and fear of the darkey, natural in those but one generation removed from slavery and but a few generations removed from the wildest savagery." Tim Fortune lambasted Roosevelt for his "criminal indiscretion," which he said was a cover for the fact that black soldiers had actually rescued Teddy's Rough Riders from death. Both black and white soldiers on the battlefield with Roosevelt subsequently contradicted his assessment, and he later recanted some of it.[4]

Whether he appointed blacks or whites in the South, Teddy was removing the dispensation of patronage in the South from Hanna, and he wanted Booker's advice. "I want to have a long talk with you," Roosevelt wrote ten days after taking office, and their conversation took place in the White House on September 29.[5] Newspapers reported that Washington was advising the president on appointments.

Two days after they met, the federal judge in Montgomery died, and a scramble for the appointment ensued. Would-be judges immediately offered themselves to Booker. Oscar Hundley, a Huntsville Populist turned Republican, made a pitch, no doubt hoping that Booker had forgotten his strong advocacy of separating the school funds by race. Former governor William Oates did not ask directly for Booker's endorsement but reminded him that a right-thinking federal judge could provide protection for blacks: "With the impending sentiment among a large class of white people in the south the greatest bulwark of protection to your race is to be found in the federal judiciary." Booker hardly needed Oates's words to know the significance of the federal judgeship to blacks. He had already decided that there was no white Republican in Alabama worthy of his support and had made a different choice, which he probably had also communicated to the president. He sent a formal letter of nomination on October 2. Thomas Goode Jones was "a gold democrat, and is a clean, pure man in every respect," Booker wrote. He explained that Jones had stood up in Alabama's constitutional convention for a fair election law and black education and against lynching. He did not write to the president about Jones's paternalistic attitude toward blacks or his belief that blacks deserved every opportunity to improve themselves, although he may have conveyed these factors in conversation. From his private communications with Jones and his observation of the former governor at the convention, Booker concluded that Jones would stand up for black rights. Jones's vociferous opposition to the grandfather clause in the Alabama constitution led Booker to think that he might be persuaded that the Alabama suffrage law violated the U.S. Constitution and, if given the chance, would overturn it from the protected authority of the federal bench. It is doubtful that the new president was thinking that far ahead: Teddy only wanted to know if Jones had voted in 1900 for Bryan, and even when he got the bad news that the former governor had, he appointed Jones.[6]

Alabama editors and political wags were slow on the uptake, but not so Josephus Daniels of Raleigh, the editorial mouthpiece of North Carolina's white-nationalist Democrats. Daniels instantly declared that Jones's opposition to the suffrage plan in the Alabama constitutional convention was the "milk in the cocoanut" that Booker Washington would drink once his challenge to disfranchisement reached Judge Jones's court. "Do you see?" Daniels demanded. "Does the light begin to break?"[7]

The light surely started shining about a week after the appointment was announced. Roosevelt had summoned Booker back to the capital for further discussion of patronage appointments. When he arrived at the Washington home of his friend Whitefield McKinlay, Booker was handed an invitation from the president to dine at the White House. Roosevelt later wrote privately that he had talked so much with Washington "it seemed to me that it was natural to ask him to dinner to talk over this work, and the very fact that I felt a moment's qualm on inviting him because of his color made me ashamed of myself and made me hasten to send the invitation." Roosevelt added wistfully that he had never thought of "its bearing one way or the other, either on my own future or on anything else." Booker discussed the invitation with McKinlay and probably with other close friends in the District. He knew that no black person had ever dined at the White House, and he surely remembered the harsh criticism of President Cleveland for hosting Queen Liliuokalani of Hawaii at the White House in 1895. But the invitation did come from the president of the United States, and one could hardly decline a request from that quarter. He later wrote privately that he accepted the dinner with his eyes open, knowing its potential consequences. He had a day to think about it and count the costs. He decided that it represented "recognition of the race and no matter what personal condemnation it brought upon my shoulders I had no right to refuse or even hesitate."[8] There was also the reality that Washington had been accepting hospitality from northern whites for twenty years, usually on terms of perfect equality. At all times courtly and acutely sensitive to whites' expectations, he often slept and ate in white homes when he was fundraising and even more commonly dined with them in hotels and banquet halls. He had attended many public events in the North at which whites treated him as an honored guest. After all, he was one of the most remarkable men in America and certainly the most interesting Negro.

At dinner at the White House, Booker sat with Roosevelt, the president's wife Edith, his seventeen-year-old daughter, Alice Lee, and three of his sons. The scene would be portrayed later as an acceptance of a Negro into the bosom of the Roosevelt family, and that interpretation was mostly accurate. It made some difference that Mrs. Roosevelt was there, and even more that the teenaged Alice had eaten dinner with Washington. She was a beautiful and lively girl with an extraordinary life of political celebrity in front of her. The presence of the marriageable daughter provoked ugly imaginings among many a white nationalist in the South. Also at dinner was Roosevelt's friend and hunting partner Philip Stewart from Colorado. After the meal, Roosevelt and Washington discussed the South and Roosevelt's plans for shaping political affairs there. The appointment of Thomas Goode Jones was to be only the first of many decisions that had to be made about patronage in the South.

Late that night a reporter saw the register of White House visitors. He noted who had come to dinner, and the story went out to the wire services. By then Washington had boarded a train for New York, where the next day he dined with another powerful white man, his friend William Baldwin. He mentioned to Baldwin his previous night's engagement, and apparently neither man felt any alarm about it. That day Booker spoke to John D. Rockefeller Jr.'s Sunday school class at the Fifth Avenue Baptist Church, another gathering of powerful white men.[9]

Booker knew well the hysteria that overtook white southerners at such displays of "social equality." He himself had been battered with the trope that any white man who invited a Negro to dine was offering him the bed of his sister or daughter. John Temple Graves and Paul Barringer had declaimed that, notwithstanding Washington's achieve-

35. Alice Roosevelt, the president's teenaged daughter, was present at the dinner with Booker Washington, a source for the race-sex hysteria among white southerners. Photo by Frances Benjamin Johnston, 1902; courtesy of the Library of Congress.

ments, no self-respecting white southerner would ever invite him to his table. And now the president of the United States had done just that. Booker had addressed such white obsessions at the Atlanta exposition with his separate-as-the-fingers metaphor, but now he had created a contradictory and even more powerful image, one that would cancel entirely the effect of the earlier symbolism. To many Americans, and to nearly all white southerners, the White House dinner represented an embrace of racial equality by the most powerful white man and the most powerful black man in the United States.

African Americans took immense pride in the honor accorded their leader. The symbolism of the event thrilled the image-conscious Emmett Scott. "It is splendid, magnificent!" he wrote to Booker the next day. "The world is moving forward." A Chicago minister hailed the president's act as "an omen of the coming of that day when we shall neither be favored nor hindered because of the color of our skin." A Birmingham minister wrote to Booker that "we negroes feel that you are greatly honored, indeed, and that you have done more to advance our interest in new territory than any living man." The intensely anti-Negro Atlanta *Journal* was for once accurate about blacks' feelings: "When the President took to his family board one of their race he kindled in the heart of thousands of negroes a desire for social recognition of a similar character."[10]

It took thirty-six hours for the event to land squarely in the consciousness of white southerners. "BOTH POLITICALLY AND SOCIALLY, PRESIDENT ROOSEVELT PROPOSES TO CODDLE DESCENDANTS OF HAM," shouted the headline in the Atlanta *Constitution*. "Men heretofore friendly to him are loud in condemnation" and "President's influence with southern white men gone" pronounced the subheads in the story. Indeed anger welled up everywhere in the white South and fed the violent imaginings of every white-nationalist leader there. "The action of President Roosevelt in entertaining that nigger," Ben Tillman announced, "will necessitate our killing a thousand niggers in the South before they will learn their place again." James K. Vardaman proclaimed that Roosevelt had insulted every white man in America: "President Roosevelt takes this nigger bastard into his home, introduces him to his family and entertains him on terms of absolute social equality." Rebecca Felton said that although Washington was reputed to be a level-headed Negro, at the White House he had thrown off the mask and revealed himself as a "disintegrator and disorganizer of both races." Booker would be wise "to lift his Tuskegee plant and move northward while he is basking in Presidential favor." The Nashville *American* said that despite Booker's respectability, "A leak in a dam is

36. Among Booker Washington's most determined southern enemies were (from left) James K. Vardaman, future governor of Mississippi, and J. Thomas Heflin, who would represent Tuskegee in the U.S. Congress. The man at right is Congressman Ollie James of Kentucky. Originally published by the Bain News Service, ca. 1908; courtesy of the Library of Congress.

dangerous to the dam's safety," and giving Washington such status would cause other blacks to demand the same privileges. "Miscegenation would follow and a mongrel race would be the result." Governor Oates, Booker's friend, reiterated the point: "No respectable white man in Alabama of any political party would ask him to dinner nor go to dinner with him."[11]

Editorial opinion across the South was universally negative, though it varied in harshness, with the Atlanta *Constitution* and the Montgomery *Advertiser* attempting to fix the blame entirely on Roosevelt. The usually friendly editor of the Birmingham *Age-Herald* surmised that the temptation of Roosevelt's invitation to the White House had been too great and "Washington fell," in the process damaging his school and undermining his life's work. Henry Watterson, editor of the Louisville *Courier-Journal* and one thought to be more absorbed in booming southern industry than upholding white nationalism, wrote that

Washington was admirable as head of Tuskegee Institute, but as head of Roosevelt's kitchen cabinet "he is to be pitied, a red rag to racial prejudice; an object of envy in those blacks who are intelligent enough to differentiate; an offense to white Republicans, a menace to white Democrats in the South." Roosevelt's having "a nigger to dine at the White House," the Memphis *Scimitar* declared, was the "most damnable outrage which has ever been perpetrated by any citizen of the United States," and it taught a frightening lesson: "Any Nigger who happens to have a little more than the average amount of intelligence granted by the Creator of his race, and cash enough to pay the tailor and the barber, and the perfumer for scents enough to take away the nigger smell, has a perfect right to be received by the daughter of the white man among the guests in the parlor of his home." The New Orleans *Times Democrat* taunted its readers: "White men of the South, how do you like it? White women of the South, how do you like it? Every one knows that when Mr. Roosevelt sits down to dinner in the White House with a negro, he that moment declares to all the world that, in the judgment of the President of the United States, the negro is the social equal of the white man." In the view of the editor of the Richmond *Times,* Roosevelt's invitation meant that Negroes should "mingle freely with whites in the social circle—that white women may receive attentions from Negro men; it means that there is no racial reason in his opinion why whites and blacks may not marry and intermarry, why the Anglo-Saxon may not mix Negro blood with his blood." The Geneva *Reaper,* a Populist weekly in Alabama, was representative of many country papers: "Poor Roosevelt! He might now just as well sleep with Booker Washington, for the scent of that coon will follow him to the grave, as far as the South is concerned."[12]

The tongue-lashing from a few northern blacks almost matched the white-nationalist wrath. The newly established Boston *Guardian* denounced Roosevelt for inviting Booker to the White House. The *Guardian*'s George Forbes echoed Rebecca Felton when he said that it would be "a blessing to the race if the Tuskegee school should burn down." William Ferris of the *Guardian* told Washington privately that the white South "only cares for you in so far as it can use you as a tool or catspaw, but that deep down in their hearts they despise you as they

37. The Birmingham *Age-Herald* typified southern newspapers with its ugly
cartoons about Roosevelt and his racial policies. Here he is shown serenading
a figure labeled "Negro Vote." The caption reads: "'Teddie,' the (color blind)
tenor, will now render his favorite ballad, entitled 'Because I Love You,' assisted
by the eminent Miss Snow Flake and chorus." Artist unknown; from the
Birmingham *Age-Herald,* November 30, 1902.

do the most ragged worthless loafer." Ferris said that "no matter how
magnificent an institution you may, by your constructive genius & tact,
erect, no matter how many nice things you may say about the white
man of the south, in his estimation you are a nigger just the same."[13]

Washington's white friends were divided over the meaning of the
uproar. J. L. M. Curry thought it would be a nine-day wonder, as did
Walter Hines Page, who saw it as part of the disfranchising hysteria.
But a week after the dinner, Edgar Gardner Murphy considered the
tensions too great for him to visit Tuskegee. The priest believed that
Booker and Roosevelt had made a foolish mistake: "When men come

to represent something greater than themselves (the President in his office and you in the leadership of your race) every act is representative, and carries, to the popular mind, a vast significance." In this case that meaning was all bad: "The average man in the street can see nothing in the incident but a deliberate attempt on the part of the President and yourself to force the issue of inter-marriage and amalgamation!!!!"[14]

Murphy's anxiety intensified when the press reported five days after the White House dinner that Washington and Roosevelt had marched side by side at Yale University and that Alice Roosevelt had dined either with or near Booker—action that prompted the *Constitution* headline "Northern Whites Feeding with Booker Washington." Murphy's warning reflected the extent of the tension: "The trouble is not superficial. The whole south has not been so deeply moved in twenty years."[15] Murphy was deferential to a fault with white nationalists, but he proved to be right about the White House dinner. He saw that this breach of racial etiquette had inflamed white southerners' political insecurity in the same way that Alex Manly's suggestion about white women's desire for black men had unleashed terrorism in North Carolina in 1898. Any symbolic hint that blacks wanted social equality only deepened the commitment to oppressing blacks politically.

For weeks reporters pursued Washington for comments and interviews, but he kept silent. Threatening letters poured into Tuskegee. A black man later confessed that he had been hired by white Louisianans to assassinate Booker and had come to Tuskegee, only to find that Washington was absent from his home. Indeed, Booker stayed in the North for months after the White House dinner. Injured while in Tuskegee, the assassin was treated so well at the Institute hospital that he felt too guilty to carry out his mission and finally confessed it.[16]

Forever the optimist, at least outwardly, Booker chose to believe those who downplayed the event's significance. Ten days after the dinner he told Roosevelt that the disfranchising campaigns were inflaming white opinion, but that he was "more than ever convinced that the wise course is to pursue exactly the policy which you mapped out in the beginning" about patronage appointments and that "not many moons will pass before you will find the South in the same attitude

THE VIOLENCE OF THEIR IMAGINATION

toward you that it was a few weeks ago." Roosevelt was astonished at the white South's reaction, telling William Baldwin that he had invited Booker to dinner not for any racial purpose but as a convenience for himself and a courtesy to Washington for helping him with appointments. Booker sensed Roosevelt's discomfiture with the outrage and feared that it would undermine the president's inclination to follow his recommendations. He silently acknowledged what others saw in Roosevelt: he was an impulsive man, one who sometimes acted hastily or arbitrarily on the basis of self-righteous certainty that could just as suddenly justify a reversal of his position. An anti-Roosevelt southern newspaper hit close to the truth about Teddy's impetuosity: "Nobody knows what he will do next under any circumstances, and each act must be taken upon its own separate deserts or demerits."[17]

The White House dinner was instantly loaded with political meaning in the South. It fueled the campaign to ratify Alabama's new constitution. The dinner had sharpened the question, as one newspaper put it, "whether the white man shall rule or the negro be forced into our churches, schools, and firesides." The convention president declared that, followed to its logical conclusion, the White House dinner meant that "the son of a black man might woo and win the daughter of the white man." Such a result made disfranchisement not just an effort for better government: "It involves the preservation of our civilization." Tom Heflin made speech after speech saying that Roosevelt had ruined the Negroes of the South and, in so doing, had spoiled his own political career.[18]

The dinner undermined Washington's acceptance in the white South well past the fall of 1901. Apparently no southern editor ever forgot or forgave him or Roosevelt for their insolence. The event became the main point of reference for all discussions of black participation in politics and for Roosevelt's handling of any southern concern for the remainder of his presidency. Almost two years later James K. Vardaman, editor of the Greenwood *Commonwealth,* insisted that the White House was "so saturated with the odor of the nigger that the rats have taken refuge in the stable." A southern minister said that Roosevelt "could never atone to the Southern people for the one act of eating with a Negro." Within a few days of the White House dinner, Democrats in

Maryland—mounting a campaign for control of the state legislature to secure the election of a white-nationalist Democratic senator—were distributing thousands of lithographs with caricatures of Washington and Roosevelt laughing while Mrs. Roosevelt poured them tea. The caption read: "It has come to this."[19]

The event entered the popular culture. Bill Arp predicted that Portia Washington, then being battered in the white-nationalist press for attending Wellesley College, would spend her school holidays at the White House and that she would soon be betrothed to one of the Roosevelt sons. Finley Peter Dunne's Mr. Dooley assessed the damage wrought by the White House dinner: "It's goin' be be th' roonation iv Prisident Tiddy's chances in th' South. Thousan's iv men who wudden't have foted f'r him undher anny circumstances has declared that under no circumstances wud they now vote f'r him . . . Onless he can get support fr'm Matsachusetts or someother State where th' people don't care anything about th' naygur exipt to dislike him, he'll be beat sure." The dinner was soon memorialized with a coon song:

> Coon, coon, coon,
> Booker Washington is his name;
> Coon, coon, coon
> Ain't that a measly shame?
> Coon, coon, coon,
> Morning, night, and noon,
> I think I'd class Mr. Roosevelt
> With a coon, coon, coon.[20]

Washington had lost control of his own image among whites. The firestorm unsettled him, but he knew that any apologetic statement would only stoke the controversy and seem cowardly. "Never since Freedom were the curses of the entire South centered upon one man for weeks as they were upon me for my dining with President Roosevelt," he wrote privately years later, but in fact he had "never uttered a word of explanation or regret." He did use surrogates to make his defense. Six weeks after the White House dinner, a columnist in the Washington *Post* wrote that Booker should go home to Alabama and attend to the business of running his school. "His dinings and winings in New England are doing no good to the black people at the South, and, if I am any judge of signs and portents, still less to himself. Washington didn't get up in the world by talking, but I begin to believe he can easily get down in that way, if, indeed, he hasn't already made the turn." The *Post* column angered Booker not only for its inaccuracies—Booker had in fact risen in the world by speaking and traveling in the North to keep Tuskegee going—but also for its terrible timing. "I wish you would go and have a frank talk with the managing editor," Booker wrote Whitefield McKinlay, his close ally in the District of Columbia. Tell him "that in no way have I changed my attitude towards the South or my actions in the North, I am simply going forward doing the work for Tuskegee in the same way that I have been doing it for twenty years and intend to make no change."[21]

But, of course, he had changed. He now staked more of his leadership efforts on getting blacks opportunities in politics. He forged ahead with the purpose that had taken him to the White House in the first place, the naming of federal appointments in the South. Both enemies and friends questioned the wisdom of his continuing political participation, but Booker calculated that the potential gains outweighed the risks. Because blacks had lost so much in the disfranchising campaigns and were suffering the relentless decline of support for black education, the patronage appointments saved a way for blacks still to participate in American democracy. Washington never said this, because doing so would have conceded too much to the hostile circumstances of the time; but such a perspective helps to explain why he continued to fill the dangerous role of political boss over the next few years. Patronage jobs offered a significant number of opportunities around the country. In addition to federal judgeships, there were federal marshals, postmasters, census takers, various collectors of federal taxes, and a multitude of appointments in Washington. By no means would all of these appointments have gone to black people or their allies, but in the absence of Booker's strong advocacy they would probably have gone only to whites selected by Lily White Republicans or even by white-nationalist senators like Ben Tillman and John Tyler Morgan.

In the months after the White House dinner, Booker advised the president on appointments all over the country. Applying the criterion of good character, Booker's investigation of the current white nominee for revenue collector in South Carolina revealed that the man had participated in a lynching; the fact disqualified him in Booker's, and finally Teddy's, eyes. He endorsed a black doctor from Missouri as minister to Liberia, an appointment that Roosevelt made and then had to rescind because of a scandal. Booker was ambivalent about a black office seeker from Mississippi because he seemed not to be "in good odor" in the Magnolia State; Booker could not ascertain the reasons, but he was unwilling to risk the consequences of ignorance. For a coveted judgeship in the nation's capital, he opposed Calvin Chase, a critic of Booker since 1895, even though Chase had the endorsement of the District's bar association. In this instance Booker told the president, in so many words, that it took a Negro to know a Negro. "It is often true, I think you will find, that white men do not have an opportunity of knowing the real character and reputation of members of our race whom they recommend." Booker's candidate got the job. To get his endorsement, a potential officeholder had to be of good character, and if he was white, he had to be fair-minded to blacks. If he was black, he needed to be an ally of—or at least not critical of—Booker Washington.[22]

Washington understood that his persistence in exercising political influence had real costs. In early 1902 William Baldwin warned him that southerners in Congress were "mightily disturbed on account of your connection with appointments in the South." The *Constitution* warned that any false step by Washington would undermine his standing as an educator. "It is up to Booker Washington to elect whether he will be a negro political boss and so lose the respect and support of the heretofore friendly white leaders of the south, or whether he will be true to his promise to let politics alone and continue on as the truest and safest Moses his people have ever known in their emancipated condition." This pronouncement made Booker worry about the potential effect on the Institute. "I wish you would watch very carefully the tone of the Southern press," he asked his secretary Emmett Scott in June 1902, "and in fact the press of the whole country for that matter, in connection with Mr. Roosevelt and colored office holders." He wanted to help Roosevelt and "the race if I can, but at the same time I must be careful not to injure our institution." Scott and others advised that he should leave the impression that he made recommendations only when asked by the president. The ruse did not generally work. Booker was managing Republican politics in several states, and his friends and enemies alike tended to believe that he was even more powerful than he actually was. In the end, Washington accepted the risk that his political activity might hurt the school.[23]

His resolve was tested in the summer and fall of 1902, when the Lily Whites in several states, capitalizing on the disfranchisement of black voters, tried to remove all blacks from power within the Republican Party. In Alabama, William Vaughan, the Hanna-appointed U.S. attorney who headed the state Republicans, instituted a rule that only registered voters could serve on the state committee—this in the aftermath of the near-total disfranchisement of blacks by the new constitution. "The complete throwing down of the few decent, property-holding Negroes," Booker wrote to the president, "just the class that you wanted to have come to the front—by the Republican leaders in Alabama, is a thing that I hope you will rebuke in no uncertain manner." Aside from the moral wrong, he warned, "the effect on the Negro voters in the North will be serious if not checked." Washington was telling him that to earn the favor of black voters in the North, he would need to deal harshly with some Lily Whites in the South. Roosevelt fired Vaughan. Booker put forward his Tuskegee neighbor, Joseph Thompson, whose Democratic brother was the local congressman but who was himself a sincere Republican known to listen eagerly to the principal of Tuskegee. Booker found two other whites, one of them a former Democrat, to stand with young Jody Thompson. Roosevelt turned patronage over to the three white men—with the clear understanding that nothing important would be decided without consulting Booker.[24]

To challenge the Lily Whites in Mississippi, Booker located a white Democrat, Edgar S. Wilson, to be patronage chief. Though connected by experience and family to entrenched power—his brother-in-law was the Democratic governor—Wilson proved to be just as wily, determined, and loyal as Washington to the cause of fair patronage—and rewarding one's friends. Wilson stopped the removal of black office-holders and got a few new appointments. Just as important, Wilson liked to operate in secret, obscuring both his and Booker's manipulation of who got what in Mississippi.[25]

The apparent defeat of Mississippi's Lily Whites set the stage for a political controversy in the little town of Indianola in the Delta. There a well-to-do, light-skinned, middle-aged black woman named Minnie Cox had been the postmistress since the Harrison administration. She had experienced no problems; the white Indianolans were apparently entirely satisfied with her service. Then James K. Vardaman rode the twenty miles over from Greenwood. He was preparing to run again in 1903 for governor of Mississippi, and he had already found the message that he believed would propel him to power. In his newspaper, Vardaman had been blistering Theodore Roosevelt without pause since the White House dinner, never missing an opportunity to lambaste the president for appointing blacks and Republican-friendly Democrats. He called Roosevelt the "coon-flavored miscegenationist in the White House," and when he learned that the president was coming to Mississippi for recreation, Vardaman ran an advertisement in his newspaper: "Wanted sixteen 'coons' to sleep with Roosevelt when he comes down to go bear hunting." In Indianola he excoriated the white citizens for tolerating a "nigger wench" as postmistress. Rather than stand against the "azure boweled bigots" of the Roosevelt administration, Vardaman railed at his neighbors, they had suffered taking their mail "from the hands of a coon." Mississippians were *not going to let niggers hold office.*" Mrs. Cox soon resigned her office and moved to Alabama. Amazed at the events, Roosevelt closed the Indianola post office.[26]

Roosevelt had got the message about demonstrating his worthiness to black voters. He, or someone in his administration, apparently released to newspapers Washington's recommendation letter for Thomas Goode Jones, in which he recounted to Roosevelt Jones's problack positions in the constitutional convention. The clear implication of Washington's letter was that those positions made Jones suitable to him and

Roosevelt, and the president wanted the credit for it. The letter did earn Roosevelt kudos among black voters, but he apparently did not consider that its publication represented real jeopardy to Washington. It sent hostility toward Booker soaring once again. Rather than maintain the public silence he had adopted after the White House dinner, Washington responded publicly. He issued a statement to newspapers that he did not promote candidates or volunteer information regarding men or measures—a claim that would not stand up under any scrutiny, because that was what the Jones letter had done. But the motives he gave for advising the president were honest. His involvement in politics was not for the sake of power but purely to advance the progress of his people: "We cannot elevate and make useful a race of people unless there is held out to them the hope of reward for right living."[27]

Roosevelt's boldest assertion of his support for black political power came with his November appointment of William Crum, a black physician, to be revenue collector for the Port of Charleston. Crum had been Booker's choice and apparently an easy decision for Roosevelt. But white Charlestonians, who until then had regarded him highly, responded hysterically to a black man's receiving a position of such high prestige and pay. Crum's appointment drove the Charleston elite into alliance with their long-standing enemy, Senator Tillman, who still resented the doctor's candidacy against Pitchfork Ben in the 1894 U.S. Senate race. "We still have guns and ropes in the South," Tillman warned, "and if the policy of appointing the Negro to office is insisted upon, we know how to use them." The violence of Tillman's imagination seemed to know no bounds. Southern newspapers echoed his anger, with many of them seeing—quite correctly—the secret hand of Booker Washington in the appointment. Even the New York *Times* asserted that Teddy was asking for trouble. On the other hand, the appointment won Roosevelt the desired praise from blacks in the North, who saw it as a test of the president's mettle. Both Roosevelt and Washington stood firm and hoped the furor would expire.[28]

At this moment, in the late fall of 1902, Congressman Edgar Crumpacker reintroduced his proposal to reduce congressional representation in the disfranchising southern states. Coming at the height of the Crum and Cox controversies, the revival of Crumpackerism further stoked the rage of southern editors. Roosevelt and the Republicans "WILL WAGE WAR ON THE SOUTH!" screamed the Montgomery *Advertiser* about the Crumpacker measure. War was exactly what it must have felt like to Booker Washington, and it was one over which he had little control, try as he might.[29]

The Crum nomination fueled Ben Tillman's determination to spread far and wide the white-nationalist appeal delivered in his lecture-hall harangue, "The Race Problem from the Southern Perspective." To a large audience in Detroit in early 1903, he shouted that Roosevelt's appointments policies meant that "more blood will flow than was shed in the civil war if you persist in trying to subject us to the domination of the blacks." His speech elicited both cheers and hisses. "Had it been known by the soldiers who surrendered with Lee that it was your devilish intent to set up the negro over the white man we would have fought you till now," he insisted. Tillman told the New York Press Club that whites would resort to the shotgun and tissue ballots they had used during Reconstruction to maintain their control, because a free vote and fair count would mean "perpetual servitude to a race of baboon men." In several long speeches on the Senate floor in February 1903, Tillman asserted that Roosevelt's courting of a few black voters in the North was dictating racial policies for fifty million white Americans. He taunted the Republicans for their hypocrisy in not imposing Negro equality everywhere. Blacks composed one-ninth of the nation's population and therefore deserved one of the nine cabinet seats. "I would vote to confirm Booker Washington as secretary of anything," he sneered at his northern colleagues. Why didn't they make blacks officers in the army and the navy and give blacks their share of all the good jobs in the economy? "You do not intend to do it; you could not do it; your people would not submit to it."[30]

The attacks became so vitriolic that Crum wanted to withdraw, and Booker had to work hard to bolster his courage. As the condemnations rained on him, Roosevelt asked Booker again for confirmation of Crum's worthiness. He had examined Crum's character thoroughly,

Booker reported, and was convinced of his uprightness. Booker sensed that Roosevelt regretted the Crum appointment, and so he bucked up the president. "You have increased the quality of Negro officials in the South and reduced the quantity," he wrote Roosevelt. "This fact I am getting into the ears of the people North and South." Booker sent word to the White House through a confidant that there was no alternative to fighting it out. Washington surely agreed with another black Republican ally that "if a man like Crum gets out of the way, it means that the idea of Tillman will prevail, and it would take us 20 years to overcome it." In March 1903 Roosevelt sent the Crum nomination forward. Tillman invoked senatorial courtesy to stop it, and his influence largely blocked its approval. Roosevelt then made a recess appointment of Crum, who was breaking physically and would have withdrawn if Washington had let him off the hook.[31]

All the while, Washington's white advisers were expressing misgivings about the Crum matter, each claiming that it was causing more antagonism among white southerners than the appointment was worth. Edgar Gardner Murphy wrote to Booker that every white friend of the Negro was on the defensive, unable to act positively, because there was more antagonism to blacks than he had ever seen. Many whites "absurdly believe that the President means to put Negroes into office practically everywhere through the South, and many believe, unjustly but sincerely, that this purpose is the reflection of your influence." The priest went to see Roosevelt and asked him to withdraw Crum's nomination. William Baldwin opined that the appointment was unwise, an indication that Roosevelt failed to see the continuing impact of the White House dinner. Roosevelt was an arrogantly naïve "sophomore," Baldwin said, warning Booker to beware of the president's weaknesses. Booker did not heed the caution; he saw Roosevelt as the one white man standing firm for black political rights. Robert Ogden hinted broadly that Booker should get Crum to withdraw. Washington answered that if he pushed Crum out, "the whole responsibility would be placed directly upon me." Booker could imagine the loud condemnations from Boston should he capitulate to the white South. "The feeling of the colored people throughout the coun-

try," he said, was that defeat on Crum meant "the end of colored people holding office in the South." The feeling of the colored people was
in fact the feeling of Booker Washington. Without explicitly contra-
dicting him, Booker let Ogden know that he was standing firm on
Crum.[32]

As the Crum controversy was building in January 1903, Roosevelt
appointed William H. Lewis assistant U.S. attorney for Boston, the
highest position a black had ever held in the federal government. The
action prompted the *Constitution* headline "'Coon' Is Put on Boston by
President Roosevelt." Previously the sharpest critic of Washington in
Boston, Lewis had reached an accommodation with him soon after
Roosevelt became president. Both men realized that to retain their influence with Roosevelt they would have to get along with each other.
Although he was the beneficiary of an elite education, Lewis had been
born into humble circumstances in Virginia quite similar to Booker's,
and the two men soon became firm allies. Booker welcomed the appointment as a signal achievement for blacks. But it did fuel the opposition to his and Roosevelt's appointments plans, and they had by no
means heard the last of Tillman and Vardaman.[33]

The furor over the White House dinner and the growing criticism of
his influence over political patronage during 1902 meant that Booker
could not afford for anyone, black or white, to know that he was behind a challenge to disfranchisement. In early 1902 Washington and
Wilford Smith, a Texas lawyer, discussed bringing a case against the
new Alabama constitution. At exactly the same time, a group of post-
office employees in Montgomery, literate men with jobs that could not
be taken from them for participation in a civil-rights lawsuit, formed
the Colored Men's Suffrage Association. They came up with $200 to
finance a case and a plaintiff, Jackson Giles, a postal worker and member of the Suffrage Association. When informed of the group's existence, Wilford Smith volunteered his services to it without its knowledge that Booker was paying his fees. All communications between
Washington and Smith passed in code through Emmett Scott, and
there was no direct contact between the Tuskegeeans and the Suffrage

Association. Starting in May 1902, Smith filed five lawsuits, all with Jackson Giles as the plaintiff. His goal in all the cases was to reach the U.S. Supreme Court to get a judgment on whether the new constitution violated the Fourteenth and Fifteenth Amendments. Smith believed that the high court had yet to rule on the substance of whether southern disfranchising laws violated the Reconstruction amendments. Even in *Mississippi v. Williams,* the 1898 case upholding Mississippi's 1890 constitution, the Court had found for the state on procedural not substantive grounds.

From 1902 into 1904, the *Giles* cases became a testament to the persistence of Wilford Smith, Jackson Giles, and Booker Washington to show that blacks were wronged in the Alabama constitution. Because the new constitution provided an appeals remedy in state courts, Smith started the first four cases there, and in each instance the courts found procedural reasons to stop the case. In the first hearing, in the Montgomery circuit court, Smith was threatened and might have been attacked but for the protection of a local judge, William Thomas, who learned of a plot and stopped it. Anxious to settle the issue as soon as possible by getting to the U.S. Supreme Court, Smith filed a fifth and final case in the federal courtroom of Thomas Goode Jones. Here was the payoff for Washington's sponsorship of Jones. Smith argued that the 1901 constitution had been enacted to disfranchise blacks and blacks alone, and he attached an extensive set of newspaper articles, convention speeches, and statistics that proved that purpose. But there was still the jurisdictional obstacle that state law provided a state appeals remedy. The state's lawyers argued that Giles had hardly exhausted his state remedy. But Judge Jones ignored their pleading even as he denied Giles relief. When Smith declared that he was appealing the judge's ruling, Jones invoked a federal procedure that allowed a trial judge to request an immediate opinion on a jurisdictional issue from the U.S. Supreme Court, and the fifth *Giles* case duly went to Washington. Here was the milk in the coconut of the Jones appointment: he got the Negroes where they wanted to go, but he did so with the kind of indirection that safely obscured his real purpose. The judge was the kindred spirit of the principal of Tuskegee.[34]

The Warring Ideals

Booker Washington's engagement with politics provoked intensified opposition from a small group of blacks in the North. The more widely known Washington had become since 1895, the firmer had grown the resolve of his black northern critics that he was the wrong man to lead the race. A group of Massachusetts men, several of them Harvard graduates, had always rejected his leadership, especially his message of conciliation with whites. The strongest denunciations had coincided with the worst atrocities in the South: the Wilmington riot, the Sam Hose lynching, the passage of disfranchising constitutions. The White House dinner, which made him look more powerful than anyone else of his race, elicited vitriol from the weekly Boston *Guardian,* founded in 1901 by William Monroe Trotter, a Harvard graduate and son of a Civil War soldier. Trotter had enjoyed a privileged upbringing in the relatively enlightened racial environment of Boston, and he looked down on blacks who had attended industrial schools in the South. Like most black Americans, he was alarmed at the decline of black rights in the 1890s—even in Boston, which was beginning to witness discrimination in some public accommodations. The *Guardian* immediately found an avid readership among Booker's Boston enemies and among whites curious about the conflict.[1]

38. William Monroe Trotter founded the Boston *Guardian* in 1901 and made Booker Washington the main object of its reporting and editorials, including its cartoons. Photographer unknown; from *Voice of the Negro* 2 (October 1906).

The *Guardian* ridiculed Washington in every issue from its inception. Among the epithets applied were "Pope Washington," "the Black Boss," "the Benedict Arnold of the Negro race," "the Exploiter of all Exploiters," "the Great Traitor," "the Great Divider," "the miserable toady," "the Imperial Caesar," and "the Heartless and snobbish purveyor of Pharisaical moral clap-trap." A *Guardian* reporter described his features as monstrous: "Harsh in the extreme," marked by "vast leonine jaws into which vast mastiff-like rows of teeth were set clinched together like a vice." His forehead was "a great cone," his chin "massive and square," his eyes "dull and absolutely characterless, and with a glance that would leave you uneasy and restless during the night if you had failed to report to the police such a man around before you went to bed." The monster was in the eye of the beholder, for the many contemporary photographs of Booker presented an entirely different physical impression. The paper's cartoonist drew Booker with big lips and beady eyes, in exactly the manner southern papers were doing at the time, and captioned it "Grave Digger Washington A Busy Man," burying equality and voting rights. Next it depicted him as a witch boiling a black child tagged "Negroes' Rights." Then the cartoonist grouped Booker with William Hooper Councill and William Hannibal Thomas as three traitors in hell. Soon Booker was drawn as Janus-faced: "The Facile and Fluent Orator is Everything to Everybody."[2]

The *Guardian*'s brief against Washington was long. Trotter accused him of belittling blacks and of publicly exaggerating their shortcomings to curry white favor. "Is there anyone then so selfish as not to know why the white people of this country call Booker Washington great? Can not every intelligent colored man see that the booming of this one man for the ideas which he holds is the undoing of the Negro personally and politically?" In 1902 and 1903 the *Guardian* flogged Washington relentlessly for saying that the disfranchising constitutions put a premium on blacks' acquiring education and property and demonstrating good character, citing a statement Washington made in re-

39. Cartoons revealed the Boston *Guardian*'s intense opposition to Booker Washington. The caption here reads: "Auntie Booker has too many irons in the fire; some of them are bound to burn up." Artist unknown; from the *Guardian*, November 1, 1902.

sponse to white attacks on his patronage activities. The *Guardian* interpreted the statement as an endorsement of disfranchisement, a misreading characteristic of its treatment. It claimed that Booker was assisting the Lily Whites in putting white men in office in the South and taking blacks out. In the midst of the Crum and Indianola post-office controversies, when white anger about Washington's patronage influence was peaking, the *Guardian* ran an editorial saying that Washington was "more interested in placing men in office (white men we mean) than he was in managing his school." An accompanying cartoon portrayed him as "Auntie Booker," a woman with too many irons in the fire. A few weeks later the paper drew Booker drowning in a sea of politics, with the caption "Parson Washington Getting in Too Deep Water—South Resents His Political Activity."[3]

Any friend of Booker Washington's was an enemy to Trotter. The *Guardian* accused Washington of co-opting the support of young black men educated at Harvard and other elite schools. He referred to men like Roscoe Conkling Bruce, son of Senator Blanche K. Bruce and a Harvard graduate, whom Booker hired as his academic dean at Tuskegee and whom he sent north to recruit teachers from Harvard and other elite liberal-arts schools. Its cartoonist portrayed Booker as the devil, tempting Bruce with money and status at Tuskegee and saying: "All these things I will give thee if thou will fall down and worship me as the only 'it.'" The *Guardian* made Tim Fortune the object of almost as much ridicule as Booker, and William Baldwin was excoriated more than any other white man except Theodore Roosevelt.[4]

Even Booker's family was fair game. The *Guardian* reported gleefully that Portia Washington, now eighteen years old, had been forced to withdraw from Wellesley College and that Booker Jr., age sixteen, was struggling academically at a Boston-area prep school. "These children of Mr. Washington are not taking to the higher education like a duck to water, and while their defect in this line is doubtless somewhat inherited, they justify to some extent their father's well known antipathy to anything higher than the three Rs for his people." The attacks on his children infuriated Booker, and he did answer the aspersions cast on Portia. The damage was done, however. Most southern newspapers reported the story just as Trotter had: Booker Washington's daughter was pretentious enough—and her father hypocritical enough—to seek an elite liberal-arts education but not smart enough to succeed at it.[5]

The relentless attacks hurt Washington's standing, though not nearly so much as Trotter intended. A New Haven minister reported that whites thought Trotter's attitude was typical of blacks in New England and asked Booker to visit to show that he had support in Connecticut. A black man from near Boston wrote to Emmett Scott that although he admired the Tuskegee educational work, "we cannot follow his lead when he counsels 'nolo contendere' in the matter of manhood and citizenship rights." Nor could he "admire, agree with, or respect his position of *passive surrender* of all rights in order to win them." Neither came close to a fair characterization of Washington's public stances, but they accurately reflected what Trotter said they were.[6]

Washington's white admirers were shaken by the attack on him. A Boston man had tried to reason with Trotter's followers, telling them that they needed perspective on why Washington said what he did and that Booker had a larger, long-term vision. But it was to no avail, the man reported. "I was astounded at this discovery that you were without honor among your own people." Washington answered that had he grown up in the North as they had, he might have felt the same way. If he had been "schooled in the high schools and colleges of that section, with no opportunity of coming into contact with the real problem of the race, I might share their sentiments." But the fact was they knew little about southern blacks, and "with no opportunity for doing effective work in their behalf," the Trotter group could not "in any appreciable degree touch or influence the real heart of the people."[7]

When Tim Fortune and Emmett Scott took firm control of the Afro-American Council in 1902, Calvin Chase of the Washington *Bee* reported that Washington's allies "trotted and pranced just as he pulled the reins and his ticket was elected and his namby-pamby policy was incorporated into the address, which was nothing more than a pronouncement of his Nibs, the boss of Negro beggars." Trotter condemned Fortune as a "me too" to Booker: "These two men have long since formed themselves into one twain in their dealing with the Negro race, Fortune furnishing whatever brain the combination needs and Washington the boodle." Trotter attempted to gather all potential anti-Washington forces. "We might have expected Prof. Du Bois to have stood in the breach here," he wrote, "but like all the others who are trying to get into the band wagon of the Tuskegeean, he is no longer to be relied upon." At the time Du Bois was maintaining a relationship with Washington, despite the negative appraisal of his leadership in his review of *Up from Slavery*. Washington was still providing financial support for Du Bois's discrimination suit against the Pullman Company. In early 1903 Washington wrote to Robert Lincoln about the recent mistreatment of a young black man on a Pullman car: "It does seem to me that a rich and powerful corporation like yours could find some way to extend in some degree, protection to the weak." As he had been doing for years, Lincoln ignored the injustice against Du Bois and every other black person. In late 1902 Washington discussed with Du Bois a possible conference to negotiate a truce with his critics. Du Bois set an agenda for such a meeting, but it never took place, because by early 1903 Du Bois was clearly planning his own final break with Washington.[8]

Washington felt that other blacks should stand with him in the fundamental competition with southern whites, and when they opposed him—and, in his view, gave comfort to the enemy—he fought back tenaciously and sometimes ruthlessly. Booker's allies warmed to the fight. "If the agitators of the antis have grown bolder," a supporter in the District of Columbia reported to Emmett Scott, "the supporters of Dr. Washington have grown correspondingly more aggressive." Booker instructed his allies to pressure black newspapers to ignore Trotter. He tried to counteract Trotter by supporting the establishment of rival black newspapers in Boston. In 1902 and 1903 he partly funded three papers, each of which failed. For all its one-sidedness, the *Guardian* was established and represented the feelings of an influential portion of northern blacks. In the end, Booker could only seethe about the assassination of his character by men who he believed did not know him or understand the obstacles he faced in the South. He had the wherewithal to defeat the Bostonians in direct competition over who should lead the race, but he could not make Trotter and his allies see that their sniping undercut him in the more important conflict with whites in the South. Indeed, their opposition to Booker echoed more and more what the white-nationalist leaders in the South were saying. Booker smoldered about how his northern critics missed the irony of that convergence.[9]

The fallout from Washington's political activities littered the South in 1903. The Louisiana State Federation of Women's Clubs withdrew an invitation to Booker to speak on his educational work. "I need not tell you," its president explained, "that the course of President Roosevelt has changed very materially the color of things throughout the South." The irony of the Louisianan's perception of changing color in the South was probably unintended, but any such withdrawal of white support worried Booker. Questions about social equality still dogged him, as was evident in June after a white chambermaid refused to make Booker's bed while he was a guest at an Indianapolis hotel. When the hotel fired her, Lulu Hadley released a statement that ran widely in newspapers. "I admire Booker T. Washington in his place," Hadley declared, "but unfortunately he is out of it most of the time." Washington was a national celebrity, she said, and he never failed to take advantage of it. "He seeks the most aristocratic and seclusive [sic] company of the white people, and what arouses my indignation is the fact that some of the members of my own race seem glad of the opportunity to welcome him into their homes." She was, of course, referring to President Roosevelt, who had "lowered himself and his country" and should be impeached. Lulu was on her way to the South, where "the negro knows his place, and he keeps it," and whence came money rewarding her for her stand.[10]

Even whites who spoke kindly of Washington were subject to condemnation. In the summer of 1903 a young history professor at Trinity College in North Carolina wrote an essay titled "Stirring Up the Fires of Race Antipathy" for *South Atlantic Quarterly*. John Spencer Bassett had probably heard Washington speak at Trinity in 1896 and had clearly followed Booker's subsequent career with admiration, because he used the article to condemn the political demagogues who had been exploiting the White House dinner for the past two years. The professor wrote that Washington "is a great and good man, a Christian statesman, and take him all in all the greatest man, save General Lee, born in the South in a hundred years." The comparison sparked hysteria at the Raleigh *News and Observer,* where the white-nationalist editor Jonathan Daniels denounced the professor and began publishing his name as "bASSett." Angry whites all over the Tarheel State demanded Bassett's firing, and only the determination of the college's president and of its chief benefactor, Benjamin Duke, kept it from happening, though the historian soon decamped to New England. Bassett shared the fate of George Washington Cable, in being exiled from the South for speaking the truth about its human relations.[11]

Bassett might have predicted the outrage from what had happened the previous year at Emory College in Georgia. There a young classics professor and Methodist minister, Andrew Sledd, had published an article in the *Atlantic Monthly* in which he denounced the mistreatment of blacks in the South, especially lynching but also the many indignities of discrimination in public accommodations. He decried white southerners' "vicious idea of the inequality of the races in the fundamental rights of human creatures." The son-in-law of Bishop Warren Candler of the Methodist Church, who was also a former president of Emory, Sledd was a popular teacher at the college, in part because he coached the football team. Little note was taken of the article when it first appeared. But then Georgia's white-nationalist firebrand Rebecca Felton discovered it and went to work. "Pass him on!" she said about Sledd. "Keep him moving! He does not belong in this part of the country. It is bad enough to be taxed to death to educate negroes and defend one's home from criminal assault . . . but it is simply atrocious to fatten or feed a creature who stoops to the defamation of the southern people only to find access to liberal checks in a partisan magazine." Sledd soon resigned, and the Emory board of trustees quickly accepted his action, notwithstanding the opposition of Emory students and Sledd's powerful father-in-law.[12]

Booker Washington admired Sledd and Bassett and chose to view their courageous statements as signs of progress among southern white men. He was not, however, surprised at what happened to them, for he knew all too well the costs of speaking the truth about race in the

South. He had paid it already, and in due course he would pay a lot more.[13]

At the height of the Crum controversy, as the Boston *Guardian's* drumbeat against him got progressively louder, Washington still worried about the decline of black schools. School boards in most southern states had escalated the practice of discriminating in the funding of black schools. The average white child in the South had at least three times as much spent on him as the typical black child, and in the Black Belts of South Carolina, Georgia, Alabama, Mississippi, and Louisiana the ratios were usually much higher—and the discrepancy was increasing all the time. Southern states typically did not provide money for school buildings for black children, and therefore most rural black education took place in ramshackle frame structures, often old churches. The pittance provided for teachers made it difficult for schools to stay open more than a few months. In 1903, as he became more and more alarmed, Booker pleaded with Oswald Garrison Villard, publisher of the New York *Evening Post* and the *Nation* magazine, to send a reporter to the South to investigate the beggaring of black education. A grandson of William Lloyd Garrison, Villard was the one white publisher willing to investigate southern racial practices. Booker told him about the black teacher who was being paid $7.50 per month to maintain a school for 200 children for five months. A while later he wrote him about Lafayette Parish, Louisiana, where there was only one school to serve 11,000 blacks. Villard dispatched reporters to write about lynching and peonage, but he showed little interest in the school-funding matter. Washington discovered that, fundamental as education discrimination was, it did not stir whites' consciences.[14]

Nor did the northern public realize the continuing insecurity of black schools and teachers in the South. This reality was dramatized in late 1902 by the destruction of one of the many schools established by Tuskegee students. Booker's keen sense of modern mass communications led him to engage the services of a professional photographer, Frances Benjamin Johnston, of Washington, D.C., to make a visual record of life on the Tuskegee campus, which the school would use in promotional efforts. When that work was done, Booker sent Johnston to make photographs of some of the little Tuskegees. She traveled by train to the Ramer Colored Industrial School, ten miles south of Montgomery, where late one evening she was met by George Washington Carver and Nelson Henry, the Ramer school's founder and principal for the past six years. As Henry drove the attractive young Johnston from the station toward his house, they were accosted by a group of white men who drew the conclusion that Henry had breached racial etiquette and shot at the couple three times. Henry fled Ramer as white patrols declared their intention of beating him to death. Carver walked all night to get away. Somehow Johnston escaped on a train. An investigation by the governor of Alabama concluded that the incident was the work of a few hotheads, not the sentiment of all whites. But Henry was unwilling to risk a return to Ramer, notwithstanding the years invested there. Blacks in Ramer had advised him not to come back. The school closed, suffering a fate similar to that of the Colored University in Marion in 1886, except white hysteria killed the Ramer school once and for all. It was an object lesson for every black principal and teacher in the South at the time.[15]

The insecurity of black education—and its spokesmen—was further imposed on Booker's consciousness a few weeks later, when William Sheats, Florida's superintendent of education, invited him to speak to a large gathering of white school officials in Gainesville. Sheats had a reputation as a Negro hater, but he had hired Tuskegee students, obtained backing from the General Education Board to promote better schools in Florida, and apparently overcome some of his old prejudices. At the same time, a group of Gainesville blacks asked Booker for his advice about building an industrial school. He had every reason to go to Florida, except for the intense hostility that his name elicited from white Floridians in January 1903. In the aftermath of the White House dinner and the Crum appointment, one newspaper had declared that there had never "lived (and please God there never will) a white man so low in the social world but he was ten times better than the most respectable negro." In response, Gainesville officials withdrew their offer of hospitality to Washington, and the local school superintendent, a political rival of Sheats, denounced the prospect of Washington's presence on the grounds that Booker stood for "social equality inconsistent with the ideas, customs and institutions of the South." Sheats insisted that Booker would be protected. Booker dispatched his white ghostwriter, Max Thrasher, to check out the situation, and was advised that it would probably be safe to go. On the way to Gainesville, his train stopped in a village where a local white farmer, apparently none too prosperous, asked to meet Washington. "Say, you are a great man," the farmer told Washington as they shook hands. "You are the greatest man in this country!" Trying to douse the adulation with a splash of modesty, Booker answered that he believed the greatest man in the country was the president, to which the farmer answered with even more excitement: "Huh! Roosevelt! I used to think that Roosevelt was a great man until he ate dinner with you. That settled him for me."[16]

In Gainesville Booker held 2,000 people, equally divided racially, in thrall for two hours. The performance led a black critic of Washington to marvel at the masterly way he handled "those Negro-hating 'crackers.'" Booker said that blacks and whites were "bound together in a way that we cannot tear ourselves asunder," and "as one race is lifted up and made more intelligent useful and honest . . . are both races strengthened." Blacks were humble, patient, and law-abiding; when wrongs were done to them, they responded not with violence but with prayers, spirituals, and faith that justice would prevail. "I do not believe, I cannot believe, that the Negro will ever appeal to the Southern white man in vain." Afterward Booker interpreted the invitation and the peaceful reception as signs of acceptance of his philosophy and influence. The visit took its toll on Sheats, however, who under Booker's influence became an advocate for longer school terms for black children and higher pay for black teachers. In 1904 he lost his race for reelection as state superintendent to the Gainesville school administrator who had opposed Booker's appearance and who during the campaign flogged Sheats about his coziness with the infamous Washington.[17]

In the climate of 1903, even nominally good things for black education were turned against the cause. In April a large meeting was held in New York to celebrate and benefit Tuskegee. This affair marked the apogee of William Baldwin's fundraising effort for the Tuskegee endowment. Former president Grover Cleveland's opening remarks overshadowed the larger purpose of the meeting. Among blacks, Cleveland said, "there is still a grievous amount of ignorance, a sad amount of viciousness, and a tremendous amount of laziness and thriftlessness," all of which meant that the white South was owed utmost sympathy for tolerating "the humiliation and spoliation of the white men of the South during the saturnalia of reconstruction" and for remaining kindly toward blacks even while "deluged by the perilous flood of indiscriminate, unintelligent, and blighting negro suffrage." Northerners needed both to be considerate of southern whites, who "stagger under the weight of the white man's burden," and to support the one Negro, Booker Washington, who could find a solution to "the vexatious negro problem of the South." If the burden of Grover Cleveland's racist views was not enough to stagger Booker, the editor Lyman Abbott piled on more. "We have tried the experiment of giving to the negro suffrage first and education afterward and bitterly has the country suffered from our blunder." Abbott extracted a moral: "No man ever should receive the power to control other men until he is able to exercise such control." Apparently it never occurred to Abbott to apply the same commandment to whites.[18]

Cleveland and Abbott were all too typical of Tuskegee's white friends in the way they adumbrated a huge, complex problem and then reduced the solution to one man's work. This odd form of support invited, even demanded, a popular perception of the Negro Problem as "vicious" and "vexatious" and a simplistic location of its solution in Booker Washington. It is scarcely surprising that his enemies, black and white, were able to focus so many wrongs on him, given that Booker's own friends laid upon him all responsibility for righting the situation.

Two days later the steel magnate Andrew Carnegie gave Tuskegee Institute $600,000 in U.S. Steel bonds, and he designated $150,000 of it for the personal benefit of Washington. He wanted Booker to be able to devote himself entirely to managing Tuskegee and uplifting the race. History knew two Washingtons, Carnegie said, one white, the other black, both the fathers of their people. "I am satisfied that the serious race question of the South is to be solved wisely, only by follow-

ing Booker Washington's policy which he seems to have [been] spe-
cially born—a slave among slaves—to establish."[19] At least with
Carnegie, the burden imposed on Booker by a white man came with
some compensation. The gift more than doubled the Tuskegee endowment and relieved some of the fundraising pressure on Washington.

To avoid controversy in the South, Carnegie's intention that so much
money go personally to Booker was not at first made public, but in the
current atmosphere of white suspicion, envy was inevitable. Bill Arp
suggested that, given Booker's faith in the toothbrush as an instrument
of racial uplift, the entire amount should go to dental care: "Anything
to get rid of the money that keeps on piling up" for black education.
Southern newspapers condemned the Carnegie gift as interference by
northern philanthropy into southern race relations: it made blacks
dangerously independent of white control. The Washington *Post* published a letter from a Montgomery lawyer condemning Carnegie for
giving a huge sum "for the benefit of this shrewd darkey and his alleged beneficial Tuskegee propaganda." Students learned best by example, Gordon McDonald declared, and "Booker the Crafty" was setting a disastrous one for young Negroes by hobnobbing with the
president on terms of social equality, getting spoiled as the petted guest
of rich northerners in their homes, and sending his daughter to a fash-
ionable school for white girls. Such behavior taught that social equality
was possible, indeed near. The thrust that no doubt cut deepest in
Booker was that "for one genuine hardworking husbandman or arti-
san sent into the world by Washington's school, it afflicts this State
with twenty soft-handed Negro dudes and loafers, who earn a precarious living by 'craps' and petit larceny or live on the hard-earned wages
of cooks and washwomen, whose affections they have been enabled to
ensnare." McDonald admitted that William Paterson, Booker's longtime enemy at the Colored University in Montgomery, had shaped his
views and that he had never in fact been to Tuskegee. But the damage
had been done in a widely read national newspaper.[20]

The Boston *Guardian's* anger at the Carnegie gift surpassed even
that of Paterson and his cat's-paw. "Are we not justified in assuming
that Mr. Washington, with his school endowed, has no further need to
travel up and down the country to talk on the Negro question?" Trot-

ter asked. "If this is true, every Negro in America is to be congratu-
lated." The next question was: "Did ever the white south have a better
representative for its side than Washington?" A cartoon showed a
"Temple of Negro Liberty" being torn down by Grover Cleveland,
Lyman Abbott, and William Baldwin and its material being used to
build Tuskegee, with the caption "It's at the Negro's Expense, After
All, That Tuskegee is Built." The next issue's cartoon depicted
Tuskegee as the road to slavery and "college"—meaning liberal-arts
institutions—as the road to "Justice" and "Equal Rights," and the
Guardian heralded an anti-Washington speech as "Thoughtful Bostonian Shows the Evil of the Wizard's Teachings." An admiring writer
had once labeled Washington the "Wizard of Tuskegee." Trotter now
appropriated it to suggest sneaky, underhanded methods. "One would
naturally suppose that when a Negro got $1,000,000 for his school
work, especially with a life provision for himself and family thrown in,
he would let up in his attacks on his race's rights. The reverse, however, seems to be true of the 'wizard' of Tuskegee." In June the *Guardian* declared that "Tuskegee has proved the most deadly enemy of Negro liberty, more deadly than the south itself, because it comes in the
guise of a friend."[21]

The bellicose opposition of the *Guardian* was one kind of threat,
representing the long-standing antagonism of some educated, middle-
class New England blacks who refused to acknowledge the constraints
imposed on southern blacks. But the full-scale resistance of Burghardt
Du Bois to Washington's leadership was something quite different. In
early 1903 Du Bois declined a position as Tuskegee's research director
for Negro life, although curiously he agreed to teach at Tuskegee in
the summer of 1903. But by then he had clearly rejected Washington's
racial leadership, a move that no one could miss knowing after *The
Souls of Black Folk* appeared in April 1903. It was a collection of fifteen
pieces, most of them essays previously published. The writing contained lyrical passages about black rural life and several observations
that have since shaped thinking about the African-American experience. For instance, he wrote that "the problem of the Twentieth Century is the problem of the color line," a prophetic statement about the
centrality of race in American life that certainly proved to be accurate.

He described a veil behind which all black life was lived, an enforced separation that marked blacks with inferiority but gave space for separate cultural development. He identified the double consciousness of the African American: "One ever feels his twoness,—an American, a Negro; two souls, two thoughts, two unreconciled strivings; two warring ideals in one dark body, whose dogged strength alone keeps it from being torn asunder." Other nineteenth-century black writers had explored this bifurcated identity, and Booker Washington had acted upon a dual racial awareness throughout his life; but Du Bois expressed the idea more elegantly and passionately than anyone else had. Remarkably for the social-science scholar who had done the most distinguished empirical studies of black life to that time, Du Bois in *Souls* adopted a romantic viewpoint in describing the Christ-like selflessness of African Americans. Negro blood had a "message for the world" that soared above the stale preoccupations of white Americans. "We black men seem the sole oasis of simple faith and reverence in a dusty desert of dollars and smartness." Du Bois's racial essentialism would inspire several generations of black nationalists.[22]

In 1903, however, his racial mysticism meant less than his sharp critique in the essay "Of Mr. Booker T. Washington and Others." In this expansion of his review of *Up from Slavery,* Du Bois declared Washington a black leader chosen by whites, having won their favor with his 1895 speech, which Du Bois dubbed "the Atlanta Compromise," because Washington allegedly had surrendered civil and political rights for economic opportunities. "The Atlanta Compromise" would prove to be one of the most enduring pejoratives ever coined in American letters. All white southerners liked Booker and his message, Du Bois insisted, calling him the most distinguished southerner since Jefferson Davis. The comparison to Davis was a not-so-sly jab: Du Bois had earlier called the Confederate president a morally obtuse Teutonic character. Washington's humble approach made few demands on behalf of blacks, and the white response, Du Bois suggested, was "if that is all you and your race ask, take it." Washington's program "practically accepts the alleged inferiority of the Negro races," including the denial of black citizenship rights, and the results of this offer of the palm branch were disfranchisement, segregation, and poverty for black higher education. Washington asked blacks to forgo political power, civil rights, and higher education. He was "striving nobly to make Negro artisans business men and property-owners; but it is utterly impossible, under modern competitive methods, for the workingmen and property-owners to defend their rights and exist without the right of suffrage." Washington had advocated elementary and industrial schooling but failed to see that such institutions could not operate without teachers trained at liberal-arts colleges.

Du Bois insisted that Washington's message left the impression that the Negro's low status justified white prejudice, that wrong education in the past accounted for his current bad conditions, and that his future progress depended entirely on his own efforts. These half-truths had encouraged whites to shift responsibility for the Negro Problem entirely onto blacks' shoulders. Washington had failed to make criticisms that whites needed to hear. By quashing dissent against his own decisions, he had perverted the natural process of choosing leaders. Still, Booker's alleged counsel of submission had elicited bitter opposition, and courageous new leaders were emerging who believed in honesty and rejected flattery. Du Bois concluded: "So far as Mr. Washington preaches Thrift, Patience, and Industrial Training for the masses"— all things Du Bois had earlier dismissed with derision—"we must hold up his hands and strive with him, rejoicing in his honors and glorying in the strength of this Joshua called of God and of man. But so far as Mr. Washington apologizes for injustice, North or South, does not rightly value the privilege and duty of voting, belittles the emasculating effects of caste distinctions, and opposes the higher training and ambition of our brighter minds,—so far as he, the South or the Nation, does this,—we must unceasingly and firmly oppose them."[23]

Elsewhere in the book, Du Bois defended higher education against Booker's alleged hostility to it. "No secure civilization can be built in the South with the Negro as an ignorant, turbulent proletariat," and industrial education would make blacks nothing more than that. "By slamming the door of opportunity in the faces of their bolder and brighter minds," the Tuskegee philosophy put their training into the hands of "untrained demagogues." Du Bois toted up the black men taught to think in institutions of higher education, North and South, and came up with about 2,000 since the Civil War, which group he designated the "Talented Tenth." "By refusing to give this Talented Tenth the key to knowledge, can any sane man imagine that they will lightly lay aside their yearning and contentedly become hewers of wood and drawers of water?"[24]

Du Bois would be complimented for his restrained tone in *Souls of Black Folk*—the kudos arising from its contrast to the Boston *Guardian*—but in fact it was an artful critique that carefully masked its intense partisanship. Du Bois understood precisely why Washington had said what he did at Atlanta. Afterward he himself had called it a settlement of the Negro Problem, which he meant as a compliment to Booker's racial diplomacy. In "Of Mr. Booker T.," Du Bois failed to note his own earlier support or to explain why he had changed his mind to cast the speech in such a negative light. He knew that Booker had neither accepted inferiority nor relinquished political or civil rights, because he had worked closely with Booker to challenge railroad discrimination and disfranchisement in Georgia. He had witnessed the racial hysteria surrounding the Sam Hose lynching and the White House dinner and most assuredly could imagine the possibility of white terrorism aimed at Tuskegee or Washington himself; yet no empathy for the precariousness of every black person's circumstances in the South of 1903 was extended to Booker. Instead Du Bois pushed the red herring that Washington opposed all higher education. He knew of Washington's support for Fisk University, his preference for hiring teachers from good liberal-arts schools, and his frequently stated position that an academic education was entirely appropriate for blacks who could put it to use. Du Bois was party to the rancor between Tuskegee and Atlanta University that was based largely on decisions made in the philanthropic foundations by white men well beyond Tuskegee control; but such complicating contextual evidence did not fit with the declaration that Washington opposed all but industrial education.

Du Bois touted the saving grace of the Talented Tenth, but his numbers in fact amounted to a much smaller fraction. His higher-education graduates accounted for about one in every 5,000 American blacks in 1903. *Souls* was silent about the fate of the other 4,999, and he gave Booker Washington no credit for his concern with educating the black masses. Du Bois called Washington's public statements propaganda, and although he may have disagreed with the strategy, it was partisan not to have acknowledged at least that Washington's public posture and rhetoric had the intended purpose of defusing white hysteria. If Du Bois truly did not understand the larger purpose of the propaganda of interracial peace, he may have been the only black man living in the South in 1903 so obtuse—and there was nothing dim-witted about Du Bois. And he had understood that larger purpose in 1895. Any man has a right to change his mind, but a fair man acknowledges that he has done so.

Booker maintained a public silence about the attack, and, amazingly, Du Bois came to Tuskegee to teach in the 1903 summer school. But Booker knew that in this man he had his most formidable black opponent yet. He deeply resented Du Bois's insinuations of his cowardice. For example, Du Bois chose not to vote, a decision that to Washington represented extreme hypocrisy given that Du Bois had condemned him for surrendering political rights. In time *Souls of Black Folk* would be remembered as much for its rendering of blacks' racial soul as for its attack on Booker Washington. No one noted the irony that a book offering so lyrical a picture of blacks also so harshly caricatured one black man. Nor did many see, then or later, that African Americans' preeminent scholar, their keenest empiricist, had forsaken careful observation and balanced assessment in favor of bias and partisanship. In his determination to bring down Washington, Du Bois had not only turned on his former ally but also left the real world for a form of racial essentialism.

In the summer of 1903 Monroe Trotter mounted a full-scale assault. He began calling Washington "His Nibs," a mocking title for a self-important man. At the annual Afro-American Council meeting in Louisville in early July, his coeditor at the *Guardian*, William Ferris, objected to the picture of Booker placed on the stage and demanded that an image be displayed of some Negro who advocated "the higher life and intellectual development" of blacks. Trotter told the council that, unlike Washington, "we northern Negroes are not going to sit supinely by and let the whites put their feet on our necks." Trotter's allies presented a resolution that "agitation is the best means to secure our civil and political rights," which was defeated by the Washington loyalists who controlled the convention. In his speech to the council, Booker ignored the attacks and focused on the recent lynchings in northern states. Lynching was a national problem that contributed to the "present season of anxiety and almost despair which possesses an element of the race."[25]

The combat was most intense between the chief lieutenants. The anti-Washington forces focused their ire heavily on Tim Fortune, who, one wrote, had earlier been the "most fearless advocate of the manhood rights of the Negro" but who now believed that blacks "should be trained for good servants and laborers only, that disfranchisement of the Negro was a blessing rather than a curse." Those were hardly Fortune's views, but in the escalating warfare of July 1903, Washington's enemies asserted them as his. Fortune in turn bragged that the Boston group saw that he, as president of the council, had been "out for the scamps all the time, with blood in my eyes and chip on both shoulders." James C. Napier, a more restrained pro-Booker businessman from Nashville, claimed that the opposition was just poorly informed: "These young men who come from Boston, with their high notions of life, with their blood-thirsty speeches," ought to visit the South and learn "something of the conditions of their people" and the value of "a gospel of peace." The *Guardian* admitted that it had lost the battle: "There was never a clearer case of being dominated to death by one man."[26]

Both sides left Louisville holding angry grudges. Attempting to discourage attention to his detractors, Booker wrote privately to the editor of the Brooklyn *Eagle* that the trouble had been raised by three men from Boston—a significant underestimation of the opposition—who made "such asses" of themselves that other blacks had paid them little attention, another misrepresentation. "Aside from gratifying a personal spite, their main object is to get their names into the newspapers which they know they can easily do by opposing some man whose name is well known to the public." Trotter now had fewer allies, but the ones who remained were almost his equal in their vitriol. "Booker

T. Washington is largely responsible for the lynching in this country," the lawyer Edward Morris told his hometown newspaper, the white-owned Chicago *Inter Ocean*. "The learned doctor teaches the colored people that they are only fit to fill menial positions. The spirit of his teaching is illustrated by a rag-time song, 'Mr. Coon, You're All Right in Your Place.'" Morris asserted that Ben Tillman did more good for blacks than Washington. "The colored people think it doesn't matter so much what [Tillman] says, since he says he is an enemy of the colored race," but they believed Booker was "their friend and look upon him as a prophet." It was an inadvertent tribute to Booker.[27]

Trouble simmered for the next three weeks, with each side plotting to hurt the other. Trotter and company were investigating Washington's alleged subsidies to black newspapers for printing pro-Tuskegee articles and editorials. Booker was indeed helping to launch newspapers that supported him. In addition to efforts in Boston, he was subsidizing a New York paper edited by Melvin Jack Chisum, whom Emmett Scott had known in Texas. Chisum in fact would spend more time over the next few years spying for Tuskegee among Trotter and other opponents. Chisum's instructions usually came from Scott through the lawyer Wilford Smith, although Chisum and Booker sometimes met on park benches in New York City. Smith was preparing a libel suit against Trotter—financed secretly by Washington—for the *Guardian*'s attack on a black student at Yale. William Pickens had given a public address critical of the black government of Haiti, which the *Guardian* said was "throwing down his own race," an act so treasonous as to warrant its calling Pickens "the little black freak student at Yale . . . with his enormous lips, huge mouth, and a monkey grin coextensive with his ears." Any irony about who was throwing down whose race was lost entirely on the light-skinned, thin-lipped Bostonians.[28]

Fighting literally broke out on July 30 as Washington was preparing to address members of the Negro Business League at a Boston church crowded with 2,000 spectators. When William Lewis first mentioned Booker's name, a cacophony of hisses, catcalls, and foot-stomping filled the church. While Lewis was still talking, a man named Granville Martin rose and shouted denunciations of Washington and was forcibly removed. Quiet was momentarily restored, but when Tim Fortune went to the pulpit, he began sneezing and coughing uncontrollably. The podium had been baited with cayenne pepper. Martin returned to the sanctuary and began hissing and stomping his feet, and Lewis again had police remove him. Then Monroe Trotter rose and shouted, "put me out; arrest me!" But in fact he took his seat when a policeman ordered it. As he was introducing Washington, Lewis chastised the audience for its disgraceful behavior in the house of God, and Fortune admonished the crowd to rebuke riot and disorder. Riot and disorder indeed ensued when Washington went to the podium. "We don't want to hear you, Booker Washington," someone shouted. "We don't like you." Trotter stood on a chair and read aloud nine questions he had prepared, including one about whether the lynching rope was "all the race is to get under your leadership." Washington ignored him, but Sam Courtney, Booker's old Malden friend, could not: "Throw Trotter out the window!" he shouted. Fights broke out across the sanctuary. People began rushing to the exits, which had become cluttered with stumbling bodies caused by the arrival of more policemen. A pro-Trotter woman in the crowd stabbed a policeman with a hatpin. Trotter and Martin were taken off to jail, and order was eventually restored. Booker finally made the speech, though he had to shout over a loud hubbub.[29]

The next day Trotter explained that "the Boston riot" resulted from Lewis's refusal to let anyone who hissed or shouted ask Washington to explain his statements favoring Jim Crow railroad cars and disfranchisement. Washington told the Boston *Globe* that "just as a few flies are able to impair the purity of a jar of cream, so three or four ill-mannered young colored men were able to disturb an otherwise successful meeting." A press release issued from Tuskegee reflected the more openly bellicose attitude of Emmett Scott: "It is very likely that Trotter's stay in the public jail will give him an opportunity to review his foolish life. From Harvard College to the gaol—the distance is great; but Trotter has traveled it in short order."[30]

The public battle in Boston induced Washington and his allies to engage all their enemies, thus matching the total-war attitude of Trotter's group. They abandoned the long-standing Tuskegee strategy of avoiding newspaper controversies, one to which Washington almost always adhered with white critics. He expected the denunciations of white men because they were bound to recognize the inherent challenge to white supremacy in his strategy of racial uplift. But he had little tolerance for criticism from blacks—at least not for that made in public—because he thought it was offered in bad faith and that it undermined the larger cause of black progress. In reality some challenge was inevitable: among almost ten million blacks, some people were bound to reject whoever was the leader of the moment. His critics represented a small portion of the black public and even a minority of the race's elite. Booker had very few critics in the South, where 90 percent of blacks lived, and a strong group of black followers in every northern city. Even in Boston, Chicago, and Washington, where his critics were most numerous, the majority of blacks probably approved of his leadership. Blacks in every northern city flocked to his appearances, and the leading black businessmen almost always supported his work and his positions. For every northern preacher, lawyer, or editor who opposed him, there were several of each who supported him. He might well have ignored Trotter and the others and lost little influence. But Booker fought them aggressively, with fierce cunning. Both sides got down into the mire, and all would inevitably get up bruised and dirty, with Booker's reputation damaged once and for all. Both sides seemed compelled to go there.[31]

Washington's response to the attacks from northern blacks surely owed something to the deterioration of conditions in the South in the summer of 1903. Senator Furnifold Simmons, a white-nationalist leader of North Carolina Democrats, denounced industrial schools as dangerous fomenters of economic competition between blacks and whites. "We are in the midst of a noisy propaganda for negro industrial education," Simmons said, in which blacks were being taught skills, but he warned that such teaching promised to bring much trouble to the Negro and the whole society. The Negro needed to stay on the farm, the senator declared. A few weeks later James Griggs, a Georgia congressman, issued a similar warning that industrial education would not, as was being promised, solve the Negro Problem. "Educate the negro to compete with the white laboring man and you may as well open wide the door to every other avenue of thought and action." Such public assaults on his work threatened Washington anew. Simmons did not know what he was talking about, Booker told Walter Hines Page. "It is all barking and no biting. Every Negro in the South that learns to do something which the South wants done finds ready employment, and in my opinion it will be a hundred years before that condition is changed, if ever." The resentment in his tone suggested that the barking worried him nevertheless.[32]

In the late summer of 1903, a single political campaign further undermined the already precarious support for black education in the South. James K. Vardaman was running for governor in the first statewide primary among Mississippi Democrats. Vardaman had campaigned for governor in 1899 on a platform of abolishing black education, and in the intervening years he had honed the most virulent anti-Negro appeal yet seen in American politics. The violence of his imagination was stunning. "We would be justified," he declared in 1901, "in slaughtering every Ethiop on the earth to preserve unsullied the honor of one Caucasian home." Having won enormous attention from his manufactured outrage over the Indianola post office, Vardaman entertained Mississippians by the thousands throughout the 1903 campaign as he railed on the hustings against Theodore Roosevelt for the president's alleged affinity for blacks—or "coons," as Vardaman habitually designated them. About Roosevelt, Vardaman said: "I hope he will be bitten by a blue-gum nigger and die of hydrophobia." He made education of white children his main campaign issue, calling for free textbooks for white children and racial separation of school funds. Time and again he said that educating blacks was foolish, because they were incapable of using real schooling and any pretense toward it encouraged black ambitions to vote. "We spent $150,000 [in 1890] disfranchising the negro," he said, "and $6,000,000 since to bring him back to the polls." He promised to abolish black education once and for all in Mississippi.[33]

The Mississippi events shook Booker Washington as much as anything else that had happened in the South. "My heart is made to feel very serious over the election of Vardaman," he wrote to Oswald Villard two days after the vote. He did not think that the northern press, apparently including Villard and the New York *Evening Post,* had taken in the election's implications. They were clear-cut to Booker. "The majority of white people in Mississippi oppose Negro education of any character," he explained. They had been the first to disfranchise the Negro and would now lead the South, he thought, to end black public education. "If Mississippi succeeds, other states will follow."[34] Friends of black education must act now, Booker pleaded. But still no exposé of discrimination in black education appeared in Villard's publications.

The day after the Mississippi vote, the principal of a black industrial school in New Roads, Louisiana, was shotgunned to death in an ambush. L. A. Planving was a carpenter, the principal of Point Coupee Industrial College, and a friend of Booker Washington. Planving had recently encouraged blacks to buy land, claiming that they would eventually have whites working for them. Newspapers reported that whites knew the identity of Planving's murderers, but no arrests were made. Francis Garrison wrote from Boston that the Louisiana events demonstrated that schools like Tuskegee rested on a powder magazine. He begged Booker not to expose himself unnecessarily to whites in the southern countryside. It was true, as William Baldwin observed at this moment, that anyone in the South in 1903 was living among insane people.[35]

At that point, Washington's instinct for survival took over. In late September he took Garrison's advice. Thoroughly beleaguered by the attacks against him, exhausted from the apparently futile effort to save black education, he boarded a ship, alone and traveling under the name Homer P. Jones, to sail for France. He left a situation even more demoralizing than what he had escaped after the Hose lynching in 1899 when he went to Europe for the first time. His various enemies seemed to be attacking in concert, only this time with more intensity and to greater effect on his leadership. Booker slept for the seven days across the Atlantic, visited Normandy and Paris, and disappeared to locations never reported; he was not heard from until he docked in New York in mid-October. The burden of racial leadership had pushed him almost to the point of collapse, and he fled—obviously for self-preservation but, in characteristic fashion, with no open acknowledgment of the trouble that pressed upon him.[36]

12

———

The Tuskegee Machine

Booker had many hours crossing the Atlantic Ocean to contemplate what to do about the trouble with Monroe Trotter and his group. He felt humiliated by their personal attacks on him. Looking respectable was a first concern among middle-class blacks of Booker's generation, and the Boston riot demonstrated the basic disregard of Trotter's group for the value of respectability. The challengers had embarrassed him in front of powerful whites. Answering Roosevelt's query about the trouble, he claimed not to be bothered by the Boston group, when in fact he was outraged. He said that a half-dozen jealous men in Boston were making all the trouble—a significant undercount of his detractors. The Boston men had not worked their way up from the bottom or paid a price for their status but had simply been given a college education, and they thought that all blacks could be put "in the same artificial position that they themselves are in." He was the scapegoat for the Trotter group: "When a people are smarting under wrongs and injustices inflicted from many quarters," Booker told Roosevelt, "it is but natural that they should look about for some individual on whom to lay the blame for their seeming misfortunes." Booker believed that the Boston group envied his influence with Roosevelt and was trying to undermine it by making the president consider him a liability. He assured Roosevelt that no president since Lincoln had been as much admired by blacks as he was. He reported that all but 5 of the 178 black newspapers supported Roosevelt editorially.[1]

Booker wanted the president to believe that blacks continued to deserve his patronage because of their loyalty to him, notwithstanding the few troublemakers. He realized that Roosevelt's popularity and his own were inextricably tied. By late 1903 Booker's authority as the leader of his race was based heavily on Roosevelt's success as president and on Booker's ability to direct the president's action. Each man looked to the 1904 election as a fateful event in his career.

Booker was sufficiently rejuvenated on his return to direct an assault against his critics. His Boston allies hired a lawyer to press charges against Trotter and Granville Martin for disturbing the peace at the Boston riot. The two were convicted and sentenced to thirty days in jail. The judge said that he might have been more lenient if Trotter and Martin had been willing to apologize and promise not to disrupt future meetings attended by Washington. Booker instructed Scott to encourage reporting of the convictions and incarcerations to the black press, and he asked Tim Fortune to do the same: "I am most anxious that the last dastardly attempt on the part of that Boston crowd to disgrace the race be made public in some way." The spy Melvin Chisum reported a plot to disturb another speech by Booker in Boston, but nothing in fact happened. Apparently unnerved by the controversy, Trotter's partner, George Forbes, decided to sell his part of the *Guardian*. Booker's allies schemed to buy Forbes's share, but Trotter's friends raised enough money for him to maintain control. Still, the riot and the jail term undermined much of Trotter's legitimacy. His opposition to Washington became less potent after the summer of 1903.[2]

Washington's black enemies smarted most under his dominance of black opinion. "Our trump card on Booker is his corrupt methods," Trotter told Du Bois. "The real issue as to Washington is his lust for power, his desire to be a political leader, to be a czar, his clandestine methods of attempting to crush out all who will not bow to him." Certainly Washington intended to be a strong leader who maximized his power, especially against those who opposed his every move, but his methods were no more unscrupulous than Trotter's. At this point Booker's enemies began to use the pejorative "Tuskegee Machine," which they believed was the mechanism with which Booker enforced his will across the country. Indeed there was a loosely organized national network of Washington supporters, but they were held together far less by coercive pressure from the top than by deference to established power and trust in the leadership strategy emanating from Tuskegee. The differences in perception between the Trotter group and the so-called Tuskegee Machine were irreconcilable, although Washington had not yet admitted it.[3]

Trotter's decline after the Boston riot ultimately mattered less than the impact of his fate on Du Bois, who by the end of the summer of 1903 was fully and finally alienated from Washington. Du Bois lived with Trotter in Boston during the weeks after the riot as the prosecution of the editor was unfolding. In the fall Du Bois wrote a letter to the philanthropist George Peabody praising Trotter's "single hearted earnestness & devotion to a great cause" and calling him "the object of petty persecution & dishonest attack." Du Bois asserted that Trotter's "sincerity and unpurchasable soul" made him "far nearer the right" than Washington, who was "leading the way backward." Trotter published a private letter from George Towns, Du Bois's Atlanta University colleague, praising Trotter for his stand. The letter angered the Atlanta trustees who admired Booker, and they demanded that President Horace Bumstead apologize to Washington. "I am sure that much of the opposition has its origin in Atlanta University," Booker said, "although I have always been kind to them there or attempted to be."[4]

Several black intellectuals hoped to mediate the conflict. Charles Chesnutt, the Cleveland novelist, had carried on a frank but friendly correspondence with Booker. He had expressed his doubts that any good results could come from Booker's policy of conciliation with the white South. "Under it, whether because of it or not I do not know, the rights of the Negro have steadily dwindled," Chesnutt thought. Booker responded that he had regularly spoken out against both disfranchisement and lynching, but he acknowledged that he did not habitually do so: "If I were saying the [same] thing all the time the world would pay no attention to my words when the proper time came." Booker knew that northern critics wanted him to condemn loudly and continuously the indignities of the Jim Crow South, but he felt that he had said as much as he practically could. After the Boston riot, Chesnutt privately condemned the actions of Trotter and company, but he also criticized Washington's "complete acquiescence" to disfranchisement. "You are willing, in your own State and county, to throw yourself upon the mercy of the whites, rather than to claim your share in your own government under a free franchise." He conceded that Booker might argue that disfranchisement was a *fait accompli,* but "you need not approve of it, thereby tying the hands of the friends of the race who would be willing and able to cry out against the injustice." Chesnutt's criticisms were not fair: Washington had not acquiesced in disfranchisement or prevented anyone from protesting, nor had he approved any disfranchising measure beyond literacy and property requirements, which he had always insisted had to be administered without regard to race.[5]

Archibald Grimké of Boston, a lawyer and diplomat in the Cleveland administration, also objected to Booker's statement—habitually quoted in the Boston *Guardian*—that property and literacy requirements gave blacks new incentives to acquire education and land. "While it is true that you have several times endeavored to prevent the disfranchisement of your race by certain Southern states," Grimké wrote, Washington had counseled "in effect, if not openly, acquiescence on the part of your people in such adverse action."[6] What Booker had accepted were the realities of a restricted ballot and the dangers inherent in any open black resistance to disfranchisement in the South. A black educator in the South put his institution and himself in jeopardy if whites perceived him to be a threat to the status quo, as the recent death of L. A. Planving in Louisiana and the terrorism aimed at Nelson Henry in Ramer, Alabama, had so clearly shown. For that matter, so did a white educator who criticized antiblack measures, as the experiences of Andrew Sledd and John Spencer Bassett demonstrated. But Washington's northern critics refused to acknowledge that this reality was not theirs. From a safe distance, they saw only the seeming repudiation of full civil rights for black Americans.

Just weeks after the Boston riot, Kelly Miller, the Howard University professor known as a perceptive observer of black life and one who tried to straddle the current partisan divide with plentiful flattery, published a widely read commentary on Washington's leadership. Miller wrote that Booker's powers of analysis revealed the "certainty and celerity of a genius," while Trotter was "as sincere a man as there is in the race." Miller noted that circumstances often dictated the nature of leadership: Frederick Douglass had lived in the epoch of moral giants like Lincoln and Garrison, whereas Washington moved in the era of merchant princes. Miller wrote that "Douglass was like a lion, bold and fearless; Washington is lamblike, meek and submissive." Douglass was a "moralist, insisting upon the application of righteousness to public affairs; Washington is a practical statesman, accepting the best terms which he thinks it possible to secure." Miller ignored the fundamental similarities in the programs and values of Douglass and Washington. His commitment to bipolarity resulted in a gross caricature of Washington's leadership: Booker moved "not along the line of least resistance, but of no resistance at all"; he retreated into "sphinxlike silence when the demands of the situation seem to require emphatic utterance"; and "the white race saddles its own notions and feelings upon him, and yet he opens not his mouth." Washington let white southerners believe that he accepted black inferiority, was "quiescent if not acquiescent to white man's superior claims," and ignored the wrongs done to blacks. "He never runs against the Southerner's traditional prejudices."[7]

The speciousness of Miller's characterizations indicated the degree of hostility to Washington's leadership among northern intellectuals in late 1903. His opponents rejected the strategy Booker had laid out in the Atlanta exposition speech: to achieve enough settlement, or interracial peace, on the Negro Problem to implement a strategy of economic and educational uplift. They placed little value on encouraging hope about the future among the nine million southern blacks at this depressing time. Nor did they acknowledge the limits on free expression in the South, even though Grimké and Miller had been born in the South and Chesnutt had lived there. Grimké wrote that he appreciated "the difficulty and danger of your relations with the South, and of those of Tuskegee also," but he did not speak as if he truly did understand.[8]

Washington might have accepted the inevitability of northern criticism and stayed silent about it, but in late 1903 he still wanted to persuade his detractors of the logic of his strategy. Nearly all black southerners understood and accepted Washington's avoidance of open conflict with whites. They lived with the oppression and knew very well the high cost a black person paid for criticizing race relations in the South. They rarely questioned Washington, feeling that to do so would be unfair to him and his leadership. "Throughout all the agitation," Booker wrote to a white confidant, "it is most encouraging to note that the rank and file of our people see matters clearly and correctly, and no man could ever have his hands held up more strongly and loyally than my hands are held up by the masses of our people." It was a self-serving appraisal but more accurate than not. At a national conference of sociologists, Washington told the country's most serious students of race relations that condemnation of wrong should always be made, but that protest alone would not improve conditions. "Now, some of us live in the section of the country where we hear of these wrongs," he said. "We eat them for our breakfast, for our dinner, for our supper. We live on them day in and day out." He asked the sociologists to embrace a positive program along with condemnations of wrong. "What we can construct," Booker said, "is what will bring us relief."[9]

By late 1903 Washington saw the wisdom of reaching a compromise, or at least of trying new tactics to bring his critics around. Du Bois was the main person to persuade. Trotter's verbal assaults put him well beyond the pale of negotiation. The previous February, when Booker had proposed a meeting of black leaders to establish a national black agenda, Du Bois had written a platform of goals to advance at such a gathering. Its planks included full black political rights; higher education for selected Negro youth but industrial education for the masses; court challenges on behalf of civil rights and a legal defense fund; a study of black problems and a national Negro periodical; and an end to the campaign of black self-deprecation. In the midst of the mounting Boston attack on Booker during the winter and spring of 1903, the meeting had not occurred. Now, in late October, Booker asked Du Bois to help convene a group of the most prominent men, from various sections of the country and various interests, to consider "quietly all the weighty matters that now confront us as a race." Suspicious that it would be just a Booker Washington "ratification meeting," Du Bois negotiated aggressively about the invitation list, and in the end about one-third of the twenty-eight black men who met at Carnegie Hall for three days in January 1904 were opponents of Booker Washington. Trotter was not invited, although he tried to crash the meeting. But his close ally Clement Morgan and Booker's bitter Chicago enemy Edward Morris joined Du Bois in the anti-Washington contingent. Before the meeting Du Bois exhorted his allies to bring Booker's published statements that damned him in his critics' eyes. "The main issue of the meeting is *Washington*," he said. "Refuse to be side-tracked."[10]

The proceedings at Carnegie Hall were not recorded, but Du Bois later reported that his group made strong objections to Washington's alleged "attacks on higher training and his general attitude of belittling the race and not putting enough stress upon voting and things of that sort." Morgan read the same nine loaded questions that Trotter had shouted at the Boston riot. Near the end of the conference both Du Bois and Washington spoke, and Booker's remarks apparently persuaded all but the hard-core opposition of his reasonableness and sincerity in pursuing blacks' best interests. Archibald Grimké was moved by Booker's words, some of which recounted the indignities he suffered after the White House dinner. He thought that Washington's arguments were unanswerable, that undoubtedly he was working for the best interests of the Negro. The problem was not ideological, but "simply a difference in method and lack of understanding." The participants produced a sense of the conference on several crucial issues: the right to vote was paramount and should be upheld and defended; all racial restrictions on public accommodations, including railroads, should be challenged in court; blacks should get thorough training, which included, first, higher education and then elementary and industrial training; lynching had to stop; and a national Negro newspaper should be established. Except for not condemning deprecatory statements about blacks, it replicated the program that Du Bois had proposed almost a year earlier. Apparently consensus had been reached readily, despite the intense hostility leading up to the meeting. The meeting called for the creation of a Committee of Twelve to coordinate future action, with Du Bois and Washington as its conveners and about nine of the members mostly friendly to Booker.[11]

The positions taken at Carnegie Hall represented clear commitments to positions that Washington's detractors had alleged that he opposed. The strong pro-Booker majority staunchly defended higher education, black voting rights, and equality of public accommodations. All the positions taken at Carnegie Hall were easily recognizable in a close reading of Booker's speeches and newspaper interviews since the Atlanta speech, even though his detractors had steadfastly refused to acknowledge that he had taken them. Indeed, considering the secret court challenges of disfranchisement and railroad discrimination that Washington was then organizing and personally funding, Booker had long since been at work on the agenda. J. C. Asbury, editor of the *Odd Fellows' Journal,* wrote to a Washington opponent that Booker was "thoroughly sound upon every question affecting the progress of the Race," but he was "just a little more diplomatic than the rest of us and consequently more successful; and as you know in times of peace diplomacy rules the world."[12]

But for Booker's opponents, it was no time of peace. Within days of the Carnegie Hall meeting, Edward Morris declared that it mattered less what Washington actually said than what people imagined he thought. Morris proceeded to assail Washington for what people thought he believed. Despite having prevailed on all policy decisions made at Carnegie Hall, Du Bois neglected his agreed-upon role in the Committee of Twelve and proposed a different, larger body. He took as another act of oppression Booker's preference for giving the Committee of Twelve a chance to succeed. In an April magazine article he offered this characterization of the Tuskegee program: "The trimmings of life, smatterings of Latin and music and such stuff—let us wait till we are rich. Then as to voting, what is the good of it after all? Politics does not pay as well as the grocery business, and breeds trouble." Kelly Miller and Archibald Grimké took responsibility for implementing the Carnegie Hall agenda, and their cooperation with Washington infuriated Du Bois: "I count it a clear misfortune to the Negro race when two clear-headed and honest men like you can see their way to put themselves under the dictation of a man with the record of Mr.

Washington," he wrote. "I am sorry, very sorry to see it. Yet it will not alter my determination one jot or tittle. I refuse to wear Mr. Washington's livery or put on his collar. I have worked this long without having my work countersigned by Booker Washington . . . and I think I'll peg along to the end in the same way."[13]

By early 1904 Washington had demonstrated that his interests in advancing the race were sincere enough, and his strategy for doing it plausible enough, to persuade an overwhelming majority of blacks that his leadership was legitimate. The general reaction to the Boston riot, as well as to the Carnegie Hall meeting, had demonstrated that fact clearly. He did not need to scheme against Trotter and Du Bois, because his position was strong enough once it was explained, and their partisan obsessions transparent enough, that he would vanquish them in a fair fight. Booker might have been well advised to have assumed the sphinxlike posture toward them that he typically took toward anti-Negro whites. But Washington by instinct was an intensely competitive man when locked in a political fight that he thought he could win. On matters of infighting within the black community, he listened to Emmett Scott and Tim Fortune, also fierce partisans. Increasingly influential with Booker at this time was the New York Republican politician Charles Anderson, who in early 1904 offered Booker this advice about dealing with adversaries: "My experience in politics is, that, he is whipped oftenest who is whipped easiest, and I long ago made up my mind to give my opponent the very best I have in my shop, when he sets himself the task of fighting me. The opposition to you and your work, is confined to a little coterie of men who have graduated from some of the best Universities of the country,—*and have done nothing else.* A good thrashing would convince these young upstarts, with their painful assumption of superior intellectuality, that they had better spend their time in some less dangerous occupation."[14] It was advice that, good or not, Booker followed.

With Booker's silent but steady backing, Wilford Smith had pushed his multiple challenges to the Alabama constitution through the courts in 1903 and 1904. The white press kept a close eye on what Smith was doing. Judge Jones's quick recognition of a jurisdictional dispute had got one of Jackson Giles's cases to the Supreme Court. Smith argued to the Court that the new Alabama constitution represented a "high-handed and flagrant" nullification of the Fourteenth and Fifteenth Amendments and that the United States was obligated to honor "its solemn constitutional guarantees made to the negro shortly after the civil war." In April 1903 the newly appointed Justice Oliver Wendell Holmes Jr., an abolitionist and Union soldier in his youth, delivered the court's majority opinion against Giles. If it was the intention of the "great mass of the white population [of Alabama] to keep the blacks from voting," and Holmes understood that to be whites' purpose, one black man's name on the voting roll would not defeat them. Any relief for Giles had to come from the state or the U.S. Congress, the justice said. No adverse Supreme Court ruling could be enforced against the state of Alabama. The Fourteenth and Fifteenth Amendments were, therefore, a dead letter in the face of white southern opposition.[15]

Booker refrained from expressing his distress publicly at the decision, but Monroe Trotter was outraged that Boston's own Holmes had dodged the issue, likening him to Roger Taney in the *Dred Scott* decision in deciding that blacks had no rights that white men were bound to respect. Trotter never figured out who was behind the *Giles* case. Similarly in the dark about Booker's efforts, Charles Chesnutt wrote after the decision that blacks should bombard the courts with suits until they reached the correct conclusion—a demand he made without considering the money necessary to make one court challenge, this coming from one who made his living as a court stenographer and surely knew the practicalities of litigation. In the context of the *Giles* decision, Chesnutt chastised Washington for conciliation of whites, another unfair condemnation that Booker had to let pass. In fact Booker and Wilford Smith had four other *Giles* cases still in the works. In two of the cases, Smith argued that the county boards of registrars were unconstitutional, and he asked the state courts to register all blacks denied the vote by any board. If the boards were unconstitutional, the state justices said, then they could not order a null body to act without becoming a party to fraud. The U.S. Supreme Court agreed to hear appeals on both cases. In early 1904 the Court essentially repeated Holmes's earlier evasion of the constitutional issue. Washing-

40. Justice Oliver Wendell Holmes Jr. gave Alabama blacks no relief in the challenges to disfranchisement arranged secretly by Booker Washington. Photo by Frances Benjamin Johnston, 1902; courtesy of the Library of Congress.

ton's allies were incensed at what Smith called the Court's dodging game, but Booker remained committed to the effort. "I believe there is a way to win, or at least put the Supreme Court in an awkward position," he wrote to Smith. "We must not cease our efforts." But facing a new round of legal fees, Booker finally gave up on the Alabama challenges in March 1904. The following month the Supreme Court ruled against disfranchised blacks in Virginia in two well-financed cases argued by two prominent white lawyers from the Old Dominion. The highest tribunal simply would not be persuaded to protect black voting rights. At the very same time the appeal of the Louisiana disfranchising constitution, which Booker had nurtured through the years, died in a state court.[16]

Simultaneously with the voting cases and also with Washington's secret sponsorship, Smith was making a criminal appeal on behalf of an Alabama convict, Dan Rogers, who had been convicted by a jury picked from an all-white jury roll. Smith had won such a jury-discrimination suit in Texas. Though unwilling to protect the political rights of blacks, the U.S. courts consistently ruled against all-white juries in protecting the rights of blacks accused of crimes. In January 1904 the Supreme Court found for Rogers and sent the case back to Alabama for retrial. The case marked the only real victory for Smith and Washington of the half-dozen pushed through the courts from 1902 to 1904. The decision gave "the colored people a hopefulness that means a great deal," Booker wrote to Smith. In June 1904 Washington reported happily to Smith that six black men in Montgomery had been summoned for jury duty.[17]

Judge Jones was further vindicating Booker's effort to get him on the bench. In early 1903 he ordered a Secret Service investigation of abuses of the criminal justice system in Coosa and Tallapoosa Counties, north of Tuskegee. Jones then convened a federal grand jury to investigate peonage in those counties. The grand jury found that a black man was often accused of a petty offense and then, to avoid being shipped as a leased convict to work in a Birmingham coal mine, entered into an agreement to pay a fine with a work contract on a local plantation. The Negro, Judge Jones explained, was "made to believe he is a convict, and treated as such." The U.S. attorney working with Jones reported that the black peon was "placed into a condition of involuntary servitude, he is locked up at nights in a cell, worked under guards during the day from 3 o'clock in the morning until 7 or 8 o'clock at night, whipped in a most cruel manner, is insufficiently fed and poorly clad." When such a debt slave was close to working off his debt, he often was charged with another crime. The system was operated by a network of corrupt justices of the peace, many of whom were themselves contractors or relatives of those who used peons—mostly planters and sawmill operators. The grand jury indicted eighteen men on ninety-nine counts of enslavement. Along the way, Jones declared Alabama's contract labor law unconstitutional. Booker encouraged Oswald Villard to expose peonage in the New York *Evening Post* and the *Nation,* and he provided information for editorials in *Outlook.* "We owe to Judge Thomas G. Jones," he told Villard, "a great debt of gratitude for what is being done in regard to exposing the peonage system in Alabama."[18]

Jones was determined to get guilty verdicts and to overcome defense lawyers' insistence that blacks were only partial citizens. "The question between us and God and our consciences," he told the all-white jury, "is can we rise above our prejudices, if we have them, so far that we as white men are able to and willing to do a negro justice." When the jury seemed confused by the applications of contract law, Jones essentially directed a guilty verdict: "There cannot be any voluntary contract in the eye of the law made in this country by which a man surrenders his liberty and his person to the dominion of another to secure an obligation." When the jury reported that it was hung, Jones reprimanded the members for refusing to enforce the laws "for no other reason than the base one that the defendant was a white man and the victim of the law he violated is a negro boy." His charge to the jury incurred the wrath of Alabama's secretary of state, Tom Heflin, who told a large gathering of Confederate veterans that Jones's actions were "wholly uncalled for and out of place and it tended in my judgment to intimidate rather than enlighten, to trespass on the domain of the jury, and to usurp its function." A man with large political ambitions, Heflin had found in Judge Jones a white traitor on whom to focus antiblack feeling. Subsequent trials turned out more to Jones's liking, and one of the accused pleaded guilty. Having exposed the problem and taught his lessons, Jones handed down light sentences and privately solicited Booker to encourage the president to pardon some defendants. "The object of all good men now is to lessen the friction between the races & to put the blacks especially on as high a plane as possible," he wrote. He asked that Booker call for clemency for the convicted men. "Would it not confound 'negro haters' and their friends to have your people take such a stand?" Roosevelt soon issued pardons.[19]

Jones's actions provided Washington with a valuable example of white goodwill in the midst of seemingly relentless white hostility. In July 1903 he told the Afro-American Council that Jones represented "the very highest type of Southern manhood, and there are hosts of others like him." There was a "class of brave, earnest men in the South, as well as in the North, who are more determined than ever before to see that the race is given an opportunity to elevate itself."[20] Booker exaggerated the size of this group, but Jones enabled Washington to counter the insistence of his critics that all southern whites were blacks' enemies.

Less hopeful were the deteriorating conditions for blacks on Pullman cars in late 1903 and 1904. Newspapers reported in October 1903 that blacks would be barred from occupying the same sleeping cars as whites in Tennessee, the result of an order from the state's governor, James Frazier. Frazier had found himself in a Pullman with five blacks who in his view took too much of the porter's time. Booker's travel often took him through Tennessee. "I cannot conceive of how I could do my work in the South and be compelled to sit up in a jim crow car night after night," he wrote to William Baldwin, whom he implored to contact Robert Lincoln and the Pullman board of directors. "It is a matter that means more to us than you can conceive." Booker organized a group of twenty leading blacks to go to Chicago to meet with Lincoln, and he sent at least two intermediaries to negotiate an audience for the group. The president's son sent word that no meeting was necessary, because he knew of the trouble already. He did not, however, offer any relief. Denials of Pullman berths occurred a while later in Cincinnati, by which time Booker and Baldwin were discussing a lawsuit against the company. "If Mr. Lincoln would stand up straight there would be little trouble regarding Negroes and the sleeping cars," Booker surmised privately. "George M. Pullman let the world understand that no discrimination was to be tolerated, consequently there was practically no trouble while he lived." But Lincoln's indifference encouraged Pullman agents in the South to discriminate as they wished. Booker kept a close tally of brave, earnest white men in America, and in defiance of his legacy, Robert Lincoln did not make the list.[21]

In the summer and fall of 1903 Theodore Roosevelt had twice resubmitted the Crum nomination to the Senate, and Ben Tillman had successfully opposed it both times. Roosevelt again made recess appointments, which kept Crum in office but did not carry with it the federal salary that a regular appointment would have paid. As a consequence, Crum, who was in poor health, had to carry on his medical practice at night to earn a living. In early 1904 Washington orchestrated a large lobbying campaign among northern and western senators to support the nomination. Covering the expenses of the effort himself, Booker ordered black leaders from California, Minnesota, New York, and West Virginia to come to the capital and apply the only kind of pressure that politicians heeded. Seeing the mounting support for Crum, Tillman feigned illness and left the capital for South Carolina. Senatorial courtesy prevented any action while Tillman was away. Crum's wife wrote to Booker that the doctor was seriously ill, his morale flagging. She was afraid that a Senate failure to confirm him would kill him, and she shared her husband's depression: "Better to be dead than an Afro-*American*."[22]

Tillman's stalling only made Booker more determined. He went to the Capitol himself and buttonholed a dozen senators. He had his black allies send telegrams "intimating unrest among the Negro people because of non-action & the possible effect of failure to confirm at this session." The implied threat was the loss of black support in the 1904 elections. Still, the Senate adjourned in the spring of 1904 without confirming Crum, and Roosevelt made yet another recess appointment. The president's persistence won him almost no white friends, not even in the North. Noting the anger that Roosevelt had stirred among southerners, the editor of the New York *Times* observed that it seemed not to matter to the president. "Nor does it make any difference to him that the wisest friends of the negro look with disfavor upon the policy of forcing men of that race into political prominence," the editor concluded. "It is by other means that the advancement of the colored people is sought by those who best understand their interests."[23]

The Crum matter represented a defeat for Booker and a millstone to the president—not to mention a great personal trial for Crum himself; yet it had its benefits. Roosevelt got strong, solid support from blacks in the 1904 election, something he would not have had if he had backed away from the appointment. Washington had organized a nationwide lobbying effort, which, though not immediately successful, had marshaled fair-minded senators against Tillman. Booker had shown his tenacity in advancing black political interests, and many blacks around the country were aware of his bold leadership on the issue. In the absence of his resolve, either Crum or Roosevelt would in all likelihood have abandoned the effort. He held them firm, and the possibility of a regular appointment remained alive.

The presidential race elicited the strongest white-nationalist rhetoric since the White House dinner. In February 1904 James K. Vardaman wrote in a national magazine that he was "opposed to the nigger's voting, it matters not what his advertised moral and mental qualifications may be." The Mississippi governor was just as much against allowing Booker, "with all his Anglo-Saxon re-enforcements"—meaning Washington's white ancestry—to have the franchise as he was to voting by "the cocoanut-headed, chocolate-colored typical little coon, Andy Dotson, who blacks my shoes every morning." It was time to repeal the constitutional amendments "which gave the nigger the right to pollute politics." Amazingly, Vardaman called himself "the nigger's best friend," although he expected a black "to live, act, and die as a nigger."[24]

In Alabama, racial tension rose as the electoral season heated up. When Washington's friend Charles Thompson, the local congressman, died in March, Tom Heflin was appointed to fill the seat, and he immediately announced his campaign for a full term. The ascendancy of Heflin marked a political disaster for Washington. More than any other Alabama politician, Heflin was adopting Tillman's and Vardaman's white-nationalist bellicosity against black education. Edgar Gardner Murphy worried about the impact of Heflin's campaign on Booker. "Tuskegee and Mr. Washington were never so intensely unpopular," Murphy wrote to Robert Ogden. "Poor fellow! I am glad he does not see—and cannot see—the situation as it is. It is partly the resentment of his success, partly the just resentment of the 'showiness' of so large an institution, partly the effect of the national & state campaigns, partly the old old feud between black and white. The demagogue is abroad—with the Evening Post as his chief ally—using the hectoring animus of Villard to drive ignorant men into a frenzy of hate and rage, a frenzy which brings profits only to the demagogue."[25] And Murphy was one of blacks' best white friends in Alabama.

The Democrats exploited Roosevelt's racial policies on behalf of their lackluster nominee, Judge Alton Parker. Southerners thrashed Roosevelt mercilessly about the Crum nomination, and newspapers ran one cartoon after another depicting the White House dinner. The Raleigh *News and Observer* portrayed King Teddy on a throne with Booker the courtier whispering in his ear. The Birmingham *Age-Herald* drew Booker as a monkey dancing to Teddy's organ. Democrats in Baltimore appropriated a Republican billboard that had depicted Uncle Sam with his hand on Teddy and captioned "He is good enough for me." They changed the image to Roosevelt's hand on a flashily dressed Negro with the same caption. "In every way throughout Maryland the race question is being pressed at the expense of other issues," one newspaper reported, and "wherever this question is brought forward Booker Washington is used as an instrument for further inspiring race hatred and as typifying the negro race in an effort to force itself into social equality with the whites." Henry G. Davis, the Democratic vice-presidential nominee, asserted that Roosevelt, "by inviting Booker Washington to his table, thereby making him his political and social equal, and by appointing negroes to offices of high trust, has so encouraged the negroes generally in all sections of the country they have committed outrages, including robbery, assault upon helpless women, and, in some cases, murder."[26]

In May, on the east plaza of the nation's capitol, a moving-picture company staged a satirical short film starring Lew Dockstader, the preeminent blackface minstrel performer of the day and an actor known for his political monologues. Dockstader played "a perfect counterfeit of the sage of Tuskegee," the Washington *Post*'s reporter wrote, noting that "the bogus Booker was made much of by the sham President, who ostentatiously rescued him from an uncomfortable position on the concrete, helped him to rise in the 'Presidential' arms, offered him a cigar with a polite bow, and finally assisted him inside his own carriage." The *Post* reported that it was "variously rumored that the 'Booker' pictures would be used for political purposes in the South and West." The New York police department, formerly under Roosevelt's control, soon confiscated Dockstader's film, preventing its use by Democrats.[27]

The 1904 Republican nominating convention dramatized the ongoing tension between the Lily Whites and Black-and-Tans in the South. Because of the hysteria about his political influence since the White House dinner, Booker did not attend the convention but relied on Emmett Scott and Charles Anderson to implement his strategies. The Lily Whites remained the big concern. Booker had fought for control of the Alabama delegation, but he finally had to accept a compromise split of delegates to the Chicago convention. He insisted to Roosevelt, however, that his Black-and-Tan Tuskegee neighbor Joseph Thompson should lead the Alabama group. He fought even harder for the Louisiana Black-and-Tans. Roosevelt argued the other way at first, and Booker feared that he and the president might break over it, but his view finally prevailed.[28]

Charles Anderson had supplanted Fortune as Washington's main adviser on Republican Party matters. In the spring of 1904 Washington and Fortune had a bitter argument over the latter's indiscretion in divulging information about Booker's secret challenges to the Alabama constitution. Fortune had probably done this when drunk. He also wrote an editorial for the New York *Age* condemning Booker for a remark he had made in a speech. Booker had said: "We must face the fact that in a large degree ours, as yet, is but a child race—very largely an undeveloped race—an undeveloped race is a far-different thing from an inferior race." Fortune ignored Booker's contextual explanation of the unfortunate use of "child race" and compared it to the writing of William Hannibal Thomas, a nasty aspersion in the context of Thomas's reputation as a traitor to his race. Fortune showed the editorial to Charles Anderson, who severely warned him against printing it and who then wrote to Booker about it. "It is very strange," Anderson said, "that whenever this man feels a little cross, he immediately turns to abusing his friends." Fortune insisted that he would run it, although it is not clear that the editorial ever appeared. But the action deepened the alienation between Fortune and Washington. They would not break entirely, but Booker's confidence in Fortune was diminished, and he began to treat Anderson as his chief political lieutenant. By all indications, this was a wise choice. A self-made businessman and successful political organizer in New York, Anderson regularly demonstrated his tough-mindedness, loyalty, and similarity to Washington in his out-look. When Booker instructed Anderson to tell the 1,000 black delegates at Chicago "just what the President has done in the face of great odds in standing up in behalf of the colored race," it got done.[29]

Emmett Scott was the emissary who took the Negro plank that Booker had written for the platform to high party officials. It positioned Republicans unalterably against racial distinctions in party councils or elections anywhere. "Equal protection to every citizen in his civil and political rights is demanded and should be guaranteed. Color is no condition precedent in the payment of taxes, and should not be made a condition precedent in the holding of public office." Through a different channel, one not traceable to Tuskegee, Booker sent another plank: "Murder in the form of lynching or burning should have no place in a civilized country." But Booker's mastery was incomplete: Monroe Trotter slipped Crumpackerism—reduction of southern congressional representation as punishment for disfranchisement—into the platform, and at the Democratic convention, where the Crumpacker plank was denounced, its presence in the Republican platform was blamed on Washington. Richmond Pearson Hobson, an Alabamian hotly promoting his own political career, told the Democrats that Booker was helping to "oppress the Southland simply because it is trying to work out how intelligence can rule." Washington, Hobson said, advocated integration of churches and schools in the South—a complete fabrication.[30]

The presence of a third-party candidate, the Populists' Thomas E. Watson of Georgia, intensified the racial rhetoric. At the start of the Populist movement in the early 1890s, Watson had advocated alliance between black and white farmers, but by 1904 he yielded to few in his hostility to blacks. On the campaign trail in 1904, he condemned the Democrats for their exploitation of race: "What a blessed thing it is for Democratic leaders that they always have 'the nigger' to fall back on! For thirty years they have been doing business on the 'the nigger,' and to-day he is their only stock in trade." But Watson questioned the sincerity of the Democrats' white-nationalist commitment. He demanded that Judge Parker answer a series of questions: Would school integration be good for the South? Would he refuse to appoint blacks to office in the South? "Would you refuse to eat at the same table with Booker Washington?"[31]

Booker urged the president to steer clear of southern questions during the campaign. Just ignore the Crumpacker plank, he advised: "The minute you mention the 'Fourteenth Amendment,' the whole Southern question looms up in the eyes of many timid people in the North and West." Roosevelt followed his advice. In contrast, the Democrats incessantly exploited race. Jeff Davis, the foot-stomping, shouting governor of Arkansas, erupted in disgust when recounting the White House dinner on the campaign trail: "Can you think of anything dirtier, nastier than that?—eating with a nigger." Every red-blooded southern white man would shoot any black who approached his daughter at church and asked to walk her home. "I would, and I am the governor of Arkansas." But Alice Roosevelt had been put in a terrible bind. "What would that sweet girl do, her having entertained Washington . . . and having dined with him in [her] own home? Let me tell you, we are not going to have any nigger equality down here as long as we can pull a trigger and there are shotguns and pistols lying around loose." In this atmosphere, Booker stayed out of the public eye. He spent the campaign season directing lieutenants about how to influence black voters in the northern and border states, where close contests were expected. He oversaw the publication of Roosevelt propaganda in the New York *Age* and arranged for five states to be blanketed with the paper. In the end, Roosevelt was so strong and Parker so weak that the black vote affected the outcome only in Maryland and Delaware.[32]

With his big victory, Roosevelt again pushed the Crum nomination in January 1905. Finally the long-suffering doctor was confirmed. Crum received back pay, served successfully without controversy for four more years, and made notable improvements at the Charleston port. None of that would have happened had Washington not fought so persistently for Crum. The nomination had cost both Booker and the president a lot of effort in the face of intense hostility, but at last they prevailed in maintaining some small, symbolic black presence in politics. For Booker, the victory rewarded his need to demonstrate black progress.

Events at the Tuskegee courthouse on the hot Monday morning of October 3 marred the eventual Roosevelt victory for Washington, because they revealed how close the violent appeal of a white nationalist could come to him. Tom Heflin was campaigning for election to Congress in a race that had turned ugly. His Republican opponent was a former Populist, Benjamin Walker, who appealed to the same poor farmers that Heflin addressed. Heflin had taken to calling Walker a "black and tan serpent hissing at the feet of honest and upright Democrats." He had accosted Walker the previous afternoon at the train station in nearby Opelika and threatened to kill the Republican for lying about him. When Walker refused to recant, Heflin beat him severely with a knife handle. Heflin had been using Washington as his whipping boy throughout the campaign, saying that if reelected Roosevelt would appoint Booker to his cabinet. He "may enjoy being 'Negro Patronage Boss' of Alabama," Heflin sneered, but "his head is turned, he is a changed negro . . . If Booker Washington didn't believe in social equality, he wouldn't do as he is doing." Inevitably he alluded to the White House dinner. "There they sat, Roosevelt and Booker," Heflin shouted to the 300 people in the courtroom, including some blacks in the back. "If some Czolgosz"—referring to McKinley's assassin—"had thrown a bomb under the table, no great harm would have been done the country." Washington was scheming to elect Walker. "If Booker interferes in this thing there is a way of stopping him," Heflin warned. "We have a way of influencing negroes down here when it becomes necessary." The threat of lynching spurred whites to a standing ovation.[33]

Heflin continued in this vein throughout his successful campaign. He condemned Judge Jones, who had stooped so low as to "puppy around" Washington to get appointed. Washington had thrown aside his cover of deference: "The real Booker is seen as he really is. Against the practice of Booker Washington plain talk is necessary." Washington said nothing publicly, but privately he dismissed Heflin's words as "so bitter and unreasonable that in a very large measure they nullify themselves." But he made a telling admission to a friend: "Of course

41. Alabama congressman Tom Heflin made Booker Washington his whipping boy in his 1904 election campaign. Photo originally published by the Bain News Service, ca. 1904; courtesy of the Library of Congress.

there is a class of ignorant and prejudiced people with whom these attacks will have influence, but I do not believe they will amount to much with the thinking and intelligent." He did not acknowledge that there were more ignorant and prejudiced white people than any other kind.[34]

Nor could he give voice to an obvious truth: the threat of assassination against him, made by a sitting U.S. congressman with a history of personal violence, issued less than a mile from the Institute campus, had to be taken seriously and must have raised urgent fears in himself and in those close to him. Regardless of his mastery of national politics and the respect he commanded among the nation's most powerful and wealthiest people, he was a Negro in the South who lived entirely at the sufferance of whites. The Heflin attack revealed a dangerous erosion of Booker's public acceptance among whites. The congressman would not have chanced the verbal assault had he not known he could get away with it. The only course for Booker was to lie low and hope the attacks passed.

By the end of 1904 Booker Washington knew that his leadership was yielding good results: the Roosevelt reelection, the Crum appointment, the successful challenge to jury discrimination, and the punishment of those perpetrating peonage. But he also had to see that his success bred not just more success but also more hostility to him. No enemy is hated more than one who keeps getting the best of the opposition. Booker surely saw, however, that his effectiveness was ultimately tied to the success of the Republican president. His ability to thwart the anti-Negro obsessions of white nationalists and the anti-Booker fixation of Du Bois and Trotter rested heavily on his standing with the national administration. As long as Theodore Roosevelt listened to him and acted as Booker suggested—and well he should, given Washington's good advice and hard work on his behalf—the Tuskegee influence would in all likelihood prevail. But if Teddy wavered, his friend was in trouble.

13

The Assault by the Toms

Politics distracted Washington from his Institute work, but the responsibilities there never ceased. The legitimacy of his leadership derived chiefly from Tuskegee as an exemplar of black achievement, a symbol of the race's upward progress. By 1905 Tuskegee Institute's enrollment surpassed that of nearly all other institutions of higher education in the South. The dozen new buildings on campus stood as tall, red-brick testaments to what blacks could do on their own. Whites who admired Booker Washington—Carnegie, Baldwin, Ogden, and Peabody—were amazed that a black man had done so much with all the obstacles posed by his color. The budget required about $100 per year per student, and with an annual enrollment of about 1,500, he needed about $150,000 per year. Few students paid any tuition. Even with the Carnegie gift in the endowment, Booker still had to raise $90,000 each year to operate the school. He estimated at the time that nine-tenths of the money spent on black industrial education in the South came from northern donors, and at Tuskegee the fraction was even larger. Because the Tuskegee student body was so much larger than those at other black industrial schools—the state-supported black land-grant colleges averaged only about 200 students, and they received far more state funding than Tuskegee did—Washington's financial responsibility dwarfed that of virtually any other higher-education leader in the South, black or white. His fundraising therefore could never cease.[1]

He hoped for another big gift from Andrew Carnegie, whose confidence in Booker was total, but for the time being he had to be satisfied with helping the increasingly blinkered eighty-year-old to decide which schools in the South should get his libraries. Booker used his influence with Carnegie in a liberal spirit: he endorsed gifts to a white Methodist college in Mississippi and a black college in North Carolina, though he had no close connection to either. He lobbied successfully to get a library for Fisk University, one of the liberal-arts colleges he was accused of opposing. He even endorsed a Carnegie library for Alabama State University, run by his underhanded nemesis William Paterson, the man behind the 1903 attack in the Washington *Post*. (Booker's good deed for Paterson did not go unpunished.) Booker wanted some of Carnegie's money to go to the South, the needs in fact were now greater outside Tuskegee, and gifts to other schools enhanced his own influence. He helped at least twenty-two black educational institutions to get Carnegie libraries, although it was often an arduous process: The applicant had first to make the request to Carnegie, who sought Washington's opinion. If Booker approved, as he always did, Carnegie offered money, usually with the stipulation of a local match to his gift. Booker had to go back to Carnegie on the institution's behalf when it could not raise the matching funds. After Booker begged him to waive the match requirement, the old man usually handed over the money.[2]

William Baldwin's long illness and then death in early 1905 made the fundraising more difficult. For a decade Baldwin had advised him on virtually all matters about the school, but especially about financial management. "None knew better than he the strong as well as the weak points of the people of my race," Booker said in his eulogy of Baldwin, "and deeply as he sympathized with the effort of the race to go forward, he never allowed himself to be controlled by mere sentiment." Other than Booker himself, Baldwin had been the main force in fundraising, guiding Washington to men with money and suggesting how to approach them. Baldwin's influence went further: he understood Republican politics, especially how to deal with Theodore Roosevelt, and he advised Booker on coping with the institutional philanthropy centered in the Ogden Movement. In these areas, Booker's efforts would be less successful after he lost Baldwin's counsel. Baldwin was also the only white man to whom he felt he could speak unguardedly about white racial attitudes. Losing Baldwin as a sounding board would handicap Washington's decisionmaking in the future.[3]

Tuskegee Institute's success belied the worsening poverty of black primary schools in the South. Ever since he had arrived in Alabama, Booker had been talking about the great difficulty in improving black education when there was no dependable financial support for school construction. In 1905 an elderly Quaker woman in Philadelphia, Anna Jeanes, endowed the building of rural schoolhouses in the South with what would eventually come to a million dollars. Tuskegee and Hampton were given dual responsibility to administer the Jeanes Fund among their graduates who returned to rural communities to teach. This effort represented a bit of good news in the otherwise bleak story. The larger problem for black schools was the steadily diminishing public funding for school operations. In July 1905 Booker sent Oswald Villard evidence of the widening disparity in spending between black and white schools in the South, and he pleaded again for the editor to send a reporter to investigate. "You will note in the enclosed letter this man says in his district $15 per capita is allowed every white child and 35 cents per capita for every Negro child. If this is true and this condition exists in large proportion of our counties, you can easily see what the results would be." But Villard was less interested in such structural injustice than he was in the more sensational misdeeds of the white South: lynching, peonage, and disfranchisement. Funding discrimination reflected white hostility to black education that was promoted constantly by white-nationalist politicians. Mississippi's Vardaman continued to decry education as the curse of the Negro. He asked the legislature to remove the constitutional guarantee of equal education in order that all money might go to "the white country boys and girls who are to rule Mississippi in the future."[4]

The Ogden Movement, the coalition of northern philanthropists and southern white educators created in 1901, had continued its shameful disregard of black education. When an Ogden party stopped in Tuskegee in May 1904, it stayed only four hours but in that time picked up what Booker thought were false impressions—wrong judgments resulting from the group's excessive fear of engaging in social equality with Tuskegee blacks. Booker's distress stemmed in part from his need to influence the philanthropists in the group. J. L. M. Curry had just retired as administrator of the Slater and Peabody Funds, and Washington feared that the foundations might begin to ignore all black schools. Later Booker pleaded with Hollis Burke Frissell, the white principal of Hampton and an influential member of the Ogden Movement, for philanthropic help for black rural schools. A great deal was being done to improve white schools across the South, "but in the country districts I am quite sure that matters are going backward." White school terms were being lengthened with new tax revenue, but no improvements were seen in black schools. In fact some black teachers were being paid as little as ten dollars per month. "This of course means no school," Booker told Frissell. The Ogden Movement's propaganda for better white schools encouraged more robbing from the black children to help the whites.[5]

Whites who hated Booker Washington did so precisely because he had so successfully lifted himself and those who followed him. Those most determined to end his racial leadership cast the whole Tuskegee enterprise as either a fraud or a threat to the racial peace of the South. In 1904 Edgar Gardner Murphy had noted the growing resentment in Alabama of the "'showiness' of so large an institution." White hostility to Tuskegee's success accounted for a bizarre attack in the spring of 1905. It came in a book purportedly written by a music teacher at the white Alabama Female College in Tuskegee, one S. Becker von Grabil. *Letters from Tuskegee, Being the Confessions of a Yankee* reported that there was rampant immorality among the students and faculty at Tuskegee Institute. The book claimed that female students were made to have sex with male professors and bore their children out of wedlock. "It is so difficult for a modest, virtuous Negro girl,—by reason of the fact of her modesty and virtue,—to preserve her chastity athwart the smooth allurement of some Negro Parson or Educator." Predatory professors were responsible for "*two to five* illegitimate matriculations in the cradle class each year," but the school covered up the births. Von Grabil alleged that Tuskegee's industrial education was fraudulent, that hired workers falsely designated as students had actually built the Institute, and that enrollment figures were inflated. Booker was too busy with politics to find whites a maid when asked, and Margaret Washington dismissed such requests out of hand. When a Montgomery matron managed to hire a Tuskegee graduate as a maid, the girl "informed the Madame, that she, being a Booker Washington graduate, considered herself as good as her mistress." Before the school was founded, the county had held only two terms of criminal court, but now it had to have six, the increase reflecting the activity of "so-called educated negroes." Every student and teacher at the Institute had only one aspiration, von Grabil wrote, "to compel the white man to cringe and do homage to his or her particularly sublime majesty."[6]

Emmett Scott attributed the attack to the Institute's rejection of von Grabil's offer to give piano recitals on campus, but the motive was more likely the animus of William Paterson. The book's allegations were suspiciously similar to those made two years earlier in the Washington *Post* by Paterson's agent. Many of the allegations in the book emanated from Montgomery. Von Grabil's mastery of the shibboleths of antiblack thought and the tropes of white-nationalist writing strained credulity when coming from a recent immigrant. Richard Massey, head of the female college, wrote a letter defending the moral conditions at the Institute, but Booker stopped its publication because it would only promote the attack. A few shameful things had occurred in twenty-four years, Booker admitted privately to Massey, but he had always dismissed the student or teacher who brought disgrace on the school. "The wonder is that there have not been more instances of wrong doing than there have been." Mailed to newspapers all across the country, the book elicited much editorial comment. The assertions of immorality, fraudulent management, and dishonest public relations resonated with prejudices already well entrenched among whites, and thus easily enjoyed credence; and for those already of a mind to challenge his legitimacy, *Letters from Tuskegee* lent strength to their efforts. But there was little that Booker could do but let the mud dry and hope that it left no lasting stain.[7]

The growing resentment of the Institute's and Booker Washington's success revealed in *Letters from Tuskegee* was reiterated in an attack a few months later from Tuskegee's state legislator, Ernest Thompson. He was the twenty-five-year-old son of the late Democratic congressman and the nephew of Joseph Thompson, whom Booker had recently made the most powerful white Republican in Alabama. Young Ernest introduced a bill to limit the Tuskegee Institute's tax-exempt status on the grounds that the school was trying to own the entire county. It had to be a bitter irony to Booker that the immature scion of a family for which he had done so much would attack the school in such a public way. Pressure from his family and the Institute's friends only made Thompson more obstinate, and he pushed through the legislature a resolution ordering the governor to audit the Institute's finances. The governor's man studied the Institute books and declared its management a model of perfection. Thompson's tax bill was defeated soundly but not before other legislators voiced their opposition to the school. "Tuskegee Institute has more income than the University of Alabama, the Polytechnic Institute [at Auburn] and the Girls' Industrial School [at Montevallo] combined," announced a Birmingham Progressive. "And they are educating them how? To hate us." Another was even more alarmed: "Booker Washington and his gang [will] prove to be the curse of the South, and if I had my way I would wipe his institute off the face of the earth."[8]

At the same time that *Letters from Tuskegee* was bringing unwanted attention in the white press, Washington was dealing with a new frontal assault in the black press. In the aftermath of the Boston riot, Trotter accused Washington of manipulating the black newspapers through financial pressure and bribery. In early 1905 Du Bois published a claim that Washington had paid $3,000 to control the black press in five cities. He probably referred at least to Boston, Chicago, Washington, and New York, where Booker was nurturing pro-Tuskegee papers to counter existing papers that opposed him; the latter included the Boston *Guardian,* Washington *Bee,* Chicago *Conservator,* Chicago *Broad Ax,* and Cleveland *Gazette.* He had been engaged in the effort in Boston since 1901 and more recently in Chicago, in each case without success. The Washington *Colored American* did provide a competent alternative to the *Bee.* Booker's clearest involvement was in the *Colored*

American Magazine, a Boston publication about to go under when he dispatched Fred Moore, a New York ally through the National Negro Business League, to purchase it and move the magazine to New York. Washington kept his involvement secret, and he did not allow Moore to write too favorably about Tuskegee. It was therefore true that Washington was subsidizing the black press, but Du Bois lacked the evidence to prove the $3,000 figure.[9]

Booker answered the criticism by insisting to black allies that he had never paid to influence any editorial opinion. He did support black newspapers by providing them with copy, buying advertisements, and getting them political contributions from the Republican Party to print campaign issues during elections. He was surely shading the truth, and it was probably an unnecessary deception. He had said openly that blacks needed a national publication to create common understandings and to advocate united positions on issues. He and Tim Fortune had discussed the need in the late 1880s. After the call for a central bureau of communication at the Carnegie Hall meeting in January 1904, Booker asked William Baldwin to help raise money for a national black newspaper to "unify the race and keep it at work along sensible and constructive directions." He predicted to Fortune that someone would soon start a dominant national weekly newspaper. Booker wanted Fortune's New York *Age* to fill that role.[10]

It made sense for Washington to want a national publication over which he had primary influence. It would be a more efficient means to promote his message of race progress, set more policy agendas for blacks, and respond to issues as they arose. White-nationalist leaders had their publications: Vardaman's Greenwood *Commonwealth* and *Tom Watson's Magazine* served their owners as open spigots of antiblack venom; and James Hemphill at the Charleston *News and Courier,* Clark Howell at the Atlanta *Constitution,* John Temple Graves at the Atlanta *News,* and Josephus Daniels at the Raleigh *News and Observer* were all white-nationalist editor-politicians who daily posted their opinions about the Negro Problem. There were columnists at big newspapers doing what Bill Arp had done for decades, retailing pernicious black stereotypes that underpinned white cultural antipathy. On the other side, Oswald Villard had the New York *Evening Post* and the *Nation* to advance his problack viewpoint. And there was Trotter, who condemned everything Booker did.

Booker's plan to expand and elevate the New York *Age* foundered on the troubled character of Tim Fortune. In 1904 Fortune was drinking heavily and intent on getting a political appointment from Roosevelt. He told Scott that he wanted to sell the *Age* and "let the Negro business go . . . and make some money, which I can do all right, if I dump the Negro load I have on my back."[11] He soon antagonized Booker by criticizing the "child race" remark and talking loosely about Booker's secret support of the Alabama suffrage cases. Washington began to encourage Fortune's partner to expand the *Age*'s mission, apparently with the expectation of buying Fortune's interest in the *Age* and shaping its editorial policies from a distance.

Booker's reluctance to act openly left a vacuum that was filled in 1904 with the appearance of a new national magazine, the *Voice of the Negro*. The magazine's general editor was the Atlanta academic theologian John Wesley Edward Bowen, a Washington ally but a man too busy to pay much attention to the new venture. The dominant influence was a young Virginian, Jesse Max Barber, who as managing editor worked to advance Du Bois's criticism, including publishing Du Bois's accusation that Washington was paying for newspaper approval. Barber asked editorially "What Is A Good Negro?" to which he replied sarcastically: "'A good Negro' is one who says he does not want the ballot. He orates before his people and advises them against going into politics. He says to them 'Keep out of politics.' Go to the farms; keep quiet and let the whites handle the government. 'A good Negro' is one who says that his race does not need the higher learning; that what they need is industrial education, pure and simple. He stands up before his people and murders the truth and the Kings English in trying to enforce upon them the evils of a College Education and the beauties of the plow." Barber's editorial outraged Washington, and he demanded privately that Bowen explain how he could publish such a censure. He did not tell Bowen, but Booker marked the *Voice of the Negro* for destruction and Max Barber for oblivion.[12]

Oswald Villard offered Du Bois space in the New York *Evening Post* to present any evidence he had that Booker was controlling the black

42. In 1904 the monthly *Voice of the Negro* became the main vehicle through which Du Bois challenged Washington's leadership. Cover of *Voice of the Negro* 2 (January 1905).

press. Du Bois turned down the offer to publish but asked to provide the evidence privately to Villard, whose favor he hoped to curry as the most influential problack editor among white journalists. Du Bois then wrote frantically to Trotter to send him the evidence. The case that Du Bois made to Villard was highly circumstantial, based mainly on the existence of new pro-Washington newspapers in Boston and Chicago and the flow of press releases from Tuskegee. Villard sent Du Bois's brief to his uncle Francis Garrison, who replied that Washington was undoubtedly influencing black newspapers but to "secure unity rather than contention & discord, & this not because he cares for the attacks on himself, but because he knows that some of his assailants would gladly see Tuskegee wrecked if necessary to discredit & pull him down." Villard then informed Du Bois that the evidence of Washington's control had not persuaded him. "I greatly regret your position and your attitude towards Mr. Washington," he wrote. "I do not think that there are any essential differences between your positions."[13]

Washington's attempts to ensure himself a favorable black press involved the expenditure of a lot of energy in what he should have seen as a hopeless cause. Inevitably some of his critics were going to publish their condemnations, but in the event these attacks were never as potent as Booker and his close allies feared. "If Trotter and his sympathizers are bound to assail you," Francis Garrison wrote to Booker, "they will do it in spite of all efforts to avert it, but personally I should not be troubled as to the result, which can only be a recoil on themselves."[14] Garrison's advice was wise, but, like most men, Booker found it hard to ignore ugly, false accusations. For all the effort expended on behalf of the *Colored American Magazine* and the anti-Trotter newspapers in Boston, and against the *Voice of the Negro,* he might have created "Booker Washington's Magazine," installed Emmett Scott as the editor, and said exactly what he thought needed saying. If Booker did consider this option, he may have concluded that everything he wrote or said would be subject to white misrepresentation and that going on the record regularly might keep him mired in controversy. He believed he could get his views aired through proxies. But the secret financial dealings and misrepresentations in which this choice involved him were unworthy of the higher purposes to which he was committed.

Washington had suspected that Du Bois and Trotter would create an organization to oppose him, and they did so in the summer of 1905. The Niagara Movement represented Du Bois's open, concerted challenge to Washington and the beginning of his campaign for recognition as the leader of the race. Most of the twenty-nine men whom Du Bois convened at Niagara Falls in July came from the black professional ranks in New England and the Midwest. Often referred to as Du Bois's "Talented Tenth," the group would have had to multiply many times to live up to that name. In fact they amounted to about one percent of the college-educated black elite, which by Du Bois's own calculations accounted for about .02 percent of the black population in the United States in 1905. Not surprisingly, this infinitesimal minority took a stand for what nearly all blacks were already on record as wanting; most of the Niagara positions in effect reiterated the agenda set at Carnegie Hall in 1904: a defense of personal liberty, civil and voting rights, opportunity for education and jobs. The group's manifesto differed only in an explicit embrace of open protest: "We refuse to allow the impression to remain that the Negro-American assents to inferiority, is submissive under oppression and apologetic before insults. Through helplessness we may submit, but the voice of protest of ten million Americans must never cease to assail the ears of their fellows, so long as America is unjust . . . Persistent manly agitation is the way to liberty."[15]

As he did in trying to cancel the impact of critical black newspapers, Washington overreached in his attempts to stifle the new group. He sent spies to find out what happened at the meeting and exhorted his allies to prevent news of the movement from reaching the public. He quashed some reporting, but his opponents were far too determined to be kept out of the public eye for long. Booker's claim that his black opponents amounted to a few men in three cities was for the most part true, but he and his allies acted as if the opposition was much greater. Washington had always been intolerant of black criticism, and much of that aimed at him was purely personal. Du Bois and Trotter exaggerated the differences between their views and his, misrepresenting Booker's positions. They also refused to acknowledge the very real restrictions that his residence in the Deep South imposed on his leader-

43. Du Bois and Trotter inaugurated the Niagara Movement in the summer of 1905 as the institutional vehicle to wrest leadership of American blacks from Booker Washington. Photographer unknown; from *Voice of the Negro* 2 (September 1905).

ship. But Booker's intolerance of his critics reflected his unwillingness to accept that among ten million people there must inevitably be some dissension. It also demonstrated the resentment he felt at their refusal to stand with him against the attacks from the white South since he dined with the president.

At the very time that Du Bois and Trotter were enjoying the gentle mists of the Niagara waters, a new storm hit the South. In June 1905, with Washington still feeling the fallout from *Letters from Tuskegee,* a prominent minister told white college students in nearby Auburn that Washington's philosophy was "the greatest piece of humbuggery that was ever presented to the minds of the American people." J. W. Stagg called Booker the greatest exaggerator ever to take a platform and the "greatest beggar that ever held out his hat to the American public." Education for blacks was a waste, Stagg said; they should be deported until disease effected their extinction. What had provoked a minister of the gospel, one apparently unknown to the principal of Tuskegee, to feel such personal animus must have perplexed Booker. It augured badly for the next few months. At the same time Washington came under attack for a story he told in a speech, one that he had used often to suggest his skepticism about the campaigns to bring white immigrants to the South. When a landlord asked his black sharecropper what he thought about the possibility of Europeans moving in, the black man answered: "Boss, we got as many white folks down here now as we can support." All of a sudden, the story was taken as an unpardonable insult to white southerners, and editorialists spewed wrath at Booker. The editor of the New Orleans *States* asserted that the story pandered to the northern idea that southern whites were "indolent and shiftless and the material prosperity of this section is created by the Negroes." Like all other Negroes, he wrote, Booker would not "hesitate to create or encourage a fake impression if by doing so he can advance his own interest."[16]

At the same moment, the Georgia congressman Tom Watson attacked Washington. Having run unsuccessfully as the Populist candidate for president in 1904, Watson was now heading back into the Democratic fold in preparation for mounting a campaign for disfranchisement in Georgia. One of the most effective propagandists ever to take the political stump in the South, or to lift the editorial pen, Watson surely had noted the white-nationalist demonization of Washington, and now he added to it with his peculiar talent for vituperation. In *Tom Watson's Magazine,* he charged that Washington believed that "the black man is superior to the white." When in a national magazine article James K. Vardaman had used statistics on black criminality to justify ending black education, Washington had launched an indirect counterattack by citing in speeches the rapid increase in black literacy since emancipation as evidence of black progress. He reported that literacy rates among African Americans were now higher than those in

European countries. But Watson reported that Washington had claimed that blacks had developed more rapidly in the thirty years of their freedom than Italians and Spaniards had in a millennium. Watson denounced Washington for not counting all the ignorant blacks in Africa and the Caribbean. "If you will number *all* the negroes, Doctor, your percentage of illiteracy *among the blacks* may run up among the nineties, and knock your calculation into a cocked hat." During the millennium when Europeans were building a civilization, "your people were running about in the woods, naked, eating raw meat . . . steeped in ignorance, vice and superstition, with an occasional lapse into human sacrifice and cannibalism." Would Roosevelt and Carnegie "like you better when they hear you putting forth a claim to race superiority?" Did it not, Watson demanded of Washington, "occur to you that you may create a feeling of resentment among *all* the whites?" That was exactly Watson's purpose. *"Whenever the North wakes up to the fact that you are teaching the blacks that they are superior to the whites,"* Watson warned, *"you are going to feel the east wind."* He ended with a rant that Western civilization owed a great debt to Latin culture: "What does Civilization owe to the negro? Nothing! *Nothing!! NOTH-ING!!!"*[17]

Reprinted in many southern newspapers, the attack was more widely quoted than anything else Watson ever wrote. Washington ignored the article until editorialists started endorsing Watson's view. Then he wrote to deny that he had ever claimed black superiority—but without naming Watson.[18] Even so, Booker knew that the mere fact of his response could fuel a public controversy.

In 1905 one assault seemed to beget another. Thomas Dixon had just published his second novel, *The Clansman,* and it was on its way to selling a million copies within a year. *The Clansman* reprised *The Leopard's Spots*—an anti-Negro melodrama of Reconstruction with a strong emphasis on black soldiers' sexual assaults of white southern women. African Americans were portrayed in the antebellum years as happy and loyal servants, and after the war mainly as dangerous beasts intent on sexual exploitation of white women, in which they were thwarted only by the emergence of multitudes of mounted Ku Klux Klansmen. Its climactic scenes described a lustful black soldier chasing a young white woman until he drove her to suicide, followed by a lynching. In the summer of 1905 Dixon was preparing a stage version of *The Clansman,* and he was angling for a media controversy to promote his novel and play. He had already been making it his business to attack Washington and his allies. In June he wrote in newspapers that Robert Ogden had walked through his New York department store with his arm around Booker, a gesture that proved Ogden to be a "negro worshiper pure and simple." If weak-minded Yankees were allowed to promote black equality, Dixon wrote, then Negro blood would "drown the national character at last in a welter of negroid mongrelization."[19]

In August Dixon published in the *Saturday Evening Post* an artful critique of Washington second only to Du Bois's *Souls of Black Folk.* Dixon identified Booker's life as a romance that appealed to the human heart, the kind of story that Dixon himself liked best. "The story of a little ragged, bare-footed piccaninny who lifted his eyes from a cabin in the hills of Virginia, saw a vision and followed it, until at last he presides over the richest and most powerful institution of learning in the South, and sits down with crowned heads and Presidents, has no parallel even in the Tales of the Arabian Nights." But Washington's vision raised false hope that the racial problem in America could be solved, Dixon declared; blacks' failure was inevitable. He reiterated the points made by his *Leopard's Spots* character Preacher Durham. Washington's educational mission was a subterfuge for racial equality and amalgamation. Booker was preparing blacks not to work in an industrial economy for white men but was "training them *all* to be masters of men, to be independent, to own and operate their own industries, plant their own fields, buy and sell their own goods, and in every shape and form destroy the last vestige of dependence on the white man for anything." This independent black nation represented a great danger. "Every pupil who passes through Mr. Washington's hands ceases forever to work under a white man. Not only so, but he goes forth trained under an evangelist to preach the doctrine of separation and independence." The real tragedy would begin when black men and white men began competing in the industrial workplace. Would the southern white man allow the Negro to master his industrial system, take the bread from his mouth, and place a mortgage on his house, as in fact Booker had promised? Dixon emphatically answered "no": "He will do exactly what his white neighbor in the North does when the Negro threatens his bread—kill him!"[20]

Dixon's indictment of Washington summarized the critique that had been mounting since the late 1890s among white nationalists. Despite Booker's constant flow of reassurances that blacks wanted to be of service to their white neighbors and to establish cordial, complementary relations, the real purpose of his strategy was equal economic status for blacks and eventually political and social equality. Ben Tillman had suggested this in the 1890s, Dixon had written it into his first novel, and much of the white South came to believe it in the aftermath of the White House dinner. The Tuskegee strategy was to get the Trojan horse of industrial education inside the walls of the industrial economy, and social equality would eventually emerge.

Dixon's attack appeared just as another firestorm broke out in Washington's life. In mid-August Booker had dinner with the department store magnate John Wanamaker at the United States Hotel at Saratoga Springs, New York. For years Booker had been going to Saratoga and other summer resort spots in the Northeast to solicit gifts from wealthy vacationers. Since 1882 he had often dined with whites in their homes and sometimes in public places, and no significant criticism had emerged before the White House dinner. But after that, he was far more vulnerable to the charge of engaging in social equality. In the summer of 1904 there had been a brief flurry of controversy over reports that Booker had dined at the home of a prominent white family in Stockbridge, Massachusetts. He had gone there to solicit funds from Alexander Sedgwick alone and found that his host had invited six other prominent whites to dine with the famous black man. That affair was reported during the heightened tension of the presidential campaign, and it probably helped to prompt the Saratoga outcry a year later. The wire services picked up a false report in William Randolph Hearst's New York *Evening Journal* about the Wanamaker dinner: a buzz had spread and necks had craned among hotel diners when Booker escorted Wanamaker's daughter to their table.[21]

Fury erupted again in the South. The editor of the Montgomery *Advertiser,* who had defended Washington after the White House dinner, now wrote that whites were "sorely grieved by his continual exhibition of desire for social equality, knowing that what he did would make a deep impression upon the more ignorant negroes of this country." To the lieutenant governor of Alabama, Washington's action showed conclusively that he was an unwise leader of his race. "It contradicts emphatically the policies he has preached and the profession he has made. It impairs his usefulness to his people, for, while he may be immune from the injury that will follow, the credulous and ignorant will suffer incalculably." A Birmingham judge declared Booker a bad Negro: "He had us all fooled . . . Booker talks one way and acts another. He educates his children in white schools while he is conducting a negro school." Vardaman asserted that it would be fortunate for Alabama "if her people could induce Booker to go north where things are more congenial with his fastidious taste." The Columbus *Ledger* opined succinctly: "Booker T. Washington passed away at Saratoga." William Hooper Council condemned Booker's action, which "could not and would not be permitted," and offered himself to Alabama's governor as a truly safe leader of blacks. A white informant warned Emmett Scott that a white man from Tallassee, the historical center of white terrorism north of Tuskegee, had vowed to kill Booker, boasting that no court in Alabama would now convict him for doing so. Scott warned Booker to stay out of Alabama, and he did so through September. By then he had engaged Pinkerton guards to travel everywhere with him.[22]

In contrast to the strict silence he maintained after the White House dinner, Washington soon issued a response about the Saratoga affair. He had not escorted Wanamaker's daughter to the table, but he admitted that he regularly dined with whites in the North. "When in the South I conform like all colored people to the customs of the South," he wrote, "but when in the North, I have found it necessary . . . to come into contact with white people in the furtherance of my work in ways I do not in the South." Privately Booker worried that the sensational reporting would prevent him from raising money. And yet the attacks that bothered him most came from the *Guardian,* which condemned him for associating with wealthy whites. Du Bois had apparently gone from Niagara to Boston and spent the remainder of the summer helping Trotter to edit the paper. When Du Bois sent word that he would like to reply to Thomas Dixon on Booker's behalf, Washington was incensed. "Certainly Dixon or no other white man has ever attempted to damage and discredit the work of this institution and my own efforts more than Du Bois has done," he wrote privately. In Booker's mind, Du Bois and Trotter had in effect joined hands with the white nationalists. "These men seem to forget that Dixon and the lower element of the Southern press are not aiming at me as an individual but at the race, and that when men join Dixon and Tillman and Tom Watson in condemning me, they are condemning at the same time the race to which they belong." Du Bois and Trotter refused to see that "it is not B. T. Washington who is attacked, but the race."[23]

In the fall of 1905 Thomas Dixon's play *The Clansman* toured from city to city in the South. The audiences were wildly enthusiastic about the melodramatic staging of the Ku Klux Klan's heroism during Reconstruction, including live horses and a burning cross on stage. Audiences in Atlanta were so riveted by the white girl's effort to escape the sex-crazed freedman, and by her ultimate leap to death to avoid being raped, that they screamed "Lynch him!" when the Klan captured the black brute (played by a white actor). When the lynching was staged, blacks in the audience hissed loudly, and fights broke out. A few months later, as his controversial play was opening in New York, Dixon sent Booker a proposal—and simultaneously informed the press of it. "I hereby offer to contribute $10,000 from the profits of 'The Clansman' to Tuskegee Institute," Dixon wrote Washington, "provided you give complete satisfactory proof that you do not desire Social Equality for the Negro and that your School is opposed to the Amalgamation of the races." Dixon sent another challenge with the assertion that "the issue of Social Equality and Race Amalgamation . . . is one which the American people will demand that you face squarely sooner or later." Washington declined without comment.[24]

The summer of 1905 had been a season of disaster for Booker Washington, though in typical fashion he never conceded that publicly. Washington worried privately to Francis Garrison that several southern newspapers had called for his assassination and the destruction of Tuskegee Institute. Threatening letters had poured in. He admitted to

A Snake in the Grass

Cartoonist Adams pictures Tom Dixon as a keen-tongued viper coiled up and ready to hurl
his poisonous saliva at race amity in America.

44. At the same time it was attacking Booker Washington, the *Voice of the Negro*
ran editorial cartoons condemning the white nationalists, especially Thomas
Dixon and James K. Vardaman, who were blasting Booker for promoting racial
equality. Cartoon by John Henry Adams; from *Voice of the Negro* 4 (October
1907).

his Boston friend that a large element of the South had decided that
black education would go no further. He feared that whites intended
to stop the progress of Tuskegee Institute as a white-nationalist object
lesson: "The explanation of this is that the colored contractor or architect or carpenter or brickmason comes into competition with the white
man while the Negro teacher or minister does not." Garrison replied
that he, too, feared violence: "I have long felt, as I have told you, the
possibility of the torch being applied even to Tuskegee in some sudden
whirlwind of passion." At the same time, Oswald Villard wrote to his
uncle that he pitied Washington, "for he is in a desperate position and
may yet prove a martyr to his cause."[25]

There was a chance for Booker Washington to redeem some of his public standing in late October, when Theodore Roosevelt made Tuskegee a stop on a tour of the South. William McKinley had visited Tuskegee in 1898 as Booker was weathering a storm of condemnations from his Peace Jubilee speech, and the occasion had raised Booker's spirits. Perhaps that might happen again, though the circumstances were even more tense now. It was not certain, however, that the president would remain constant. As he moved through the South, Roosevelt had made one saccharine overture of sectional reconciliation after another to Confederate Veterans and Ladies' Memorial Associations. White southern observers noted a distinct change: the president seemed to have seen the light and was now "as much opposed to negro domination as any Southerner."[26] Everyone who knew him realized that he was an impetuous man, one who often acted without careful deliberation. He had privately expressed his regret at having entertained Booker at the White House and at having appointed William Crum, and Booker probably suspected Roosevelt's doubts if he did not know them for a fact.

Two days before the president's party arrived, Pinkerton agents Number 58 and Number 22 met with Emmett Scott and were briefed on the threats made against Booker's life. Scott asked them to discover the sentiment among the whites of Tuskegee and "to learn whether any party or parties in outlying towns or districts had any evil designs upon Dr. Washington." Scott was especially concerned about Tallassee. The Pinkertons investigated a white stranger on the grounds and then mingled among the travelers at the local railroad terminal, where they heard threatening remarks from disreputable-looking young men. In the lobby of the local hotel that night, they heard S. Becker von Grabil condemn Washington's methods for elevating his race, saying, according to Number 58, that "Dr. Washington advocated social equality and endeavored to impress upon the colored people the idea that they do not need to indulge in manual labor in order to live." As the agents continued to circulate among people arriving to see the president, they heard a young soldier, assigned to accompany Roosevelt, say he would "like to exterminate Dr. Washington and his people; that they were a menace to the community." The agents met privately with Booker and then spent the day questioning whites in the town. "Some of the young men were disposed to 'rail' about Dr. Washington and his school," they found, "but the best and most reputable citizens of the town spoke very highly of Dr. Washington and his work."[27]

Roosevelt's visit went off without a problem. The president was impressed with the spectacle staged for his benefit and offered warm words about Booker before delivering the careful, noncontroversial speech that Washington had helped prepare. The event pleased Booker for the positive message it projected. Francis Garrison complained privately to him that "the outcries of the South about the White House incident have made [Roosevelt] so timid that he could not break bread under your roof," but it may have been Booker himself who was unwilling to chance yet another event that might be interpreted as a breach of racial etiquette.[28]

The attacks on Booker had almost entirely overturned his earlier image in the white South, as well as perceptions of his original purpose. By end of 1905 most southern whites had encountered incessant perversions of almost every public word and action. In the past year an angry trio of Toms—Heflin, Watson, and Dixon—had transformed Washington into the power-hungry, deceitful "Wizard of Tuskegee." Du Bois was promoting precisely the same image in the hope of displacing him as leader of the race. Ever on the alert to discover flaws in a celebrity, the press did its part to tumble the mighty during the Wanamaker controversy. By then Booker had to ask whether he could regain control of what he stood for, restore his good name, and otherwise overcome the damage done to him. If he could not do those things, he had failed as the leader of his people.

Washington had never failed at anything he had undertaken, and not for a moment did he concede defeat. He had faith that, given exposure to the real Booker Washington, many whites and nearly all blacks would embrace his message and reject the white nationalists. The best way to restore faith in his purpose after the disasters of 1905 was to go among the masses and deliver his message of black progress. His public tours had always restored his faith in his leadership. He believed he could turn the tide of white opinion in his direction, toward a more positive view of blacks and an optimistic outlook for race relations.

First he needed to take the pulse of black opinion. Theodore Roosevelt was not long gone from Tuskegee when Booker left for Chicago and the National Baptist Convention, where he spoke twice, each time to crowds of 5,000 African Americans who continually roared their agreement with him. Every race that had risen had been misunderstood, had suffered and been persecuted, Washington said, and the black race was no exception to the rule. Jews and even Anglo-Saxons had fought their way up through difficult circumstances. "My main concern just now about my race is that it shall be worthy, that it shall be within itself all that we represent it to be, that it shall continually practice frugality, industry, modesty, and self-control." Blacks should never imitate the habit of cherishing hatred and ill will toward another race. They must turn the other cheek. Nothing would sooner stop their progress than engaging in racial hatred. Black Americans must instruct their children that the powerful men of the world had risen above racial considerations. Then he shifted from teacher to prophet: "The black race will come into its reward, and will be counted among the successful peoples of the earth just in proportion as it keeps its eyes steadfastly fixed upon the substance rather than the shadow, just in proportion as it seeks continually to accomplish real things and builds its houses upon the rock." After each speech, listeners rushed to Booker to touch him.[29]

After the onslaught of criticism in 1905, questions were raised about Washington's popularity and his ability to lead his race. Du Bois, Trotter, and their followers insisted that Washington was not popular among blacks. Other African Americans saw matters differently. "No man in America has ever had such a hold on these people as B. T.," one observer wrote about the huge turnouts in Chicago. When the Federal Writers' Project interviewed former slaves in the 1930s, many were asked their opinion about Washington. Virtually all were positive, typically seeing him as a great man in the same way that Abraham Lincoln had been. "Booker T. Washington was a man of de fust magnitude," one declared. Another said that "everybody thinks he is a great man for the colored race." "He used to live in a cabin jest lak I done," an Oklahoma woman observed. "He was sho' a great man." Booker was "the first Negro to represent the Negroes in Washington," another said. "He was a great leader." An Alabama woman said that "Booker T. Washington was one of de greates' niggers dat ever lived, he always tried to raise de standard of de race."[30]

A more immediate measure of Booker's standing existed in the naming practices of black parents for their newborns during the years of Booker's leadership. In 1902 more than 100 black babies were named Booker T. In 1905 there were 335 infants named Booker, and 212 of them were Booker T.'s. In 1906, 245 newborns would be called Booker T. At the height of the attacks from the Niagara Movement, Booker seemed to be gaining in popularity among southern blacks. The number of black babies named Booker in 1905 represented eleven times the number of black men who attended the founding of the Niagara group. In 1905 there was only one black newborn named Du Bois and another named Frederick Douglass. The average number of babies named Booker for the years from 1902 through 1916 would be almost 260, and among these the average number with the middle initial *T* was 185. The 1930 census located almost 3,000 Bookers in the United States. In 2007 the Social Security Death Index recorded 7,142 Bookers, 2,601 Booker T.'s, and 173 Booker T. Washingtons—117 of whom were born after their namesake had died. Given that the death index missed all the Bookers who died before the creation of the Social Security Administration in the late 1930s, the popularity of the name was surely even greater than these numbers suggest.[31]

After meeting with the Baptists in Chicago, Washington embarked on a ten-day speaking tour through Arkansas and the Oklahoma and Indian Territories, a part of the country he had not previously visited but where he now found huge and enthusiastic crowds. A Pinkerton guard was with him at all times, but the protection proved unnecessary. At Muskogee, in the Indian Territory, 4,000 blacks met him at the train depot; and at Guthrie, Oklahoma, he was greeted by a huge mixed crowd that formed a parade a mile long as it followed him to the lecture hall. The opera house in Little Rock was overrun with blacks and whites clamoring to hear him, and Booker was amazed to see blacks refusing to relinquish their seats to whites. At Pine Bluff, in

45. At Tuskegee's twenty-fifth anniversary celebration in the spring of 1906, Robert C. Ogden (seated at far left) and Andrew Carnegie joined Booker Washington, Maggie Washington, and the Tuskegee faculty in a commemorative group portrait. The man seated at far right is unidentified. Photo by Frances Benjamin Johnston, 1906; courtesy of the Library of Congress.

the Arkansas delta, the local newspaper had threatened any white man who attended Booker's speech with social ostracism; yet the white mayor welcomed him, Booker thought, "as boldly as any man would have done in Boston." The Arkansas response pleased him because Jeff Davis, the governor and U.S. senator-elect, had often condemned Booker. "I think the negro would do much better if Booker Washington and Andrew Carnegie, with their so-called philanthrophy [sic], would let them alone," Davis had said. "The negro's natural place is in the [cotton] field, where his activity and usefulness is greatest." The tour convinced Booker that Davis and the white-nationalist press were losing their hold on southern whites. "A large element of Southern white people are simply sick of the slavery in which they have been held by the radical newspapers and political demagogues," he told Francis Garrison.[32]

The celebration of Tuskegee Institute's Silver Jubilee in April 1906 presented another occasion for Washington to reclaim control of both his message and his own meaning. As with every previous commencement and the recent presidential visit, the twenty-fifth anniversary celebration was a carefully orchestrated parade of black progress, one witnessed by a throng of southern blacks and a sizable collection of supportive or merely curious whites. The congregation represented a gathering of the disparate elements of American society that approved of the Tuskegee experiment: captains of industry and commerce; the journalists Oswald Villard and Lyman Abbott; the presidents of Harvard, Hampton, the University of Alabama, and the University of the South; a brace of bishops, black and white; Secretary of War William Howard Taft, already the favorite to succeed Roosevelt as Republican Party leader; and William Lloyd Garrison Jr., legatee of the abolitionist cause. All the main speakers highlighted the racial progress that was manifest at Tuskegee. Robert Ogden, who had promoted black education as long as any other white man in the United States, called Tuskegee "the unmatched example of the possibilities of an institution entirely controlled" by blacks. Andrew Carnegie surveyed the Institute campus and wryly concluded that money might be the root of all evil, but it was also the root of all universities, colleges, churches, and libraries. Blacks would permanently reside in the South, Carnegie said, their labor a necessity for progress. They therefore should be "carefully guarded, fostered and educated and hence improved" in the manner "urged and adhered to by the Moses of his people, Booker Washington."[33]

Booker spoke prophetically about race in America. "If this country is to continue to be a Republic," he declared, "its task will never be completed as long as seven or eight millions of its people are in a large degree regarded as aliens and are without voice or interest in the welfare of the Government." Disfranchisement meant not only injustice to blacks but also a bleak future for democracy: that "the world will say that free government is a failure." The economic and political

weaknesses forced upon blacks undermined the American community. *"It requires no courage to inflict injustice upon the unprotected.* The
lifting up of the black man will be a double *blessing—a blessing to the
weak, a blessing to the strong."* At the end he mused about what had
been Tuskegee's signal contribution in its twenty-five years. It was, he
thought, "in putting a new spirit into the people, a spirit that makes
them feel that they have friends right about them, a spirit that has filled
them with the idea that they *can* make progress, that they *will* make
progress, and fulfill their mission *in this republic."* This indeed had
been his unwavering message in the quarter-century at Tuskegee.[34]

The one discordant note came from John W. Abercrombie, president of the University of Alabama and a Democratic politician who
had advocated improving white schools. Abercrombie claimed that
slavery had been of greater benefit to slaves than to their owners and
that enfranchisement had been the colossal mistake of Reconstruction
in wresting control of society from the superior race. As for universal
education, Alabama's purported educational leader pronounced: "If
the continued inaction of the national government renders it necessary
for one of the races to receive meager educational advantages, it is best
for the Negro, that for a season, the advantages should go to the dominant race." As state superintendent of education, Abercrombie had
been party to the growing disparity in school expenditures on black
and white children, and he knew full well that the educational advantages of the white race were neither meager nor attributable to federal
inaction. His hypocrisy and bad manners incensed Washington, but
Booker was far too polite—and too politic—to contradict Abercrombie himself. When Governor William Oates had cast slurs upon blacks
during a commencement ceremony in 1896, Washington had politely
ended the convocation. But on this occasion, when Abercrombie sat
down, Booker diverged from the announced program. He recognized
in the audience William Lloyd Garrison Jr., a seventy-year-old Boston
investment banker. After long applause, Washington summoned Garrison to the podium for impromptu remarks—without referring to
Abercrombie.

Booker knew his white people. In a vibrant, penetrating voice, the
white-bearded Garrison proceeded to tear into Abercrombie. He first

announced that he spoke not as a member of the superior race but only as one of the human race. Slavery was no benefit to any black man, and it was a humiliation to him as a white man. Abercrombie's insistence that it had been a blunder to enfranchise the Negro was the "veriest nonsense." The anniversary crowd loudly registered its agreement. "The way to teach a man to vote is to put a ballot in his hand." When Garrison turned away from the podium, the audience burst into shouting and applause.[35]

When the glorious days of celebration were over, the criticism from the Niagara Movement still loomed over Tuskegee. The movement had lost some of its original tiny cadre, but the opposition of Du Bois and Max Barber to Washington had grown even stronger. Barber had turned the *Voice of the Negro* into the voice of the Niagara Movement. His account of the silver jubilee pronounced Washington's economic emphasis wrong. "Food and raiment are not the most important elements in human progress. Rather the march of human progress is characterized by the language evolved, the literature created and the historical events humanity has figured in." Instead of meddling in "every three and six penny affair that pertains to the Negro," the twenty-seven-year-old pontificated, Washington should concentrate on his original work: "The black belt of Alabama needs him more than any other section of the country." At the same time, Du Bois was justifying the Niagara Movement by saying that the Afro-American Council had failed and that Washington's influence tainted the Committee of Twelve and the National Negro Business League. But Booker's partisan feelings matched Du Bois's and Barber's. He sent a spy to the second Niagara meeting in 1906. Told that Du Bois would share the podium with him at a Fisk University event, Booker abruptly withdrew. The Fisk president decided that he needed Booker's favor and rescinded Du Bois's invitation.[36]

The Niagara Movement condemned Roosevelt and the Republican Party for not enacting the Crumpacker proposal. Having managed to get the plan slipped into the 1904 platform, Trotter now said that the failure to reduce southern representation in Congress amounted to a premeditated breach of promise that made Republicans guilty of obtaining votes under false pretenses. Reduction of southern representation was a far-fetched possibility and one Fortune and Washington had long believed would encourage disfranchisement in places where it did not now apply. In March 1906 the *Voice of the Negro* ran a cartoon depicting Washington with a padlock on his lips, caricaturing his refusal to speak out for reduction of representation—this at precisely the time Booker was making his strong statement about political rights at the anniversary celebration. The reduction of southern congressional representation became a central aim for a new white organization called the Constitution League, created by John Milholland, a wealthy Irish-immigrant businessman in New York and an advocate for black political rights. Originally a supporter of Washington, Milholland broke with Booker when Washington asked him not to discuss congressional reduction in a speech to the Negro Business League. Booker had decided that such "a professional friend of the Negro" as Milholland was "a man to be watched."[37]

Only their common antipathy to Washington held the Niagara Movement together, but that was not strong enough for long. By the second meeting, Du Bois and Trotter were already at odds over control. The organization hardly warranted all the attention it drew in Tuskegee, because it had only a few members from Boston, Chicago, and Washington and a smattering of supporters from other places. Booker's supporters dominated New York and Philadelphia, and even the places with a Niagara contingent had stronger pro-Booker followings. But Booker and his confidants, ever sensitive to press reports, let themselves be distracted by their opponents' noise. An ally noted that Booker's critics in Chicago appeared to be superior in "brain, tact, and influence: the opposing faction has the ear of the public and the courtesy of the press; while we have neither." Although this was clearly an exaggeration of the Niagara Movement's influence, such reports kept Washington and his allies in action against those he perceived as his archenemies. In fact his real enemies lay elsewhere.[38]

14

The Tragedy of Color

The 1906 campaign for governor of Georgia set in motion events that forced Booker Washington to confront defeat. Two powerful, well-known Georgians engaged in a fierce contest: Hoke Smith, former editor of the Atlanta *Journal;* and Clark Howell, editor of the *Constitution.* Under the influence of Tom Watson, Smith had forsaken the genial racial paternalism of his earlier career for the shrill demand on the political stump that Georgia join the rest of the South in disfranchising blacks. His campaign ads promised "THE ELIMINATION OF THE NEGRO FROM POLITICS . . . WITHOUT DISFRANCHISING A SINGLE WHITE MAN." If an educated black tried to register to vote, Smith said, fraudulent questioning should be contrived to reject him, and "should it ever become necessary we can handle them as they did in Wilmington." Eight years after the fact, the North Carolina riot remained for whites the ultimate means of racial control. Opposition to black voting still reinforced hostility to black education. Howell responded that Smith's disfranchising measures would actually "draw the negroes of Georgia out of the cotton patch into the negro colleges," and blacks would get "bow-legged with the burden of carrying their books to school." Whites should remember, Howell said, "whenever the nigger learns his [hic], haec, hoc, he right away forgets all about gee-whoa-buck."[1]

As the gubernatorial campaign was reaching a climax in August 1906, three sensational allegations of rape of white women reverberated through Atlanta. The city's four newspapers competed fiercely to provide the most lurid accounts of the outrages that had purportedly been done by black men and that together left the strong impression that black brutality was rampant in the city. The Atlanta *News* and the Atlanta *Georgian* openly called for the lynching of the fiends responsible. In this volatile atmosphere, Hoke Smith was seen as the stronger antiblack candidate, and his victory was understood as a mandate for disfranchisement. In its next session, the Georgia legislature did finally take away most blacks' voting rights.[2]

A few days after the election, Washington came to Atlanta for the annual meeting of the National Negro Business League. He encouraged the editors of the four daily newspapers to spotlight the upstanding black citizens attending the meeting, only to have the *Constitution* report on his speech under the headline "LAW-BREAKING NEGROES WORST MENACE TO RACE."[3] The gross misrepresentation of Booker's upbeat emphasis on black progress foreshadowed trouble.

Any hope for optimism was lost three weeks later, when a sudden spate of rape allegations filled the Atlanta newspapers. On September 20 and 21 there were reports of attempted rapes, which resulted in the formation of two separate lynch mobs that police thwarted. On the third day, a Saturday, three newspapers published afternoon extra editions reporting the many rumors of black assaults on white women then circulating the city. "NEGRO ATTEMPTS TO ASSAULT MRS. MARY CHAFIN NEAR SUGAR CREEK BRIDGE" ran an Atlanta *Journal* extra's headline. The *Evening News* extras simply screamed "TWO ASSAULTS" and then "THIRD ASSAULT." A subsequent investigation cast doubt on whether the alleged assaults were in fact rape, and at least some of the attacks were simply imagined. By the early evening, angry whites filled downtown Atlanta. One man stood on a box and shouted: "Are we Southern white men going to stand for this?" Despite pleas from Atlanta's mayor to disperse, a mob of whites rolled toward the black saloon district, pushing through a line of policemen, and began beating any black man they came upon. A part of the mob attacked blacks on a trolley stopped in the area and beat three people to death, despite fierce attempts by policemen to pull them off the car. Others arriving later on trolleys were beaten, several to death. The mob attacked barbershops, pulling black men shaving white customers away from their chairs and beating them mercilessly. A crippled black bootblack was dragged to the street and killed. Eventually the mob spread out of downtown and began looting white-owned stores. When the Atlanta police failed to stymie the mob, the governor of Georgia, whose mansion was only a few blocks from the center of the violence, called out the state militia.[4]

Over the next two days, blacks in outlying neighborhoods armed themselves and fought off attempted incursions. Whites attacked the middle-class neighborhood of Brownsville, where a thirteen-year-old was armed and barricaded in his home beside his father, a postal worker. The boy heard a shout from the mob heading toward his house: "That's where that nigger mail carrier lives! Let's burn it down! It's too nice for a nigger to live in!" To the common explanation among whites that the rioters were out to punish criminals, one black editor replied that "the mob was not after the worst Negroes so much as they were after the best." The Atlanta riot shared this fundamental similarity with the Wilmington atrocity: the white mob sought out the wealthiest blacks for special violence to punish their superior economic status. The state militia, mostly concerned with the blacks who were carrying guns, came into black areas, confiscated weapons, and arrested many. At least four blacks died in the Brownsville section during the militia roundups. Although white officials actively thwarted an accurate reckoning of the total number of deaths in three days of trouble, it was probably as high as thirty blacks and two whites.[5]

The shooting had yet to stop when competing interpretations of the riot's causes began to circulate. In the New York *World,* John Temple Graves attributed the eruption to rampant black crime; northerners would have rioted, too, if faced with the degradation of their women. Max Barber, editor of the *Voice of the Negro,* cabled an unsigned rebuttal to Graves's article, describing the savagery and blaming the trouble on sensationalist newspapers and Hoke Smith. The governor-elect, Barber wrote, was a "vicious snake" whose supporters had blackened their faces and committed the rapes attributed to Negroes. Someone at the telegraph office identified Barber. Summoned before a grand jury to explain his article, Barber fled to Chicago, where he announced that he was prepared to die for his people but not to chance a Georgia chain gang. Powerful white men in the North, especially President Roosevelt, should rescue blacks and force whites to control their savages, Barber declared.[6]

Washington was in New York when the riot occurred, and he said nothing until a semblance of order was restored. But then he gave the *World* a statement urging blacks not to retaliate. Blacks were just as opposed to criminal behavior as whites, and as a black man he grieved for the innocent of both races who had died because of the "despicable acts of a few criminals." He purposely left ambiguous the race of the "despicable," but he meant to arrange an investigation of what had caused the riot. Three days after the riot he arrived in Atlanta and began meeting with black and white leaders of the city. Powerful white Atlantans were anxious to accommodate black desires, and they started listening to black concerns. An interracial group came together to map a strategy for restoring peace and preventing further violence. All saloons were closed for ten days, and whites quickly agreed to support an expansion of public industrial schools. They formed the interracial Civic League, and 5,000 Atlantans committed to preventing riots, lynching, and other forms of racial oppression. Three white lawyers, members of the new Civic League, defended a black man accused of one of the preriot attacks on a white woman and secured an acquittal. A former governor organized a movement among white Christians to preach racial reconciliation and concern for fairness to blacks.[7]

Booker called these efforts "the most radical, far-reaching, and hopeful solution of the race problem" attempted by southern whites. They were the kind of steps within a southern community that he believed would bring long-term solutions to current racial problems. Although Max Barber had demanded federal intervention and northern blacks had reiterated his plea, Booker knew that federal intervention in such situations as Atlanta was not going to happen, because police power was vested in state governments. "I had absolutely *no* authority under the circumstances to send troops to Atlanta," Roosevelt wrote to Booker in response to the demands. Similar demands made in the aftermath of the Wilmington riot had also proved futile. Nor did Washington think that federal intervention would be a good thing in the long run. He wrote to a northern critic that black southerners believed that their security and rights depended on getting "the leading classes of Southern white people to shoulder the responsibility of the protection of the Negro," and he was convinced that the correct attitude was emerging among Atlanta whites.[8]

The Atlanta riot galvanized Washington's critics. Du Bois, who had been visiting an industrial school in Alabama when the riot started, wrote a poem in the form of a Christian prayer on the train back to Atlanta. His "A Litany of Atlanta" pleaded for the innocent victims of the white mob, but even so, Washington seems not to have been far from Du Bois's mind: "Behold this maimed and broken thing; dear God, it was an humble black man who toiled and sweat to save a bit from the pittance paid him. They told him: *Work and Rise.* He worked. Did this man sin? Nay, but some one told how some one said another did—one whom he had never seen nor known. Yet for that man's crime this man lieth maimed and murdered, his wife naked to shame, his children, to poverty and evil." Critics of Booker alleged that his Business League address a few weeks before had actually sparked the white violence. Emmett Scott and Washington responded by questioning the courage of Du Bois and Barber because they had absented themselves from Atlanta during the violence. In Du Bois's case, the suggestions were unfair, but Barber's departure was widely condemned. "Threats have been made against dozens of other leading Afro-Americans in Atlanta," read an unsigned editorial probably written by Scott, "and they have stood their ground and have faced in some cases death and in other cases they have been led very near death's door."[9]

Blame settled on Washington anyway. Once again, a catastrophe for American blacks undermined his leadership. Fortune wrote that Hoke Smith should be "tried in the proper way and convicted and sentenced and shot." There had to be some sane white people in Atlanta, Fortune wrote, "but they give no sign"—an unfair statement given the white response to the riot. Fortune had called for retaliatory violence after Wilmington but had defended Washington's silence at the time. Now he criticized Booker in the New York *Age* for counseling blacks against exacting an eye for an eye. Blacks who defended themselves would inspire the respect of white hoodlums, Fortune said, and the failure to retaliate only resulted in massacre of blacks. He wished he could be in Atlanta "with a good force of armed men to help make Rome howl." Washington had little tolerance for such rhetoric. He feared that it would dominate the October meeting of the Afro-American Council, which he wanted to remain a viable alternative to the Niagara Movement. Observing that the council set forth a reform program closely resembling Niagara's, in his speech to the group he pleaded with northern blacks to mute their protests: "In your enthusiastic desire to be of service to your brethren in the South . . . be careful not to assist in lighting a fire which you will have no ability to put out." As he had after Wilmington, Booker worried that indiscriminate condemnation of whites would incite white backlash. Blacks should talk more about their white friends than about whites who wished them evil. But in the tense weeks after the riot, such admonitions were ignored. The president of the council in 1906 was Bishop Alexander Walters of New York, formerly a close ally of Washington but now a critic. "The object of our enemies is to make us serfs," Walters pronounced. "It is nonsense to cry peace when there is no peace. We are determined to rise or die in the attempt to obtain our rights."[10]

Washington kept working to shape the meaning of the riot. The New York *World* attributed the violence to white labor's hostility to black competition. Booker dismissed this explanation privately to a northern philanthropist: "Neither of our races in the South has reached the point where it is willing to fight for the opportunity of working." Such talk undermined industrial education. He was more honest with Francis Garrison, to whom he acknowledged that some southern whites might be more opposed to industrial education than to higher education for blacks. In public Booker declared that the riot had changed Atlanta for the better by inspiring blacks and whites to come together afterward in positive ways. White Atlantans were discussing the appointment of black policemen and a public defender to ensure justice in the courts. Nothing like this had occurred in the aftermath of the Wilmington riot, although both conflagrations had taken place amid tense political divisions among whites, had been impelled to violence by psychosexual fears, and had resulted in the wholesale destruction of black lives and property and finally in black disfranchisement. Both had brought scorn on the communities that had allowed it to happen, but afterward in Atlanta many leading men had asserted that such a shameful thing should not happen again.[11]

Still, the riot severely damaged Washington's standing as blacks' leader. The outpouring of blame on him after the Wilmington riot and the Hose lynching had shown that when unspeakable horrors were visited on black people, Booker became a scapegoat. Whatever goodwill emerged in Atlanta in its aftermath, the riot produced scenes of ugliness and horror that trumped Booker's positive perspective. The riot raised doubts about his stewardship among those previously uncommitted, caused some old friends to withdraw from him, and gave enemies fresh ammunition to fire at him. He needed a respite from controversy, a time for anger to burn itself out as it had done in the months after Wilmington and the Hose lynching. But this time he would have no relief: another atrocity against blacks, also far beyond Booker's control, was already afoot.

Just a few weeks earlier, on August 13, 1906, shots fired on a Brownsville, Texas, street had killed a bartender and injured a policeman. Racial tensions had been high in the area in the three weeks since the arrival at Fort Brown of the mostly black 25th United States Infantry Regiment. The black soldiers had been refused entry to bars, and they were threatened, beaten, and accused of assaulting a white woman. Whites in Brownsville now blamed the August 13 shootings on black soldiers. The white commanders at the fort reported, however, that all the black soldiers had been in their barracks at the time of the shooting. None of the 167 black soldiers confessed to shooting, nor did any of them accuse any fellow infantryman. The mayor of Brownsville presented their commanding officer with empty shell casings, the kind used in army rifles, and a soldier's cap, found in the area of the shootings. The evidence was purely circumstantial, probably planted, and certainly weaker than the fact of the commanding officer's report. Yet an investigation of the affair by a U.S. inspector general, a white South Carolinian, encouraged a presumption of the black soldiers' guilt. "The colored soldier is much more aggressive in his attitude on the so-

cial equality question than he used to be," he declared. The inspector
general alleged a conspiracy of silence among the soldiers. "The secretive nature of the race, where crimes to members of their color are
charged, is well known," he declared, then pronounced the men guilty
and recommended that all of them be discharged. It would never be
clearly established who had done the shooting, but the most likely culprits were whites who then falsely blamed the soldiers to get them
transferred from Brownsville. At worst, only a few black soldiers may
have been guilty. Yet all 167 were dismissed and lost their army pen-
sions. Some had served twenty-five years, and six were Medal of Honor
winners, among them First Sergeant Mingo Sanders, who had fought
in Cuba in 1898 and shared hardtack and bacon with Colonel Theodore Roosevelt.[12]

The president studied the inspector general's report and ordered
Secretary of War William Howard Taft to implement its recommendation. Summoned to a meeting with Roosevelt on October 30, Booker
supposed that the purpose was to discuss what the president would say
about the Atlanta violence in a forthcoming address. At the meeting,
Roosevelt informed him of the impending dismissal of the soldiers.
Horrified at Roosevelt's arbitrariness, Booker pleaded with him not to
act until a further investigation, overseen from Tuskegee, could be
made. Two days later he wrote to Roosevelt: "If you possibly can avoid
doing so, I very much hope you will not take definite action regarding
the Negro soldiers in the Brownsville affair, until after your return
from Panama. There is some information which I must put before you
before you take final action." It is unlikely that Washington had yet
gathered information, but he surely intended to send investigators in
quest of the truth, just as he was currently doing in connection with
the Atlanta riot. Roosevelt replied on November 5 that he could not
possibly refrain from firing the soldiers. The president's essential arro-
gance trumped any other element of his message: "You can not have
any information to give me privately to which I could pay heed, my
dear Mr. Washington, because the information on which I act is that
which came out in the investigation itself."[13]

Here was evidence of the Roosevelt character about which William
Baldwin had cautioned Booker. The late railroad executive had told

him that Roosevelt was a sophomore, a foolishly naïve and arrogant man who happened to have great power. He could do great good or great harm and in either case be absolutely certain that he was right. Roosevelt apparently never reckoned with the consequences of his Brownsville decision, except as they affected him personally. Beyond Baldwin's warning, Washington had spent enough time with Roosevelt to see his propensity for attributing to blacks as a group—if not to individuals like Washington—a disregard for the law and an impulse to protect a wrongdoer in their midst. Booker surely remembered Roosevelt's aspersions on the courage of black troops in Cuba. He was too acute a judge of human behavior not to suspect that Roosevelt's quick acceptance of the unsubstantiated allegations against the Brownsville soldiers was based on the president's racial bigotry and his hostility to black men in uniform. And Booker surely considered the possibility that Roosevelt's action was compensation to southern whites for having vested power in such black men as William Crum and Washington himself.

On November 7, the day after the national elections, in which Republicans won a big majority with overwhelming black support, Taft dismissed the black soldiers. The timing of the dismissal was interpreted as purely cynical. One newspaper insisted that, had the black vote been turned against the Republicans—as it might well have been had public action on the Brownsville situation been taken earlier—the party's majority in Congress would have dropped by three-fourths. Another editor surmised that Roosevelt's son-in-law, Nicholas Longworth, would surely have been defeated in his congressional election. On election day blacks had sung "'we are coming brother Theodore, three hundred thousand strong," one Yankee editor wrote, "but they would have been coming in a different temper had they known that on brother Theodore's desk was an order to disgrace and humiliate the entire colored battalion."[14]

Fury exploded in black communities across the country. Tim Fortune wrote that the president was "carrying into the Federal Government the demand of the Southern white devils" to hand over innocent black men to mob action. "The hand of Ben Tillman nor Vardaman never struck humanity as savagely as did the iron hand of Theodore

addition, have entailed considerable extra ex-   Blockson also wrote to Secretary Taft that

BUSTER BROWN IN A NEW ROLE— Courtesy of the *Chicago Republic*
Columbia—I consider it most unjust and unworthy of you, Buster, to treat your colored soldiers
in that way.

46. The *Voice of the Negro,* like many other American publications, lampooned Roosevelt as Buster Brown, an impetuous boy who had his way regardless of the consequences to others. Artist unknown; from *Voice of the Negro* 3 (December 1906).

Roosevelt," a black editor in Atlanta wrote. "His new dictum is lynch-law, bold and heartless." Over the next few weeks, black churches and community groups organized protest meetings across the country. "No one, for a moment, believes that these companies would have been dishonorably discharged if they had been composed of white soldiers," declared a North Carolina Baptist convention. In a time of "tension between the races, and of fear, forebodings, uncertainty, unrest, and heartaches on the part of the colored people . . . the Chief Executive of a great nation has estranged 10,000,000 of his hitherto ardent admirers and supporters." At a meeting in Washington attended by 2,000 angry blacks, the editor Calvin Chase called Roosevelt a permanent enemy and urged blacks to become Democrats. When the meeting was called on to sing "America," only hisses were heard. Roosevelt had "shot us when our gun was empty," a New York minister declared, but their slogan in 1908 would be "a Democratic President to resent the insult heaped upon us." Booker's allies reported the outrage to him. "Negroes are depleting the dictionary of adjectives in their denunciation of the President," one wrote from Ohio. From Chicago: "You cannot find a Negro who is not denouncing the President in frightful terms of abuse."[15]

Condemnations of Roosevelt also filled white newspapers. The New York *World* blasted Roosevelt for not knowing how many soldiers were guilty of shooting, or how many knew who the guilty ones were. The *World* declared that no amount of ignorance made any difference to the president. The angriest of all white editors was Oswald Garrison Villard, editor of the New York *Evening Post.* The Garrisons viewed Roosevelt as a dangerous internationalist and a grandstander, and they suspected that he was not sincere in his support of black interests. They were particularly protective of blacks' reputation as soldiers, probably because at least one of William Lloyd's sons had served in a mostly black unit in the Civil War. Villard's editorial asserted that blacks were historically more loyal to the colors than whites and that the dismissal of the troops renounced blacks' patriotism and the rights that flowed from it. Villard told Booker privately that the nation was "awakening to the instability" of Roosevelt, which he had known would eventually come. He said that he could prove that Teddy was the worst president in twenty-five years.[16]

The Brownsville affair predictably won Roosevelt new respect in the white South, which was perhaps its real purpose. "These nigger loving Yankees are sending all sorts of protests to Washington against the discharge of the negro soldiers," observed the Nashville *American.* "Their dismissal is the most praiseworthy thing the President has done." The *Constitution* commended Roosevelt's investigation on the grounds that "unless outlawry and its concealment were summarily checked, the army would speedily became a hotbed of mutiny and disorganization." The New York *Times,* often sympathetic to the white South, reported that the dismissal was needed to correct the impudence among black soldiers—described as a "strange development of 'cockiness'"—that Roosevelt had encouraged when he invited Washington to dinner at the White House.[17]

Washington knew that 167 soldiers would not be the only Negroes victimized by the Brownsville events. He had done all he could to keep Roosevelt from making this terrible blunder, Booker told Charles Anderson, but "the enemy will, as usual, try to blame me for all of this." He had already decided that he would remain silent. "They can talk," he said of his detractors. "I cannot, without being disloyal to our friend, who[m] I mean to stand by throughout his administration." It was a serious misjudgment of the bounds of loyalty. The New York City minister Adam Clayton Powell did indeed begin to talk, telling the New York *Times* that some blacks believed that as Roosevelt's adviser Booker Washington was responsible for the president's change in attitude toward blacks. "The awful march of events since the famous Roosevelt-Washington [dinner] makes a thoughtful man ask: Has the colored race been sold for a mess of pottage?"[18]

The gross miscarriage of justice, perpetrated arrogantly and impetuously, would forever taint Roosevelt in the eyes of black Americans and their white liberal allies. The stain spread instantly to Washington, his ally and adviser. Booker should have publicly renounced the decision and put some distance between himself and the president in order to preserve his standing as the advocate for and protector of his race. But he said nothing publicly. The summary punishment of the soldiers was in no way justifiable. Washington knew that, and said so to Roosevelt, but then kept quiet.

Washington's refusal to disavow Roosevelt's decision openly may have been the worst mistake of his public career. He may have believed that some of the men were in fact guilty. The weakness of the case against them did not become clear until a congressional investigation was completed several months later. Du Bois always thought that some of the black soldiers were guilty. Booker hoped that he might effect a reversal on the Brownsville dismissal, or at least a modification of Roosevelt's decision. He appealed privately to Taft to change the order: "I have never in all my experience with the race, experienced a time when the entire people have the feeling that they have now in regard to the administration," he wrote. "The race is not so much resentful or angry, perhaps, as it feels hurt and disappointed." Taft did suspend the order, but Roosevelt overrode him, saying that the dismissal was made "after due deliberation" and that he cared "nothing whatever for the yelling of either the politicians or the sentimentalists."[19]

Understanding why Washington did not publicly disown Roosevelt's decision requires some reflection on both Booker's circumstances and his personality. Keeping silent about events beyond his control had generally proved to be the correct strategy; controversies usually died down and were eventually forgotten. The exception to this pattern was the furor following the White House dinner, and in that instance he had no real alternative but to remain stoic. There, too, he had approved of the president's action, as he had Roosevelt's resolve on the Crum nomination. Indeed, Roosevelt's loyalty to Booker in those situations, probably more than anything else, earned him Booker's silence about the Brownsville affair. Washington was intensely loyal to people who had helped him, even when they became critics. Despite Fortune's intemperate behavior and proclivity for violent verbal attacks, sometimes on his friends, Booker had forgiven and helped him time and again, because they had been close helpmates for long periods in the past. With whites, Booker had lower expectations of loyalty, and therefore lower standards for maintaining friendship. He had tolerated disagreements with, and the frequent cowardice and bad judgment of, Edgar Gardner Murphy, Robert Ogden, and any number of white politicians and editors, in part because he needed them and in part because there was no viable alternative. Booker understood that human behavior was often inconsistent and that today's nemesis might be tomorrow's savior, and vice versa. He broke finally with people only when they made ugly, personal criticisms of him or his family.

He knew that Theodore Roosevelt, the most powerful man in the United States, was a rash personality with a Manichean habit of mind and latent racial bigotry. He had seen enough of the arrogant president to know that Roosevelt's attitude toward him could change instantly if he said the wrong thing. Booker's public criticism might precipitate a break with Roosevelt and therefore an end to any positive influence Washington might have in the White House and on the Republican Party. He did not entertain the possibility of supporting a Democrat, because, whatever Roosevelt's faults, the southern-dominated Democratic Party offered nothing but scorn for blacks. Booker knew that much of his power as leader of his race was based on his close relations with the president. By late 1906 Booker may have known, or guessed, that Roosevelt was contemplating running again in 1908, and the possibility that he might be the president for another six years also surely played a role in his silence.[20]

Part of Washington's mistake lay in his failure to accept that his influence with Roosevelt was already waning. The president made overtures to the white-nationalist South during his 1905 tour of the region, an attempt to make amends for the Crum appointment, which, like the White House dinner, he privately viewed as a mistake. Since his election in 1904 he had made fewer black patronage appointments, and Washington in early 1906 had brought this fact to his attention: "I find that colored people throughout the country are very sensitive on the subject of your making any move in the direction of reducing the number of colored people holding office in the South." But no new jobs had resulted. Charles Anderson and Emmett Scott had worried that Roosevelt's failure to appoint blacks would provide ammunition for Booker's enemies.[21]

Booker would never know if open criticism of Roosevelt might have saved him from the damage Brownsville did to his leadership. He could have made a public statement critical of the Brownsville decision, asking Roosevelt to reconsider and perhaps risking only a further diminution in influence that was diminished already. He might have said what in fact he explained privately to Roosevelt in order to prepare the president to deal with blacks who soon descended on him to register their anger: the Brownsville decision came when blacks were already upset about the Atlanta riot; at least some wholly innocent men were being punished; and the order had been cynically held in abeyance until the black vote had been secured in the election. Such a statement probably would not have quashed all the condemnations that came down on Booker, but his silence left it possible to think that he approved of the decision.

Booker at first regarded the protests as serving the useful purpose of venting anger, but as they continued he concluded that they were alienating white allies. To a supporter in Ohio he declared that "one thing the American people will not stand for any length of time, and that is abuse by any group of people of the President of the United States, and if our people make the mistake of going too far, there will be a reaction in the North among the people and newspapers who have stood by us." He added that he was "doing all I can to check that folly." In a speech in December, Washington warned a group of blacks that "civilization soon tires of a race, as of an individual, that continually whines and complains." When asked by reporters to comment on the discharge of the troops, he answered that he would neither applaud nor condemn the action; "I have nothing to say on that subject."[22]

Roosevelt added insult to injury in his annual address to Congress in early December. Booker had advised him on the speech, strongly urging changes in the language, but Roosevelt again rejected Booker's counsel. In denouncing lynch law, the president said that "the greatest existing cause of lynching is the perpetration, especially by black men, of the hideous crime of rape—the most abominable in all the category of crimes, even worse than murder." To prevent it, Roosevelt said, "the respectable colored people must learn not to harbor their criminals, but to assist the officers in bringing them to justice." He believed that blacks' protection of criminals had led to the Atlanta riot—just as black soldiers' alleged lying for other black soldiers justified the wholesale dismissal in Brownsville. "Every colored man should realize that the worst enemy of his race is the negro criminal, and above all the negro criminal who commits the dreadful crime of rape; and it should be felt as in the highest degree an offense against the whole country, and against the colored race in particular, for a colored man to fail to help the officers of the law in hunting down with all possible earnestness and zeal every such infamous offender."[23]

For black observers not already entirely alienated from the president, Roosevelt's speech was the final straw. Booker got more warnings about Teddy's liability to him. "The Negro is held up as a race of criminals and rapists, banded together to uphold one another in crime, with only occasional exceptions," Kelly Miller wrote to Washington. The speech did "more to damn the Negro to everlasting infamy than all the maledictions of Tillman, Vardaman, Dixon and John Temple Graves." Miller warned Washington that he would be held responsible for Roosevelt's behavior. "When Mr. Roosevelt requested you to act as his adviser and when you accepted that delicate responsibility, the world may be expected to believe that he is guided by the advice of his own seeking." Tim Fortune insisted that Roosevelt's adoption of white-nationalist attitudes compelled Booker to disengage from the president. "He has two years more as President, and you the remainder of your life as the controlling genius of the Tuskegee Institute and leader of the Afro-American people, and your future will depend largely on how far you allow it to be understood that you are sponsor for what he says and does."[24]

It was sound advice, but it was hard for Booker to follow. The damage was done, and he wanted to be in a position to influence Roosevelt on subsequent decisions that might affect African Americans. He enjoyed his influence as leader of his race at least in part through his connection to the president, and he would lose it if he publicly broke with Roosevelt. Having been told that his Roosevelt connection was now a great detriment to his leadership, Washington listened but stayed his course. In the end, Roosevelt did not make it up to Washington or to blacks in general.

The Constitution League, John Milholland's new black-rights organization, tried to present Roosevelt with evidence of the injustice at Brownsville, but the president refused to meet with the league's representative. That evidence was then turned over to Senator Joseph Foraker of Ohio, a Roosevelt critic and would-be Republican presidential candidate in 1908. Foraker initiated a congressional investigation that exposed the weakness of the evidence against the Brownsville soldiers, including information that undermined the alleged conspiracy of silence among the soldiers. In January 1907, at a meeting of the Gridiron Club in Washington, D.C., Roosevelt attacked Foraker for the Brownsville investigation, whereupon the senator rose and answered with an equally vehement condemnation of the president's action. The Senate committee's majority report supported the president's decision, but the minority positions raised doubts and kept the criticism of Roosevelt alive for the next few years. Foraker was convinced that the Brownsville soldiers were innocent and said so repeatedly, though in doing so his motives were also political. He hoped to undermine Roosevelt's political future, and that of Teddy's protégé William Howard Taft, by courting black voters. Although exposure of Foraker's financial ties to Standard Oil ruined his political career, in 1910 14 of the 167 black soldiers would be declared eligible for reinstatement in the army.[25]

The more condemnations he received about Brownsville, the angrier Roosevelt became at blacks. Furious at the way the black press had made a martyr of Mingo Sanders, his fellow soldier in Cuba, Roosevelt later wrote that this model infantryman with twenty-five years in uniform was "as thoroly [sic] dangerous, unprincipled and unworthy a soldier as ever wore the United States uniform, and that under no conceivable circumstances should he ever be allowed again in the army." In early 1907 he wrote privately that the Brownsville affair depressed him "not so much by the attitude of the colored troops themselves, although that was sufficiently ominous, but by the attitude taken by the enormous majority of the colored people in regard to the matter." Roosevelt said that he no longer doubted the presumption of southern whites that "decent Negroes would actively or passively shield their own wrong-doers." Had the troops been white, the president insisted, no whites would have defended them, but "the colored people have made a fetich [sic] of the innocence of the troops and have been supporting in every way the political demagogs and visionary enthusiasts who have struck hands in the matter of their defence."[26]

Washington grew increasingly annoyed with and defensive about blacks' continuing preoccupation with Brownsville. The longer blacks' attention remained fixed on it, Washington believed, the greater would be the delay in moving toward new, positive action. He may not have grasped how deeply the injustice was felt by blacks or how far the anger about Brownsville deepened the scrutiny of his failure as leader of the race.

Earlier in 1906, before the Atlanta riot and Brownsville, Booker had met with Herbert George Wells, a not-yet-famous British writer of science fiction doing a book about America's future, for which he needed the opinions of a noteworthy black man. H. G. Wells liked

Washington's "rather Irish" face, soft voice, and slow speech, and correctly surmised that Booker "looks before and after, and plans and keeps his counsel with the scope and range of a statesman." He asked Washington if blacks would ultimately be integrated fully and equally into American life. Feeling the sting of the 1905 attacks on him, Booker knew better than to declare himself for racial equality and ensure another round of public excoriation. "May we not become a peculiar people—like the Jews?" Booker asked, meaning that blacks could succeed economically but live separate socially. Wells's article "The Tragedy of Color" ran in *Harper's Weekly* the same week as the Atlanta riot. The Englishman treated him fairly, but Booker disliked the suggestion that he was party to any racial tragedy. He remained unwilling to entertain the possibility of a sad outcome to the history of blacks in the United States. Only when an individual, or a race, suffered from its own folly, he believed, did it become tragic. Blacks had too little control over their lives to make a tragic mistake.[27]

Perhaps because Booker consciously embraced his public image as an exemplar of black success, he resisted the notion that his life contained tragic elements. He had fought ardently for his cause, but in the end his efforts might fail because of the awful circumstances in which he lived; too many obstacles might stand in his way to allow him to achieve his purposes. Or he might fail because men he had chosen to trust betrayed him. Booker instinctively rejected that possibility, because he had yet to accept the implications of Roosevelt's treachery. Indeed, he would never openly confront the full meaning of the president's betrayal.

The back-to-back disasters of the Atlanta riot and the Brownsville injustice, coming on the heels of the relentless attacks in 1905, marked the beginning of the tragic end of Washington's leadership. His influence had risen steadily from 1895 through 1904, when he personified hope for progress among black Americans. It reached its zenith with the permanent appointment of Crum and the legal victories in Alabama. In reality these were minor triumphs, rendered important in Booker's eyes because they stemmed from his unrelenting determination to defeat the insanity of the white South. His greatest successes as

THE TRAGEDY OF COLOR

47. The stress of recent events showed on Booker Washington's face by 1908. Photo by Waldon Fawcett, copyright June 17, 1908; courtesy of the Library of Congress.

a racial leader had derived from his ability to shape Roosevelt's policies from 1901 through 1904; but what Teddy had given Booker, he took away with Brownsville. Washington knew this, but he did not admit the extent of its damage to his leadership. In this denial he was typical of powerful men, who rarely rush forward to acknowledge their own mistakes. By 1907 Washington's leadership appeared to many to be on its way to a tragic end, its demise the result of his mistaken loyalty to Theodore Roosevelt.

Booker never publicly acknowledged the defeat or its effect upon him, but it could be seen in his face, which revealed a rapid aging: his once-clear gray eyes now seemed clouded, and the flesh around them thicker and sagging—all the cost of too much worry and too little rest. He looked much older than he had just months earlier. After 1906 his mastery came harder and would never be as comprehensive as it had been earlier. He was fifty years old, and in 1906 that represented an age by which most men had long since accepted the limits on fulfilling their ambitions.

Booker Washington began to make that adjustment, but it would not be easy. His larger achievements lay in the building of black morale and the inspiration of hope, but his career as the leader of his race would be judged more on political wins and losses, and after 1906 there were not many victories. He kept doing most of the same things, but he looked less successful, and the appearance of vulnerability and defeat fed the enthusiasm and efforts of those who intended to displace him once and for all.

15

The Man Farthest Down

Booker Washington's life occurred on many levels, and his work after 1906 in arenas other than politics often yielded more positive results. His large family was mostly happy. Having enjoyed her study of music in Europe, Portia in 1906 contemplated staying in Germany to avoid racial problems in America. Booker counseled against becoming a permanent exile, saying that she would make a mistake if she dwelt too much on race. Portia dutifully returned home and soon became engaged to Sidney Pittman, a Tuskegee graduate and favorite of her father. Booker had helped Pittman to be educated as an architect, and the young man had begun a successful practice in Washington, D.C., helped along by his father-in-law's influence among the wealthy and powerful. Their wedding in October 1907 was the social event of the season in Tuskegee. Portia and Sidney had three children, and Booker took time to be a grandfather, at one point dropping for two weeks all other duties to help Portia when his first grandson became very ill.[1]

When Booker T. "Baker" Washington Jr. left Phillips Exeter Academy suddenly after only a few weeks, the press made a sensation of it. Though never thoroughly satisfied with his oldest son's behavior, Booker defended the twenty-year-old's departure and got him admitted to Fisk University, where Baker enjoyed his education. Most of this time his father was supporting him, even when he married suddenly in

48. Booker, Maggie, and their two sons in 1906. Photo copyright Underwood and Underwood, 1906; courtesy of the Library of Congress.

1913. Booker T. Washington III arrived soon thereafter. Baker then attended a pharmacy school, not successfully, before returning to Tuskegee to work on agricultural-extension projects. Eventually he ended up in Los Angeles, where he spent most of his adult life in the real-estate business. Dave, the younger son, was a worry to his father because of his precarious health. After a short stint at a North Carolina medical school, Dave enrolled at a New York City secretarial school. In 1914 he returned to Tuskegee with a new wife and began a lifelong career as an administrator and fundraiser at the Institute.[2]

Booker's family life extended well beyond Maggie and the three children. In 1904 he and Maggie adopted her orphaned niece and nephew, Laura and Thomas Murray. Laura, only four at the time, lived from then on as part of the Washingtons' nuclear family. Booker indulged her even more than he did his own offspring, sending her to Spelman College in Atlanta and writing to her often and affectionately. His brother, John Washington, remained a central figure at Tuskegee Institute, teaching trades and tending relations with whites in town. John and his large family saw much of his brother's brood, and Booker sometimes watched over John's children. Booker was close to his nephew Albert Johnston, who also worked at the Institute. Albert's mother, Booker's beloved younger sister, Amanda, still lived in Malden. He visited her when he could arrange it; she was his last direct tie to his West Virginia boyhood—and to his dear Jane, of whom the hardworking Amanda was always a sweet reminder. The adopted brother James ran the Tuskegee Institute post office. When in 1905 the postmastership was upgraded to one appointed by the president, Booker told Theodore Roosevelt's secretary that James Washington was *"no relation of mine"*—a literal but highly misleading truth made so that James could keep his job and the White House would not think, Booker said, that "I would recommend one of my relatives for such a position."[3]

Washington tended always to the Institute's financial well-being. The school had matured, having essentially reached its physical completion by about 1905. In the next decade, only two new dormitories and an agricultural hall were added to the campus. Also by 1905 the student enrollment had reached the plateau it would maintain until after World War I. But the Tuskegee Endowment had also leveled off in that period; Booker still had to raise more than $100,000 a year to balance the budget. He searched constantly for new sources of money, and by 1904 his regular calls at the investment house of Kuhn, Loeb and Company in New York had begun to yield results. Jacob Schiff, the firm's leading partner and second only in influence to J. P. Morgan among financial capitalists in the United States, contributed to Tuskegee and later gave Booker a substantial amount of money each year to distribute among ten smaller industrial schools that Washington deemed worthy. In 1904 Washington arranged for the appointment of Paul Warburg of Kuhn, Loeb to the Tuskegee Institute board, the first Jew to serve. Warburg and his brother Felix became significant contributors to the school, and their involvement enabled Tuskegee soon to count among its supporters bankers named Seligman, Goldman, Sachs, and Lehman. The generosity of Schiff and the Warburgs rewarded Booker for having overcome insensitivity, if not outright antisemitism, that he had manifested earlier. In 1894 he had been taken to task by the editor of the *American Israelite* for having several times designated a man as "the Jew" in an article for a Christian publication. Actually an admirer of Jewish entrepreneurial spirit and assimilation, Booker never made that mistake again. Still, in late 1904 he warned the Institute business agent that too much of the school's business was being placed in the hands of a few Jewish businesses in Montgomery when "in creating public sentiment in favor of the institution the Jews cannot be of much service." If, however, the business was going to go to some Jewish merchant, Booker wanted it given to Jacques Loeb, who in earlier hard times had extended credit to the Institute in the face of gentile merchants' collusive threats to boycott Loeb if he helped the Tuskegeans. Booker rarely forgot a slight but never a friend.[4]

Black private education in the South still depended entirely on northern money, although it was coming to Tuskegee from some new places. In 1912 the school solicited five-year pledges, and the donors included no Carnegie, Rockefeller, Huntington, Peabody, Wanamaker, Ogden, or Baldwin—all of whom had been so crucial in the building of the school. About one-fifth of the money still came from Boston, chiefly from the Mason family, which had been contributing heavily since the 1880s. But a tenth now came from Chicago, from donors who included the farm-implement maker Cyrus McCormick, the electricity entrepreneur Samuel Insull, and, most notably, the mail-order magnate Julius Rosenwald. A third of the donors worked on Wall Street, including Messrs. Schiff, Goldman, Sachs, Lehman, Kuhn, and Warburg. Almost a third of the $50,000 came from Jewish philanthropists. Of the seventy-five pledges made, only one came from the South: Mr. and Mrs. Booker T. Washington.[5]

Booker generally got involved in the administration of the school only when problems or criticisms arose. He was in Tuskegee only

about half the time, and when there he was distracted by the responsibilities of leading his race. The Institute bore the burden of Booker's
distractions in both work neglected and expenses incurred. In 1907
Seth Low, the former New York City mayor and Columbia University
president and now the chair of the Institute board, noted the high administrative costs at the school. Booker explained that he received up
to 100 letters a day about things unrelated to the school. He was unable
to neglect entertaining an unending flow of visitors to Tuskegee, attending meetings about racial matters, and assisting President
Roosevelt on political appointments. "Hundreds of matters bearing
upon the interests of the ten millions of Negroes in this country center
at Tuskegee," Booker told Low, and "those matters help to pile up the
expenses of the administration." After examining the curriculum,
Charles W. Eliot, president of Harvard, doubted that the nursing and
ministerial training were up to standards elsewhere, and he believed
that industrial skills were emphasized at the expense of adequate academic training—evidence that the tension between industrial and liberal education never eased at Tuskegee. The school should be more
rigorous, Low thought, in requiring students to matriculate for complete terms, rather than dropping in and out more casually. Booker replied to Low, whose life experience ranged all the way from Brooklyn
to Morningside Heights, that 75 percent of the students remained dependent on income from planting and harvesting the cotton crop; they
could not enter school until late in the fall and had to leave early in the
spring. Low thought the school put too much emphasis on agriculture
and owned more cropland than was warranted. Booker agreed that
the landholdings were too large, but he believed that the farming had
to continue because the campus building program was largely complete and students in the future would need work opportunities to earn
their board. In truth, the Institute's landholdings meant too much to
Booker's sense of his own achievement for him to let much acreage
go.[6]

Only serious personnel problems now drew Booker into the daily
administration of the school, and the worst arose in 1907, when Edgar
D. Penney, the longtime chaplain and head of the Phelps Bible School,
was charged with molesting a female student who lived with his fam-

ily. Booker had recruited Penney to come to Tuskegee in 1891, the Washingtons and the Penneys had been good friends, and Penney had set the tone for religious life on campus. The girl's word was the only evidence against Penney, and he strongly denied the charge, but another student earlier had made a similar allegation. In that instance Booker had given Penney the benefit of the doubt; but confronted with this second incident, Booker resolved that Penney had to go. "I do not in any degree attempt to pass judgment upon your guilt or innocence, upon your discretion or lack of discretion," Booker told him. "I am simply facing the hard, stubborn fact that you cannot in the present state of mind of all connected with the institution, render service of value." The scandal attracted newspaper reporters and provoked a demand for explanation from Horace Bumstead, president of Atlanta University, Penney's alma mater, on whose board of trustees the theologian now sat. When Booker refused information on the grounds that it was an internal Tuskegee matter and no business of his, Bumstead blasted him: "Is the voice of wicked slander so powerful there that the record of a long, useful, unblemished life counts for nothing against it? Is it possible that even you, with your great influence, are unable to overcome it?"[7]

Only Booker could come close to managing George Washington Carver. Presented with a report in 1904 that the poultry yard was nowhere nearly as well managed as Carver claimed, Booker asked his most famous faculty member to make improvements. "To be branded as a liar and party to such hellish deception," Carver replied, was "more than I can bear, and if your committee feel that I have willfully lied . . . my resignation is at your disposal." Booker soothed Carver's feelings with encomiums to the scientist's devotion to the school. But Carver habitually resisted the direction of the school's head of agriculture, whom he viewed as a rival. Told to plant certain crops on the school's experimental farm, Carver schemed to get the order changed. Although Booker appreciated Carver more than most others at the Institute, who considered the scientist a prima donna, he could not tolerate the refusal to take direction. "There are few people anywhere who have greater ability to inspire and instruct as a teacher and as a lecturer than is true of yourself," Booker wrote to Carver, but when it came to managing classes or Institute staff or the experimental farm, "you are wanting in ability." Carver took any suggestion for changing or improving his management of the experiment station as a personal affront. He complained to Booker that he was "being annoyed by committees that sometimes say very unhandsome and unbecoming things," which he admitted caused him "to indulge in the same spirit." In 1912 Washington had to tell Carver that suggestions from the Institute's executive council were simply a polite way of giving him orders. When Booker took him to task for reporting three times as many chickens in the poultry yard as actually resided there, Carver replied that he would be gone in thirty days, but he was still there to resign again six months later, and yet again two months after that. Exasperated, Washington told Carver that if necessary they would part ways after the 1913–14 academic year, but in fact Carver would be in Tuskegee long after Washington was gone. He brought fame to the school that would not have accrued had Booker not been able to balance Carver's difficult personality with his ability to demonstrate to the public a black scientist's achievement.[8]

By 1907 Tuskegee Institute had a decade and a half of experience in extending its agricultural knowledge to the rank and file of black farmers, and it was therefore ready to expand its efforts when philanthropic groups and the federal government began to show interest in that work. A new outreach effort had emerged in 1906 with the inauguration of the Jesup Agricultural Wagon, a rolling school for farmers that Booker had conceived in 1904 and then pitched to the New York banker Morris K. Jesup, who paid for the building of a twelve-foot-long, twelve-foot-high canvas-covered wagon and for filling it with the latest farming tools, including a revolving churn, a mechanical planter, a cotton chopper, different kinds of fertilizers, the latest seeds, and a milk tester. A faculty member drove the Jesup Agricultural Wagon into a field and demonstrated how farmers could improve their methods: "Where a man is running one furrow," the professor explained, "he is shown how he can run seven by using a different plow." Instead of a farmer having his wife and children spread fertilizer, "he is shown how he can take a fertilizer distributor and do the same work and do it in less time, thus allowing his wife and children to do something else." During its first summer of use, the Jesup Wagon taught new techniques to more than 2,000 farmers in Alabama. A related development was the appointment of the first black county farm agent. Seaman Knapp, the Texas agricultural reformer working to eradicate the boll weevil, had interested the General Education Board in supporting farm demonstration agents, the genesis of what would become the Cooperative Extension Service of the U.S. Department of Agriculture. News of the Jesup Wagon brought Knapp to Tuskegee to discuss with Carver the appointment of a black demonstration agent. Knapp thought that Carver's rival in the agriculture department was the right man, but Booker, to avoid injuring Carver's tender ego, recommended Thomas M. Campbell, a recent Tuskegee graduate. Washington negotiated a grant from the board to pay Campbell to advise black farmers in Macon County on the best farming practices, especially the use of improved seed. With the passage of the Smith-Lever Act in 1914, the U.S. Department of Agriculture expanded the system of farm extension agents, and Campbell became head of all the black agents in the South.[9]

In 1906 the Institute began publishing the *Messenger,* a magazine for black farmers like Clarence Poe's *Progressive Farmer* for whites. The *Messenger*'s articles encouraged thrift, temperance, and school improvements along with instruction on building better farms and improving family life. Washington directed the editor to campaign at all times for landownership. "Hold out the advantages of the school, cheap land, good race relations, etc. Emphasize constantly before the teachers the importance of teaching agriculture and other industries in the public schools." In 1913 the Institute inaugurated a fortnightly newspaper, the *Negro Farmer,* "in the interest of Negro landowners, tenant farmers and of those who employ Negro labor," another effort to meet the need for communication among rural blacks.[10]

The 1910 census heartened Washington with reports of an increase in black farm ownership. The main obstacle was the capital required to get started. Going back to the idea of the Southern Improvement Company of 1901, which had enabled a few black families to become landowners, Washington in 1914 instigated another landowners' farming colony on 1,800 acres of land north of Tuskegee. Named Baldwin

Farms, it sold 40-acre plots to Tuskegee graduates. The project staff provided educational support to the young farmers and admonished them "to pay as much as possible on the debt; to use rainy days to improve the interiors of the houses; because of the nature of the soil, to keep it stirred all the time so as to conserve moisture; to can and preserve everything possible; and to raise as many pigs and fowls as possible." Like the Southern Improvement Company, Baldwin Farms was only marginally successful. In 1914 rising landownership and a decade of good cotton prices made land reform for black farmers seem like a worthwhile effort, but Baldwin Farms attempted to improve black economic security in an agricultural economy that in the long run was not promising for small landowners regardless of color. Washington would not be the last reformer to believe that landownership was the salvation of southern blacks. The Tuskegee efforts were models for the Resettlement Administration, through which Franklin Roosevelt's New Deal addressed the crisis of displaced farmers. Even then, those concerned with how to improve the lives of black farmers looked to Tuskegee.[11]

The conditions of black primary education remained Washington's single greatest worry. "Much of the advance in the way of white education in recent years has been made at the expense of Negro education," he told one philanthropist. "That is, money has been actually taken from the Negro schools to advance the education of the white people." Every southern state now had funds for building white schools, but nothing was provided for blacks. When the General Education Board funded a program to promote the construction of high schools in the South, Booker discovered that only white high schools were built. "I very much fear," he wrote to Rockefeller's man in charge, "that if the General Education Board continues to employ people to encourage white high schools, and does nothing for Negro high schools, the southern white people will take it for granted that the Negro is to have few if any high schools." Nothing changed, at least not then. By 1910 Washington had started to point his students away from the creation of little Tuskegees and toward work in the public schools. Only a few poor blacks would in the end get to go to a large industrial school like

Tuskegee, whereas "the masses must depend upon the public school in their neighborhood for whatever education they get." If the black public schools continued to fail, generations would grow up in ignorance. Every black person needed to take a personal interest. Each must push authorities for a just distribution of school funds. "This kind of appeal should be repeated again and again until we do receive our just share. We should not give up or stand still."[12]

Still, Washington knew that northern philanthropy was the quickest way he had to improve black education. He had interested Anna Jeanes of Philadelphia in the problem in 1906, and the Jeanes Fund had underwritten the costs of forty-six schools built by Tuskegee Institute graduates. Booker decided that outside philanthropy should provide no more than half the costs of a new school; the local community should have to raise the balance as a means of assuring genuine appreciation and ownership of the new building. He used the money to build new schools as quickly as possible. "I find that when the people get a good schoolhouse in their midst . . . that it settles a lot of other problems," he told George Peabody. "In the first place, it means a better teacher, a longer school term and the schoolhouse becomes a social center for the neighborhood."[13]

His faith in the uplifting power of a new school pushed Booker to keep looking for more private money. By 1913 he had marked his man. Julius Rosenwald had made a fortune at Sears, Roebuck and Company in Chicago by the time he was fifty, and he began to think intensely about stewardship of his money. At Booker's behest, Rosenwald looked at the needs in black education. Starting in 1911, he donated large lots of shoes and hats for black industrial-school students in the South. Then he pledged $5,000 for five years to Tuskegee Institute and agreed to go on its board of trustees. By that time, Rosenwald and his wife were enamored of Tuskegee and persuaded that black education in the South should be a particular mission of theirs. Washington in turn had found a white man who respected and deferred to his knowledge about how to help black southerners. Not since William Baldwin had Washington related so easily and closely to a white supporter.[14]

When asked to support the building of primary schools, Rosenwald responded with the offer of prefabricated buildings, then being sold by

49. "Before" and "after" images of an Alabama schoolhouse, ca. 1911. Photographer unknown; from Booker T. Washington, *My Larger Education: Being Chapters from My Experience* (Garden City, N.Y.: Doubleday, Page, 1911).

Sears, Roebuck. Booker gently guided him away from that idea, because it took the construction process away from the black residents. Rosenwald agreed to underwrite 6 schools at a cost of $2,800. When they were completed, Washington sent him photographs and an accounting of his money to the penny. "You do not know what joy and encouragement the building of these schoolhouses has brought to the people of both races in the communities where they are being erected," Booker told him. The photographs hooked Rosenwald, and in 1914 he committed $30,000 to build 100 schools in three Alabama counties. There was immediate pressure to build larger, better-appointed school buildings, but Booker was wary: whites might "have a feeling that the colored people are getting ahead of them, therefore something might be done to bring about an awkward position regarding the Negro school." Booker knew his white people, especially their status anxieties about blacks' rising in the world. Even as modest structures, the Rosenwald schools were a vast improvement over what blacks formerly had.[15]

Having been led to black problems in the South, Julius Rosenwald stayed involved long after Washington was gone from the scene. Hundreds more schools were built after World War I, although administration of the program passed out of Tuskegee hands to a foundation, the Rosenwald Fund. Through this foundation Rosenwald also supported medical care for blacks, research into American racial problems, legal challenges to discrimination, fellowships for black artists and intellectuals (including Du Bois), and the activities of interracial organizations in the South. Rosenwald's example nurtured a broader philanthropic interest in the South; other foundations followed the Sears magnate's path into southern racial issues. In New Orleans Rosenwald's daughter Edith and her husband, Edgar Stern, established the lone southern philanthropy making grants to civil-rights organizations in the 1960s. Much of the good work of Rosenwald and his progeny was a legacy of Washington's encouragement.[16]

Among colleges, Booker directed philanthropy to Fisk, and he worked to be evenhanded in his treatment of Atlanta University despite the harsh criticisms of him emanating from there. He openly preferred Fisk, whose board of trustees he joined in 1909. In his view, there ought to be "at least one strong central institution in the South for the higher education of the Negro," and he believed that Fisk served that purpose. Still, he recommended to Andrew Carnegie that he fund a building for Atlanta Baptist College, situated adjacent to Atlanta University. He advised the agnostic Carnegie not to be put off by the "Baptist" in the school's name, "as it does not mean much in this case"—a characterization that would not have been appreciated within the denomination. Notwithstanding that John Hope, the school's president, was Du Bois's confidant and a consistent critic of the principal of Tuskegee, Washington told Carnegie that Hope was "a man of the highest and cleanest character." The school got Carnegie's money.[17]

Washington remained steadfast in his commitment to discover and disseminate information on black progress. In the spring of 1908 he finally found a man for the position of research director, the job he had tried for years to interest Du Bois in filling. He hired Monroe N. Work, a University of Chicago–trained sociologist, former member of the Niagara Movement, and research colleague of Du Bois. When he got to Tuskegee, Work later said, the hopeless view of the Negro still prevailed, and therefore "from 1908 on I was compiling a day by day record of what was taking place with reference to the Negro." In 1912 Work produced the first *Negro Year Book: An Annual Encyclopedia of the Negro,* which promised to meet the demand for "accurate and concise information in regard to the history and progress of the Negro race." It was a compendium of historical and statistical information, with a heavy emphasis on the successes achieved by black people. But it also reported on lynchings, disfranchisement, and the other forms of discrimination facing blacks at the time. Thousands of African Americans would pay twenty-five cents to own and consult the *Negro Year Book* to discover the good news and the bad news about themselves. At the same time, Washington launched, and Monroe Work produced, the Tuskegee reports on lynching. Work kept track of every alleged lynching and investigated the circumstances surrounding the killing. Then, using Work's summaries, Booker issued press releases that gave comparative figures on what had happened semiannually and annually. In the 1914 report, he explained that the number of lynchings, fifty-two, represented the lowest figure in many years. "Although the number of lynchings has not increased, there appears to be an increasing tendency to lynch for any cause, however trivial, and also to disregard sex." Only seven of those lynched had been charged with rape, and two of those were white.[18]

Washington resumed his efforts to shape how Americans thought about blacks. In 1910 and 1911 he brought to fruition several writing projects that had long been in the works but were delayed by the sudden death in 1904 of his first ghostwriter, Max Bennett Thrasher, and his preoccupation through 1906 with politics. Starting in 1905, Robert Ezra Park took over most writing and editing responsibilities. Booker had worked with Park in the Congo Reform Association and admired the sharp analytic abilities of the white Midwestern journalist who had earned a German doctorate in sociology. The two men often traveled together, and they developed a close personal relationship. Typically Booker dictated his thoughts about a subject to a stenographer, and Park then shaped those thoughts into a coherent manuscript. The Tuskegee work gave Park a feeling of relevance to the real world that academia had failed to provide. Washington was no intellectual but a man engaged realistically in a crucial task, one "who knows what should be done, and how to do it." Park would say that he learned more about human nature and society with Booker than in all his academic study. "The problem of Tuskegee is the problem of the Negro everywhere," he wrote while working beside Washington. "It is an experiment to determine whether the Negro can be made an independent citizen living peaceably and happily side by side with the white man or whether the position of subordination and tutelage in which he now stands every where is permanent and unchangeable."[19]

In 1910 they brought to fruition two books that other ghostwriters had failed to complete. One was a biography of Frederick Douglass, a competent but mostly hagiographic celebration. The two-volume *Story of the Negro* compiled articles and life histories that covered the whole experience of black people. No doubt reflecting the new influence of Park, *Story of the Negro* has a warmer, more intimate feel than *Up from Slavery*. He noted, for example, that it was only after they were freed that blacks began to think of themselves as having a past or a future distinct from those of their white owners. Booker's own first encounters with Africa had come through geography books that portrayed blacks as naked savages, people who diverged far from the norms he had been taught. He instinctively rejected the demeaning interpretation, for any race that could "produce as good and gentle and loving a woman as my mother must have some good in it that the geographers had failed to discover." His opinions about race and civilization were decidedly less accommodating to whites than they had been ten years earlier. He firmly rejected the racial essentialism that most whites embraced. Africa was home to people of many shades of color, and he believed that pigmentation meant nothing beyond a visual difference. "No one question, I may say right here, is more frequently asked me than this: 'What is the relative ability of the Negro of mixed and unmixed blood?' I usually answer that my experience and observation convince me that, where the environment has been equally favorable, there is no difference in ability."[20]

In 1911 Park and Washington produced the autobiographical *My Larger Education.* Like *The Story of the Negro,* this book was more honest in its opinions and revealing of Booker's feelings than the earlier autobiographies. He thought that nine out of ten black intellectuals believed that their race entitled them to "the special sympathy of the world, and they have thus got into the habit of relying on this sympathy rather than on their own efforts to make their way." The intellectuals understood theories, but they did not understand things, by which he meant the realities of the world. "I have long been convinced that, if these men could have gone into the South and taken up and become interested in some practical work which would have brought them in touch with people and things, the whole world would have looked very different to them." He finally declared that Roosevelt had been wrong about Brownsville, but then he let "the Colonel" off the hook: "I do not think that the criticisms and denunciation which he received had the effect of swerving him in the least from the general course that he had determined to pursue with regard to the coloured people of the country." Booker suspected correctly that he had not seen the last of him in national politics, and he did not want to alienate a powerful ally.[21]

The last important work that Park and Washington produced was *The Man Farthest Down,* based on a trip they took in 1910 to examine the lives of poor Europeans in order to compare the conditions of American blacks. Washington was looking for proof that there were people in the most civilized portions of the world who were not as well off as Booker's own in America. "I believed that if the black people in America knew something of the burdens and difficulties under which the masses of the people in Europe live and work they would see that their own situation was by no means so hopeless as they have been sometimes taught to believe." He found what he wanted and committed it to his notebook: in Bohemia, peasants suffered religious discrimination and women were exploited; in Naples fifty beggars followed him—"negro seldom begs," he noted—and there were "secret criminal societies not know[n] to Negro"; in Hungary, "Negro farmer is using more up to date machinery than white farmer in Europe—is less conservative." Overall, "Negro farmer in the South has 50% more comforts than European farmer." Booker's chauvinistic responses led Park to doubt that he had actually learned much. "When he was abroad he was not interested in the common people as I thought he would be," Park later said privately. "They were just foreigners. He was an American and thought everything in America surpassed anything in Europe."[22]

Park left his disappointment out of the book, but he had identified a fixity of vision that was both Washington's great strength and at times his deep flaw. His determination to emphasize the progress of African Americans to blacks and whites alike led him to extol the positive features of American life at the expense of his open engagement with its many negative aspects. No one knew better than Booker what was wrong for blacks in the United States, but he had long since decided to emphasize its good for the sake of bolstering black morale and winning white friends to the African-American cause. That stubborn commitment sometimes limited his perspective.

As part of a continuing engagement with Africa, in 1907 Washington took on by far his most important role. In Liberia, the nation established and governed by colonized American slaves but weakened in the late nineteenth century by English and French encroachments on its territory and by German efforts to collect Liberian debts, the indigenous people had begun to resist the governance—and heavy taxation—of the Americo-Liberian minority. In 1907, with the nation nearing both civil insurrection and British invasion, Americans living in Liberia asked Washington to negotiate American intervention. In 1908 Booker hosted Liberian officials in the United States and sat with them while they pleaded with government officials for help. Booker declined a request from Roosevelt to head a Liberian investigating commission but arranged for Emmett Scott to serve. The commissioners recommended action that, when implemented, represented the largest American foreign-policy involvement in Africa up to that time: Liberia became a U.S. protectorate like Puerto Rico, and American bankers took over the nation's debt. In return, Liberians accepted U.S. oversight of its defense forces. Washington later advised both the Liberians and Americans about future action. Liberians, he told that nation's president, needed to develop a more sensitive approach to the indigenous people and to build a more productive and self-sufficient economy. Booker found a donor for scholarships to bring Liberians of both tribal and Americo-Liberian backgrounds to study at Tuskegee. Eventually there would be a Booker T. Washington Industrial Institute in Liberia.[23]

In the aftermath of the Atlanta riot and Brownsville, Washington resumed the southern speaking tours that he believed strengthened his popularity and influence among southerners black and white. More and more he drew a contrast with the message of white nationalists like Tillman, who bragged that at Chautauquas all over the North he had "preached the gospel of white supremacy straight from the shoulder and . . . told them to their teeth that they didn't believe that the negro was equal to the white man; that they were hypocrites and liars when they said it." Booker did not challenge Tillman explicitly but instead spread his own message about the certainty of black progress, the benefits of black education, and the necessity of interracial goodwill. "The white men in the South cannot get along without the Negro," he typically declared, "any more than the Negro can get along without them." Only the bad news of race relations was reported, he often said, when in fact blacks and whites lived together peaceably most of the time and helped each other daily. When Booker toured in South Carolina in 1909, whites and blacks attended his speeches in equal numbers. At Sumter, Booker recalled, the white Baptist minister who introduced him said that "the time had come when Southern white people must stop lying about the Negro . . . and deceiving themselves and face the facts."[24]

50. Booker remained the master of the speaking platform even after the troubles of 1905 and 1906. Here he is shown in Lakeland, Florida, around 1912. Photographer unknown; courtesy of the Library of Congress.

In his 1908 Mississippi tour, Booker challenged the influence of James K. Vardaman more directly. He spoke to huge, enthusiastic crowds of blacks and whites as he moved from Holly Springs to Jackson to Utica—the last a visit to the Little Tuskegee begun by William Holtzclaw, a tangible rebuttal of Vardaman's insistence on the uselessness of black education. From there he moved on to Natchez, Vicksburg, Greenville, and Mound Bayou, the last being an all-black town that he liked for its demonstration of black entrepreneurship and political self-governance. Each stop brought a huge gathering; Mississippians came, one man recounted, "from bottom and hill, in every conceivable mode of conveyance, from the rattle-trap to the carry-all" but also in "phaetons and carriages as glittering, as new" as any seen anywhere. A white youth in Holly Springs arrived on a saddled yearling bull, from which he kept shouting, "Where is Booker T.?" At each venue, the tall, dark-skinned Major Robert R. Moton, commandant of cadets at Hampton and now one of Booker's closest allies on racial matters, would lead the throng in singing "Climbing Jacob's Ladder" and "Swing Low, Sweet Chariot." Washington's inspirational speeches addressed his nemesis only with satire. He told about a farmer who had offered to supply a hotel with enough frog legs to feed the whole dining room, only to show up with a single pair. The nearby swamp positively screamed at night with croaking, the chagrined farmer reported, but when he went for the harvest, he found only one big frog making all the noise. One big frog in Mississippi, Booker suggested, was making all the ugly noise, while the other denizens of the swamp got along quietly. The white Methodist bishop Charles Galloway, who accompanied Washington on the tour, afterward preached against "the big frog" whom white Mississippians should ignore.[25]

In place after place, white Mississippians showed their approval of Booker's message. "If I could spend a week longer in this state I think I could change the Vardaman sentiment regarding Negro education," he wrote to Seth Low. After the tour, Vardaman attacked whites who had attended the speeches. At Jackson a bleacher had collapsed, dropping several whites on top of blacks seated below; Vardaman commented: "The white people who attended were out of place and . . . being sat upon by a few rancid negro women were [sic] no more than they deserved." This was just what he wanted, Booker told Francis Garrison: a division of white opinion. "Many of them did not give much attention to Vardaman so long as he was attacking the colored people, but now, as he has attacked the white people, they are waking up to the harm that he is doing, and are vigorously defending themselves, and disapproving of his course."[26]

In 1909 he delivered speeches in eighteen villages in Virginia and another five in West Virginia. "Throughout the trip," a man who accompanied Booker later wrote, "Dr. Washington spoke to the colored people frankly of the simple, practical, fundamental affairs of life," and he always emphasized both "the duty and possibilities of improving their condition." Then he went to Tennessee and Kentucky, speaking to 50,000 people, about half of them white, in more than twenty towns. He reminded white Tennesseans of a great responsibility. "Wherever I have gone in Tennessee or any other state," Booker declared to 7,500 in Nashville, "I have found the Negro very much what the white man is." Where the whites were ignorant, lawless, and immoral, so were the blacks. "If I find an intelligent, law-abiding, and cultured class of white people, the Negro is certain to be also intelligent, law-abiding, and cultured." And everywhere he promoted interracial reconciliation, which he said already existed at one level: "Every Negro in the South has a white friend, and every white man has a Negro friend." A white judge in western Tennessee likened Booker to an Israelite prophet with a message to inspire all: "By helping you he helps us," he proclaimed to blacks. "By helping you he helps every man, woman and child in all this broad land of ours."[27]

In the fall of 1910 Washington toured North Carolina for a week, visiting all the major towns and cities, speaking in opera houses, tobacco warehouses, and schoolhouses and making several whistle-stop speeches from train cabooses in smaller places. Everywhere, it was reported, the whole black population of that part of the Tarheel State turned out to see the first man of their race. "He was their friend and their champion," a sympathetic observer wrote, and "they were correspondingly proud of him and happy to see and to be with him and to hear what he had to say." They listened to the simple, direct language used to narrate his funny stories and assert his plain morals. "If I were a white man sitting upon a jury and called upon to decide the guilt or innocence of a Negro accused of a crime," Washington said to whites all over North Carolina, "I would lay my hand on my heart and ask myself upon my conscience and before my Maker, whether I had given that black boy a fair chance to know right and wrong, to curb and restrain his passions and desires, to know the law and to obey it."[28]

In Wilmington, where a dozen years earlier the terrible pogrom against blacks had left many dead and run thousands more out of the city, Washington took the stage at the city's elegant Academy of Music, with blacks in the orchestra seats on one side and whites on the other side. Booker's message echoed the themes he had long stressed: interracial peace, mutual responsibility, black progress, but also the need for white-mandated reform in education and the criminal justice system. The Negro boy could not learn as much in three months of school as the white boy could in six, he said; but when the uneducated black boy committed a crime, his sentence was never half as long as the white boy's. Booker, ended, as always, on an optimistic note: "If we learn to be frank with each other," a typical one went, "to trust each other and cultivate love and toleration instead of hatred we will teach the world a lesson, how two races different in color can live together in peace and harmony and in friendship."[29]

Washington saw it as his responsibility to shape the thinking of both whites and blacks in the South; surely that was the real role of a racial leader. He was confident that he could accomplish that mission by getting out among the people and giving them an opportunity to hear what he had to say. But there were still times when distasteful tasks distracted him, and a series of these in 1910 and 1911 took him to the low point of his career and his life.

16

The Leader of the Race

In August 1908 Americans were shocked again by racial violence, but this time it came in the North—indeed, in the hometown of the Great Emancipator, Springfield, Illinois. From 1903 through 1906, white mobs had invaded black neighborhoods, attacked the residents, and destroyed their property with the intent of obliterating all black presence from Evansville and Greensburg, Indiana, and Springfield, Ohio. Americans' tendency to associate racial violence with the South prevented these northern instances of bloodshed and destruction from finding a clear place in the nation's consciousness. Springfield, Illinois, changed that. There a lynch mob became enraged at the safe removal of two black men, one charged with rape and the other with murdering the rape victim's father, from the local jail. In a replay of the mob action elsewhere, including Wilmington, North Carolina, and Atlanta, whites tried to drive all blacks from Lincoln's beloved home. The mob destroyed the homes of forty poor black families and several black-owned businesses. Rioters lynched two black merchants. Once again, rioters pursued most viciously not the criminal or dishonest Negroes but the successful ones. They ransacked the homes of Springfield's well-to-do blacks. The most common explanation for the violence among Springfield whites was "the niggers came to think they were as good as we are!"[1]

In the aftermath of the Illinois violence, Booker Washington issued a condemnation of mob action, but he did not go to Springfield as he had Atlanta, probably because he had far less at stake in the disorder in a small northern town. The trouble in Atlanta meant far more to his leadership, and he had far more influence there than he would in central Illinois. In 1908 he was still discouraging blacks in the South from migrating northward, because he still believed the economic competition in the North made the South a better place for them. But others would pay keen attention to Springfield, and their focus would affect Washington's leadership in a powerful way. Violence against blacks anywhere in the United States undermined Booker's standing.[2]

Washington could not have been surprised by the Springfield events; a recent journalistic exposé had predicted northern racial violence. In the aftermath of the Atlanta riot, Booker and Oswald Villard had asked the muckraking journalist Ray Stannard Baker to investigate the causes of the Atlanta riot. Baker in fact gave a full and complex first report in *American Magazine* on the causes and consequences of the Atlanta trouble and in subsequent articles reported on the full range of racial problems in the United States, including the rising tensions in the North. With the growth of black populations in Philadelphia, New York, and Chicago in the 1890s had come increased discrimination. "Generally speaking," Baker wrote, "the more Negroes the sharper the expression of prejudice." In trades in which blacks had enjoyed a strong presence in the nineteenth century, competition from white immigrants often drove them out of jobs after 1890. Strikebreaking remained a major entrée for blacks to higher-paying jobs, but blacks had acquired the reputation of being a scab race—even though whites also worked as strikebreakers. Starting in New York in 1900, riots in northern cities and midwestern towns had revealed the potential seriousness of racial conflict.[3]

In articles throughout 1907 and 1908, collected in the book *Following the Color Line* in late 1908, Ray Stannard Baker offered the most comprehensive analysis of American racial relations yet seen. He was struck by the South's absorption with race. "In the North we are mildly concerned in many things," he wrote, but "the South is overwhelmingly concerned in this one thing." The black man in the South was "both the labor problem and the servant question; he is pre-eminently the political issue, and his place, socially, is of daily and hourly discussion." He told of a young black man, recently employed at a prosperous white home, who was asked by his family what the whites talked about at mealtime. "Mostly they discusses us culled folks." Asked if blacks talked about race much, a black waiter replied that "we don't talk about much else," explaining that "it's sort of life and death with us." White southerners insisted to Baker that he could not know blacks as they did. "I know the Negroes like a book," whites typically said; "I was brought up with them. I know what they'll do and what they won't do." Baker insisted that they did not know well-to-do, educated blacks. "Many Southerners look back wistfully to the faithful, simple, ignorant, obedient, cheerful darkey and deplore his disappearance," Baker observed. "They want the New South, but the old darkey." It was surely necessary, "as a problem in human nature, to know how the Negro feels and what he says, as it is to know how the white man feels."[4]

Baker found much evidence of economic motivation for white aggression against blacks. He wrote about whites' terrorizing blacks out of towns in Arkansas and Oklahoma in 1907. A white man in northern Georgia told Baker about a black peach grower, a landowner, who was driven violently from his farm by poor whites: "The shiftless element of the whites . . . say, 'I will work or not, as I please, and when I please, and at my own price; and I will not have Negroes taking my work away from me.'" Baker recognized the divided minds of whites about black labor. "In one impulse [whites] will rise to mob Negroes or to drive them out of the country because of Negro crime or Negro vagrancy, or because he is becoming educated, acquiring property and 'getting out of his place,'" he wrote, but "in the next impulse laws are passed or other remarkable measures taken to keep him at work—because the South can't get along without him." Baker put much credence in the opinion of a white Atlanta railroad worker: "When the skilled negro appears and begins to elbow the white man in the struggle for existence, don't you know the white man rebels and won't have it so?" Although Washington acknowledged privately that white economic competition undermined black opportunities, including industrial education, he wrote to Baker that few communities had driven out blacks. Whitecapping was such an affront to his materialist strategy that he did not want it highlighted in a national magazine. But the fact was that racial competition was growing more acute as more white farmers moved to towns and competed with blacks for jobs. White, unionized railroad workers had been pushing out black workers since 1898. In 1909 the Brotherhood of Locomotive Firemen struck the Georgia Railroad over the use of black firemen. "Will the people of Georgia back their own men," the union leader dared publicly, "or will they back the Georgia railroad in trying to ram negro supremacy down the throats of its white firemen?" Soon white mobs all over the Peach State were pulling black firemen from trains and beating them.[5]

Following the Color Line vindicated Washington's leadership. Baker witnessed support for Booker among the "thousands of common, struggling human beings" to whom he had given hope and a plan for how to improve their lives. Booker was like Abraham Lincoln: each had "the simplicity and patience of the soil," immense courage and faith, and, "to prevent being crushed by circumstances," a strong sense of humor—"they laugh off their troubles." Wherever Baker found "a prosperous Negro enterprise, a thriving business place, a good home, there I was almost sure to find Booker T. Washington's picture over the fireplace or a little framed motto expressing his gospel of work and service." In contrast, Baker characterized Du Bois as an intellectual with the temperament of the "scholar and idealist—critical, sensitive, unhumorous, impatient, often covering its deep feeling with sarcasm and cynicism." He found a parallel between him and the white nationalists: both Tillman and Du Bois exhorted their races to agitate. Washington, on the contrary, told his people to work. But Baker thought that both men were needed: Washington was the opportunist and the optimist who did his work "with the world as he finds it: he is resourceful, constructive, familiar," whereas Du Bois was the idealist, the agitator, and the pessimist who saw the world "as it should be and cries out to have it instantly changed."[6]

Baker had done a remarkable job of showing the depth and breadth of white hostility to black interests in the United States, and as a result, one could not leave the work with a sense of progress. The book encompassed Washington's propaganda dilemma: Americans needed to know the truth about racial conditions in their country, but with things as bad as they were, the whole truth risked promoting anger at current leaders and despair about the future. Booker well knew who was the likely victim of those reactions.

Following the Color Line appeared as Washington was again preoccupied with presidential politics. Among blacks, the dark cloud of the Brownsville affair still hung over Theodore Roosevelt, and it cast a shadow over his designated successor, William Howard Taft. Booker had encouraged blacks to move on from the Brownsville issue, and most of his close allies had followed his lead, but Tim Fortune was irreconcilable. He continued in 1907 to denounce Roosevelt, and that criticism accelerated Washington's determination to get control of the New York *Age*. He kept his ownership secret by having Emmett Scott hold his stock, and he continued to deny ownership in a dishonest attempt to avoid the criticism that Trotter and Du Bois had been making since 1903 about his manipulation of the black press. "I do not hold a single share of stock in connection with the *Age* and have no financial interest in it," he falsely told a disgruntled former employee. From January 1907 forward, he directed Fred R. Moore, his partner in the ownership and the acting editor, on editorial and reportorial policy. Fortune, drinking heavily, stayed on a few months as an editorial writer, but then sold his remaining interest to Moore, who bought it with Booker's money. When Moore stopped discussing the Brownsville affair, Fortune was irate, quit the paper finally, and moved to Chicago. There he took up with Max Barber and bought an interest in the *Voice of the Negro,* which soon went bankrupt. Thus added to the list of Brownsville casualties were Booker's affiliation with Fortune and, in one instance at least, his commitment to the truth.[7]

Booker argued that in nine cases out of ten Roosevelt and Taft had done right by blacks, but this exaggeration apparently persuaded few, and he did not use it widely. He sensed correctly that Taft would give more favor to the Lily Whites in the South, and he warned Taft's campaign manager that it would be a battle to get blacks back into the Republican fold. Booker and his advisers rewrote Taft's acceptance speech to the nominating convention after Taft had submitted to them a draft

51. Booker Washington liked William Howard Taft but recognized that "our big friend" was not nearly as friendly to blacks as he wished. Photo by George W. Harris, copyright Harris and Ewing, 1904; courtesy of the Library of Congress.

clearly favoring southern whites. There were other bad signs: Taft appointed a white man to run the party's Negro bureau, traditionally the mechanism through which a strong black vote was secured. The white bureau chief started courting Monroe Trotter, apparently unaware that the Bostonian and his allies had already declared for the Democrat William Jennings Bryan. Washington thought two things about the 1908 election: Taft was a poor replacement for Roosevelt, whom despite Brownsville he still admired as one who was not afraid "to place power and responsibility in the hands of Colored people"; and blacks had nowhere else to go, because Bryan staunchly defended the white South's anti-Negro policies at every turn, including lynching. Taft won easily, and most blacks voted for him, although the large margin of his victory indicated that he did not need them.[8]

Taft immediately began to snub his black supporters. He demanded William Crum's resignation, believing that the doctor, who by all reports had done a fine job as revenue collector in Charleston, represented an unnecessary political liability. Washington got Crum appointed ambassador to Liberia, where he caught a tropical fever and died in 1912. Taft announced that he would appoint no blacks in the South if whites objected—therefore ensuring white protests every time a black's name was mentioned. The Lily Whites completed their take-over of the southern Republican operations that Washington had fore-stalled under Roosevelt. A few black appointments in the North went to Booker's allies, but his influence in politics was clearly diminished. His friends treated with Taft over a few jobs, but more and more they did so without Booker's direct involvement.[9]

Booker kept his own counsel regarding his declining political influ-ence. His choice was to remain on friendly terms with men in power and wait for things to change or to withdraw from politics. He did the former, but he also began gradually to disengage from the fray. It was too costly and exhausting a business if one was unable to achieve good results.

The violence in Springfield accelerated Washington's demise as the leader of his race. The riot prompted three white socialists to start or-ganizing a new civil-rights organization. William English Walling, a settlement-house worker and journalist, had investigated the riot and been appalled by its brutality. Mary White Ovington, another settle-ment-house worker and sometime journalist, shared Walling's convic-tion, as did Henry Moskowitz, a physician and urban reformer. They approached Oswald Garrison Villard of the New York *Evening Post* to support their move to create an interracial organization to defend black rights. It was an opportune moment for a new organization. Both the Afro-American Council and the Niagara Movement had es-sentially become defunct in 1908. The council's demise followed its public condemnations of Roosevelt and the Republicans after Browns-ville, moves that had caused Washington and his allies to withdraw their participation; and the Niagara Movement fell victim to the nasty infighting that accompanied Monroe Trotter wherever he went.

For several years Villard had been talking about a legal-defense group for blacks, and he took the prompt from the social workers to launch his effort. In May 1909 he assembled settlement workers, pro-fessors, lawyers, journalists, and clergymen for what would eventually be called the National Association for the Advancement of Colored People (NAACP). Du Bois, Trotter, Max Barber, and Ida Wells-Barnett were among the black critics of Washington at the inaugural meeting of the NAACP. Also present was the white businessman John Milholland, founder of the Constitution League, the organization known for pushing the Crumpacker plan for enforcement of the Fourteenth and Fifteenth Amendments and demanding redress for the Brownsville wrongs. There were strong affinities among the settlement-house workers, the socialists, and the most enthusiastic anti-Washington partisans. A bridge among the groups was Ovington, who had earlier brought blacks and whites together socially in New York's Cosmopolitan Society. She reported for Villard's *Evening Post*. She apparently was also Milholland's lover and definitely an admirer of Du Bois's genius and his "African passion." But there was also some discord within the NAACP group: Villard disapproved of Du Bois's personal animus toward Washington, and Du Bois believed that Villard thought himself superior to all blacks. Each had an accurate sense of the other's prejudices, if not of his own. Each had just published biographies of the abolitionist John Brown, and Villard had written a negative review of Du Bois's book. Despite their mutual distrust, the two were united from a distance in their commitment to replacing Booker Washington as the leader of American blacks.[10]

Villard's alienation represented a substantial loss for Washington. Like his father and his Garrison uncles, Villard had been a strong supporter of Tuskegee and at times had been Booker's confidant, the person most likely to take William Baldwin's place as Washington's tough-minded white adviser. Indeed, Villard had raised $150,000 for the William Baldwin memorial fund at Tuskegee. But differences between Washington and Villard grew after 1906. Villard and the Garrisons detested Theodore Roosevelt, and Booker's loyalty to Teddy had bothered them before Brownsville and infuriated Villard afterward. They did not really understand his loyalty to Roosevelt, and Villard did not respect Booker's independent view on the matter. Villard changed his views about the role of black protest at the same time that Booker refused to condemn Roosevelt over Brownsville. Villard now insisted that protest was the only means for black uplift. The belief may have grown stronger while he was writing his John Brown biography, which apparently made him even more conscious of his Garrisonian legacy. "There is too much agitator blood in me to feel that the colored people should ever stop their political agitation," he told Ray Stannard Baker. "I am much too radical and outspoken to make him feel comfortable," Villard said about Washington after a 1909 speech in Tuskegee.[11]

This perspective represented a new understanding of his Garrison inheritance. In 1905 he had accused Du Bois of exaggerating the difference between himself and Washington. At that point Villard agreed with the position his uncle William Lloyd Garrison Jr. expressed in 1908 when he insisted that the Niagara aspersions against Washington were cruel and untrue. Booker set "no metes or bounds to the Negro's aspiration for learning, nor does he acquiesce in the annulment of the Fifteenth Amendment," Garrison wrote. "He not only carries the burden of a great university, but upon his shoulders has fallen the mission to disarm sectional hostility, to draw support from Southern whites with inherited prejudices that must be delayed, ever to keep a hopeful front, under circumstances which must at times chill his heart." Villard's motives were based far less on his Garrison legacy than on his anger at Washington's loyalty to the Republicans. "I am one of your warm friends who is unhappy about your political activism," Villard wrote. He claimed to be worried about the danger of Booker's "being forced against your will into the untenable position of being the political clearinghouse for the colored race, a position no one can fill in the long run with success, or without causing the most intense hostility on the part of your colored fellow-citizens." Villard wanted Washington out of politics, and to effect that end he had decided that Booker had to be replaced as leader of the race.[12]

But Villard did not want Booker to oppose the new organization and invited him to the founding meeting of the NAACP. Although his larger purpose was to depose Washington, Villard knew that the new organization would be handicapped if it was perceived as just an anti-Booker group. "It is not to be a Washington movement, or a Du Bois movement," he said, without disavowing that it might be a Villard movement. Declining the invitation, Booker reminded Villard of what he had often told him: "There is a work to be done which no one placed in my position can do, which no one living in the South perhaps can do." If Villard recognized this—as his uncles had always been able to do—then Booker would reiterate that he knew the value of "sane agitation and criticism, but not to the extent of having our race feel that we can depend upon this to cure all the evils surrounding us."[13]

The NAACP's founding meeting demonstrated the organization's anti-Washington purpose. When a white participant suggested that Booker serve on its steering committee, blacks exploded in opposition. With the NAACP established, Du Bois wrote publicly that Washington had been the sole political referee for ten million blacks and had rewarded only those who agreed with his policy of "non-resistance, giving up agitation, and acquiescence in semi-serfdom." Washington's leadership amounted to substituting monarchy for democracy. Villard knew from Booker's work against peonage since 1903 that the accusation of submission to serfdom was unfair. But because his larger purpose was to overthrow Washington, he quoted Du Bois's misrepresentations in his newspaper and wrote that Booker should keep silent on political matters. Villard thus took the position that Booker's Boston critics had espoused in 1898 and that Trotter had advocated since 1901: that Washington should cloister himself at Tuskegee and leave politics to the men in the North who knew better.[14]

The irony of the false characterizations about Washington's motives and actions was that they arose in opposition to political power that, by May 1909, was largely eroded. Indeed, so well-organized a challenge to his leadership could come only because Roosevelt's and Taft's indifference had already reduced Washington's political influence. In an age so thoroughly hostile to black interests, powerful white men did in fact set the terms under which black men exercised authority—or lost what little influence they had. Villard was in the process of making that reality manifest.

But in 1909 neither Washington nor his opponents knew that the rise of the NAACP represented the next phase in the Tuskegee descent from power. Booker kept a sharp eye on the new group, using spies whom he or Charles Anderson, the New York Republican politician who was now Booker's closest black ally outside Tuskegee, sent or who volunteered on their own. As Washington put it to Baker, a few perennial black naysayers, people with little standing in their own communities, had allied with insincere whites who were deceiving blacks into believing that "they can get what they ought to have in the way of right treatment by merely making demands, passing resolutions and cursing somebody." Booker's opposition hardened in 1910 when Du Bois went to work for the NAACP as research director, where he created the new magazine *Crisis*. Within a few years it became the successful national publication about black interests that Booker had long envisioned. Its acceptance bothered Booker, who saw that it was usurping his New York *Age*. Through *Crisis* Du Bois gained broad influence on the thinking of African Americans. Otherwise, the NAACP was largely a white-run organization into the 1920s.[15]

The leaders of the NAACP continued to attack Washington. Villard wrote to a cabinet minister in the Taft administration—whose policies he scorned—that the great majority of prominent black men considered Washington "a traitor to the race" because he attempted to be the office broker for blacks. The NAACP's hostility to Washington made international news in the fall of 1910, when Washington spoke in London to the Anti-Slavery and Aborigines Protection Society. Booker gave his standard speech emphasizing the progress of blacks and the importance of industrial training, but there was no verbatim account of it. John Milholland, who was in London but did not hear the speech, distributed a letter castigating the speech before its delivery. Milholland repeated the old misrepresentations of Washington's policies: he was responsible for the inadequate education of his race, accepted the violation of blacks' constitutional rights, and believed that it would take 100 years to qualify blacks for citizenship. "Dr. Washington stands for private, spasmodic schemes of education based upon private charity; condones the disfranchisement of the Negro, in fact if not in form, negatively if not positively; deems it unwise to denounce lynching or peonage, or protest against the numberless shameless outrages perpetrated upon his Race throughout the country."[16]

Booker was still steaming when Du Bois wrote his own open letter to the "People of Great Britain and Europe." Washington's financial responsibilities had made him dependent upon the wealthy, who compelled him "to tell, not the whole truth, but that part of it which certain powerful interests in America wish to appear as the whole truth." This letter appeared beneath the letterhead of the National Negro Committee, the original name for the NAACP. Booker pointed out to Villard that the use of the organization's stationery made it look like official policy. Villard dismissed it as merely a clerical error and then delivered Booker a history lecture: "If my grandfather had gone to Europe say in 1850 and dwelt in his speeches on slavery upon certain encouraging features of it . . . as evidences that the institution was improving, he never would have accomplished what he did, and he would have hurt, not helped, the cause of freedom. It seems to me that the parallel precisely affects your case." Booker denied the validity of the parallel. "Your grandfather faced a great evil which was to be destroyed. Ours is a work of construction rather than a work of destruction. My effort in Europe was to show to the people that the work of your grandfather was not wasted and the progress the Negro has made in America justified the word and work of your grandfather." As for Villard's contention that there was growing black opposition to him, Washington answered that most of the people opposing him now had been against him since the Atlanta speech in 1895. Reports of black discouragement were misinformed: in the North, he heard only discouraging things about the South, but when he went home, he saw "what is being done and how it is being done, and what the actual daily connection between the white man and the black man is," and he became encouraged again.[17]

In early 1911 Booker wrote to Tim Fortune, with whom he was temporarily reconciled, that Villard and Milholland were "attempting to run and control the destinies of the Negro race through Du Bois." He thought that the two white men would have a tough time doing it, however, because the Negro was "going to do his own thinking and own acting and not be second fiddle to a few white men, who feel that the Negro race belongs to them." Booker was clearly pointing Fortune, now writing for the New York *Amsterdam News,* in a direction to challenge the NAACP and Du Bois in particular. "When we get done with Dr. Du Bois," Fortune answered, "I am sure that he will have some trouble in handing over the leadership of the race to white men." It remained largely true, however, that the creation of the NAACP marked the advent of white leadership of blacks, whether or not Washington could yet admit it.[18]

The irony of Washington's displacement by the NAACP was that he had anticipated almost all of the NAACP's civil-rights agenda. Over the previous two decades he had protested discrimination on railroads, lynching, unfair voting qualifications, and discriminatory funding in education. He had organized and financed court challenges to disfranchisement, jury discrimination, and peonage. The NAACP likewise focused on segregated public accommodations, lynching and the criminal justice system, and disfranchisement. It would eventually echo Washington's concerns about economic discrimination and equal educational rights. Its efforts to lobby Congress for legislation against lynching and for civil-rights protections closely resembled Washington's pressure at the Capitol to confirm William Crum. The NAACP would also regularly condemn the ugly stereotypes prevalent in American life. Indeed, a consensus on the measures needed to protect black rights had emerged as early as 1900. By 1910 there was little debate among African Americans about the necessity for direct challenges to discrimination. The argument was whether they should be mounted aggressively and defiantly, or carefully and indirectly. There was a case for each method, but any rational discussion of strategy and tactics was made subordinate to the personal acrimony that had emerged between Washington and anti-Booker groups. The personal hostility to Washington—more potent from powerful whites than from blacks in 1909 and 1910—made the method of racial uplift the overriding issue.

There was further irony for Washington: coincidental with his loss of influence in national politics and the usurpation of his racial leadership was a waning of the white-nationalist domination of thinking. Part of this change reflected the natural ebb and flow of events and people: Vardaman was no longer in office; Tillman was suffering a long illness; Heflin had become the object of some opprobrium after the shooting, apparently with questionable provocation, of a black man on a Washington, D.C., streetcar in 1908; Dixon no longer occupied a spot in the national celebrity spotlight. White racial hysteria dissipated somewhat with the formalization of the Jim Crow system: disfranchisement had been accomplished in every southern state, and segregation had been imposed on virtually all places of public accommodation. The streetcar boycotts had ended after 1905, and with them expired the heightened tensions that naturally came with protest efforts. Lynchings, which put communities and entire regions on edge, by 1909 and 1910 had shrunk to half their number in the early 1890s. Economic competition between blacks and whites continued, but rising prices for cotton in 1909 and 1910 brought an agricultural prosperity not seen in the South in a generation. Better economic times made human relations easier.

Washington attributed the easing of racial tension to a change in the tone of public information. "A large part of our race troubles in the South," he said, "are in the newspapers," because "when a man is running for office he will say most anything" to get his name mentioned. Drawing a lesson from the Atlanta riot, southern newspapers were paying less attention to black crime and noting the educational and commercial successes among blacks. The Memphis *Commercial Appeal* instructed its reporters to "bear down as lightly as possible on Negro crime and to say as much as possible about Negro strivings for betterment." The Nashville *Banner* and the Columbia *State* had joined the ranks of newspapers trying to be fair to blacks. Things were getting better, but Booker Washington would not get to enjoy much of the improvement.[19]

He lost much of his chance to benefit from the easing racial mood on the night of March 19, 1911. Washington was in New York at the Manhattan Hotel in midtown, his long-standing residence when in the city. He had arrived there the night before from speaking engagements in Chicago and Detroit. The main reason for going to Michigan had been to get a health evaluation at the Battle Creek sanatorium of the physician and health reformer John Harvey Kellogg. Margaret Washington had asked Kellogg for his help in addressing her husband's declining health. Booker knew that he could also use his visit for fundraising, because Kellogg's hospital was well known for ministering to the wealthy with its long-term regimens of diet reform, baths, and exercise. Like many of those near him, Margaret had become alarmed at Booker's physical condition. He had suffered with severe headaches at least since the 1890s, and indigestion had become a chronic problem. He seemed exhausted much of the time. Much of the decline was a result of stress and overwork, but Washington was also ill with heart and kidney disease. Arteriosclerosis was probably well advanced in the fifty-five-year-old, and his blood pressure had in all likelihood been very high for some time. Diabetes had probably already set in. Throughout his life Washington had enjoyed the high-fat, low-fiber diet typical of southerners black and white; he loved pork and 'possum. Kellogg, however, clearly made an impression: a nurse was soon dispatched from Battle Creek to Tuskegee to reform his diet, and Washington was directed away from meat and toward vegetables and Graham flour. But before those changes were put in place, Booker suffered another serious setback.

March 19 was a Sunday, and in the afternoon Booker Washington spoke at two churches, one black and one white. In the early evening he left his room at the Manhattan Hotel and took the subway to an address on West 63rd Street, not far from the southern end of Central Park. At an apartment house across from a theater, he rang a doorbell marked "Cleary." While he was waiting for an answer, a white woman left a nearby apartment building with her dog. No one answered Booker's ring, and he left and walked up and down the street, where he passed the woman and the dog. He then reentered the building. While he was studying the names on the register of residents in the entranceway, two young women walked out of the building. Washington again rang the bell marked "Cleary" but still received no answer, and he stepped outside again and paced the block. Across the street, in the darkened entrance to the theater, a heavy-set, forty-year-old white man named Henry Ulrich, the live-in companion of the woman with the dog, now watched Booker. Ulrich was alarmed, probably because his girlfriend, Laura Alverez, was involved in a custody battle in which her estranged husband had recently tried to snatch their ten-year-old daughter, with the aid of a black accomplice.[20]

When Booker entered the building a third time, Ulrich followed him in and asked: "What are you doing here? Are you breaking into my house? You have been hanging around here for four or five weeks." When Washington tried to reply, Ulrich slugged him on the side of his head. Again Booker tried to explain, but Ulrich hit him several more times. After attempting unsuccessfully to defend himself from the younger, stronger man, Booker fled the building. Ulrich followed him into the street and was handed a heavy walking stick by a bystander. He beat Washington over the head with the stick, hitting him twelve times and causing severe cuts. "Don't beat me this way," Booker pleaded, and begged Ulrich to call the police. Booker ran down 63rd Street toward Central Park with Ulrich and the owner of the walking stick in pursuit. He tripped on a trolley track, fell sprawling, then picked himself up and continued running until, at Central Park West, he fell into the arms of a policeman, Chester Hagan. Ulrich ran up to Hagan and shouted that Booker was a thief and a peeping Tom. Another policeman arrived and asked Ulrich whether a thief would have entered the building through the front door. Someone in the gathering crowd shouted that maybe Booker was after the two young white women who had earlier left the building. Ulrich insisted that the police charge Booker with attempted sexual assault. The policemen took him to a nearby station, not to a hospital, although he was bleeding profusely.

Booker presented documents to persuade the police of his identity. They then dismissed their charges and allowed Washington to press an assault claim against Ulrich. Only then was Booker taken to a nearby hospital, where his cuts required sixteen stitches and his head was wrapped in gauze. With Ulrich now in the lockup, Laura Alverez, claiming to be Mrs. Ulrich, told the police that Booker had said to her, "Hello, Sweetheart." Washington vehemently denied this allegation. "It is strange that a man cannot protect his wife and daughter from insult and keep out of jail," Alverez pronounced indignantly.

The next morning's New York newspapers carried sensational stories of the beating. They reported the "Hello, Sweetheart" allegation, and some suggested that Washington had been drunk. At the hospital Booker had told newspapers that he had gone to the apartment building to meet Daniel Smith, a white accountant who audited Tuskegee's finances, as directed by a telegram from Emmett Scott. Reporters telephoned Smith's residence only to be told that the accountant was in Tuskegee. When they asked Booker about the discrepancy, he said that it had been not a telegram but a letter from Scott that had informed him that Smith was visiting relatives at the address of the attack. He had thought that the name of these relatives was McCreary but had not been certain because he had destroyed the letter providing the information. Speculation then began to fly in the New York press: the 63rd Street address was not far from the Tenderloin District, a notorious center of vice in Manhattan, and Washington had gone there for an assignation with a white prostitute.

During the next day Charles Anderson, Wilford Smith, and Seth Low attempted damage control as the questions mounted about why Washington had gone to meet someone who was not in the city—and whom he had not attempted to call, although Daniel Smith's home and office had telephones. The letter that Washington claimed to have received from Scott might have quashed the ugly rumors, but it did not materialize. At Ulrich's arraignment on Tuesday, the white man insisted that Booker was drunk and was peeping through keyholes. Ulrich claimed that Booker had hit him first, saying that it was "None of your damn business" when the white man had asked what he was doing in the building. Booker told the judge that Ulrich "made the mistake of thinking that perhaps I was a burglar." Ulrich was ordered to stand trial on the assault charge.

Letters of support for Washington poured in, including statements of continuing confidence from President Taft and Andrew Carnegie. Many magazines and newspapers declared the beating a case of mistaken identity, an unfortunate but ultimately insignificant event in Washington's virtuous life. Charles Anderson organized a rally of support at a black church in the New York. And the immensely resourceful Anderson did much more: he discovered that the alleged Mrs. Ulrich was in fact only a live-in Manhattan companion, that Henry Ulrich had a legal wife and children in New Jersey, and that he had recently been convicted of felony dog theft. New Jersey authorities soon took him off to jail for desertion and nonsupport of his family.

Legitimate questions about why Washington was on 63rd Street on a Sunday night did not go away. Emmett Scott arrived in New York and corroborated Booker's explanation about the letter directing him where to find Daniel Smith. The accountant then appeared and told reporters that he had made no arrangements to meet Washington, and that if Scott had sent Booker to 63rd Street, it was the secretary's mistake. Francis Garrison and Oswald Villard discussed the holes in Booker's story. To remove suspicion, Garrison believed, Washington needed to remember the name of Daniel Smith's alleged family connection in the building and to present the letter from Scott that had prompted him to go that address. One Tuskegee trustee demanded from Seth Low answers to the same questions. But the facts were that Booker did not know the name for a certainty and did not have the letter—if it ever existed. To many people, his story seemed concocted. Not all the doubters were white. Gilchrist Stewart, a Tuskegee graduate who had become a successful New York lawyer, explained frankly to Booker that the average black New Yorker did not "exactly understand your reasons for being in that locality" but believed that "there was some particular and special motive of a character not explained to the public, i.e. there is an indefinite assumption that a laxity of morals was involved in looking for something or somebody." The evolving story about the telegram or lost letter had, Stewart intimated, "given rise to some doubt upon which a thousand interpretations have been stretched."[21]

Booker Washington could not clear his name to the satisfaction of even some natural allies, and he would never do so. If his purpose on 63rd Street had been something other than what he said, it was never revealed. Laura Alverez's accusations of his forward remarks to her were in all likelihood a lie, but the speculation that Booker had gone to 63rd Street to rendezvous with a woman was plausible. The address was not known as a haunt for prostitutes—as it would often be misrepresented—but it could have been the home of an entirely respectable woman whom he was seeking to visit. Washington had never before been tainted with sexual impropriety, as Fortune was regularly, but living as he did so much of the time in hotels far from home, he had ample opportunities for extramarital affairs. Plenty of prominent men of the day, including Du Bois, Milholland, and J. P. Morgan, had mistresses that they kept with varying degrees of discretion. Booker was practiced about secrecy and had loyal male friends, especially in New York, where he stayed for extended periods, who would have guarded his reputation. But never before the Ulrich affair had there been a whiff of scandal involving a woman, notwithstanding the intense hatred for Washington among his northern black and southern white-nationalist enemies. They would certainly have exposed any peccadillo. Booker's marriage to Margaret is largely walled off from the historical record, and the circumstantial evidence is conflicting: there were no children from their union and little evidence of continuing romantic attachment, but she originally was deeply attached to him and always very concerned about his physical well-being. If what he was up to that Sunday night on 63rd Street was different from what he said it was, it has stayed hidden.

Booker and his advisers worked to salvage his reputation. The two doctors who had seen Booker that night swore that he had been sober and perfectly courteous. Booker and his men eventually began to discuss ways to get Laura Alverez to retract her story about his making sexual advances, which was the rumor that most bothered Washington. He was willing in return to drop the assault charge against Ulrich, but the Washington camp feared that Ulrich would publicize the offer, and it was never made. A New York lawyer discussed terms with Ulrich for dropping the charges in exchange for a public statement avowing that the beating resulted from his mistake about Washington's purpose. But no agreement was reached, and Booker had no choice, he felt, but to go through with the prosecution.

During the wait for the trial, Booker's black enemies further besieged his injured reputation. Harry C. Smith, the editor of the Cleveland *Gazette* and a persistent if minor anti-Booker voice, asserted that the demise of Washington's national reputation had brought down the whole race. He needed to explain what he was doing in that "free and easy" neighborhood in the late evening, "and on a Sunday, too." Trotter published an open letter to Booker—without in fact sending it to him—proclaiming that "this condition of affairs, by which you are actually suspected and accused by many white persons at least, of having been in the 'tenderloin' of New York City for improper reasons, with the charges of drunkenness and seeking after white women now followed up by the prosecution of the accuser, does great injury to the entire colored race."[22]

Ulrich was tried before three judges who heard testimony that had long since been aired in the press. Laura Alverez repeated her claim that Booker had greeted her with "Hello, Sweetheart!" and that she had seen him peeping through a keyhole. A policeman quoted Ulrich as having said that Washington was "after two young girls who live in the house, and officer, if you hadn't come along I would have knocked his black head off." In the dock, Booker, wearing his usual blue sack suit and black bow tie, told how Ulrich had surprised him in the vestibule of the building and started beating him. "What were you doing in that hallway?" Judge Lorenz Zeller demanded; "Whom were you looking for?" another judge asked. A friend, Washington replied, to which Ulrich's lawyer responded, "Colored or white?" Washington then explained about the auditor Smith and the confusion about the name of his supposed friends in the building. The prosecutor asked Booker if had said "Hello, Sweetheart!" to Alverez. "I never opened my mouth to a man, woman or child," Booker answered. "I have never spoken to a strange woman in all my life." Zeller and another judge voted to acquit Ulrich on the grounds that his vicious motive was not proved beyond a doubt. The yellow press reported that the judges had decided that the attack was "provoked and justifiable." Charles Anderson later discovered that Zeller had a long record of ruling against black rights, a fact that Anderson used in the judge's next—and unsuccessful—campaign.[23]

The trial's outcome left Booker deeply injured, emotionally if not physically, because his reputation was severely sullied. Booker admitted that he was most bothered by the suggestion that he had acted immorally toward a white woman: "The hardest part of the whole outrage was the conspiracy to make it appear that I addressed indecent words to a woman, something I never did in my life." Two years later, well after it would have done any good, a friend of Alverez in a fit of conscience wrote to Washington. She had been visiting Alverez that night and verified Booker's account of the events, including the fact that the "Hello, Sweetheart!" accusation was a fabrication to justify Ulrich's violence. Friends believed that the humiliation aggravated Booker's already failing health. "I think he has grown older since the assault," an old friend wrote to Scott in April 1911. "I know that he is as sensitive as a woman about his moral status." If Booker had doubts about the extent of the damage done to him, the proprietors of the Manhattan Hotel made it clear: they informed him that he was no longer welcome to stay there.[24]

Villard did not believe Booker's story about what he was doing that night, and he saw the Ulrich affair as an opening to get Washington to relinquish leadership once and for all. Since the appearance of Milholland's and Du Bois's letters denouncing Washington's London speech, the Tuskegee forces had returned the NAACP's nastiness in kind. Booker promoted exposure of interracial dinners given by Ovington's Cosmopolitan Society, although it had not taken much to get New York's yellow press to write salacious stories about white women's rubbing shoulders with black men. At Booker's instigation, the New York Age had condemned the NAACP founder William English Walling for a breach-of-promise suit brought against him. Still, soon after the assault, Villard engineered an NAACP resolution expressing the organization's "profound regret at the recent assault on Dr. Booker T. Washington in New York City in which the Association finds renewed evidence of race discrimination and increased necessity for the awakening of the public conscience." The sympathy resolution had been controversial, however, and a stronger statement affirming Washington's version of the events was rejected. Villard thought that his troubles had made Washington see that divisions among blacks had to end. He sent word to Booker that the NAACP's sympathy statement showed that he should call off "his papers like the Age that have been so villainous in their attacks upon us." The present was "no time for the colored people to be divided; they should present a solid front to the enemy." While keeping up the charade that he did not own the Age, Booker promised Villard that he would encourage the Age and other black newspapers to stop their criticism of the NAACP. Washington suggested a détente between the NAACP and the National Negro Business League, to be achieved by sending delegates to each other's annual meetings. "It will be a happy day for my race," Booker wrote to Villard, "when all of the forces and organizations while still remaining individually separate can sympathetically and heartily cooperate and work together for its larger good."[25]

With his personal reputation damaged and his health failing, Booker was ready to cease hostilities. Coming on top of Roosevelt's and Taft's withdrawal of political influence and Villard's aggressive action to supplant Washington's racial leadership, the Ulrich matter moved him further toward acceptance of the reality that his leadership had been undermined. The humiliation had given him more firsthand experience of the insecurity of being black in the United States than he had known in a long time. All the white woman had had to do was allege that Washington had spoken to her in a suggestive way, and public opinion had convicted him of being the typical black sexual predator of white women. The ease with which immoral, felonious whites had brought him down to their level and got away with unprovoked violence and character assassination undercut his lifelong determination to see the best in his circumstances. As an old Alabama black friend put it, the Ulrich incident "illuminates the actual conditions existing in this country so far as . . . relates to Colored People regardless of their standing as to wealth, education and morality and puts to flight the opinion entertained in some quarters that the Negro who 'behaves himself' is never lynched, assaulted or unmercifully treated in and out of the Courts of the land."[26] Booker had wanted to believe that the "behaving" Negro was safe, but he could no longer do so. The Ulrich matter left him a shaken and, at some level, defeated man, even if pride kept him from acknowledging openly how diminished he was.

Du Bois smelled blood in the Ulrich scandal. He told people that Washington had gone to 63rd Street to get a white prostitute and had done so before. In defiance of Villard's offer of the olive branch, Du Bois reopened fire in *Crisis* over the misrepresentations he perceived in *The Man Farthest Down,* which provided the pretext for an overall indictment of Booker's leadership, delivered with typically artful elegance. "Awful as race prejudice, lawlessness and ignorance are, we can fight them if we frankly face them and dare name them and tell the truth," he wrote. "But if we continually dodge and cloud the issue, and say the half truth because the whole stings and shames; if we do this, we invite catastrophe. Let us then in all charity but unflinching firmness set our faces against all statesmanship that looks in such directions."[27]

17

The Morning Cometh

Washington's response to personal scandal was to return to his work in the South. He conducted statewide speaking tours through Texas in 1911, Florida in 1912, and Louisiana in 1915. His purpose remained to influence white thinking about blacks, but in these years he was not provoked in the intense way he had been in Mississippi in 1908 by Vardaman's ugly white nationalism. During the Florida tour, however, he made a point of stopping at the courthouse in the town of Lake City in the immediate aftermath of the lynching of six black men—just as he had gone to Wilmington in 1910 because it had been the scene of the terrible riot. But it was only his presence, not his words, that was defiant. From the podium in Lake City, Booker looked down to see a white man sitting with a pistol in his lap. It was perhaps the most flagrant threat made to him in more than thirty years of living on the color line in the South. "I am glad to see many of our white friends here," he declared warmly. "In these trying circumstances, it is gratifying to know that some of them are here to see that my friends and I are well protected."[1]

To blacks across the South, it was the presence of the great race man in their midst that mattered. A stooped, white-haired former slave pushed her way to the front of the crowd in New Orleans, peering up into one face after another, speaking in a voice no stronger than a whisper: "Whar Booker? Whar Booker? I want to see Booker."[2]

Perhaps the least rewarding part of Booker's work now was politics. As the 1912 election approached, he faced the unhappy prospect of choosing between the Republican incumbent William Howard Taft and the third-party challenge of Theodore Roosevelt. "The Colonel" had become so disaffected with the leadership of his handpicked successor that he gave in to the powerful sense that only he knew what was best for the United States. To Booker, Taft had been polite but inattentive. His minions now listened only to the Lily White Republicans in the South. "Our big friend," as Booker referred to the 320-pound president privately, did put Washington's closest black allies in the North into good federal jobs, including William H. Lewis as assistant attorney general, the highest office to which a black had ever been appointed. Booker was disappointed in Taft overall, but he would have had a hard time supporting any other party, even when Teddy Roosevelt created his Bull Moose Party in 1912. The Tuskegee board of trustees, which now included Roosevelt, gave him the way out: he should take no part in the election, it concluded. He followed this dictate, and it is not clear how he voted. Roosevelt got the support of some Booker allies, but when he ejected all southern black delegations from the Bull Moose convention, the former president demonstrated again that he did not deserve their loyalty.[3]

At the same time, Du Bois, Trotter, and their friends condemned both Taft—"utterly lacking in initiative and ideal"—and Roosevelt. "How many black men, with the memory of Brownsville, could support such a man passes our comprehension," Du Bois wrote. Wilson, on the other hand, "will treat black men and their interests with farsighted fairness," Du Bois promised. He might not be blacks' friend, but he would not be a captive of the Tillmans and Vardamans. "He will not seek further means of 'Jim Crow' insult, he will not dismiss black men wholesale from office, and he will remember that the Negro in the United States has a right to be heard and considered." Within weeks of his taking the White House, it was clear that Tillman and Vardaman could hardly have improved on Wilson's advancement of Jim Crow. His mostly southern cabinet secretaries ordered segregated toilets, lunchrooms, and work areas in the Treasury and Post Office Departments. To facilitate discrimination, photographs were now required on applications for federal civil-service jobs. Whites replaced blacks in the attorney general's office and the Navy Department. Du Bois, Trotter, and Villard—another Wilson admirer—were outraged. Washington had little contact with the president or his men. Trotter, on the other hand, went to the White House and vented his outrage at Wilson, who then ordered him from the Oval Office.[4]

Booker's one foray to the capital during the Wilson years was undertaken to fight a measure proposed in early 1915 to exclude all immigrants of African descent, including people from the Caribbean and South America. It had the strong support of the southern Democrats, who now controlled the Congress. Booker pulled together a broad lobbying campaign, commanding that all members of the Negro Business League and all black newspaper editors advance aggressively on their members of Congress. He dispatched all available allies in the District of Columbia to the Capitol to buttonhole congressmen. Washington wrote letters to major American newspapers saying that black immigrants had been especially valuable additions to the American population as laborers on the building of the Panama Canal. He objected, too, on the grounds of fairness, for the measure treated blacks the same way that the United States handled alien criminals. Black people had never been anarchists, he said, and to be treated like criminals through this legislation would be intensely discouraging. "Certainly," he wrote, "we have enough to contend with already without having this additional handicap and discouragement placed in our pathway." The campaign finally yielded a sound defeat of the bill. Booker may have been powerless at the White House in 1915, but he still had real influence in the country at large.[5]

In 1911 Washington brought to fruition an important legal challenge that he had long supported surreptitiously. In 1908 he had begun financing a court challenge to Alabama's 1903 contract-labor law, which was written, Booker explained, so that "any white man, who cares to charge that a Colored man has promised to work for him and has not done so, or who has gotten money from him and not paid it back, can have the Colored man sent to the chain gang." Judge Jones's pursuit of peonage in Alabama in 1903 had encouraged a state judge, William H. Thomas, to look for challenges to the Alabama law. One materialized when the case of Alonzo Bailey was brought to Thomas's court. Bailey had signed a contract to work on a farm, received an advance of wages, did not work the required period before leaving the farm, and was now being prosecuted under the 1903 law. At Thomas's behest, two young white lawyers in Montgomery agreed to challenge the Alabama law in federal court if Washington raised the money for the appeal. Booker supplied the money, some of it from his own pocket, and in 1911 *Bailey v. Alabama* became a landmark constitutional decision against peonage.[6]

Booker watched with concern the increasing migration of blacks to cities. Always skeptical of the big-city environment for blacks, he paid particular attention to employment conditions in cities. In 1910 he be-

52. Booker pushed the case of the Alabama farm worker Alonzo Bailey to challenge Alabama's contract-labor law, and with the help of some determined white lawyers and a judge, the law was finally overturned. Image of Alonzo Bailey, photographer unknown; from *American Magazine* 2 (1911).

gan advising William Baldwin's widow, Ruth Standish Baldwin, on an organization to improve opportunities for the black urban working class, an effort that became the National Urban League. He directed an Institute survey of the labor movement in which labor leaders were asked their attitudes about including blacks in their unions. The findings, though critical of many unions' discriminatory practices, suggested a softening of Booker's long-standing opposition to organized labor. The survey convinced him that white unionists would accept blacks not because, as Samuel Gompers had promised, it was a matter of principle, but because it was in their interest to do so. His optimism would prove to be misplaced.[7]

By 1912 a change could be detected in the way Washington talked and wrote about the wrongs done to black people. He had always spoken out against discrimination and exploitation, but he had usually done so with extreme care—the restraint he thought necessary given the complete intolerance of white southerners for criticism of their racial practices. But about 1912 his language began to show more assertiveness, more emphatic rejection of injustice, and he would maintain that new tone for the rest of his life. He admitted no change, because he said little that he had not said before, but now he placed less blame on blacks for their conditions and more on whites for their unfairness. Why Washington's attitude shifted is a matter only for speculation, because he did not acknowledge the change. The hardening reality of disfranchisement and segregated public accommodations may have overridden his earlier caution, which had been based on his assumption that race relations were in flux and that protest against discrimination only fueled whites' determination to oppress blacks further. Booker's increased assertiveness perhaps also resulted from some small improvement in conditions; his greater willingness to condemn unequal educational opportunities may have reflected his sense that the move to abolish black education had been defeated. His loss of national political influence may have liberated him from concern about white southern opinion. The humiliations of the Ulrich affair may have so personalized the injustices of being black that he shed some of his natural caution. The beating and his declining overall health may have led him to see the need for a legacy of more resistance to the ugly realities of his world. Conjecture could so proceed endlessly.

Regardless of the causes, whatever his motives, Washington maintained a more resistant bearing from 1912 forward. It was seen in his public insistence that lynchings happened because white opinion allowed them and that blacks were usually not even guilty of the crimes that provoked the terrorism. The new attitude was apparent in his emphatic demands for better treatment of black schoolchildren and his sardonic criticism of whites for allowing the huge disparities in spending. And although he still issued specific directions on how blacks should improve themselves, he spent less time elucidating black shortcomings and more on what whites were doing wrong.

Washington's 1912 article in *Century* magazine, "Is the Negro Having a Fair Chance?," marked the clearest point of departure. From the outset, he declared that the conditions of American blacks were not satisfactory, that the Negro was not getting a fair chance in all things. Blacks in the West Indies had a better chance to get an academic education and to gain justice in the courts than did those in the United States. Jamaica had "neither mobs, race riots, lynchings, nor burnings, such as disgrace our civilization." Blacks in the islands did not face the trouble that American blacks did, with whites' confusion of civil rights with social intermingling. Booker still insisted that American blacks had a reasonably fair chance for economic opportunity in the South, but in the North and the border states, he said, labor unions ensured that the Negro, "when compared with the white man, does not have a fair chance." In the construction of a new brick building at Howard University in the nation's capital, for example, every man laying brick was white and every one carrying a hod was black. Blacks in the North had political rights and more nearly equal educational opportunities, but job discrimination left them unable to use their education, a situation that resulted in bitterness and despondency. In the criminal-justice system, blacks faced insurmountable discrimination in the South. "With few exceptions, colored lawyers feel, as they tell me, that they do not have a fair chance before a white jury when a white lawyer is on the other side of the case." When wronged, blacks in the South had no recourse. Not only were the courts unfair, but blacks also lacked representation in the legislatures, and the white press rarely listened to their complaints. Much of the unfairness about segregation in public places lay in blacks' uncertainty about where and how separation was enforced. In the South, railway travel caused more anger among blacks than did any other issue. "In the matter of education," Washington jibed, "the negro in the South has not had what Colonel Roosevelt calls a 'square deal,'" pointing to the Alabama county that spent $15 on each white schoolchild every year and thirty-three cents on each black one. Southern states placed a higher monetary value on leased convicts—$46 per month—than they did on black schoolteachers, who earned only $30. Blacks were paying their fair share of taxes and deserved a far fairer share of educational opportunities in the South.[8]

Washington's response to the question "Is the Negro Having a Fair Chance?" was so negative that it prompted positive acknowledgment from Du Bois: "We note with some complacency that Mr. Booker T. Washington has joined the ranks." Du Bois knew that the article reiterated what Washington had said many times earlier, but he correctly perceived the change in tone.[9]

To maximize the article's impact, Washington had copies mailed to railroad executives with a personal letter appealing to them to do something about the embittering black experience on common carriers. Several executives replied that the piece had raised their sensibilities about black treatment. Washington honed in on the Louisville & Nashville Railroad, a main connector between the Deep South and the Midwest. He had already been lobbying Milton H. Smith, the president of that line, about the miserable conditions in the black coaches. In 1913 he demanded that the officers of the National Baptist Convention pressure the L & N for fair treatment before its members traveled to their convention. He had Emmett Scott send out anonymous editorials to black newspapers denouncing the line. A year later Washington organized what he called "Railroad Days," a time when blacks all over the country were to go to railroad managers and air their grievances. Two or three blacks should see each railroad manager in each town, Booker commanded, and discuss accommodations in station restaurants, waiting rooms, and on the cars themselves. They were not to call it a protest, Washington instructed, but he stressed the importance of "*going to see* the R.R. officials, not merely talking *about* it among themselves." Washington wrote to Du Bois asking that he promote Railroad Days in *Crisis,* but the request was ignored. Still, thousands of blacks around the country did as Booker instructed, and many of them had fruitful conversations with officials about improving treatment. Railroad Days by no means ended the practice of Jim Crow on the railroads, but the campaign represented the kind of activism that Booker Washington had always believed in—and that he increasingly advocated.[10]

Having seen to the tabulation of facts about lynching in the annual Tuskegee report, Washington campaigned continuously against it, analyzing its causes and effects in most speeches and publicly praising southern governors who openly decried the practice. He asserted in a national magazine that most blacks lynched were innocent of any crime and consequently most blacks in the South knew that innocence offered them no security against being lynched. In 1913 he declared that lynching occurred because the community tolerated it, and therefore hostile public opinion was the prevention for lynching. In 1915 he expressed profound shock that two black men and two women had been lynched in Georgia for fighting a policeman; he was sure that a court would have punished the four blacks adequately if they had in fact been in the wrong. To integrated crowds in Louisiana, he said that both races suffered because the outside world heard of crime, mobs, and lynchings but not about interracial friendship. "The best white citizenship must take charge of the mob and not have the mob take charge of civilization."[11]

Efforts to segregate residential space summoned Washington's determined opposition. In 1913 Clarence Poe, editor of the *Progressive Farmer,* began pushing to segregate rural areas in the South when a white majority so requested. This would have amounted to a kind of legalized whitecapping—something approximating the "homelands" created under apartheid in South Africa. Poe claimed that his plan would reduce racial tension and purify rural communities. He acquired some following, but Washington knew that white planters would oppose the idea, therefore dooming it, and he refused to help draw attention to Poe by publicly denouncing the plan. But he did supply Poe's white opponents with arguments, such as his observation that the average southern white man "likes to have just as many black people in 'calling distance' as possible."[12]

A far more potent threat lay in the emerging efforts to segregate space in cities. Between 1900 and 1910 a half-million blacks and even more whites moved to southern cities. Competition for housing was especially intense in border-state cities, and violence began developing there around 1910. In Kansas City, for example, there were five separate bombings in 1910 and 1911 in a two-block area of formerly all-white housing after two black families moved there. Such violence only convinced whites that they needed residential segregation laws. Responding to blacks' purchase of homes on previously all-white streets in middle-class areas of Baltimore, that city in 1910 made it illegal for citizens to occupy a house on a street that was currently populated entirely by people of another race. Between 1911 and 1914 many southern cities passed such ordinances. By 1912 the NAACP had launched a challenge to the Baltimore law as a violation of property rights, and its challenge of a Louisville ordinance would lead to a landmark decision against such action, although that did not come until 1917. Washington was convinced from their first appearance that these laws were unconstitutional and had to be challenged. He noted that in border cities blacks voted freely, but action at the polls had not stopped the trend. Blacks would have to protest openly to city officials. When a segregation ordinance was proposed in Birmingham, Washington told the mayor that it would stir up racial strife, and that the law was unnecessary anyway because blacks did not want to live where they were not wanted—a classic example of Booker's strategy of indirection. He advised the mayor to meet with the black leaders in Birmingham and find out what they wanted. After the meeting occurred, the proposal was withdrawn; for the time being, residential segregation laws had been defeated in Birmingham. As with Railroad Days, Washington instigated protests among blacks, but he worked behind the scenes.[13]

In 1915 he prepared a strong statement against residential segregation in the *New Republic*. "My View of the Segregation Laws" was unique for Washington in its candor and disparagement of the latest efforts at racial control. The leading men in politics, including the president of the United States, had been raised in intimate circumstances with black people, but in most instances blacks and whites naturally chose to live in racially exclusive circumstances. In places where a few well-to-do blacks lived among whites, Booker observed, everyone got along just fine. Blacks strongly opposed the residential segregation laws not because they wanted to live next door to whites, but because any residential area designated black would soon suffer declining municipal services. Even without statutory segregation, black sections tended to be overwhelmed with vice. Segregation was ill advised because it was unjust, encouraged more injustice, and bred resentment among blacks. It was unnecessary and inconsistent, because whites were not prohibited from doing business in black neighborhoods. "There has been no case of segregation of negroes in the United States that has not widened the breach between the two races. Wherever a form of segregation exists, it has been administered in such a way as to embitter the Negro and harm more or less the moral fibre of the white man."[14]

Washington now exerted less energy in promoting a positive black image, but he had not given up his concern with how his people were perceived in American popular culture. He was perplexed by the controversies surrounding the boxer Jack Johnson. To restore fan excitement in 1908, Tommy Burns, the white heavyweight boxing champion, agreed to fight the powerful Johnson, a break with whites' customary refusal to join blacks in the ring. Johnson knocked out the champion and then quickly dispatched five other white opponents. His victories sparked both a movement to ban boxing and another to find a "White Hope" to beat Johnson. In 1910 a retired champion, James J. Jeffries, put his gloves back on and met Johnson in a match ballyhooed as a showdown for racial supremacy. When Johnson thrashed Jeffries, racial violence erupted in many places, North and South. If he had not already threatened white domination enough, Johnson married a white woman and then took a nineteen-year-old white girl on an interstate trip. The law against crossing a state line for immoral purposes was intended to stop prostitution, and the girl was neither a prostitute nor acting against her will, but Johnson was prosecuted and convicted in 1913. Blacks were divided over Johnson, although the vast majority delighted in his pugilistic success, filling movie theaters to watch films of his fights. The movies were quickly banned in southern theaters. To Booker Washington, Johnson was a public-relations nightmare—a black man who threatened white domination in both his physical and sexual prowess, one who flagrantly used white women. "In misrepresenting the colored people of the country, this man is harming himself the least," Booker said. "I wish to say emphatically that his actions do not meet with the approval of the colored race." Monroe Trotter quickly accused Washington of pandering to blacks' enemies with his criticisms of Johnson.[15]

There was no dissent among blacks in 1915 about David W. Griffith's *Birth of a Nation,* the celluloid version of Thomas Dixon's novels. *Birth of a Nation* took racial stereotyping in American popular culture to new extremes. The film's most provocative scenes reprised *The Clansman's* sexually charged episode in which a lustful black soldier chased a white girl until she leapt to her death. The NAACP responded quickly to its Los Angeles opening with protests and demands for censorship. Booker knew that Dixon relished the controversy; in 1906 he had hired a black man in New York City to distribute flyers protesting the play *The Clansman.* Even so, Booker decided to try to stop the film from being shown, fearing that it would stir up racial strife. He believed that southern cities would ban it for precisely that reason, perhaps thinking of the precedent of the Johnson fight films. Booker's first instinct proved correct. Dixon took the film to the White House and screened it for his graduate-school friend Woodrow Wilson. "It's like writing history with lightning," the president said. "My only regret is that it is all so terribly true." Dixon sent Wilson word that the film would "transform every man in my audience into a good Democrat" and a "Southern partisan for life"; its critics would be limited to the tiny minority from "Villards [sic] Intermarriage Society." The film opened in New York City, and despite the presence of many protestors, three million people would see it there during the next year. Booker was wrong in his prediction that southern cities would not allow the film to be screened. When *Birth of a Nation* was screened in Atlanta, the streets near the theater were filled with whites on horseback wearing full Ku Klux Klan regalia.[16]

Clearly, the chorus of protest that Washington joined accomplished little good, at least not at the time. The new medium of film made the old images more powerful than ever, and against that influence black protests seemed powerless. For Washington, the fight to eradicate the Negro-as-beast image from American popular culture was an old one. By late 1915 he must have felt that the more things changed, the more they stayed the same. The fate of Jack Johnson and the triumph of *Birth of a Nation* each revealed the unrelieved racial competition in American society—among whites insisting on enforcing supremacy in every place and among blacks struggling to achieve equality, or at least some fairness, in the areas where it was warranted. And still blacks lost.

Both the fall of Jack Johnson and the plot of *Birth of a Nation* turned on whites' hysteria about black men's sexual desire for white women. Did Booker connect these developments to the great damage to his own reputation caused by the allegation that he pursued white women? Did he draw a line back to those black newspapermen in the 1880s and 1890s who had been run out of southern towns for discussing interracial sex? Did he recognize that the terrible troubles in his own life that arose from his alleged pursuit of social equality—the White House dinner, the Wanamaker incident, and the Ulrich affair—were not that far removed from the persecution of Jack Johnson in 1913? Booker must have seen the larger truth: whites were most fundamentally committed to stopping black men from consorting with white women, because such association represented equal power to white men. But he remained too practical to acknowledge that truth openly.

Washington's more open efforts to protest wrongs earned him no credit at the NAACP. His 1912 assessment of the unfair treatment of blacks overall apparently counted for nothing with the organization. The refusal to recognize the similarity of purpose between Washington's leadership and the NAACP persisted even as the Tuskegeean's methods became more like Du Bois's and Villard's. Joel Spingarn, the white English professor who chaired the NAACP's executive committee, publicly condemned Washington as unworthy of racial leadership for his failure to attack Clarence Poe's rural segregation plan. Villard mistakenly saw Poe's movement as the greatest menace yet, one that would undoubtedly lead to legislation, "thus giving the lie to Washington's advice to his people that if they will only be good and buy land they will be let alone and will flourish." Washington was "like Nero, fiddling while Rome burns," silent while "one right after another is being taken away from the colored people, one injustice after another being perpetrated." He was becoming anathema to the educated blacks, Villard said, "and he is drifting further and further [to] the rear as a real leader."[17]

That was the real issue: Washington's standing as the leader of the race. Du Bois, Villard, Spingarn, and other insiders at the NAACP continued to view Washington as an opponent because most Americans, including most blacks, still considered him the preeminent black man among them. Any continuing influence he had for good, including his direct protests against wrongs, seemed to discomfit the NAACP leadership because it presented a challenge to their own dominance. Villard was angry when Washington declined to come to the NAACP offices in 1913 for a meeting on black industrial education, an area that Booker thought lay more in his bailiwick than in Villard's. "In giving way to prejudice as much as you do," Villard lectured Washington, "you increase prejudice and weaken yourself." Villard wanted Washington to "take to heart the lesson of my grandfather's life and know no such thing as compromise with prejudice or with evil." If Booker would only listen to him, Villard promised, "then a nation of whites and blacks would rise up and call you blessed." Villard sent a copy of this admonition to Seth Low, chairman of the Tuskegee board of trustees and nominally Booker's boss. Low answered Villard that Washington did not lack courage, but simply had his own way of addressing the problem, and in the matter of leading industrial education, "Dr. Washington's judgment is far more likely to be correct than either yours or mine."[18]

Washington thought of the NAACP as Villard's organization, and in due course so did its black members. Whites dominated the committees and let their paternalistic condescension show, something that the prickly Du Bois especially resented. The organization was held together mostly by its members' antipathy to Washington. Even anyone associated closely with Booker came in for criticism. In his obituary of

Robert Ogden, who had begun supporting black education when Du Bois was a toddler, the black sociologist wrote that "a self-helping Negro was beyond" the genial businessman's conception, because Ogden had "looked upon the Negro as an incomplete man." Still, the perceived threat of Washington could contain the NAACP's oversupply of self-righteousness only so long. Du Bois brooked no interference, or even suggestions, regarding his conduct of *Crisis*. When white members voted that the magazine should acknowledge and condemn black criminality, Du Bois flatly refused to do it—though he had made such judgments in the past. Nor would he report in *Crisis* on Trotter's bad behavior in Woodrow Wilson's office. But Villard was a full sponsor of the organization's racial dysfunction. Eventually black members began to quit the organization over his high-handedness. Not even in the NAACP were blacks ready, as Washington put it, "to be taken charge of bag and baggage by any white man." Other whites recognized that Villard had to be replaced, and the equally arrogant but less strong-willed Spingarn finally assumed its leadership. Villard thus lost his bid to be leader of the black race. Du Bois consolidated his autonomy over the magazine and used *Crisis* to advance his own agenda and indulge his personal prejudices, but it cannot be said that he assumed the leadership of the race. Washington would have to leave the scene altogether for that to become a possibility.[19]

The signs of Booker's declining health persisted even after the nurse from Battle Creek reformed his diet. He still showed signs of exhaustion, suffered constantly from indigestion, and worried all those close to him. He needed, more than anything else, rest and relaxation. In 1913 Emmett Scott arranged a fall fishing trip in the Gulf of Mexico, hosted by a Mobile undertaker. The fishing was so good and the atmosphere so relaxing that they repeated the excursion in the two years following. Booker bought a summer house on Long Island where the family spent summers, although he traveled and spoke much of the time the family was relaxing on the beach. In 1914 Booker was planning another trip to Europe, in large part because he had learned that to relax entirely he had to leave the country—out of the reach of newspapers, stenographers, and train rides to speaking engagements. But when war broke out in Europe in August, the opportunity was lost.

In late 1914 Washington's health began to deteriorate further. In addition to the frequent headaches and near-constant indigestion, he was now showing symptoms of diabetes: inordinate thirst, constant urination, failing vision, fatigue, and weight loss. He experienced coldness in his feet. In February 1915 he became acutely ill with gastrointestinal distress. In response to the various ailments, he quit drinking coffee and tea and gave up the cigar or two he had been smoking daily. In September he obtained his first pair of eyeglasses. His personal physician, George Cleveland Hall of Chicago, was alarmed at Booker's blood pressure, and he and Booker made plans to go to the Mayo brothers' clinic in Minnesota. In the meantime Scott, Hall, and others implored Washington to stop and rest.[20]

There was something compulsive about Booker Washington's lifestyle, especially his need to travel across the United States to preach his gospel of racial progress and to raise money for Tuskegee Institute. Beginning in about 1910 he made several long trips to the West, but instead of resting at home afterward, he immediately boarded a train to the East. In 1913 he spoke at college convocations, prep schools, church meetings, Chautauquas, and academic congresses. He could not resist appearing at events to mark a positive black achievement. He spoke to a throng of 15,000 at the 1912 opening of a cottonseed-oil mill in his favorite Mississippi place, the all-black town of Mound Bayou. The black-owned and black-operated mill marked a "unique and distinct step in the progress of the negroes of America . . . the largest and most serious undertaking in a purely commercial and manufacturing enterprise in the history of our race." He could not resist saying again in Mound Bayou what he had said earlier in a dozen other places: there was much academic discussion about race relations in the South, "but when we get down beneath the surface of this discussion and get into the individual communities it is found that every Negro has a white friend and every white man has his Negro friend, and that in nine cases out of ten in our Southern communities, as is proven here, that the relations between white people and black people are peaceful and happy."

He kept his deep faith in object lessons: "As we go on year by year demonstrating our ability to make good and law abiding citizens and our ability to create something that the white man wants and respects, in the same degree will our relations be further cemented in the direction of peace and prosperity."[21]

Booker's faith was justified nowhere more solidly than among the members of the Negro Business League. In his presidential address at the 1913 convention, which celebrated the fiftieth anniversary of the Emancipation Proclamation, Booker exhorted members to stay hopeful, notwithstanding the resentments felt at the moment about Woodrow Wilson's segregation orders. "Once in a while even those in high places may seem to seek to insult and humiliate and harass us." But Booker the prophet promised that this situation would not last. "'The morning cometh,'" he said, just as the watchman had promised the Israelites. "Those who treat us unjustly are losing more than we are. So often the keeper of the prison is on the outside but the free man is on the inside . . . Let us go from this great meeting filled with a spirit of race pride, rejoicing in the fact that we belong to a race that has made greater progress within fifty years than any race in history, and let each dedicate himself to the task of doing his part in making the ten millions of black citizens in America an example for all the world in usefulness, law abiding habits and high character."[22]

Prophets expire before their promises are fulfilled, and so it was with Booker Washington in the fall of 1915. In late October his tired body rapidly shut down. His kidneys ceased to function, probably as a result of chronically soaring high blood pressure, and he endured attacks of intense pain. He suffered almost continuously with a headache. He knew that he was seriously ill, and he still planned to go to the Mayo clinic. But he kept delaying to fulfill one more speaking engagement. In late October he spoke at Yale and at a black church in New Haven on the same day. Back in New York, he reluctantly canceled a series of appearances and entered a hospital. Various New York physicians were brought in to consult on his condition, including one who announced to the press that Washington was exhausted, extremely nervous, and showing signs of hardening of the arteries. "Racial characteristics are, I think, in part responsible for Dr. Washington's break-

53. Booker Washington lying in state at the Tuskegee Institute chapel. Photographer unknown, 1915; courtesy of the Library of Congress.

down." Such a statement in the vernacular speech of 1915 amounted to a signal that he had syphilis. The doctor may have been referring to the greater propensity of people of African descent to suffer from hypertension and other circulatory problems, but he did not clarify his remark. George Hall was infuriated by the implication and privately railed against both the wrong diagnosis and the breach of patient confidentiality.[23]

Booker realized the seriousness of his situation and sent for Margaret. By the time she arrived, the New York doctors had given up, and Washington declared that he wanted to go home. Margaret got him on a train on November 12, and they arrived in Tuskegee late the next evening. Just before dawn on November 14, lying in his bed at his home, the fifty-nine-year-old Booker T. Washington died.

Three days later, thousands gathered at the Institute chapel for a funeral, where Booker's body lay in state. Isaac Fisher, the editor of the *Negro Farmer,* described the funeral for the Montgomery *Advertiser:*

"No labored eulogies; no bastings of his great work; no gorgeous trappings of horses; no streaming banners; no mysterious ceremonies of lodges—just the usual line of teachers, trustees, graduates, students and visitors which so often marched to the chapel just as it did Wednesday, and the simple and impressive—impressive because simple—service for the dead, said for the humblest, said so often for those who die, in all walks of life."

An elderly black couple had entered the chapel, and the man, his eyes moist and his voice trembling, approached a professor.

"Do you reckon they will let us see Booker?" He and his wife had walked a long way, the man haltingly explained, "to see him de las' time." He waited a moment.

"Do you reckon they will mind us looking at him?"

The two pilgrims were escorted forward to cast a last gaze on their leader and their inspiration.[24]

18

———

The Veil of History

Tributes to his life and career flooded Tuskegee and the public media in the days after Booker's death. Some were merely extravagant declarations of his standing in the world: "The greatest man America ever knew," declared Madame C. J. Walker, the black businesswoman. Others provided more acute assessments. An emotional Charles Anderson wrote to Emmett Scott that he felt like demagnetized steel, but he managed to observe that Washington had "the rare gift of keeping his eyes fixed on the goal and not the prize, and of steadily urging his way onward, while the hounds of Acteon were in full cry and baying at his heels." The editor of the *New Republic* wrote that Washington had a unique capacity for "exciting in his people a healthy pride of race without employing the means of invidious disparagement of other races," for elevating blacks "in their own eyes and in the eyes of the whites." The lone dissenting view came in Du Bois's eulogy in *Crisis:* Washington "never adequately grasped the growing bond of politics and industry; he did not understand the deeper foundation of human training and his basis of better understanding between white and black was founded on caste." Booker's failings, he continued, went beyond ignorance: "In stern justice, we must lay on the soul of this man, a heavy responsibility for the consummation of Negro disfranchisement, the decline of the Negro college and public school and the firmer establishment of color caste in this land." Du Bois understood as well as anyone the true context of Booker's life, and there was no justice in placing so much responsibility for so many bad things upon him. Even with Booker dead, Du Bois's personal antipathy overrode his capacity for objective judgment.[1]

Who would replace Washington as head of Tuskegee—and leader of the race—became a preeminent question within days of his death. Most of Booker's close black allies outside of Tuskegee wanted Emmett Scott to succeed him. Margaret Washington thought that neither Scott nor Warren Logan, the longtime financial manager, would be an appropriate choice, apparently because the appointment of either would divide the Tuskegee Institute community. An outsider would be best, she advised, and it turned out that most of the trustees agreed. They favored Robert Russa Moton, the commandant of cadets at Hampton, as the new principal of Tuskegee. Major Moton soon took the reins at Tuskegee, but he did not attempt to be the leader of the race. Though a staunch supporter of Washington, Moton had little taste for the extensive political engagement and constant speaking that leadership of the race required. His lack of desire to exercise racial leadership and his noncombative personality made him more acceptable to the anti-Washington group.[2]

Washington's departure from the scene allowed the already-existing consensus on a protest agenda to emerge fully. Having lost its original *raison d'être,* opposition to Washington, the NAACP found constructive purpose in a comprehensive pursuit of black civil rights. It pushed an assimilationist agenda similar to what Washington had pursued, and it did so openly, whereas Booker had been forced to act indirectly much of the time. Over the next decades the NAACP became the main advocate for black interests as it challenged many aspects of segregation. In 1916 the NAACP appointed James Weldon Johnson, the noted lyricist, novelist, and diplomat, to be its field secretary and then executive director. Washington had arranged a series of diplomatic appointments for Johnson, and the appointment of a Bookerite signaled an easing of the long-standing tension between the Tuskegee forces and the NAACP. Johnson expanded the NAACP's membership and gently made the organization a mostly black-led operation. A man of great personal charm and commanding presence, Johnson was like Washington in his ability to inspire the masses and treat with the powerful with equal skill, but somehow he never captured a huge public following. Through *Crisis,* Du Bois became influential with the wider black public in shaping opinion toward protest, but in 1934 he rejected the integrationist goals of the NAACP in favor of a racial nationalism infused with Marxist ideology and left the organization.[3]

The nearest thing to a mass leader came in the early 1920s in the person of Marcus Garvey, the Jamaican-born founder of the Universal Negro Improvement Association. Washington's emphasis on self-help had inspired Garvey, and they had occasionally corresponded, but Garvey based his organization on a racial nationalism, including a back-to-Africa movement, that Booker had always rejected. Still, Garvey's movement had a strong appeal among the black working class, including rural southerners. The NAACP leadership, led by Du Bois, fought bitterly against Garvey, who disparaged the light-skinned elitism of the NAACP by calling it the National Association for the Advancement of Certain People. More potent opposition to him arose in the U.S. government, where officials were suspicious of his growing popularity. Convicted of mail fraud, Garvey was jailed for two years and in 1927 deported to Jamaica.[4]

In the years after Washington's death, more evidence of his appeal to ordinary African Americans emerged. Public institutions across the United States used the name extensively to memorialize black achievement. For almost two generations after his death, scores of schools, parks, community centers, libraries, and streets were named for Booker T. Washington. When the first public high schools for blacks were eventually built in many southern communities in the 1920s and 1930s, most were named for Booker T. Washington or George Washington Carver. The symbolism of this practice was perhaps elastic: the Tuskegee legacy may have been viewed as acceptable to powerful whites in the Jim Crow South when other blacks of note might not have been, but blacks independently embraced these names as symbols of their own success. Black-owned businesses often adopted Booker's name and his image to signal racial pride, and they needed no white consent to do so.[5]

The first assessments of his life by black scholars in the 1920s affirmed that popularity. Horace Mann Bond noted that no other African American had commanded the personal following among the masses of southern blacks that Washington had gained through direct contact with them. Washington "alone represented a well defined school of opinion which was supported by the rank and file of the race." Kelly Miller, the Howard University professor, in 1903 had criticized Washington as "lamblike, meek and submissive," a man who moved "not along the line of least resistance, but of no resistance at all"; but five years after Washington's death, he understood the basis of Washington's popularity among blacks. His critics denounced Booker for not having demanded everything to which blacks were entitled, Miller wrote, "but no one has ever demonstrated that he ever asked for less than it was probable, or even possible, to secure." Washington was "the philosopher of the possible" who believed in "reaching the ideal by gradual approximation." In his effort to document a constructive history of black progress, Carter G. Woodson wrote that "no president of a republic, no king of a country, no emperor of a universal domain of that day approached anywhere near doing as much for the uplift of humanity as did Booker T. Washington."[6]

The most sophisticated defense of Washington's career came in 1928 from the black sociologist Charles S. Johnson, a Virginian who had studied American race relations under Robert Ezra Park, Booker's ghostwriter, at the University of Chicago. White fears of blacks were based on assumptions of black inferiority, to which had been added, Johnson wrote, "fear of the competition of Negroes, fear of an enforced social equality, fear of political domination, and fear of losing the black labor." Washington saw that white fears were a threat constantly on the verge of explosion, and they had to be abated or at least controlled if blacks were to make progress. Believing that aggressive black action would not overcome whites' fears, in the Atlanta address he had "reversed the position of Negroes in the south from that of a menacing burden to that of a possible ally, and linked the fortunes of Negroes publicly with the fortunes of the south." Washington knew that the vicious images of blacks had to be proved false by objective demonstration, not by mere verbal assertions. Blacks needed to acquire land,

wealth, skill, health, education, and sensitivity to beauty and order—
the foundations of civilization and culture. Once blacks had demonstrated that they were civilized, their status would rise, and whites
would accept them.[7]

Johnson's assessment hardly registered, in part because the Great
Depression, signaling as it apparently did the demise of capitalism, led
scholars to question Washington's acceptance of capitalism, his emphasis on blacks in agriculture, and his skepticism about unions. In 1931
Sterling D. Spero and Abram L. Harris, social scientists studying black
workers, asserted that Washington had misled blacks in his opposition
to organized labor and that industrial education at Tuskegee had failed
to prepare students for the highly mechanized twentieth-century
American factory. They missed the real purpose of a Tuskegee education: the training of teachers and businessmen and not industrial workers. Their interpretation of Washington's goals launched a decades-
long trend to judge him by presentist concerns and to disregard the
contextual constraints of his day. He was hardly the first historical figure to be subjected to the anachronistic fallacy, but few reputations
would be so thoroughly devastated by it.[8]

The most influential critique came in Du Bois's 1940 memoir *Dusk
of Dawn*. Du Bois's memory focused selectively on the ideological differences between himself and Washington. He claimed that Booker
had prevented him from getting the school superintendency in the
District of Columbia, and he placed the dates of that episode and of the
Boston riot later than they occurred, creating the impression that he
had constantly been responding defensively to aggressive attacks by
Washington. Du Bois claimed that Washington had pandered to
northern industrialists' desire for a big supply of cheap, docile black
labor and had undermined support for Atlanta University among the
big philanthropies. "After a time almost no Negro institution could
collect funds without the recommendation or acquiescence of Mr.
Washington." The Tuskegee public-relations efforts were aimed only
at advancing Booker's power and defeating his critics. He denounced
Washington's alleged hypocrisy about political involvement: "It did
not seem fair, for instance, that on the one hand Mr. Washington
should decry political activities among Negroes, and on the other hand

dictate Negro political objectives from Tuskegee." He exaggerated Booker's political influence: "Few political appointments were made anywhere in the United States without his consent." He claimed that Washington had excused the South's discrimination and always blamed the poor black man himself for his own predicament. "Booker T. Washington was not an easy person to know," Du Bois concluded. "He never expressed himself frankly or clearly until he knew exactly to whom he was talking and just what their wishes and desires were." Twenty-five years after Booker's death, Du Bois remained angry about him.[9]

Dusk of Dawn reinforced the negative view set forth in *The Souls of Black Folk,* a critique that became much more influential several decades after Washington's death than it had been in 1903. Few men in an open society get to set the terms for the historical memory of their avowed enemy, but W. E. B. Du Bois was one who did.

Few Americans paid attention to how Booker Washington's materialist strategy worked out in its place of birth, but if they had, they would have discovered that its outcome was ambiguous and open to competing interpretations. Under Major Moton's less ambitious leadership, Tuskegee ceased to be what Du Bois resentfully called "the capital of the Negro nation." By the late 1920s the Great Migration had moved the headquarters for black imagemaking to Harlem, home of the black cultural Renaissance, the New Negro, and the NAACP. Moton did manage to maintain the Tuskegee tradition of maximizing black opportunities in the little Alabama town and making the latter a demonstration of black achievement. In 1921 the Veterans' Administration (VA) announced that it would build a hospital for black veterans of the Great War, and with the encouragement of local whites like the Varner family, who anticipated economic benefits to the town, Moton persuaded the agency to build the hospital in Tuskegee. Shortly before its opening, however, other whites objected vociferously to the hospital's being staffed by black doctors and nurses, notwithstanding that an Alabama law prohibited white nurses from tending to black men. In the finest Booker Washington tradition, Moton kept silent in response to the mounting hysteria and absented himself while it raged. The Ku

Klux Klan paraded through the Tuskegee Institute campus, and the student cadets prepared for an armed defense. But the final decision was made in Washington, D.C., and the federal bureaucrats held firm to their original plan on the staffing. The state senator from Tuskegee, a loud opponent of black doctors and nurses at the hospital, announced that the whole business demonstrated "clearly and conclusively how rapidly a Negro grows in presumption, courage and the attempted assertion of power, when he is dealt with on the basis of a white man, and treated with consideration and courtesy." The senator resented that the Negroes were "gradually taking things away from us by contesting every inch of the ground, resisting all compromise, and fighting to a finish." The remarks resonated with the old accusation that Booker Washington had constantly schemed to pull the Trojan horse of black equality inside the walls of the Jim Crow South.[10]

On the other hand, the Tuskegee approach had failed in the pursuit of agricultural prosperity. Charles S. Johnson studied 612 black farm families in Macon County in the 1930s and found little evidence of progress. More and more were becoming sharecroppers in spite of the Institute exhortations to own their farms. A large majority of black farmers were trapped in the vise of crop-lien debt and as a consequence had no real autonomy. The crop-lien system undermined blacks' faith in education, because, Johnson learned, farmers with much schooling usually quit the plow. Tuskegee Institute, of course, bore no responsibility for the structural problems of southern agriculture—including a worldwide depression in prices, a vast overproduction of cotton, a scarcity of credit, and a large overpopulation on southern farms.[11]

World War II brought the first significant reshaping of whites' perceptions of blacks, something that Washington had tried to hard to achieve. The war forced Americans to be more sensitive to the racial bigotry in their midst; Hitler, it was said, finally managed to give racism a bad name in America. The U.S. government made a positive black image a public-policy objective, and such agencies as the Office of War Information campaigned against negative racial stereotypes and promoted in the popular media information about black patriotic contributions and good citizenship. Under government sponsorship, awareness of black achievement became what Washington had intended it to be: the antidote to the ugly images of blacks promoted in American popular culture. The elevation of black exemplars was part of the wartime effort, and Booker Washington became the first black to be celebrated with official symbols issued by the U.S. government. In 1940 the U.S. Post Office Department issued a ten-cent stamp displaying his image. In 1942 a cargo vessel was named the SS *Booker T. Washington* and given the merchant marine's first black captain and a multiracial crew. In 1946 the United States Mint produced a Booker T. Washington half-dollar. Soon after these recognitions, both Frederick Douglass and George Washington Carver were given similar honors.[12]

World War II also brought blacks a twofold opportunity to benefit from federally imposed segregation, when in 1941 the U.S. army established its training camp for black flyers near Tuskegee. The army's plans to separate the black airmen drew loud objections, especially from the NAACP, and the Institute administration was roundly criticized for cooperating with the government in perpetuating Jim Crow. The plans proceeded nevertheless, and several thousand black soldiers became Tuskegee Airmen—and future exemplars of black skill, patriotism, and success. Many other blacks benefited economically from providing the support services needed for the airfield. Thus the town experienced a surge in federal jobs and in black prosperity; but it also underwent an increase in white anxiety about all the Negroes in military uniform, some of them carrying guns. Racial violence was barely averted on several occasions. Local blacks had firsthand exposure to the democratic ideology that accompanied the American spirit of wartime sacrifice. At the end of the war there were a good many soldiers around town who had been overseas fighting for democracy and were now ready to enjoy it at home.[13]

Booker Washington's promise that economic success would ultimately bring political rights received only partial vindication in Tuskegee. As late as the mid-1930s only a handful of blacks could vote in Tuskegee and Macon County, and Institute administrators constituted most of the blacks on the voting roll. There were several hundred well-educated Institute and VA employees who did not vote,

54. World War II brought the realization of some of Booker Washington's goals and some celebration of his importance in American history. This image shows students in the Reserve Officer Training Corps at Tuskegee Institute, in front of Charles Keck's statue *Lifting the Veil of Ignorance.* Photo by Arthur Rothstein, March 1942; courtesy of the Library of Congress.

though in many instances they had not attempted to register. About 1935 a young Institute sociologist named Charles G. Gomillion began to encourage members of the Tuskegee Men's Club to register to vote. The local board of voter registrars required every new black applicant to have a white voucher for his or her good character. Gomillion had acquired his white voucher only by making his successful voter registration a condition for signing a contract with a white builder to construct his new home. The board of registrars required black applicants to meet both the property and literacy requirements for voting, whereas the Alabama constitution clearly made them alternate prerequisites. Local whites were determined to keep the several hundred well-educated blacks as politically powerless as the poor and illiterate blacks. Black economic success in Tuskegee had not yielded political rights in the manner that Washington had seemed to promise it would.

On the other hand, the economic independence of blacks in Tuskegee enabled them to mount a determined challenge to get the right to vote. Starting in 1941, Gomillion led the Institute faculty and the VA staff in demanding their constitutional rights. His organization threatened court action and followed through with a suit against the board of registrars. It monitored board practices and assembled large groups to demand to register at each registrars' meeting. It exerted pressure on political figures in Alabama to appoint registrars who were more receptive to black rights. When in 1957 Tuskegee officials redrew the city boundaries to remove nearly all black voters, all blacks in Tuskegee boycotted local businesses for the ensuing three years. Gomillion's organization attracted attention from the new United States Commission on Civil Rights, and the organization sued all the way to the U.S. Supreme Court to have the original city limits restored. By 1961 enough blacks voted to determine the outcome of every local election.[14]

The constant confrontations with the local board, the lawsuits, the persistent lobbying of state and federal governments, and the long boycott were made possible by the economic independence of so many blacks in Tuskegee. The salient reality was that although material autonomy enabled protest and demands for political rights, economic success did not on its own bring political rights, as Washington had suggested it would. On the other hand, neither did the opposite proposition hold. Most African Americans in Tuskegee, rich and poor alike, had assumed that black political power would result in new and better economic opportunities. Political freedom, it was thought, would lead to material prosperity, especially for those at the bottom of the socioeconomic order. During the 1970s and 1980s, the black-controlled city and county governments in Tuskegee advanced many projects to bring new jobs to the community, using taxpayer subsidies and public authority to attract industries and a dog-racing track. Some of the efforts failed, and the ones that survived did not produce much growth. In the end, poor Tuskegeeans were deeply disappointed that political rights had not wrought the changes in their lives they most wanted.[15]

In the end, the Tuskegee experience suggested a fundamental disconnect between political rights and economic opportunity. Booker was proved wrong, but so, too, were his critics, who had insisted that political rights were prerequisites to getting and holding economic gains. Economic and political strategies are parallel and must be complementary. In fact, while he publicly stressed the economic purpose, Washington had persistently pursued political goals, often quietly or secretively, and therefore had engaged in both at once.

Such complexity was seldom apparent in the assessments of Washington's historical significance during the civil-rights movement of the 1950s and 1960s. At first Martin Luther King Jr. invoked Booker as a moral authority for King's ethic of love and his posture of passive resistance to white hatred. He quoted Washington's saying "Let no man pull you so low as to make you hate him" in speeches and twice in his 1958 book, *Stride toward Freedom*. But when King said much about Washington after that, he was criticized. His call for a Washington-like program of self-help was condemned in Los Angeles in 1958 as a "dolled-up Uncle Tomism." As direct resistance to segregation increased starting in 1960, younger blacks began to dismiss Booker as an unworthy hero, one who had sold out his people to racist white power. To students accepting the risks of white violence by protesting in the streets, and in many cases getting quick white capitulation to change, Washington's failure to challenge discrimination directly was seen as having delayed the day of freedom. His presumed acceptance of segregation became the preeminent example of how blacks were *not* supposed to behave. At the other pole was Du Bois, now perceived as the foremost exponent of protest. John Lewis, the chairman of the Student Nonviolent Coordinating Committee (SNCC) in the early 1960s, a man born and reared not far from Tuskegee, claimed that Washington was "ridiculed and vilified by his own people for working so closely with white America"—an assertion true for only a tiny minority of blacks during Booker's life but for a mounting majority during Lewis's. By 1963 King had revised his position on Washington. "Be content . . . with doing well what the times permit," he erroneously paraphrased Booker, which King now dismissed as cowardly resignation. But his revision did not satisfy young activists. Lewis reported that SNCC leaders dismissed King's March on Washington speech as the same kind of "candy-coated, conciliatory gesture to white America" that Washington had made in the "Atlanta Compromise." As younger activists usurped the national spotlight by launching the Black Power movement, King suffered a similar demonization. The Black Power radical Eldridge Cleaver called Booker "the Martin Luther King of his day." Washington was for segregation, Cleaver said, Du Bois against it.[16]

Thus interpretations of Washington's historical meaning were used not only to condemn the past but also to demonize those in the present who did not demand maximum, immediate change. To serve the purposes of the present, Washington's historical meaning was extracted from its original context and misrepresented.

In the end, the student activists and the radicals did little damage to King with their specious analogies. For most people, King represented the polar opposite to Washington, the leader who knew that blacks must take and hold a posture of protest. King was prophetic, many assumed, and Washington complacent. King was a lion, Washington not even a fox but a lamb, and there really was no place for foxes. Lost altogether were the similarities between the two. King and Washington shared a commitment to shaping the way whites thought about racial character in order to elicit fairer treatment for blacks. Each followed Frederick Douglass's precedent in applying the promise of the Constitution to blacks. Each warned of the danger of hate, the power of love and reconciliation. Just as Washington portrayed blacks as decent and moral, King presented blacks as loving and unworthy of the terrible treatment that southern segregationists visited upon them. Although King was harder on whites than Washington had been, he preached that the worst of them could be redeemed. Each appealed to democratic values as the imperative for reforming race relations and prophesied that it would happen. The difference was that pricking the American conscience worked for King, whereas it usually had not for Booker. But that was a function of the harsher time in which he lived. To be sure, their styles were different: King depended on religious metaphor in the oratorical style of the funeral oration. Washington's allusions were commonplace, his speaking more informal, indirect, and ironic. But those surface differences should not be allowed to obscure the similarities of their purpose and appeal.

They lived in disparate times. Booker Washington's was truly a different country from the one Americans occupied during the 1960s. The ideology of the United States had changed; freedom and equality had altogether new and larger meanings, thanks primarily to World War II. White nationalism was no longer a legitimate ideology, even in the South. Power had shifted dramatically from states to the federal government. The federal judiciary had declared itself firmly and finally against racial discrimination. African Americans had a much larger endowment of resources on which to base a challenge to discrimination. And yet the leadership of Martin Luther King Jr. became the foil for denigrating the historical reputation of Booker Washington. Notwithstanding King's greatness and his unsurpassed influence in support of human rights throughout the world in the twentieth century, his career was in no way a fair measure for judging Washington's historical significance.

Even more than activists, academics disparaged Washington's historical reputation. In contrast to the public celebration of Washington's memory during and just after World War II, two young black historians, John Hope Franklin and Rayford W. Logan, offered critical assessments in the postwar years. Franklin picked up the earlier criticism that Tuskegee taught outdated skills, although he resisted Du Bois's wholesale rejection. A measured estimate of Washington's career emerged in the work of a white scholar, August Meier, who mastered the sources on black thought in the age of Booker Washington more completely than any other historian, black or white. Meier demonstrated that Washington's emphasis on self-help represented the mainstream of black opinion well before he began to promote it, and he placed Booker fairly in the complex evolution of both Frederick Douglass's and Du Bois's careers. Meier discovered the secret legal challenges that Washington made to discrimination, credited him with practicing the art of the possible, and noted carefully Booker's impulse to undermine his black opponents. But for all his enterprise and determination in uncovering black history, Meier failed to place Washington plausibly within the ugly environment of the turn-of-the-century South, and he cast Booker's approach as "accommodationist" in contrast to the protest commitments of Douglass and Du Bois. The protest-accommodation dichotomy made sense within Meier's complex understanding, but when extracted and adapted by those who knew far less, it became an invidious distinction.[17]

"No American success story could match the Master of Tuskegee's *Up From Slavery!*" began the sardonic commentary of unquestionably the most influential postwar review of Washington's life, C. Vann Woodward's 1951 *Origins of the New South.* Du Bois's views reverberated through this work. Woodward adopted his pejorative "Atlanta Compromise" and repeated his blame for disfranchisement: "In so far as Washington's pronouncement constituted a renunciation of active political aspirations for the Negro it had an important bearing upon the movement for disfranchisement." Woodward echoed Du Bois on the inconsistency between Washington's disavowal of black political activism and his own political influence: "The power this man came to wield over the destinies of his race and over the New South stood in striking contrast to his incorrigible humility." Even more severely than Du Bois, Woodward faulted Washington for not condemning the "prejudices and injustices of the caste system and the barbarities of the mob (subjects he rarely mentioned)." He seconded Du Bois's criticism of Washington's embrace of materialist values: "The businessman's gospel of free enterprise, competition, and *laissez faire* never had a more loyal exponent than the master of Tuskegee." Reflecting both Du Bois and the anticorporate influence of the Progressive historian Charles A. Beard, Woodward indicted Washington for his close ties to Carnegie, Huntington, and Baldwin, men who in his view had perpetrated a weak, colonial economy on the South. Washington's hostility to unions was "a compound of individualism, paternalism, and antiunionism in an age of collective labor action." And, Woodward argued, the skills taught at Tuskegee failed to serve his wealthy friends, for they had "more relevance to the South of Booker Washington's boyhood than to the South of United States Steel."[18]

Few historians have been more conversant than Woodward with the historical sources for Washington's time and place, and yet he failed to acknowledge most of the circumstances that vexed Washington or to see the strategy that he was pursuing. He did not acknowledge the intense demonization of black character and culture that preoccupied Washington. Woodward surely knew that throughout his career Booker was fighting a defensive battle to save black education from official abandonment, but the historian refused to grant that much black education would not have existed but for the northern philanthropy that Washington promoted. To have acknowledged the good works of the rich men would have undermined his argument about the evil influence of big corporations on the South. Woodward may not have known about Washington's secret challenges to disfranchisement, but he surely knew that by the time Booker's public statements about voting were heard in the mid-1890s, disfranchisement was an unstoppable movement in the South. Although he covered the antiblack rhetoric of Vardaman and Tillman, Woodward made no mention of their condemnations of Washington. With this omission, Woodward left the unmistakable impression that Washington had more freedom to speak and act than he actually did. He ignored Washington's efforts to bolster black morale at an awful time and maintained total silence on Tuskegee as a symbol of black achievement and competence.

In Woodward's schema, Washington was guilty of perpetrating the fraudulent "New South" by his collaboration with white oppressors. His interpretation was seminal: for at least fifty years after its publication in 1951, *Origins of the New South* was without question the most influential book on the post-Reconstruction South, and Woodward until his death in 1999 by far the most influential historian of that subject. His views on Washington became the most important after Du Bois's. He had a large contingent of admiring students who became the next generation of influential historians of the South, and they jealously protected his positions.

Many academic historians had themselves been activists, and certainly nearly all admired the achievements of civil-rights protest. Activism became an imperative among many historians who came of age in the 1960s, and activism dictated protest driven by idealism, not measured appeals to slow prescriptions based on material and educational improvement. A presumption entered the thinking and writing that protest was the correct, and for most the only legitimate, means of improving minority conditions. By the mid-1960s Washington was understood to have been the enemy of activism, the Uncle Tom who delayed the day of freedom. From then on, the present-mindedness of historians writing about race went mostly unquestioned.

One of Woodward's students, Louis R. Harlan, stepped forward as the next influential interpreter of Washington with the publication in 1972 of the first installments of both his two-volume biography of Washington and the fourteen-volume *Booker T. Washington Papers.* Harlan recycled his mentor's pejoratives, condemning Washington as "master of the Tuskegee plantation, ruling his campus and its people personally, absolutely, and with infinite attention to detail, delegating none of his authority." Harlan reached for ever-more-vivid symbolic language to capture Washington's personality. "If we could remove those layers of secrecy as one peels an onion, perhaps at the center of Washington's being would be revealed a person with a single-minded concern with power." Harlan mimicked Monroe Trotter in flinging epithets at Washington: he was "a minotaur, a lion, a fox, or Brer Rabbit, some frightened little man like the Wizard of Oz, or, as in the case of the onion, nothing—a personality that had vanished into the roles it played. Seeking to be all things to all men in a multifaceted society, Washington 'jumped Jim Crow' with the skill of long practice, but he seemed to lose sight of the original purposes of his dance." The ugly images piled up: driven by an "intense, faustian ambition," Washington was like Moses, "the king of a captive people." Harlan volunteered that before he began his research he had thought of Washington "entirely in terms of the Uncle Tom stereotype—a stereotype, I might add, with many elements of truth"; but the discovery of Washington's secret ways put him in mind of Richard Nixon, who was not "what he seemed to millions who thought they had observed him closely." Harlan made Washington's "'dirty tricks' and his mealy-mouthed moderation in the face of racial injustice" the main theme of the biography's second volume. Winner of the Bancroft Prize for history and the Pulitzer Prize for biography, *The Wizard of Tuskegee* developed the Tricky-Dick interpretation to perfect the Du Bois and Trotter indictment of Washington for his hypocritical disavowal of politics while influencing appointments, for his power with the black press, and for his punishment of enemies.[19]

Instead of putting these events in the context of groups competing for political power—southern blacks versus white nationalists, southern blacks versus northern blacks, and southern blacks in pursuit of northern help—Harlan situated them in a Manichean struggle between northern black idealists of "distinction and dignity" and the Tuskegee Machine, ruled by the power-hungry Wizard. He accepted the arguments of Du Bois and Trotter, mostly ignoring their personal rancor, and then piled up evidence of spite from Washington's camp. Harlan chose not to show the mounting white hysteria about Washington's role in politics. He vastly underreported the impact of the White House dinner. He did not discuss the sustained attacks made by Vardaman, Tillman, Heflin, Watson, Dixon, or the half-dozen other white-nationalist politicians who openly hated Booker. He neglected the intensifying opposition to black education, even though he had written an earlier book on the weak and declining support for it. He largely ignored Washington's effort to raise black morale and missed entirely his prophetic purpose. The positive symbolism of Tuskegee Institute got hardly a note.[20]

But because he drove his thesis well and paraded vivid images before the reader, Harlan shaped virtually all the writing on post-Reconstruction race relations published after 1972, including the interpretations purveyed in college textbooks of American history. His work appears to have influenced all scholarly interpretations of the period from Reconstruction to Wilson's presidency. Studies of black politics in the South took for granted that Washington opposed black voting rights. Examinations of civil-rights activism presumed that Washington was the friend of segregationists and the enemy of equality. Studies of Du Bois, including David Levering Lewis's much-celebrated biography, were unrelenting in their negative portrayal of Washington.[21]

By the end of the twentieth century, the perception of Booker Washington, at least among the intelligentsia, was profoundly negative. Du Bois left a body of elegant criticism that almost irretrievably distorted his historical memory. The ideological imperatives of C. Vann Woodward marked a second stage in the demolition of Washington's reputation and significance, and again the detractor was a brilliant rhetorician—and one of the most influential American intellectuals of the twentieth century. The civil-rights movement prompted a rethinking of racial strategies, and any approach other than direct-action protest came to be viewed as illegitimate. In that environment, Du Bois's life became a paradigm of correct black leadership, and Booker's a model of what had to be avoided. After the 1960s the terms of Washington's memory were dictated chiefly by Harlan, the biographer almost universally regarded as definitive and one who viewed his subject as a sellout. Given the status of Harlan and his mentor Woodward in the academic world and the post-1960s elevation of Du Bois to the position of unquestioned authority on African-American culture and thought, it is little wonder that history brought Booker so low.

Washington deserved to be remembered with more understanding. Great obstacles stood in his way as he tried to put African Americans on a trajectory of progress at a time when the thoroughly white-dominated society believed that blacks were declining into criminality—and even oblivion. He faced a public discourse and a popular culture that were relentlessly hostile to his people. He confronted personal and political enemies in the South who fought to keep him from projecting his message of black progress and who, starting in 1901, stirred racial hatred by attacking Washington for his defense of black officeholders and black education. Those attacks undermined his ability to pursue

symbolic action on behalf of black progress, but he never stopped trying. He suffered irreparable harm with Theodore Roosevelt's betrayal
in 1906. Afterward he kept working to raise black morale and reduce
white hostility to his people, even though his influence as the leader of
his race was clearly diminished. Still, he remained immensely popular
with African Americans, and his leadership lasted until he died.

Washington has often been portrayed as the symbol of the age of
segregation, usually with the presumption that he acquiesced in Jim
Crow. In light of the evidence of Washington's challenges to white
domination, that view seems wrong. He has often been called conservative. At the very least, that claim conveys an unacceptably imprecise
meaning. Washington's purpose was to change conditions for African
Americans. He should be considered a conservative only with regard
to his belief that capitalist enterprise offered blacks their best opportunity to rise in America and his skepticism that much help would be
forthcoming from governments. The almost universal characterization of Washington as an accommodationist to segregation is also inac-
curate. Having conditions forced on him, with the threat of destruction clearly the cost of resistance, does not constitute a fair definition of
accommodation. It is coercion. The accommodation-protest binary has
obscured the fundamental similarity of the substance of Washington's
action to the protest agenda put forward by the NAACP. Washington
made public protests against Jim Crow on railroads, lynching, disfranchisement, disparities in education funding, segregated housing legislation, and discrimination by labor unions. He arranged and partly financed lawsuits challenging disfranchisement, jury discrimination,
and peonage. And he campaigned constantly against the pernicious
images of blacks projected in the media and popular culture. The
NAACP would do those same things after him.

Led by Du Bois, however, many have confused the Washington
style with the substance. African-American leaders must always be li-
ons like Frederick Douglass or Martin Luther King Jr. They cannot be
foxes, or else they are accused of being Uncle Toms or resembling
Richard Nixon. Franklin Roosevelt's cagey style of leadership has not
been acceptable for a black leader. Washington was dismissed during
his time and afterward as a leader chosen by whites, but in fact he was

selected in much the same fashion as Douglass and King: he was a powerful voice who got the attention of white opinionmakers at the same time he earned the respect and admiration of the black masses by helping them imagine a better future. Even on the matter of leadership style, Washington should be credited for exercising the prophetic leadership that is expected of black leaders.

Honest interpreters should recognize that direct-action protest has yielded the desired results more episodically than consistently. It is misleading to teach that change is the result exclusively, or even predominantly, of protest. Other strategies for change have worked better at other times, and external influences—wars, depressions, technological developments—have been determinants of change at many points. The accumulation of human capital through better health, education, morality, and enterprise seems irrefutably a good strategy for advancement in American society. One can imagine that if Booker Washington lived today, he would insist that every disadvantaged group in American society—and blacks especially—should be working internally to improve their home lives, schools, and reputations to be ready to exploit the opportunities that arise in a rapidly evolving world. And when an injustice is identified, any group should object to mistreatment firmly but carefully. A rising people must operate on more than one track to lift themselves. As he did in his day, Washington might warn that there is a cost to be paid for appearing constantly aggrieved. Many Americans soon stop listening to the complaint and start blaming the complainer, he in effect said. Constructive action and clear demonstrations of virtue are crucial means for lifting a group. That faith in object lessons was a more popular message in his day, when such demonstrations were much harder to accomplish, than it would be later, when opportunities for progress became more available to disadvantaged groups. It remains today a valid strategy but one that is suspect to all those who privilege the protest posture in their thinking.

Although Washington's approach was appropriate to the harsh circumstances of his world, it by no means changed his world. In that sense he was a heroic failure. In a hundred different ways he expressed his faith that a black person who acquired economic independence would command the respect of white neighbors, and that ultimately with autonomy would come the full rights of citizenship. He did not acknowledge publicly that most whites objected to the rise in status achieved by a black skilled worker, business proprietor, or landowner. To concede that political rights would not follow from economic success would have undermined his materialist strategy. And in his day there was no other realistic avenue to progress. Certainly neither politics nor protest worked in the South of 1895 or 1901 or even 1915. Booker insisted that blacks would improve their lives through education and economic success. To a certain extent, events after his death vindicated this view: the wars, migrations, and vastly expanded national government of the twentieth century did bring enough economic opportunity to free many African Americans from the white South's opposition to black progress. But those events also brought a better chance for political solutions, and it would be political action in the 1960s that ended segregation and disfranchisement.

There was a tragic dimension to Washington's effort to remake the black image in the American mind. During his lifetime the obstacles to that purpose were simply insurmountable. His efforts could not overcome the intense political and cultural authority of white nationalism. But neither did the efforts of the NAACP succeed in that regard until World War II, when the demands of defeating racist enemies sparked the rejection of racial stereotypes in American culture. The fact remains that Washington was the first to identify it as a necessary challenge, although it was left to others to meet it. Washington should receive credit for anticipating the modern world in which image was more readily manipulated than reality, in which prophecies were often self-fulfilling and pessimism had little social utility.

Though largely overlooked, his effort to sustain blacks' morale at a terrible time must be counted among the most heroic efforts in American history. Booker T. Washington told his people that they would survive the dark present and, as far as possible, he showed them how to do so. By building an institution that demonstrated blacks' potential for success and autonomy, he gave them reasons to have faith in the future. Indeed, his life itself was an object lesson in progress, providing hope

NOTES

ACKNOWLEDGMENTS

INDEX

Notes

The following abbreviations are used in the notes.

BTW	Booker T. Washington
BTWP	*The Booker T. Washington Papers,* ed. Louis R. Harlan, Raymond W. Smock, and Geraldine McTighe, 14 vols. (Urbana, 1972–1989)
Harlan, *Making*	Louis R. Harlan, *Booker T. Washington: The Making of a Black Leader* (New York, 1972)
Harlan, *Wizard*	Louis R. Harlan, *Booker T. Washinton: The Wizard of Tuskegee* (New York, 1983)
Larger Education	Booker T. Washington, *My Larger Education: Being Chapters from My Experience* (Garden City, N.Y., 1911), with page references to *BTWP,* vol. 1
Story	Booker T. Washington, *The Story of My Life and Work* (Napierville, Ill., 1900; rev. 1901, 1915), with page references to *BTWP,* vol. 1
Up	Booker T. Washington, *Up from Slavery* (Garden City, N.Y., 1901), with page references to *BTWP,* vol. 1

Prologue

1. Atlanta *Constitution,* October 24 and 25, 1905.

2. "Three Reports of Pinkerton Detectives, October 22, 23, 24, 1905," in *The Booker T. Washington Papers,* ed. Louis R. Harlan, Raymond W. Smock, and Geraldine McTighe, 14 vols. (Urbana, 1972–1989) (hereafter cited as *BTWP*), 8: 418–421.

3. Dewey W. Grantham Jr., "Dinner at the White House: Theodore Roosevelt, Booker T. Washington, and the South," *Tennessee Historical Quarterly* 18 (June 1958): 112–130.

4. Montgomery *Advertiser,* October 4, 1904; undated Tuskegee *News* article re-

printed in Nashville *American,* October 19, 1904; Ruperth Fehnstoke [S. Becker von Grabil], *Letters from Tuskegee, Being the Confessions of a Yankee* (Montgomery, Ala., 1905); *Tom Watson's Magazine,* June 1905, 392–393; Thomas Dixon Jr., "Booker T. Washington and the Negro: Some Dangerous Aspects of the Work of Tuskegee," *Saturday Evening Post,* August 19, 1905.

5. Cotton States Exposition Address, reprinted in Booker T. Washington (hereafter BTW), *Up from Slavery* (Garden City, N.Y., 1901) (hereafter cited as *Up,* with page references to *BTWP,* vol. 1), 330–334.

6. Waldo E. Martin Jr., *The Mind of Frederick Douglass* (Chapel Hill, 1984), 55–91, 275–277.

7. "A Press Release, October 24, 1905," in *BTWP,* 8: 421–427.

8. Ibid.

9. Ibid., 427.

10. "An Address by Theodore Roosevelt, October 24, 1905," in *BTWP,* 8: 428–431.

11. Ibid., 428, 429, 430.

12. Ralph Ellison, *Invisible Man* (1952; reprint, New York, 1972), 36.

13. John Lewis with Michael D'Orso, *Walking with the Wind: A Memoir of the Movement* (New York, 1998), 18; Waldo Martin, "In Search of Booker T. Washington: *Up from Slavery,* History, and Legend," in *Booker T. Washington and Black Progress:* Up from Slavery *100 Years Later,* ed. W. Fitzhugh Brundage (Gainesville, 2003), 40.

14. Robert J. Norrell, *Reaping the Whirlwind: The Civil Rights Movement in Tuskegee,* 2d ed. (Chapel Hill, 1998), 182.

1. The Force That Wins

1. *Up,* 218.

2. *Up,* 225; BTW, *The Story of My Life and Work* (Napierville, Ill., 1900; rev. 1901, 1915) (hereafter cited as *Story,* with page references to *BTWP,* vol. 1), 12–13.

3. *Story,* 10; Louis R. Harlan, *Booker T. Washington: The Making of a Black Leader* (New York, 1972) (hereafter cited as Harlan, *Making*), 4–5, 325.

4. *Up,* 216.

5. *Story,* 11; *Up,* 216–218; Booker T. Washington, *My Larger Education: Being Chapters from My Experience* (New York, 1911) (hereafter cited as *Larger Education,* with page references to *BTWP,* vol. 1), 420.

6. *Story,* 415; "A News Item in the *Tuskegee Student,*" in *BTWP,* 9: 635–640; *Up,* 215, 221.

7. *Up,* 217; *Story,* 415–416.

8. *Story,* 12.

9. *Story,* 9–10; *Up,* 228.

10. *Up,* 227.

11. Ibid.

12. Ibid., 233–234.

13. *Story,* 15; *Up,* 228–229.

14. *Up,* 228–231.

15. *Up,* 231–232.

16. *Up,* 237–238.

17. Gilson Willetts, "Slave Boy and the Leader of His Race," *New Voice* 16 (June 1899): 3.

18. Harlan, *Making,* 40–44.

19. *Up,* 254–255.

20. *Up,* 255.

21. "The Minutes of a Republican Rally at Tinkersville," July 13, 1872, in *BTWP,* 2: 21.

22. *Up,* 238–240.

23. *Up,* 240, 243.

24. James D. Anderson, *The Education of Blacks in the South, 1860–1935* (Chapel Hill, 1988), 33–78; Joe M. Richardson, *Christian Recontruction: The American Missionary Association and Southern Blacks, 1861–1890* (Athens, Ga., 1986); James M. McPherson, *The Abolitionist Legacy: From Reconstruction to the NAACP* (Princeton, 1975), 187–188.

25. Robert Francis Engs, *Educating the Disfranchised and Disinherited: Samuel Chapman Armstrong and Hampton Institute, 1839–1893* (Knoxville, 1899), 80–114; Engs, *Freedom's First Generation: Black Hampton, Virginia, 1861–1890* (Philadelphia, 1979), 139–160.

26. Engs, *Freedom's First Generation,* 142–4; Engs, *Educating the Disfranchised,* 78.

27. *Up,* 241, 245.

28. *Story,* 21; *Up,* 243–244; *Southern Workman* 6 (February 1877): 10.

29. *Up,* 245–246.

30. *Story,* 23; *Up,* 249; Nathalie Lord, "Booker Washington's School Days at Hampton," *Southern Workman* 31 (May 1902): 255–259.

31. BTW, The *Story of the Negro: The Rise of the Race from Slavery,* 2 vols. (New York, 1909), excerpt in *BTWP,* 1: 402; *Larger Education,* 423.

32. *Up,* 302–303; Engs, *Freedom's First Generation,* 131–132.

33. Engs, *Educating the Disfranchised,* 98–106; *Larger Education,* 420–421.

34. New York *Times,* June 15, 1875; Harlan, *Making,* 7.

35. New York *Times,* June 15, 1875.

36. Peter A. Coclanis, "What Made Booker Wash(ington)? The Wizard of

Tuskegee in Economic Context," in *Booker T. Washington and Black Progress: Up From Slavery 100 Years Later,* ed. W. Fitzhugh Brundage (Gainesville, 2003), 81–106.

37. William T. McKinney to BTW, September 11, 1911, in *BTWP,* 11: 304–308; Harlan, *Making,* 84–87.

38. McKinney to BTW, September 11, 1911; Harlan, *Making,* 67, 95.

39. *Up,* 260–261.

40. *Up,* 260–262.

41. *Story,* 26–27; Lord, "Washington's School Days."

42. *Up,* 265–266.

43. Samuel Chapman Armstrong to George Washington Campbell and Other Trustees of Tuskegee Normal School, May 31, 1881, in *BTWP,* 2: 127.

44. *Up,* 271.

2. The Model Community

1. Thomas McAdory Owen, "Macon County," in *History of Alabama and Dictionary of Alabama Biography,* 4 vols. (Chicago, 1921), 2: 918–922.

2. *Up,* 272; *Story,* 34.

3. Emmett J. Scott and Lyman Beecher Stowe, *Booker T. Washington: Builder of a Civilization* (Garden City, N.Y., 1916), 6–8.

4. Robert J. Norrell, *Reaping the Whirlwind: The Civil Rights Movement in Tuskegee,* 2d ed. (Chapel Hill, 1998), 12–13, 15.

5. *Confederate Veteran* 40 (1932): 97–99; New York *Times,* November 12 and 20, 1865; Montgomery *Advertiser,* June 12, 1906; Case Files of Applications from Former Confederates for Presidential Pardons ("Amnesty Papers"), reel 1, group I, Alabama, AB–Bo, National Archives Microfilm Publications m1005; *Testimony Taken by the Joint Select Committee to Inquire into the Condition of Affairs in the Late Insurrectionary States, Alabama,* 42d Cong., 2d sess., vol. 2, 1136–39 (hereafter cited as *Late Insurrectionary States*); Thomas McAdory Owen, "Cullen Andrews Battle," in *History of Alabama,* 3: 115.

6. *Up,* 255; *Late Insurrectionary States,* 3: 1548; 1: 140.

7. *Late Insurrectionary States,* 2: 1020–22, 1059–72.

8. Ibid., 1026–41, 1094–97.

9. Ibid., 1026–40, 1070, 1104–12; 1: 236.

10. On ethnic nationalism, see Anthony D. Smith, *The Ethnic Origins of Nations* (New York, 1986); and Liah Greenfeld, *Nationalism: Five Roads to Modernity* (Cambridge, Mass., 1992).

11. New York *Times,* August 18, 1868; January 26, 1869; October 5, 1874.

12. Tuskegee *News,* June 17, March 11 and 25, April 22, June 3, 1875; August 23, 1877.

13. Macon *Mail,* April 5, 1876; December 4 and August 28, 1878; October 1, 1879; July 10, 1878; July 2, 1879; Tuskegee *News,* October 21 and 28, 1880.

14. Scott and Stowe, *Booker T. Washington,* 3–4; Harlan, *Making,* 115–117; BTW to James Fowle Baldwin Marshall, December 22, 1885, in *BTWP,* 2: 286–289.

15. Tuskegee *News,* June 9, 1881.

16. BTW to J. F. B. Marshall, June 29, 1881, in *BTWP,* 2: 135.

17. *Up,* 272; BTW to editor of *Southern Workman,* July 14, 1881, in *BTWP,* 2: 140.

18. William H. Holtzclaw, *The Black Man's Burden* (1915; reprint, New York, 1970), 13–24; *Up,* 274–275.

19. *Up,* 276.

20. *Up,* 280; Scott and Stowe, *Booker T. Washington,* 6.

21. Harlan, *Making,* 116; *Up,* 278–280.

22. Horace Mann Bond, *Negro Education in Alabama: A Study in Cotton and Steel* (1939; reprint, New York, 1969), 142; Daniel W. Crofts, "The Blair Bill and the Electronic Bill: the Congressional Aftermath to Reconstruction" (Ph.D. diss., Yale University, 1968), 177–178; Stephen Kantrowitz, *Ben Tillman and the Reconstruction of White Supremacy* (Chapel Hill, 2000), 216.

23. Crofts, "The Blair Bill," 177–178; Montgomery *Advertiser,* February 4, 1888.

24. *Christian Advocate,* December 28, 1882; Atlanta *Constitution,* March 19, 1882.

25. *Up,* 273; William Warren Rogers and Robert David Ward, *August Reckoning: Jack Turner and Racism in Post–Civil War Alabama* (Baton Rouge, 1973).

26. Tuskegee *News,* September 21, 1882.

27. Montgomery *Advertiser,* August 27, 1882; Tuskegee *News,* August 31, 1882.

28. Harlan, *Making,* 146–147. On the difficulty of discovering the internal content of black marriages in the late nineteenth century, see Patricia A. Schechter, "'Curious Silence'? African American Women in *Up from Slavery,*" in *Booker T. Washington and Black Progress:* Up From Slavery *100 Years Later,* ed. W. Fitzhugh Brundage (Gainesville, 2003), 131–148.

3. The Self-Made Men

1. *Story,* 34; *Up,* 294.

2. BTW, *The Story of the Negro: The Rise of the Race from Slavery,* 2 vols. (New York, 1909), excerpt in *BTWP,* 1: 414.

3. BTW to Abby E. Cleaveland, January 19, 1888, in *BTWP,* 2: 409–410; information on Logan, ibid., 47; information on Courtney, ibid., 289.

4. Information on Davidson, ibid., 137–138.

5. Harlan, *Making,* 126; *Story,* 32; *Up,* 281–285.

6. *Up,* 309.

7. *Up,* 308–309, 282–283.

8. *Up,* 285, 290.

9. *Up,* 289, 290–291.

10. "Three Items from a Notebook," in *BTWP,* 2: 197–201; *Up,* 291–292.

11. Moses Pierce to BTW, January 1882, in *BTWP,* 2: 162–164.

12. James Fowle Baldwin Marshall to BTW, March 4, 1883; Atticus Greene Haygood to BTW, November 7, 1883, ibid., 221–222, 244–245.

13. Ellen Weiss, "Tuskegee Landscape in Black and White," *Winterthur Portfolio* 36 (Spring 2001): 19–37; L. Albert Scipio, *Pre-War Days at Tuskegee: Historical Essay on Tuskegee Institute (1881–1943)* (Silver Spring, Md., 1987).

14. *Up,* 295–296.

15. *Up,* 297.

16. Ibid.

17. *Up,* 292, 310.

18. BTW to Morris Ketchum Jesup, April 29, 1893, in *BTWP,* 2: 316.

19. Adella Hunt to BTW, July 20, 1887; "A Report on the Summer State Teachers' Institutes, November 1888," ibid., 374, 494.

20. *Southern Letter,* March and December, 1887; Missouri C. Strong to BTW, December 1, 1887; Virginia L. Adams to BTW, May 15, 1888, in *BTWP,* 2: 393–394, 453–454.

21. *Southern Letter,* June, September, and November 1886; June, November, and December 1887; January and June 1888; April 1889.

22. "A Speech before the Alabama State Teachers' Association, April 7, 1882," in *BTWP,* 2: 193–195.

23. Harlan, *Making,* 146–147; *Story,* 34; "The Inscription on the Tombstone of Fanny Norton Smith Washington, May 4, 1884," in *BTWP,* 2: 250–251.

24. BTW to J. F. B. Marshall, December 22, 1885, in *BTWP,* 2: 286–289.

25. Information on John Henry Washington, ibid., 5–6.

26. Information on James, Amanda, and Albert, ibid., 7, 20, 477–478.

27. BTW to Samuel Chapman Armstrong, October 31, 1885; Olivia A. Davidson Washington to Mary Elizabeth Preston Stearns, April 11, 1887, ibid., 283, 338–340.

28. Harlan, *Making,* 149–151; Announcement of wedding of BTW and Olivia A. Davidson, August 11, 1886, in *BTWP,* 2: 306–307.

29. *Up,* 273–274.

30. BTW to editor of Montgomery *Advertiser,* April 30, 1885, in *BTWP,* 2: 271–273.

31. George M. Elliott to BTW, April 30, 1885, ibid., 274–275.

32. Louis D. Rubin Jr., *George W. Cable: The Life and Times of a Southern Heretic* (New York, 1969), 157–159; BTW to Frederick C. Jones, December 21, 1885, in *BTWP,* 2: 285.

33. BTW to J. F. B. Marshall, December 22, 1885, in *BTWP,* 2: 286–289; *Southern Letter,* September 1886; W. Fitzhugh Brundage, *Lynching in the New South: Virginia and Georgia, 1880–1930* (Urbana, 1993); Philip Dray, *At the Hands of Persons Unknown: The Lynching of Black America* (New York, 2003).

34. Jesse C. Duke to BTW, January 20, 1887, in *BTWP,* 2: 325–326. The characterization of Dorsette as a "big head" is from Editor's Note, ibid., 326.

35. Lovejoy's letter quoted in ibid., 474–475.

36. Robert Charles Bedford to Olivia A. Davidson Washington, August 4, 1888; George W. Lovejoy to BTW, August 12, 1888; BTW to editor of Tuskegee *Weekly News,* August 14, 1888, ibid., 474–479.

37. "Two News Items from the Springfield *Daily Republican,* May 8, 1882," ibid., 203–204.

38. "A Speech before the Unitarian National Conference, September 21, 1886"; BTW to George Washington Cable, February 1, 1889; BTW to editor of *Southern Workman,* February 18, 1886, ibid., 308–313, 511–512, 296–297.

39. Charles Darwin, *The Descent of Man,* vol. 1 (London, 1877), 201; John Tyler Morgan, "The Future of the American Negro," *North American Review* 139 (July 1884): 83–84; Edward C. Gilliam, "The African Problem," ibid. (November 1884): 417.

40. "A Speech before the National Educational Association, July 16, 1884," in *BTWP,* 2: 255–262.

41. August Meier, *Negro Thought in America, 1880–1915* (Ann Arbor, 1963), 74, 39; Frederick Douglass, "Self-made Men," 549–550, 560, http://memory.loc.gov/ammem/doughtml.

42. BTW to John Elbert McConnell, December 17, 1885, in *BTWP,* 2: 284.

43. "A Speech before the Unitarian National Conference, September 21, 1886."

44. Henry Woodfin Grady to BTW, in *BTWP,* 2: 320–321.

45. Horace Mann Bond, *Negro Education in Alabama: A Study in Cotton and Steel* (1939; reprint, New York, 1969), 204; William Hooper Councill to BTW, September 3, 1887, in *BTWP,* 2: 382–384; Harlan, *Making,* 168–170.

46. Atlanta *Constitution,* July 29, 1900; Meier, *Negro Thought,* 110; BTW to William Hooper Councill, September 9, 1886; J. F. B. Marshall to Samuel Chapman Armstrong, January 31, 1887; Marshall to BTW, April 21, 1887, in *BTWP,* 2: 307–308, 330–331, 340–341.

47. Robert Charles Bedford to BTW, November 20, 1890; Warren Logan to BTW, December 6, 1890, in *BTWP*, 3: 100–101, 111–112.

48. Robert J. Norrell, *A Promising Field: Engineering at Alabama, 1837–1987* (Tuscaloosa, 1990), 36–39.

49. BTW to Warren Logan, April 14, 17, 18, 19, 1889, in *BTWP*, 2: 523, 525; BTW to Samuel Chapman Armstrong, April 21 and May 18, 1889, ibid., 523–525, 531–532; *Southern Letter*, March and May 1889.

50. BTW to Armstrong, August 13, 1889, in *BTWP*, 3: 4.

4. The Survival of the Race

1. Allen Johnston Going, *Bourbon Democracy in Alabama, 1874–1890* (University, Ala., 1951), 164–167.

2. BTW to Robert Charles Bedford, August 22, 1893; BTW to Hollis Burke Frissell, October 2, 1893, in *BTWP*, 3: 360, 368.

3. "A Speech at Old South Meeting House, Boston, December 15, 1891," in *BTWP*, 3: 199–201; BTW to Grindall Reynolds, August 11, 1893, ibid., 355–356; BTW to William Addison Benedict, February 8 and May 11, 1892; and January 28, 1893, ibid., 211–212, 228–229, 288–289; "An Article in *Unity*, November 16, 1889"; BTW to Samuel Chapman Armstrong, December 13, 1889; Olivia Egleston Phelps Stokes to BTW, September 20, 1890, ibid., 16–17, 21–22, 83.

4. BTW to William LeRoy Broun, October 15, 1890; "A Speech before the New York Congregational Club, January 16, 1893"; "An Interview in the Chicago *Inter Ocean*, January 26, 1895," ibid., 87–90, 279–288, 502–506.

5. Ralph E. Luker, *The Social Gospel in Black and White: American Racial Reform, 1885–1912* (Chapel Hill, 1991), 20–22.

6. August Meier, *Negro Thought in America, 1880–1915* (Ann Arbor, 1963), 89–99; BTW to Warren Logan, April 15, 1893, in *BTWP*, 3: 308; BTW, "The Awakening of the Negro," *Atlantic Monthly*, September 1896, 322–328.

7. "Proceedings of the Triennial Reunion of the Hampton Alumni Association, May 28, 1893"; "A Sunday Evening Talk, February 10, 1895," in *BTWP*, 3: 336–339, 510–515.

8. BTW, "The Awakening of the Negro," 326.

9. William Jenkins to BTW, March 3, 1889, in *BTWP*, 2: 514–515; Harlan, *Wizard*, 288.

10. Margaret James Murray to BTW, July 24, October 26, and November 1, 1891, in *BTWP*, 3: 160–161, 174–175, 177–179.

11. Portia Marshall Washington to BTW, November 19, 1893, ibid., 375.

12. BTW to James Nathan Calloway, June 27, 1892; BTW to Charles W. Greene,

April 24, 1893; Jabez Lamar Monroe Curry to BTW, April 17, 1894; BTW to Alice J. Kaine, September 5, 1894, ibid., 240–241, 311–312, 404, 466–467.

13. BTW to the Faculty Committee on the Course of Study, September 15, 1893; BTW to Robert Hannibal Hamilton, September 23, 1894, ibid., 366–367, 471–472,.

14. Jane Gottschalk, "The Rhetorical Strategy of Booker T. Washington," *Phylon* 27 (Spring 1966): 388–395; "Reading as a Means of Growth," "Self Denial," "Sowing and Reaping," "Unimproved Opportunities," "The Work to Be Done by Tuskegee Graduates," in *BTWP*, 3: 91–94, 129–132, 138–146, 508–515, 548–553.

15. "A Sunday Evening Talk, May 12, 1895," in *BTWP*, 3: 554–556.

16. Washington was teaching his students to embrace what the German sociologist Max Weber would later call "hidden honor," something that oppressed people such as blacks in the United States needed to have in order to sustain themselves. Weber discussed American blacks as a "pariah people" who developed means to give one another status even as the dominant authority in the society attempted to deny them any of the honor or prestige that conveyed status to whites. See Weber, *Essays in Sociology*, trans. and ed. H. H. Gerth and C. Wright Mills (New York, 1946), 189–190.

17. William J. Edward, *Twenty-five Years in the Black Belt* (Boston, 1918); Rose Herlong Ellis, "The Calhoun School, Miss Charlotte Thorn's 'Lighthouse on the Hill' in Lowndes County, Alabama," *Alabama Review* 37 (July 1984): 183–201; BTW to Mabel Wilhelmina Dillingham, August 15, 1891, in *BTWP*, 3: 163–164.

18. "A Circular Announcing the Tuskegee Negro Conference, January 1892"; "The Declaration of the First Tuskegee Negro Conference, February 23, 1892," in *BTWP*, 3: 209–210, 217–219.

19. BTW, "The Awakening of the Negro."

20. Harlan, *Making*, 189–190.

21. Allen W. Jones, "The Role of Tuskegee Institute in the Education of Black Farmers," *Journal of Negro History* 60 (April 1975): 252–267; *Ladies' Home Journal*, May 1907, in *BTWP*, 9: 289–294; BTW to Samuel Chapman Armstrong, February 26, 1892, in *BTWP*, 3: 219–221; Jacqueline Anne Rouse, "Out of the Shadow of Tuskegee: Margaret Murray Washington, Social Activism, and Race Vindication," *Journal of Negro History* 81 (Winter 1996): 31–46; BTW to William Torrey Harris, May 4, 1892, in *BTWP*, 3: 226.

22. BTW to Warren Logan, July 5, 1995, in *BTWP*, 3: 663–664.

23. "A Speech before the Boston Unitarian Club, 1888," in *BTWP*, 2: 503; Luker, *Social Gospel in Black and White*, 132–142.

24. "An Article in the *Christian Union*, August 14, 1890," in *BTWP*, 3: 71–75;

BTW to Edgar James Penney, April 30, 1890; June 13 and 23, 1891, ibid., 52–53, 156–158; Olivia Egleston Phelps Stokes to BTW, September 20, 1890, and November 5, 1891, ibid., 83, 180.

25. David Sehat, "The Civilizing Mission of Booker T. Washington," *Journal of Southern History* 73 (May 2007): 344.

26. Daniel Alexander Payne to BTW, November 3, 1890; Ida B. Wells to BTW, November 30, 1890, in *BTWP,* 3: 97–98, 108; Francis J. Grimké to BTW, December 12, 1890, and November 28, 1891, ibid., 114–115, 196–197.

27. "A Speech before the New York Congregational Club, January 16, 1893"; "An Article in *The Congregationalist,* August 31, 1893," ibid., 279–288, 361–364.

28. "An Address at a Mass Meeting in Washington, D.C., November 20, 1891," ibid., 184–194; "An Article in *The Congregationalist,* August 31, 1893."

29. George Washington Campbell to BTW, July 16, 1890, in *BTWP,* 3: 66–67; J. Morgan Kousser, *The Shaping of Southern Politics: Suffrage Restrictions and the Shaping of the One-Party South, 1880–1910* (New Haven, 1974); Sheldon Hackney, *From Populism to Progressivism in Alabama* (Princeton, 1969), 148–150.

30. Montgomery *Advertiser,* February 4 and 5, 1891.

31. BTW to Francis James Grimké, November 27, 1895, in *BTWP,* 4: 85–86; Harlan, *Making,* 171–175.

32. Mitchell quoted in *BTWP,* 3: 567.

5. The Settlement of the Negro Problem

1. "An Article in *The Congregationalist,* August 31, 1893"; John J. Benson to BTW, April 2, 1895, in *BTWP,* 3: 361–364, 544.

2. George M. Fredrickson, *The Black Image in the White Mind: The Debate on Afro-American Character and Destiny, 1817–1914* (1971; reprint, Middletown, Conn., 1987), 247; Thomas Nelson Page, "A Southerner on the Negro Question," *North American Review* 154 (April 1892): 411–412; Frederick Ludwig Hoffman, "Vital Statistics of the Negro," *The Arena* 4 (April 1892): 529–542; "Race Traits and Tendencies of the American Negro," *Publications of the American Economic Association* 11 (1896); Southern Society for the Promotion of the Study of Race Conditions and Problems in the South, *Race Problems of the South: Proceedings of the First Annual Conference* (Richmond, Va., 1900), 155–156.

3. Page, "A Southerner on the Negro Question," 403; Philip Alexander Bruce, *The Plantation Negro as a Freeman* (New York, 1889); J. L. M. Curry, "The Negro Question," *Popular Science Monthly* 55 (June 1899): 181.

4. New York *Times,* April 25, 1892; Edwin S. Redkey, *Black Exodus: Black Nationalist and Back-to-Africa Movements, 1890–1910* (New Haven, 1969), 62.

5. Frederick Douglass, "The Nation's Problem," April 16, 1889, in *Frederick Douglass: Selected Speeches and Writings,* ed. Philip S. Foner (Chicago, 1950), 728; Henry A. Scomp, "Can the Race Problem Be Solved?" *Forum* 8 (December 1889): 365–376; John Tyler Morgan, "Shall Negro Majorities Rule?" *Forum* 6 (1888–89): 586–599; "The Race Question in the United States," *The Arena* 2 (September 1890): 385; Wade Hampton, "The Race Problem," ibid. (April 1890): 133; James Bryce, "Thoughts on the Negro Problem," *North American Review* 153 (December 1891): 648–649, 654; Page, "A Southerner on the Negro Question," 406.

6. Atlanta *Constitution,* May 1, 1900; Rayford Logan, *The Betrayal of the Negro: From Rutherford B. Hayes to Woodrow Wilson* (originally *The Negro in American Life and Thought: The Nadir, 1877–1910*) (London, 1954), 242–275; BTW to John Addison Porter, November 30, 1898, in *BTWP,* 4: 522; Atlanta *Constitution,* February 1, 1891, and February 2, 1900.

7. Thomas D. Clark, *The Southern Country Editor* (New York, 1948), 195–207; David B. Parker, *Alias Bill Arp: Charles Henry Smith and the South's "Goodly Heritage"* (Athens, Ga., 1991), 77–177; Atlanta *Constitution,* April 28, February 2, April 28, and March 16, 1890; October 14, 1891; August 1, 1897; January 25 and October 14, 1891.

8. David A. Jasen and Gene Jones, *Spreadin' Rhythm Around: Black Popular Songwriters, 1880–1930* (New York, 1998), 1–10; Robert C. Toll, *Blacking Up: The Minstrel Show in Nineteenth-Century America* (New York, 1974); Nashville *Banner,* September 15, 1906; Union Springs (Ala.) *Herald,* June 13, 1900, and October 5, 1904. See also Atlanta *Constitution,* October 8, 1899, and May 26, 1901.

9. Jasen and Jones, *Spreadin' Rhythm,* 8–43; Eugene Levy, *James Weldon Johnson: Black Leader, Black Voice* (Chicago, 1973), 79–81; Atlanta *Constitution,* July 23, 1893.

10. Harlan, *Making,* 205–221.

11. *Story,* 71.

12. "An Article in the New York *World,* September 18, 1895," in *BTWP,* 4: 5 (quotation), 3–8 (description).

13. Ibid., 8–9.

14. The quotations from the Atlanta exposition speech in the following paragraphs are drawn from *Up,* 330–334.

15. "An Article in the New York *World,* September 18, 1895," in *BTWP,* 4: 3; second Howell quote from BTW to editor of New York World, September 19, 1895, ibid., 17; *Up,* 334.

16. "An Article in the New York *World,* September 20, 1895," in *BTWP,* 4: 15–17.

17. Chicago *Times-Herald,* December 12, 1895; Mary Elizabeth Preston Stearns to BTW, September 19, 1895; Ellen Collins to BTW, September 28, 1895, ibid., 90, 17–18, 33.

18. William Still to BTW and Samuel Laing Williams to BTW, September 19, 1895, ibid., 18–19; Edward Wilmot Blyden to BTW and William Edward Burghardt Du Bois to BTW, September 24, 1895, ibid., 26–27.

19. August Meier, *Negro Thought in America, 1880–1915* (Ann Arbor, 1963), 75–78.

20. Ibid., 80–82; Ida B. Wells-Barnett, *Crusade for Justice: The Autobiography of Ida B. Wells* (Chicago, 1970).

21. Timothy Thomas Fortune to BTW, September 26, 1895, in *BTWP,* 4: 31; Emma Lou Thornbrough, *T. Thomas Fortune: Militant Journalist* (Chicago, 1972), 162.

22. Meier, *Negro Thought,* 32, 36.

23. Redkey, *Black Exodus,* 231; Harlan, *Making,* 225–226, 344–346; Thornbrough, *Fortune,* 168–169; Francis James Grimké to BTW, November 7, 1895, in *BTWP,* 4: 74–75.

24. BTW to Francis James Grimké, November 27, 1895; Andrew F. Hilyer to BTW, March 28, 1896, in *BTWP,* 4: 85–86, 149–150.

6. The Rising People

1. Karl R. Wallace, "Booker T. Washington," in *A History and Criticism of American Public Address,* ed. William Norwood Brigance (New York, 1943), 407–432; "A Book Review by William Dean Howells, August 1901," in *BTWP,* 6: 194.

2. "An Excerpt from the Diary of Claude Gernade Bowers, October 20, 1897"; "An Article in *Our Day,* February 1896"; "An Address before the National Educational Association, July 10, 1896"; "A Speech at the Institute of Arts and Sciences, September 30, 1896"; "An Address at the Opening of the Armstrong-Slater Memorial Trade School, November 18, 1896," in *BTWP,* 4: 330–332, 124–125, 188–199, 211–223, 232–235.

3. Wallace, "Booker T. Washington," 420–421.

4. Max Bennett Thrasher, "Booker Washington's Personality," *Outlook,* November 9, 1901.

5. James Hardy Dillard quoted in *Selected Speeches of Booker T. Washington,* ed. E. Davidson Washington (Garden City, N.Y., 1932), xiv–xv.

6. "A Book Review by William Dean Howells, August 1901"; Atlanta *Constitu-*

tion, July 23, 1893; Caroline H. Pemberton, March 30, 1897, in *BTWP,* 4: 268–269.

7. "Excerpt from Diary of Claude Gernade Bowers, October 20, 1897," 331.

8. "An Open Letter to Benjamin Ryan Tillman, November 4, 1895," in *BTWP,* 4: 71–73.

9. Stephen Kantrowitz, *Ben Tillman and the Reconstruction of White Supremacy* (Chapel Hill, 2000), 217–222.

10. Robert Wesley Taylor to William Henry Baldwin, September 23, 1895; Baldwin to BTW, October 4, 1895; Washington *Post,* June 21, 1896; *Our Day,* June 1896, in *BTWP,* 4: 22–23, 47–48, 186, 187.

11. Washington *Evening Star,* March 18, 1896; *Our Day,* April 1896, ibid., 138–140, 124–125; information on American Federation of Labor, ibid., 351; John Stephens Durham to BTW, March 15, 1898, ibid., 389–391; "An Article in the *Southern States Farm Magazine,* January 1898," ibid., 374–375; BTW to Timothy Thomas Fortune, March 1, 1899, in *BTWP,* 5: 47.

12. "An Article in the *Southern States Farm Magazine,* January 1898," 376; Fred H. Matthews, *Quest for an American Sociology: Robert E. Park and the Chicago School* (Montreal, 1977), 63–64; BTW to Francis Jackson Garrison, May 20, 1905, in *BTWP,* 8: 287.

13. "A Speech at the Institute of Arts and Sciences, September 30, 1896"; "An Address before the National Educational Association, July 10, 1896"; "An Address before the Christian Endeavor Society, July 7, 1898," in *BTWP,* 4: 213–216, 189, 440–441.

14. Buffalo *Courier,* July 12, 1896; Chicago *Inter Ocean* December 20, 1897, ibid., 200, 353–354.

15. Fortune to BTW, December 31, 1896, ibid., 250.

16. C. Vann Woodward, *Origins of the New South, 1877–1913* (Baton Rouge, 1951), 262, 326; Robert J. Norrell, *Reaping the Whirlwind: The Civil Rights Movement in Tuskegee,* 2d ed. (Chapel Hill, 1998), 19–20; George Washington Albert Johnston to BTW, August 10, 1896, in *BTWP,* 4: 206–207.

17. BTW to Warren Logan, July 27, 1897; "A Speech at the Institute of Arts and Sciences, September 30, 1896"; William E. Benson to BTW, December 6, 1896, in *BTWP,* 4: 315–316, 215–216, 243–244.

18. Emmett J. Scott and Lyman Beecher Stowe, *Booker T. Washington: Builder of a Civilization* (Garden City, N.Y., 1916), 312–313.

19. "An Address at the Harvard University Alumni Dinner, June 24, 1896," in *BTWP,* 4: 183–185.

20. "A Speech at the Unveiling of the Robert Gould Shaw Monument, May 31, 1897," ibid., 285–289.

21. Thomas Junius Calloway to BTW, October 29, 1896; J. Francis Robinson to

BTW, June 6, 1897, ibid., 228–230, 293–294; Scott and Stowe, *Booker T. Washington,* 314–315.

22. Robert Lloyd Smith to BTW, July 9, 1897; Emmett Jay Scott to BTW, December 4, 1897; Robert Charles Bedford to BTW, August 26, 1897, in *BTWP,* 4: 295, 346, 321.

23. "A Sunday Evening Talk, February 10, 1895," in *BTWP,* 3: 508–515; "An Article in *The Independent,* January 27, February 3, 1898," in *BTWP,* 4: 366–374.

24. BTW to Emmett Jay Scott, August 23, 1898, in *BTWP,* 4: 456.

25. "To the Faculty Committee on the Course of Study, April 3, 1896," ibid., 154–155; BTW to Charles G. Harris, ibid., 281–282; BTW to William Jenkins, March 6 and 26, 1898, ibid., 386–387, 396; Jenkins to BTW, March 26, 1898, ibid., 397; Atlanta *Constitution,* March 8, 1896, and February 25, 1897; Allen W. Jones, "The Role of Tuskegee Institute in the Education of Black Farmers," *Journal of Negro History* 60 (April 1975): 252–267.

26. Collis Potter Huntington to BTW, October 28, 1898, in *BTWP,* 4: 409–410.

27. BTW to Charles Gordon Ames, February 29, 1896; BTW to Hollis Burke Frissell, March 19, 1891; Amory Howe Bradford to BTW, June 7, 1898; Collis Potter Huntington to BTW, November 14, 1898, ibid., 123, 392, 434, 511; "An Article in the New York *Evening Post,* May 29, 1909," in *BTWP,* 10: 122–126.

28. August Meier, *Negro Thought in America, 1880–1915* (Ann Arbor, 1963), 95–96; BTW to Hollis Burke Frissell, March 24, 1896; Henry Villard to BTW, June 28, 1897, in *BTWP,* 4: 141–143, 303–304.

29. New York *Times,* January 12, 1905; John Graham Brooks, *An American Citizen: The Life of William Henry Baldwin, Jr.* (Boston, 1910), 244–245; *Up,* 329; Baldwin to BTW, October 4, 1895, and December 4 and 8, 1898, in *BTWP,* 4: 47–48, 525–526, 528.

30. "An Account of Addresses by Washington and Mrs. Washington Delivered at Charleston, September 12, 1898," in *BTWP,* 4: 461–469.

31. BTW, *Black Belt Diamonds: Gems from the Speeches, Addresses, and Talks to Students* (New York, 1898), 5, 11, 36, 28, 115.

32. Ibid., 12, 22, 37, 50–51.

33. Ibid., 17, 54, 23, 58, 68, 58–59.

7. THE LION AND THE FOX

1. Philip Dray, *At the Hands of Persons Unknown: The Lynching of Black America* (New York, 2002), 3–15.

2. New York *Times,* October 13, 1898.

3. H. Leon Prather Jr., "We Have Taken a City: A Centennial Essay," in *De-*

mocracy Betrayed: The Wilmington Riot of 1898 and Its Legacy, ed. David S. Cecelski and Timothy B. Tyson (Chapel Hill, 1998), 15–42.

4. Ibid., 25.

5. Glenda E. Gilmore, "Murder, Memory, and the Flight of the Incubus," in Cecelski and Tyson, *Democracy Betrayed,* 84–85.

6. Prather, "We Have Taken a City," 30–39; James Benson Dudley to BTW, August 28, 1903, in *BTWP,* 7:271–272.

7. Stephen Kantrowitz, *Ben Tillman and the Reconstruction of White Supremacy* (Chapel Hill, 2000), 257.

8. BTW to John Davis Long, March 15, 1898; "An Address to the Christian Endeavor Society, July 7, 1898"; Horace Bumstead to BTW, September 7, 1898, in *BTWP,* 4: 389, 439, 461; Bernard C. Nalty, *Strength for the Fight: A History of Black Americans in the Military* (New York, 1986), 63–77; "An Address to the National Peace Jubilee, October 16, 1898," in *BTWP,* 4: 490–493.

9. "An Address to the National Peace Jubilee, October 16, 1898," 492.

10. Atlanta *Constitution,* October 18, 1898; Emmett Jay Scott to BTW, November 4, 1898, in *BTWP,* 4: 501–502.

11. Emma Lou Thornbrough, *T. Thomas Fortune: Militant Journalist* (Chicago, 1972), 182–186; New York *Times,* December 21, 1898; John Haley, "Race, Rhetoric, and Revolution," in Cecelski and Tyson, *Democracy Betrayed,* 210.

12. Washington *Post,* December 4, 1898.

13. Birmingham *Age-Herald,* November 13, 1898, in *BTWP,* 4: 508–509.

14. William Henry Baldwin to BTW, November 27 and December 4, 1898, ibid., 522, 525–526; Thornbrough, *Fortune,* 187; Fortune to BTW, September 5, 1899, in *BTWP,* 5: 195; J. M. Holland to BTW, December 20 and 21, 1898, in *BTWP,* 4: 542–544.

15. "An Address Welcoming President McKinley and Others to Tuskegee Institute, December 16, 1898," in *BTWP,* 4: 531; *Up,* 378–381.

16. Edward Henry Clement to BTW, January 2, 1899; Emmett Jay Scott to BTW, January 10, 1899; BTW to Fortune, April 4, 1899, in *BTWP,* 5: 5, 7–8, 70–71.

17. "An Article in the *A.M.E. Church Review,*" in *BTWP,* 3: 420; August Meier and Elliott Rudwick, "The Boycott Movement against Jim Crow Streetcars in the South, 1900–1906," in Meier and Rudwick, *Along the Color Line: Explorations in the Black Experience* (Urbana, 1976), 267–289.

18. Peter Jefferson Smith Jr. to BTW, April 28, 1899, in *BTWP,* 5: 93–94.

19. BTW to Fortune, March 1, 1899; "An Abraham Lincoln Memorial Address in Philadelphia, February 14, 1899," ibid., 46–47, 32–38.

20. Harlan, *Making,* 262; Atlanta *Constitution,* May 14, 1899; Birmingham *Age-Herald,* April 26, 1899; New York *Times,* May 11, 1899.

21. Atlanta *Constitution,* June 22, 1899; BTW, *The Future of the American Negro,* in *BTWP,* 5: 370–375.

22. Harlan, *Wizard,* 109.

23. Ibid., 116, 115.

24. Jacqueline Anne Rouse, "Out of the Shadow of Tuskegee: Margaret Murray Washington, Social Activism, and Race Vindication," *Journal of Negro History* 81 (Winter 1996): 31–46.

25. *Up,* 360–368; Francis J. Garrison to BTW, March 23, 1899; Margaret James Murray Washington to Francis Jackson Garrison, August 7, 1899, in *BTWP,* 5: 60–61, 169–170.

26. *Up,* 364; BTW to editor of Washington (D.C.) *Colored American,* June 1899, in *BTWP,* 5: 141–144.

27. *Up,* 365.

28. *Up,* 367.

29. Albert D. Kirwan, *Revolt of the Rednecks: Mississippi Politics, 1876–1925* (Lexington, Ky., 1951), 145–147; Atlanta *Constitution,* April 30 and August 27, 1899; Fortune to BTW, August 29, 1899, in *BTWP,* 5: 187–188.

30. Thornbrough, *Fortune,* 190; Theophile Tarence Allain to BTW, August 29, 1899, in *BTWP,* 5: 187–188; Fortune to BTW, August 25 and 28, 1899, ibid., 182–183, 185–186.

31. Fortune to BTW, September 16, 1899; BTW to Fortune, September 18, 1899, ibid., 207–209.

32. BTW to Fortune, September 16, 1899; BTW to Francis J. Garrison, September 23, 1899, ibid., 206, 211–212; Atlanta *Constitution,* September 3, 1899; William H. Councill, "The Future of the Negro," *Forum* 27 (1899): 570–577.

33. E. Davidson Washington, ed., *Selected Speeches of Booker T. Washington* (Garden City, N.Y., 1932), 78–86; Atlanta *Constitution,* October 13, 1899.

34. Sheldon Hackney, *From Populism to Progressivism in Alabama* (Princeton, 1969), 186–188.

35. Memphis *Commercial Appeal,* December 17, 1899, in *BTWP,* 5: 275–282.

8. THE TRAIN OF DISFRANCHISEMENT

1. Sheldon Hackney, *From Populism to Progressivism in Alabama* (Princeton, 1969), 147–179; quotation on 179.

2. J. Morgan Kousser, *The Shaping of Southern Politics: Suffrage Restrictions and the Shaping of the One-Party South, 1880–1910* (New Haven, 1974), 152–165; "An Open Letter to the Louisiana Constitutional Convention, February 19, 1898," in *BTWP,* 4: 381–384; BTW to Warren Easton, May 15, 1900, in *BTWP,* 5: 523–525.

3. Edgar Dean Crumpacker to BTW, November 7, 1899, in *BTWP*, 5: 258–259; Michael Perman, *Struggle for Mastery: Disfranchisement in the South, 1888–1908* (Chapel Hill, 2001), 225–230.

4. Joseph Eugene Ransdell to BTW, January 24, 1900; Fortune to BTW, February 20, 1900, in *BTWP*, 5: 421–422, 444–445.

5. Atlanta *Constitution,* November 10, 1899; BTW to Fortune, November 10, 1899; BTW to Francis J. Garrison, November 29, 1899, in *BTWP*, 5: 260, 273.

6. Robert Volney Riser II, "Prelude to the Movement: Disfranchisement in Alabama's Constitution and the Anti-Disfranchisement Cases" (Ph.D. diss., University of Alabama, 2005), 273–278; Louis R. Harlan, "The Secret Life of Booker T. Washington," in *Booker T. Washington in Perspective: Essays of Louis R. Harlan,* ed. Raymond Smock (Jackson, Miss., 1988), 113–114.

7. *Race Problems of the South: Report of the Proceedings of the First Annual Conference Held under the Auspices of the Southern Society for Promotion of the Study of Race Conditions* (Richmond, 1900), 42, 178.

8. Ibid., 50, 55, 52.

9. Ibid., 52.

10. BTW to Emily Howland, June 19, 1900, in *BTWP*, 5: 562–563.

11. BTW to Ellen Collins, January 9, 1901, in *BTWP*, 13: 499.

12. Atlanta *Constitution,* May 27, 1900; John Roach Staton, "Will Education Solve the Race Problem?" *North American Review* 70 (June 1900): 785–801; BTW, "A Reply," ibid., 71 (August 1900): 221–232.

13. Nashville *American,* May 4, 1900; Washington *Post,* February 12, 1902; James D. Anderson, *The Education of Blacks in the South, 1860–1935* (Chapel Hill, 1988), 96; Louis R. Harlan, *Separate and Unequal: Public School Campaigns and Racism in the Southern Seaboard States, 1901–1915* (1958; reprint, New York, 1968), 70; Ray Stannard Baker, *Along the Color Line: An Account of Negro Citizenship in the American Democracy* (New York, 1908), 241; Atlanta *Constitution,* July 7, 1901.

14. Harlan, *Separate and Unequal,* 75–80; Harlan, *Wizard,* 187; Harlan, *Making,* 298–299.

15. Atlanta *Constitution,* April 25, 1901.

16. BTW to Hollis Burke Frissell, November 1, 1901, in *BTWP*, 6: 283–284; Harlan, *Wizard,* 190–193; Harlan, *Separate and Unequal,* 85–89.

17. William H. Baldwin to BTW, August 10, 1903, in *BTWP*, 7: 259–261.

18. Oswald Garrison Villard to Francis Jackson Garrison, May 16, 1902, in *BTWP*, 6: 465–466.

19. Max Bennett Thrasher, "Booker Washington's Personality," *Outlook,* November 9, 1901; New York *Times,* November 9, 20, and 23, 1900; "Extracts from an Address at a Dinner for Oliver Otis Howard, November 8, 1900";

BTW to Emmett Jay Scott, November 23, 24, 1900; BTW to editor of Montgomery *Advertiser,* November 24, 1900; BTW to editor of Atlanta *Constitution,* November 26, 1900, in *BTWP,* 5: 670–672, 678–679, 681–685.

20. Harlan, *Wizard,* 213.

21. Francis Jackson Garrison to Oswald Garrison Villard, February 11, 1906, in *BTWP,* 8: 518–520; William H. Holtzclaw, *The Black Man's Burden* (1915; reprint, New York, 1970).

22. Louis R. Harlan, "Booker T. Washington and the White Man's Burden," in Smock, *Booker T. Washington in Perspective,* 83.

23. Beno von Herman auf Wain to BTW, September 3, 1900; BTW to von Herman auf Wain, September 20, 1900, in *BTWP,* 5: 633–636, 639–642.

24. Harlan, "Washington and White Man's Burden," 75–77.

25. Riser, "Prelude to the Movement," 70, 78, 103.

26. "A Petition to the Members of the Alabama Constitutional Convention, May 28, 1901," in *BTWP,* 6: 129–133; Riser, "Prelude to the Movement," 112.

27. Riser, "Prelude to the Movement," 97–98; Malcolm Cook McMillan, *Constitutional Development in Alabama: A Study in Politics, the Negro, and Sectionalism* (Chapel Hill, 1955), 305.

28. Perman, *Struggle for Mastery,* 186; McMillan, *Constitutional Development in Alabama,* 228, 264.

29. George Washington Campbell to BTW, June 4, 1901; BTW to Thomas Wilkes Coleman, June 4, 1901; Hilary Abner Herbert to BTW, June 7, 1901, in *BTWP,* 6: 143–145, 152–153; Riser, "Prelude to the Movement," 251; Washington *Post,* June 4, 1901; Thomas Goode Jones to BTW, June 10, 1901, in *BTWP,* 6: 154–155.

30. Riser, "Prelude to the Movement," 294.

31. *Official Proceedings of the Constitutional Convention of the State of Alabama 1901,* vol. 2 (Montgomery, 1901), 1437; Joseph Oswalt Thompson to BTW, September 3, 1903, in *BTWP,* 7: 277.

32. Horace Mann Bond, *Negro Education in Alabama: A Study in Cotton and Steel* (1939; reprint, New York, 1969), 190.

33. Hackney, *Populism to Progressivism in Alabama,* 205.

34. Riser, "Prelude to the Movement," 362; Thomas Goode Jones to BTW, September 20, 1901; BTW to Jones, September 23, 1901, in *BTWP,* 6: 213–216.

9. THE LEOPARD'S SPOTS

1. "An Article in the *Southern States Farm Magazine,* January 1898," in *BTWP,* 4: 374–377; BTW to editor of Washington *Colored American,* May 4, 1900, in *BTWP,* 5: 496; "An Item in the Boston *Transcript,* January 6, 1900," ibid.,

403–405; BTW to Francis Jackson Garrison, May 20, 1905, in *BTWP,* 8: 287–288.

2. Atlanta *Constitution,* May 29, 1900; March 1, 14, 23, July 1, and November 15, 1901.

3. Lafayette (Ala.) *Sun,* October 2, 1901; S. A. Steele to Paul Barringer, n.d. [1900], Paul Barringer Papers, University of Virginia Library, Charlottesville.

4. BTW to Randall O. Simpson, October 22, 1903, in *BTWP,* 7: 302–304; BTW to Louis G. Gregory, January 19, 1904, ibid., 401–403; Cleveland *Gazette,* September 12, 1903, in *BTWP,* 5: 599–600.

5. "The Awakening of the Negro," *Atlantic Monthly,* September 1896, 322–328; "The Case of the Negro," ibid., November 1899, 577–587; Walter Hines Page to BTW, December 31, 1899, in *BTWP,* 5: 296–297; Carla Willard, "Timing Impossible Subjects: The Marketing Style of Booker T. Washington," *American Quarterly,* December 2001, 624–669.

6. BTW, *The Future of the American Negro,* in *BTWP,* 5: 345, 340, 335.

7. Ibid., 359, 374.

8. *Story,* 14, 12.

9. Lyman Abbott to BTW, December 9, 1899, in *BTWP,* 5: 288; information on Madison Square Garden meeting, ibid., 284.

10. *Up,* 215–216.

11. *Up,* 254–255, 259.

12. *Up,* 266, 340.

13. *Up,* 323, 347, 321, 232, 294, 229, 347.

14. *Up,* 254–255, 235, 297, 297, 338.

15. James Cox, "Washington and Autobiography," *Sewanee Review* 85 (Spring 1977): 235–261; *Up,* 279, 284, 290.

16. Barrett Wendell to BTW, April 12, 1901, in *BTWP,* 6: 87; Harlan, *Making,* 248.

17. Harlan, *Wizard,* 277–278.

18. George Eastman to BTW, January 2, 1902, in *BTWP,* 6: 370; Belton Gilreath to BTW, April 24, 1901, ibid., 94; Harlan, *Wizard,* 130–131; BTW to E. Julia Emery, February 27, 1903, in *BTWP,* 7: 100–101; Harlan, *Wizard,* 133–134.

19. "A Book Review by William Dean Howells, August 1901," in *BTWP,* 6: 194, 198.

20. "A Book Review by William Edward Burghardt Du Bois, July 16, 1901," ibid., 176–177.

21. W. E. B. Du Bois, *Results of Ten Tuskegee Negro Conferences* (Tuskegee, 1901), 1–2.

22. For background on Du Bois, see David Levering Lewis, *W. E. B. Du Bois:*

Biography of a Race, 1868–1919 (New York, 1993); Harlan, *Making,* 256–258; Harlan, *Wizard,* 50–51.

23. Du Bois to BTW, February 17 and 26, 1900, in *BTWP,* 5: 443, 450; Lewis, *Du Bois,* 233–234; William A. Pledger to BTW and Fortune to BTW, March 16, 1900; Du Bois to BTW, April 10, 1900, in *BTWP,* 5: 465–466, 480. David Lewis makes much of Washington's request that Du Bois not use the original letter of recommendation after Washington said that he had written the second letter. Washington said that use of the first letter would have made Du Bois look overly anxious for the job. Lewis insists that this is evidence of Washington's betrayal of Du Bois, but he presents no hard evidence. It is quite likely that Du Bois had already forwarded the letter to the school system. Washington's announced reason for making the request is as plausible as Lewis's belief that Booker was double-crossing Du Bois. Lewis, *Du Bois,* 236–237.

24. Lewis, *Du Bois,* 244–245, 634–635; BTW to Robert Lincoln, January 2 and October 28, 1903, in *BTWP,* 7: 3, 312–313.

25. William Ivy Hair, *Carnival of Fury: Robert Charles and the New Orleans Race Riot of 1900* (Baton Rouge, 1976); Seth M. Scheiner, *Negro Mecca: A History of the Negro in New York City, 1865–1920* (New York, 1965), 121–125.

26. John Howard Burrows, *The Necessity of Myth: A History of the National Negro Business League* (Auburn, Ala., 1988).

27. BTW to Emmett Jay Scott, July 21, 1900, in *BTWP,* 5: 589.

28. W. E. B. Du Bois, "The Conservation of Races," in *The Oxford W. E. B. Du Bois Reader,* ed. Eric J. Sundquist (New York, 1996), 46; Du Bois, *The Philadelphia Negro* (Philadelphia, 1899).

29. W. E. B. Du Bois, "Jefferson Davis as a Representative of Civilization," in Sundquist, *Oxford Du Bois Reader,* 244; Du Bois, "The Conservation of Races," 44.

30. "An Address before the National Educational Association, July 10, 1896," in *BTWP,* 4: 194; BTW to George Washington Taylor, July 5, 1904, in *BTWP,* 8: 4–5.

31. S. P. Fullinwider, *The Mind and Mood of Black America* (Homewood, Ill., 1969), 47–71; Arnold Rampersad, *The Art and Imagination of W. E. B. Du Bois* (Cambridge, Mass., 1976), 69–87.

32. Paul B. Barringer, *The American Negro: His Past and Future* (Raleigh, N.C., 1900), 5, 13–14; Charles Carroll, *The Negro a Beast . . .* (St. Louis, 1900); William P. Calhoun, *The Caucasian and the Negro in the United States. They Must Separate. If Not, Then Extermination. A Proposed Solution: Colonization* (Columbia, S.C., 1901). For examples of racial bigotry in articles in just one jour-

nal, see, in *North American Review,* Marion L. Dawson, "The South and the Negro" (February 1902); Clarence H. Poe, "Suffrage Restriction in the South: Its Causes and Consequences" (October 1902); Henderson M. Somerville, "Some Co-operating Causes of Negro Lynching" (October 1903); Thomas Nelson Page, "The Lynching of Negroes—Its Cause and Its Prevention" (January 1904); William Garrott Brown, "The White Peril: The Immediate Danger of the Negro" (October 1904). See also Alfred Holt Stone, *Studies in the American Race Problem* (New York, 1908).

33. John David Smith, *Black Judas: William Hannibal Thomas and* The American Negro (Athens, Ga., 2000), 174–176, 191–195.

34. Atlanta *Constitution,* March 3, 1901; Smith, *Black Judas,* 192.

35. "A Book Review in *Outlook,* March 30, 1901," in *BTWP,* 6: 69–75; Smith, *Black Judas,* 197; Robert Wesley Taylor to BTW, January 29, 1901, in *BTWP,* 6: 24–25.

36. Joel Williamson, *The Crucible of Race: Black-White Relations in the American South since Emancipation* (New York, 1984), 151–158.

37. Thomas Dixon Jr., *The Leopard's Spots: A Romance of the White Man's Burden, 1865–1900* (New York, 1902), 244, 263.

38. Information on book sales in *BTWP,* 1: xxxiv.

10. The Violence of Their Imagination

1. Theodore Roosevelt to BTW, September 14, 1901, in *BTWP,* 5: 206; William H. Harbaugh, *The Life and Times of Theodore Roosevelt* (1961; reprint, New York, 1975), 132–135, 140–144; John Morton Blum, *The Republican Roosevelt* (Cambridge, Mass., 1954), 46.

2. Thomas G. Dyer, *Theodore Roosevelt and the Idea of Race* (Baton Rouge, 1980), 103–116.

3. Willard B. Gatewood Jr., *Theodore Roosevelt and the Art of Controversy: Episodes of the White House Years* (Baton Rouge, 1970), 24.

4. Dyer, *Roosevelt and Idea of Race,* 89–100; Timothy Thomas Fortune to BTW, April 6, 1899, in *BTWP,* 5: 75.

5. Roosevelt to BTW, September 24, 1901, in *BTWP,* 6: 218–219.

6. Robert Volney Riser II, "Prelude to the Movement: Disfranchisement in Alabama's Constitution and the Anti-Disfranchisement Cases" (Ph.D. diss., University of Alabama, 2005), 375; Oscar Richard Hundley to BTW, October 5, 1901; William Calvin Oates to BTW, October 2, 1901; BTW to Roosevelt, October 2, 1901; BTW to Timothy Thomas Fortune, February 8, 1902, in *BTWP,* 6: 231, 222–223, 221, 394.

7. Riser, "Prelude to the Movement," 395.

8. Harlan, *Making,* 312; Gatewood, *Roosevelt and Art of Controversy,* 32; BTW to Charles Waddell Chesnutt, July 7, 1903, in *BTWP,* 7: 196–198.

9. Harlan, *Making,* 313.

10. Emmett Jay Scott to BTW, October 17, 1901; William Reuben Pettiford to BTW, October 24, 1901, in *BTWP,* 6: 250, 259, 269–271; New York *Times,* October 21, 1901; Washington *Post,* October 22, 1901.

11. Dewey W. Grantham Jr., "Dinner at the White House: Theodore Roosevelt, Booker T. Washington, and the South," *Tennessee Historical Quarterly* 18 (June 1958): 117; William F. Holmes, *The White Chief: James Kimble Vardaman* (Baton Rouge, 1970), 99; newspaper clipping, provenance unclear, Papers of Booker T. Washington, reel 718, Library of Congress; Nashville *American,* October 23, 1901; Chicago *Tribune,* October 19, 1901.

12. Birmingham *Age-Herald,* October 20, 1901; Chicago *Daily Tribune,* October 22, 1901; New Orleans *Times Democrat* quoted in Chicago *Tribune,* October 19, 1901; Grantham, "Dinner at the White House," 116–118; Riser, "Prelude to the Movement," 398.

13. Samuel Courtney to BTW, October 27, 1901; William H. Ferris to BTW, [January 1902], in *BTWP,* 6: 280–281, 384–386.

14. Edgar Gardner Murphy to BTW, October 19, 23, and 24, 1901, ibid., 256, 262, 271–272.

15. Atlanta *Constitution,* October 24, 1901.

16. Emmett J. Scott and Lyman Beecher Stowe, *Booker T. Washington: Builder of a Civilization* (Garden City, N.Y., 1916), 117–118.

17. BTW to Roosevelt, October 26, 1901; William Baldwin to BTW, November 21, 1901, in *BTWP,* 6: 274, 321; Washington *Post,* October 22, 1901.

18. Riser, "Prelude to the Movement," 405; Nashville *American,* October 24, 1901.

19. Grantham, "Dinner at the White House," 122–125; Gatewood, *Roosevelt and Art of Controversy,* 36–44; New York *Times,* October 27, 1901.

20. Washington *Post,* November 10, 1901; Birmingham *Age-Herald,* January 27–29 and 31, February 1, and March 12, 1903; Grantham, "Dinner at the White House," 116–118; Gatewood, *Roosevelt and Art of Controversy,* 35–40.

21. BTW to D. Robert Wilkins, May 19, 1904, in *BTWP,* 7: 508–509; Washington *Post,* December 8, 1901; BTW to Whitefield McKinlay, December 17, 1901, in *BTWP,* 6: 352.

22. Emma Lou Thornbrough, *T. Thomas Fortune: Militant Journalist* (Chicago, 1972), 226; BTW to Roosevelt, November 6, 1901; BTW to Whitefield McKinlay, November 6, 1901, in *BTWP,* 6: 289–293.

23. William Baldwin to BTW, February 10, 1902, in *BTWP,* 6: 399; Atlanta *Con-*

stitution, June 23, 1902; BTW to Emmett Jay Scott, June 23, 1902, in *BTWP,* 6: 487.

24. Harlan, *Wizard,* 9–10; BTW to Roosevelt, September 27, 1902, in *BTWP,* 6: 527.

25. Harlan, *Wizard,* 11–13.

26. Gatewood, *Roosevelt and Art of Controversy,* 74.

27. Riser, "Prelude to the Movement," 484–485; Birmingham *Age-Herald,* November 28, 1902.

28. Gatewood, *Roosevelt and Art of Controversy,* 112.

29. Riser, "Prelude to the Movement," 484–485.

30. Atlanta *Constitution,* March 25, 1903; New York *Times,* February 15, 24, and 25, 1903; *Congressional Record,* 57th Cong., 2d sess., vol. 36 (1903), 2515.

31. BTW to Roosevelt, December 1 and 16, 1902, in *BTWP,* 6: 600–601, 612; BTW to Roosevelt, February 3, 1903, in *BTWP,* 7: 27–28; Harlan, *Wizard,* 20–22.

32. Edgar Gardner Murphy to BTW, January 31, 1903; William Baldwin to BTW, February 16, 1903; Robert Ogden to BTW, February 25, 1903; BTW to Ogden, March 2, 1903, in *BTWP,* 7: 16–17, 79, 97, 103.

33. Atlanta *Constitution,* January 13, 1903; Scott and Stowe, *Booker T. Washington,* 314–315.

34. Riser, "Prelude to the Movement," 426–465.

11. The Warring Ideals

1. Emmett J. Scott and Lyman Beecher Stowe, *Booker T. Washington: Builder of a Civilization* (Garden City, N.Y., 1916), 314–315; Stephen R. Fox, *The Guardian of Boston: William Monroe Trotter* (New York, 1970), 34–38; Roscoe Conkling Bruce to BTW, February 8 and 22, 1902, in *BTWP,* 6: 396, 408–410.

2. Fox, *The Guardian of Boston,* 39–42.

3. Ibid., 37; Boston *Guardian,* December 6, 13, and 27, 1902; January 10, 1903; July 26, September 27, October 4, and November 1 and 22, 1902.

4. Roscoe Conkling Bruce to BTW, February 22, 1902, in *BTWP,* 6: 408–410; Boston *Guardian,* September 27 and October 25, 1902; March 25, 1903.

5. Boston *Guardian,* October 4, 1902; BTW to Fortune, November 6, 1902, in *BTWP,* 6: 577–578.

6. Adam Clayton Powell to BTW, September 13, 1902; Edwin B. Jourdain to Emmett Jay Scott, August 19, 1902, in *BTWP,* 6: 508–509, 502–505.

7. Charles Fleischer to BTW, February 11, 1903; BTW to Charles Fleischer, February 17, 1903, in *BTWP,* 7: 66–68, 81–83.

8. Emma Lou Thornbrough, *T. Thomas Fortune: Militant Journalist* (Chicago,

1972), 227–229; Boston *Guardian,* July 26, 1902; Du Bois to BTW, November 22, 1902; BTW to Du Bois, November 28, 1902, in *BTWP,* 6: 590, 597–598; BTW to Robert Lincoln, January 2, 1903, in *BTWP,* 7: 3.

9. Washington *Post,* February 3, 1903; Richard W. Thompson to Scott, February 4, 1903; BTW to Du Bois, February 12, 1903; BTW to Alexander Walters, February 13, 1903; BTW to Alexander Walters, February 26, 1903, in *BTWP,* 7: 71–74, 98.

10. Lavinia Hartwell Egan to BTW, February 9, 1903; "A Statement by Louise Hadley in the Philadelphia *North American,* June 7, 1903," in *BTWP,* 7: 63–64, 173–175.

11. "Stirring Up the Fires of Race Antipathy," *South Atlantic Quarterly* 2 (October 1903): 297–305; Joel Williamson, *The Crucible of Race: Black-White Relations in the American South since Emancipation* (New York, 1984), 262–263.

12. Henry Y. Warnock, "Andrew Sledd, Southern Methodists, and the Negro: A Case History," *Journal of Southern History* 31 (August 1965): 258.

13. BTW to Bliss Perry, August 23, 1902, in *BTWP,* 6: 506.

14. BTW to Oswald Garrison Villard, April 21 and July 9, 1903, in *BTWP,* 7: 124, 204.

15. George Washington Carver to BTW, November 28, 1902; Robert Charles Bedford to BTW, December 3 and 8, 1902, in *BTWP,* 6: 595–597, 602–604, 608–610.

16. *Larger Education,* 444–445.

17. Arthur O. White, "Booker T. Washington's Florida Incident, 1903–1904," *Florida Historical Quarterly* 51 (January 1973): 227–249; Harlan, *Wizard,* 251; "An Article by J. Douglas Wetmore, February 8, 1903," in *BTWP,* 7: 56–60.

18. New York *Times,* April 15, 1903.

19. Andrew Carnegie to William Baldwin, April 17, 1903, in *BTWP,* 7: 120.

20. Atlanta *Constitution,* May 17, 1903; Washington *Post,* April 30, 1903; Gordon Macdonald to editor of Washington *Post,* April 28, 1903, in *BTWP,* 7: 132–135.

21. Boston *Guardian,* April 25, May 2, 9, and 23, and June 13, 1903.

22. S. P. Fullinwider, *The Mind and Mood of Black America* (Homewood, Ill., 1969), 47–71.

23. W. E. B. Du Bois, *The Souls of Black Folk,* in *Three Negro Classics* (New York, 1965), 213–221, 240–252.

24. Ibid., 283–284.

25. New York *Times,* July 3, 1903; Thornbrough, *Fortune,* 245–246.

26. Thornbrough, *Fortune,* 246; Fox, *The Guardian of Boston,* 48–49.

27. BTW to editor of Brooklyn *Eagle,* July 9, 1903; "An Interview of Edward H.

Morris in the Chicago *Inter Ocean,* July 28, 1903," in *BTWP,* 7: 204–205, 226–227.

28. W. Allison Sweeney to Emmett Jay Scott, July 17, 1903; R. C. Black [Emmett Jay Scott] to J. C. May [Wilford H. Smith], July 23, 1903; Smith to Scott, June 3, 1903, ibid. 212–213, 219, 166–167.

29. Harlan, *Wizard,* 44–46; "An Account of the Boston Riot in the Boston *Globe,* July 31, 1903," in *BTWP,* 7: 229–240.

30. "A Statement in the Boston *Globe,* July 31, 1903"; "An Account of the Boston Riot, July 31, 1903," in *BTWP,* 7: 240–243.

31. "A Press Release, August 8, 1903," ibid., 258.

32. New York *Times,* May 21, 1903; Atlanta *Constitution,* June 19, 1903; BTW to Walter Hines Page, June 11, 1903, in *BTWP,* 7: 176–177.

33. Albert D. Kirwan, *Revolt of the Rednecks: Mississippi Politics: 1876–1925* (Lexington, Ky., 1951), 146–161; Atlanta *Constitution,* August 25 and 29, 1903.

34. BTW to Oswald Garrison Villard, August 31, 1903, in *BTWP,* 7: 273.

35. Baldwin to BTW, August 10, 1903, ibid., 260.

36. Harlan, *Wizard,* 282–283.

12. The Tuskegee Machine

1. BTW to Hollis Burke Frissell, November 3, 1903; BTW to Theodore Roosevelt, September 15 and October 20, 1903, in *BTWP,* 7: 325, 284–285, 297.

2. BTW to T. Thomas Fortune, September 10, 1903, ibid., 280.

3. BTW to Emmett Jay Scott, August 29, 1903, ibid., 272; Stephen R. Fox, *The Guardian of Boston: William Monroe Trotter* (New York, 1970), 38.

4. Fox, *The Guardian of Boston,* 62–63; Horace Bumstead to BTW, December 5, 1903; BTW to Robert C. Ogden, October 10, 1903; BTW to Hollis Burke Frissell, November 3, 1903, in *BTWP,* 7: 360, 298, 325.

5. Charles Waddell Chesnutt to BTW, May 2, 1903; BTW to Chesnutt, July 7, 1903; Chesnutt to BTW, August 11, 1903, in *BTWP,* 7: 136, 196–198, 262–264.

6. Archibald Henry Grimké to BTW, June 6, 1903, ibid., 170–171.

7. Kelly Miller, "Washington's Policy," in *Booker T. Washington and His Critics,* ed. Hugh Hawkins (Lexington, Mass., 1974), 87–94.

8. Archibald Henry Grimké to BTW, June 6, 1903, in *BTWP,* 7: 171.

9. BTW to Hollis Burke Frissell, November 3, 1903; "An Extract from the Proceedings of the Washington Conference of the National Sociological Society, November 10, 1903," in *BTWP,* 7: 325, 340–342.

10. Harlan, *Wizard,* 70.

11. "Summary of the Proceedings of the Conference at Carnegie Hall, January 6, 7, 8, 1904," in *BTWP,* 7: 384–387; David Levering Lewis, *W. E. B. Du Bois: Biography of a Race, 1868–1919* (New York, 1993), 308.

12. Harlan, *Wizard,* 75–76.

13. Louis G. Gregory to BTW, January 15, 1904; Cyrus Field Adams to BTW, January [ca. 18], 1904; BTW to Fortune, January 19, 1904, in *BTWP,* 7: 391–392, 397–398, 400–401; Lewis, *Du Bois,* 309–311.

14. Charles William Anderson to BTW, January 26, 1904, in *BTWP,* 7: 413–414.

15. Robert Volney Riser II, "Prelude to the Movement: Disfranchisement in Alabama's Constitution and the Anti-Disfranchisement Cases" (Ph.D. diss., University of Alabama, 2005), 506, 508.

16. Chesnutt to BTW, May 2, 1903, in *BTWP,* 7: 136–137; Riser, "Prelude to the Movement," 540–562.

17. BTW to Wilford H. Smith, February 2 and June 16, 1904, in *BTWP,* 7: 423, 534.

18. Pete Daniel, *The Shadow of Slavery: Peonage in the South, 1901–1969* (Urbana, 1990), 3–64; BTW to Oswald Garrison Villard, July 9, 1903, in *BTWP,* 7: 204.

19. Thomas Goode Jones to BTW, August 17, 1903, in *BTWP,* 7: 268–269.

20. "An Address before the National Afro-American Council, July 2, 1903," ibid., 188.

21. BTW to William H. Baldwin, October 28 and December 3, 1903; BTW to Francis Jackson Garrison, February 22, 1904, ibid., 313, 357, 446.

22. BTW to William Demosthenes Crum, February 19, 1904; Ellen A. Craft Crum to BTW, April 15, 1904, ibid., 444, 481.

23. New York *Times,* April 29, 1904.

24. *Leslie's Weekly,* February 4, 1904.

25. Edgar Gardner Murphy to Robert C. Ogden, March 8, 1904, Robert C. Ogden Papers, box 7, Library of Congress.

26. Newspaper clipping, Papers of Booker T. Washington, reel 719, Library of Congress; Washington *Post,* October 17, August 7, and June 13, 1904.

27. Washington *Post,* March 13 and May 20, 1904; New York *Times,* May 21, 1904.

28. BTW to James Sullivan Clarkson, January 18, June 14 and 17, 1904; BTW to Henry Clay Payne, February 24, 1904; BTW to William Howard Taft, June 11, 1904, in *BTWP,* 7: 394–395, 532, 534, 450–451, 529–530.

29. Harlan, *Wizard,* 24; Emma Lou Thornbrough, *T. Thomas Fortune: Militant Journalist* (Chicago, 1972), 258; "A Fragment of an Address at the Metropolitan A. M. E. Church, March 18, 1904," in *BTWP,* 7: 468–476; Charles William Anderson to BTW, May 25 and 27, 1904, ibid., 513–516; Harlan, *Wizard,* 25.

30. Harlan, *Wizard*, 25–26; BTW to Emmett Jay Scott, November 28, 1904; Roosevelt to BTW, August 18, 1904, in *BTWP*, 8: 148, 51; Chicago *Tribune*, July 9, 1904.

31. C. Vann Woodward, *Tom Watson: Agrarian Rebel* (New York, 1938), 380; New York *Times*, September 2, 1904.

32. BTW to Roosevelt, July 29, August 24 and 27, 1904, in *BTWP*, 8: 34–35, 57–58; Dallas *Morning News*, October 13, 1904; BTW to Charles William Anderson, August 15, 1904, in *BTWP*, 8: 49–50.

33. Lafayette (Ala.) *Sun*, October 5, 1904; newspaper clippings, Heflin Scrapbook 6, J. Thomas Heflin Papers, box 848, Gorgas Library, University of Alabama, Tuscaloosa; Atlanta *Constitution*, September 16, 1904; BTW to editor of Chattanooga *Times*, September 21, 1904, in *BTWP*, 8: 71; Malcolm C. McMillan, *Constitutional Development in Alabama, 1798–1901: A Study in Politics, the Negro, and Sectionalism* (Chapel Hill, 1955), 305; Montgomery *Advertiser*, October 4, 1904; undated Tuskegee *News* article reprinted in Nashville *American*, October 19, 1904.

34. Washington *Post*, November 6, 1904; BTW to N. P. T. Finch, October 24, 1904, in *BTWP*, 8: 108–109.

13. The Assault by the Toms

1. New York *Times*, November 19, 1904; BTW to William Elroy Curtis, April 13, 1905, in *BTWP*, 8: 258.

2. Atlanta *Constitution*, January 4, 1905; BTW to James Griswold Merrill and BTW to John Campbell Dancy, March 14, 1905, in *BTWP*, 8: 216–217; Neal L. Anderson to BTW, April 14, 1905; BTW to Charles Betts Galloway, April 15, 1905, ibid., 259–261; Harlan, *Wizard*, 137–138.

3. New York *Times*, January 12, 1905; John Graham Books, *An American Citizen: The Life of William Henry Baldwin, Jr.* (Boston, 1910), 244–245.

4. Harlan, *Wizard*, 194–197; BTW to Oswald Garrison Villard, July 10, 1905, in *BTWP*, 8: 322; New York *Times*, January 20, 1904; *Leslie's Weekly*, February 4, 1904.

5. BTW to William H. Baldwin, January 22, May 19, and March 12, 1904; BTW to Samuel Abbott Green, January 21, 1904, in *BTWP*, 7: 409–411, 505, 467, 405; BTW to Hollis Burke Frissell, July 18, 1906, in *BTWP*, 9: 43; Louis R. Harlan, *Separate and Unequal: Public School Campaigns and Racism in the Southern Seaboard States, 1901–1915* (1958; reprint, New York, 1968), 254–256; John Hope to BTW, November 29, 1906; BTW to Hope, December 13, 1906, in *BTWP*, 9: 150, 164–165.

6. Edgar Gardner Murphy to Robert C. Ogden, March 8, 1904, Robert C. Ogden

Papers, box 7, Library of Congress; Ruperth Fehnstoke [S. Becker von Gra-bil], *Letters from Tuskegee, Being the Confessions of a Yankee* (Montgomery, Ala., 1905).

7. Emmett Jay Scott to BTW, March 17 and April 20, 1905; BTW to Richard Massey, May 29, 1905, in *BTWP,* 8: 219, 264–265, 291–292.

8. *Official Proceedings of the Constitutional Convention of the State of Alabama, 1901,* vol. 2 (Montgomery, 1901), 1437; Joseph Oswalt Thompson to BTW, September 3, 1903, in *BTWP,* 7: 277; BTW to Ernest W. Thompson, December 15, 1906; BTW to Braxton Bragg Comer, January 19, 1907, in *BTWP,* 9: 166–167, 192–194; Harlan, *Wizard,* 167–169.

9. Boston *Guardian,* March 12 and May 21, 1904; BTW to John Asbury, February 22, 1904; BTW to Edward Elder Cooper, April 28, 1904, in *BTWP,* 7: 445, 488–489; BTW to Robert Curtis Ogden, August 9, 1904, in *BTWP,* 8: 42–43; August Meier, "Booker T. Washington and the Negro Press: With Special Reference to the *Colored American Magazine,*" *Journal of Negro History* 28 (January 1953): 67–90.

10. BTW to Timothy Thomas Fortune, November 5, 1903; BTW to Baldwin, January 19, 1904; BTW to Fortune, January 27, 1904, in *BTWP,* 7: 333, 400, 416.

11. Fortune to Emmett Jay Scott, February 15, 1904, ibid., 440–441.

12. *Voice of the Negro* 1 (December 1904): 618; Louis R. Harlan, "Booker T. Washington and the *Voice of the Negro,* 1904–1907," *Journal of Southern History* 45 (February 1979): 45–62; BTW to John Wesley Edward Bowen, December 27, 1904, in *BTWP,* 8: 167–168.

13. W. E. B. Du Bois to Oswald Garrison Villard, March 24, 1905; Francis Jackson Garrison to Villard, April 9, 1905; Villard to Du Bois, April 18, 1905, in *BTWP,* 8: 224–242, 251–252, 261–263.

14. Francis Jackson Garrison to BTW, May 8, 1905, ibid., 274.

15. David Levering Lewis, *W. E. B. Du Bois: Biography of a Race, 1868–1919* (New York, 1993), 321; Harlan, "Washington and *Voice of the Negro.*"

16. Wilkes-Barre *Times,* June 8, 1905; Emma L. Thornbrough, "Booker T. Washington as Seen by His White Contemporaries," *Journal of Negro History* 53 (April 1968): 161–182.

17. *Tom Watson's Magazine,* June 1905, 392–393; C. Vann Woodward, *Tom Watson: Agrarian Rebel* (New York, 1938), 380.

18. BTW to editor of Columbia (S.C.) *State,* July 8, 1905, in *BTWP,* 8: 319–320.

19. Atlanta *Journal,* June 9, 1905, Papers of Booker T. Washington, reel 433, Library of Congress.

20. Thomas Dixon Jr., "Booker T. Washington and the Negro: Some Dangerous Aspects of the Work of Tuskegee," *Saturday Evening Post,* August 19, 1905.

21. Editorial, Montgomery *Advertiser,* August 16, 1905; BTW to editor of Montgomery *Advertiser,* in *BTWP,* 8: 341–344.

22. Kansas City *Star,* August 14, 1905; Nashville *Banner,* August 15, 1905; Columbus *Ledger,* August 22, 23, and 25, 1905; Belleville (Ill.) *News-Democrat,* August 18, 1905; BTW to Charles William Anderson, September 13, 1905, in *BTWP,* 8: 356–357; "Three Reports of Pinkerton Detectives, October 22, 23, and 24, 1905," ibid., 418–421.

23. Montgomery *Advertiser,* August 21, 1905; BTW to Charles Woodroph Hare, August 22, 1905; BTW to John C. Asbury, October 2, 1905; BTW to George H. Woodson, September 13, 1905, in *BTWP,* 8: 344–345, 387–388, 357–358.

24. David Fort Godshalk, *Veiled Visions: The 1906 Atlanta Race Riot and the Reshaping of American Race Relations* (Chapel Hill, 2005), 36; Thomas Dixon Jr. to BTW, January 22 and 23, 1906, in *BTWP,* 8: 508–509.

25. BTW to Francis Jackson Garrison, October 5, 1905; Garrison to BTW, October 12, 1905, in *BTWP,* 8: 394–396, 402.

26. C. Vann Woodward, *Origins of the New South, 1877–1913* (Baton Rouge, 1951), 466.

27. "Three Reports of Pinkerton Detectives," 418, 419, 420.

28. Francis Jackson Garrison to BTW, October 25, 1905, in *BTWP,* 8: 433.

29. Chicago *Tribune,* October 29, 1905.

30. Samuel Laing Williams to Emmett Jay Scott, October 31, 1905, in *BTWP,* 8: 434–435; "Narratives in the Slave Narrative Collection by State," at http://memory.loc.gov/ammem/snhtml/snintro18.html. The following life histories discuss Booker T. Washington: Perry Sid Jemison, Ohio narratives, vol. 12, 54; ex-slave, South Carolina narratives, vol. 14, 27; Jane Montgomery, Oklahoma narratives, vol. 13, 229; Bert Luster, Oklahoma narratives, ibid., 206; Mary Ella Grandberry, Alabama narratives, vol. 1, 7.

31. To find persons named Booker and Booker T., go to www.ancestry.com.

32. BTW to Francis Jackson Garrison, November 25, 1905, in *BTWP,* 8: 449–450; Fort Worth *Star-Telegram,* May 10, 1903, and November 22, 1905; Kansas City *Star,* November 19, 1905; BTW to Robert Curtis Ogden, November 16, 1905; BTW to Garrison, January 10, 1906, in *BTWP,* 8: 443–444, 491–492.

33. Atlanta *Constitution,* April 5 and 6, 1906.

34. "An Address on the Twenty-fifth Anniversary of Tuskegee Institute, April 4, 1906," in *BTWP,* 8: 564–565.

35. Montgomery *Advertiser,* April 7, 1906.

36. "An Account of the Twenty-fifth Anniversary of Tuskegee Institute by Jesse Max Barber [in *Voice of the Negro*], May 1906," in *BTWP,* 9: 15–24; Archibald Grimké to BTW, January 10, 1906; Emmett Jay Scott to James Griswold

Merrill, December 4, 1905; BTW to Fortune, February 21, 1906, in *BTWP*, 8: 495, 460, 531.

37. Fortune to Jesse Max Barber, April 5, 1906; BTW to Charles William Anderson, September 29, 1905, in *BTWP*, 8: 568–569, 380–381.

38. Stephen R. Fox, *The Guardian of Boston: William Monroe Trotter* (New York, 1970), 101–102; Theodore W. Jones to BTW, January 28, 1904, in *BTWP*, 7: 417–419.

14. The Tragedy of Color

1. C. Vann Woodward, *Tom Watson: Agrarian Rebel* (New York, 1938), 374; Dewey W. Grantham, *Hoke Smith and the Politics of the New South* (Baton Rouge, 1958), 150–151.

2. Grantham, *Hoke Smith*, 152–155.

3. Harlan, *Wizard*, 297.

4. David Fort Godshalk, *Veiled Visions: The 1906 Atlanta Race Riot and the Reshaping of American Race Relations* (Chapel Hill, 2005), 85–114, quotations on 85–86; Mark Baurlein, *Negrophobia: A Race Riot in Atlanta, 1906* (San Francisco, 2001), 142–172.

5. Walter White, *A Man Called White* (New York, 1948), 3–12, quotations on 11.

6. Godshalk, *Veiled Visions*, 85–114.

7. Harlan, *Wizard*, 301–303.

8. "An Article in *Outlook*, December 15, 1906"; Theodore Roosevelt to BTW, October 8, 1906; BTW to Christopher James Perry, October 5, 1906, in *BTWP*, 9: 168, 92, 86–97.

9. David Levering Lewis, *W. E. B. Du Bois: Biography of a Race, 1868–1919* (New York, 1993), 336; BTW to editor of New York *Age*, October 1, 1906, in *BTWP*, 9: 82–83.

10. Emma Lou Thornbrough, *T. Thomas Fortune: Militant Journalist* (Chicago, 1972), 279; Harlan, *Wizard*, 299–300; "Extracts from an Address before the Afro-American Council, October 11, 1906," in *BTWP*, 9: 94–96; Thornbrough, *Fortune*, 280–281.

11. BTW to Wallace Buttrick, September 30, 1906; BTW to Francis Jackson Garrison, October 2, 1906; BTW to Charles Waddell Chesnutt, October 29, 1906; "An Article in *Outlook*, December 15, 1906," in *BTWP*, 9: 78–80, 92–94, 112, 168–174.

12. John D. Weaver, *The Senator and the Sharecropper's Son: Exoneration of the Brownsville Soldiers* (College Station, Tex., 1997), 109; Edmund Morris, *Theodore Rex* (New York, 2001), 453–467.

13. BTW to Roosevelt, November 2, 1906, in *BTWP,* 9: 113.

14. William Henry Harbaugh, *The Life and Times of Theodore Roosevelt* (1961; reprint, New York, 1975), 291; Emma Lou Thornbrough, "The Brownsville Episode and the Negro Vote," *Mississippi Valley Historical Review* 44 (December 1957): 471.

15. Thornbrough, *Fortune,* 282; Lewis N. Wynne, "Brownsville: The Reaction of the Negro Press," *Phylon* 33 (2d quarter, 1972): 155; Washington *Post,* November 16 and 22, 1906; Atlanta *Constitution,* November 14, 1906; Thornbrough, "Brownsville Episode," 472–473.

16. Oswald Garrison Villard to BTW, November 16, 1906, in *BTWP,* 9: 129.

17. Washington *Post,* November 20, 1906; Atlanta *Constitution,* November 27, 1906; New York *Times,* November 8, 1906.

18. BTW to Charles William Anderson, November 7, 1906; Anderson to BTW, November 10, 1906, in *BTWP,* 9: 118–119, 123–124; New York *Times,* December 16, 1906.

19. BTW to William Howard Taft, November 20, 1906, in *BTWP,* 9: 141; Harlan, *Wizard,* 313.

20. Morris, *Theodore Rex,* 458–459, 490.

21. Thomas G. Dyer, *Theodore Roosevelt and the Idea of Race* (Baton Rouge, 1980), 105; BTW to Roosevelt, January 4, 1906; Charles William Anderson to Emmett Jay Scott, February 3, 1906, in *BTWP,* 9: 486, 516–517.

22. BTW to Samuel Laing Williams, December 3, 1906; BTW to Ralph Waldo Tyler, December 5, 1906, in *BTWP,* 9: 152–154; Thornbrough, "Brownsville Episode," 472–473.

23. New York *Times,* December 5, 1906.

24. Kelly Miller to BTW, November 16, 1906; Timothy Thomas Fortune to BTW, December, 8, 1906, in *BTWP,* 9: 129–131, 156–158.

25. Roosevelt to Ray Stannard Baker, March 30, 1907, Ray Stannard Baker Papers, reel 25, Library of Congress; Morris, *Theodore Rex,* 471–474, 478–480.

26. Wynne, "Brownsville," 158; Roosevelt to Baker, March 30, 1907.

27. H. G. Wells, *The Future in America* (1906; reprint, New York, 1987), 147–149; Wells, "The Tragedy of Color," *Harper's Weekly,* September 15, 1906.

15. THE MAN FARTHEST DOWN

1. BTW to Portia Marshall Washington, November 15, 1906, in *BTWP,* 9: 127.

2. Harlan, *Wizard,* 107–123.

3. BTW to George Bruce Cortelyou, September 15, 1905, in *BTWP,* 8: 361–362; Harlan, *Wizard,* 123–127.

4. Marcus M. Marks to BTW, May 24, 1904, in *BTWP,* 7: 512; information on

Jacob Schiff, in *BTWP,* 8: 254; Harlan, *Wizard,* 140; information on attitudes to Jews, in *BTWP,* 3: 412; BTW to Lloyd G. Wheeler, October 17, 1904, in *BTWP,* 8: 96–97.

5. "A List of Pledges to the Tuskegee Institute Five-Year Fund, 1912," in *BTWP,* 12: 96–98.

6. Seth Low to BTW, May 29, 1907; BTW to Low, June 18, 1907; Charles William Eliot to BTW, September 7, 1906, in *BTWP,* 9: 281–284, 297–300, 71–72.

7. BTW to Edgar James Penney, January 19, 1907; Horace Bumstead to BTW, April 10, 1907; Edgar James Penney to BTW, January 16, 1907; BTW to Estelle C. Penney, January 19, 1907; Edgar James Penney to BTW, February 6, 1907, in *BTWP,* 9: 195, 259, 187–190, 195–196, 212–216.

8. George Washington Carver to BTW, October 14, 1904, in *BTWP,* 8: 95; BTW to Carver, February 26, 1911, in *BTWP,* 10: 594; Carver to BTW, September 14, 1911; BTW to Carver, June 12, 1912, in *BTWP,* 11: 312, 551–552; BTW to Carver, December 27, 1912; Carver to BTW, December 28, 1912; BTW to Carver, August 14, 1913, in *BTWP,* 12: 93–95, 251–252; Harlan, *Wizard,* 146–149.

9. "An Item in the *Tuskegee Student,* November 17, 1906"; "An Article in *World's Work,* December 1906," in *BTWP,* 9: 132, 175–181; Allen W. Jones, "The Role of Tuskegee Institute in the Education of Black Farmers," *Journal of Negro History* 60 (1975): 252–267.

10. Harlan, *Wizard,* 212; Jones, "Role of Tuskegee in Education."

11. Robert E. Zabawa and Sarah T. Warren, "From Company to Community: Agricultural Community Development in Macon County, Alabama, 1881 to the New Deal," *Agricultural History* 72 (Spring 1998): 468.

12. BTW to James Hardy Dillard, July 30, 1909, in *BTWP,* 10: 152–153; BTW to Wallace Buttrick, June 19, 1908, in *BTWP,* 9: 583; Harlan, *Wizard,* 192–194; "An Account of Washington's Louisiana Tour by William Anthony Acry, June 19, 1915," in *BTWP,* 13: 321–330.

13. BTW to George Foster Peabody, April 2, 1909, in *BTWP,* 10: 83–84.

14. Peter M. Ascoli, *Julius Rosenwald: The Man Who Built Sears, Roebuck and Advanced the Cause of Black Education in the American South* (Baton Rouge, 2006), 135–158.

15. Ibid., 139; BTW to James Longstreet Sibley, May 26, 1915, in *BTWP,* 13: 294.

16. Mary S. Hoffschwelle, *The Rosenwald Schools of the American South* (Gainesville, Fla., 2006); Edwin R. Embree and Julia Waxman, *Investment in People: The Story of the Julius Rosenwald Fund* (New York, 1944).

17. BTW to George Augustus Gates, October 7, 1909; BTW to Andrew Carnegie, November 13, 1909, in *BTWP,* 10: 181–182, 196.

18. Linda O. McMurry, "A Black Intellectual in the New South: Monroe Nathan Work, 1866–1945," *Phylon* 41 (4th quarter, 1980): 333–344.

19. Fred H. Matthews, *Quest for an American Sociology: Robert E. Park and the Chicago School* (Montreal, 1977), 62; Park statement, n.d., Robert E. Park Papers, box 11, folder 1, Special Collections, University of Chicago Library.

20. BTW, The *Story of the Negro: The Rise of the Race from Slavery,* 2 vols. (New York, 1909), excerpt in *BTWP,* 1: 403, 410.

21. *Larger Education,* 418–458, quotations on 428, 431.

22. "A Notebook of Washington's Tour of Europe, August 28–October 7, 1910," in *BTWP,* 10: 368–376; Matthews, *Quest for an American Sociology,* 66; Harlan, *Wizard,* 292–294.

23. Harlan, *Wizard,* 271–273.

24. Howard Dorgan, "'Pitchfork Ben' Tillman and 'The Race Problem from a Southern Point of View,'" in *The Oratory of Southern Demagogues,* ed. Cal M. Logue and Howard Dorgan (Baton Rouge, 1981), 51; BTW to James Hardy Dillard, March 20, 1909; BTW to Edgar Gardner Murphy, April 1, 1909, in *BTWP,* 10: 73–74, 79–80.

25. "An Article in the *A.M.E. Church Review* by Hightower T. Kealing, October, 1908"; BTW to Oswald Garrison Villard, October 21, 1908, in *BTWP,* 9: 674–675, 666–667.

26. BTW to Charles Banks, February 1, 1910, in *BTWP,* 10: 266–267; BTW to Seth Low, October 8, 1908; BTW to Francis Garrison, October 10 and 21, 1908; BTW to Oswald Garrison Villard, October 30, 1908, in *BTWP,* 9: 647–649, 664–665, 671–672.

27. "An Address by William Taylor Burwell Williams on Washington's Tour of Virginia, July 4, 1909," in *BTWP,* 10: 73–74, 79–80, 128, 143–149; "Accounts of Washington Tour of Tennessee, November 18–December 10, 1909," ibid., 202–236.

28. "An Account of Washington's North Carolina Tour by William Henry Lewis, November 12, 1910," ibid., 456, 467.

29. Ibid., 468.

16. The Leader of the Race

1. Roberta Senechal, *The Sociogenesis of a Race Riot: Springfield, Illinois, in 1908* (Urbana, 1990), 2, 108–148, 195.

2. "A Statement on Lynching, August 19, 1908," in *BTWP,* 9: 611–613.

3. Ray Stannard Baker, *Following the Color Line: An Account of Negro Citizenship in the American Democracy* (New York, 1908), 109–134.

4. Ibid., 26–27, 44.

5. Ibid., 80–84; BTW to Ray Stannard Baker, May 23, 1907, in *BTWP,* 9: 272; John Michael Matthews, "The Georgia 'Race' Strike of 1909," *Journal of Southern History* 40 (November 1974): 613–630.

6. Baker, *Following the Color Line,* 220–223.

7. BTW to Thomas Jesse Jones, July 2, 1910; BTW to Benjamin Jefferson Davis, October 16, 1910, in *BTWP,* 10: 352, 405–406; Emma Lou Thornbrough, *T. Thomas Fortune: Militant Journalist* (Chicago, 1972), 312.

8. Harlan, *Wizard,* 323–337; BTW to Frederick Randolph Moore, July 7, 1908, in *BTWP,* 9: 590.

9. Paolo Coletta, *The Presidency of William Howard Taft* (Lawrence, Kans., 1973); Henry F. Pringle, *The Life and Times of William Howard Taft* (New York, 1939).

10. Mary White Ovington to Ray Stannard Baker, November 12, 1906; Ovington to Ida Tarbell, n.d., Ray Stannard Baker Papers, reel 25, Library of Congress; Ovington to Baker, October 17, 1907, ibid., reel 26; William Henry Ferris to BTW, January 24, 1908, in *BTWP,* 9: 446–447; David Levering Lewis, *W. E. B. Du Bois: Biography of a Race, 1868–1919* (New York, 1993), 349; Harlan, *Wizard,* 376–377.

11. Oswald Garrison Villard to BTW, January 27, 1908, Oswald Garrison Villard Papers, folder 405-9, Harvard University; Villard to Ray Stannard Baker, August 29, 1908, Ray Stannard Baker Papers, reel 26; Villard to Francis Jackson Garrison, April 15, 1909, folder 1460, Villard Papers; Villard to Garrison, August 19, 1910, ibid., folder 1461.

12. William Lloyd Garrison Jr. to editor of Boston *Transcript,* January 11, 1908, in *BTWP,* 9: 438–440; Villard to BTW, May 26, 1909, in *BTWP,* 10: 118.

13. Villard to BTW, May 26, 1909; BTW to Villard, May 28, 1909, in *BTWP,* 10: 116–119.

14. "An Editorial in the New York *Evening Post,* April 1, 1910," in *BTWP,* 10: 309–310; Charles Flint Kellogg, *NAACP: A History of the National Association for the Advancement of Colored People, 1909–20* (Baltimore, 1967), 9–46; Lewis, *Du Bois,* 386–434.

15. BTW to Ray Stannard Baker, May 24, 1910, in *BTWP,* 10: 333–334.

16. Villard to Charles Dyer Norton, September 20, 1910; "A Circular Letter by John Elmer Milholland, October 6, 1910"; "A News Item in the London *Times,* October 7, 1910," in *BTWP,* 10: 385–387, 394–404.

17. "An Open Letter to the People of Great Britain and Europe by William Edward Burghardt Du Bois and Others, October 26, 1910"; Villard to BTW, December 13, 1910; BTW to Villard, January 10, 1911, ibid., 422, 506, 541.

18. BTW to Timothy Thomas Fortune, January 20, 1911; Fortune to BTW, January 23, 1911, ibid., 555, 557.

19. "Accounts of Washington's Tour of Tennessee, November 18–December 10, 1909," ibid., 229, 232.

20. The description of the incident in this and the following paragraphs is drawn from Harlan, *Wizard,* 379–404.

21. Gilchrist Stewart to BTW, March 28, 1911, in *BTWP,* 11: 50–51; Harlan, *Wizard,* 394.

22. Harlan, *Wizard,* 394–395.

23. "An Article in the New York *World,* November 7, 1911," in *BTWP,* 11: 359–362.

24. BTW to Francis James Grimké and Archibald Henry Grimké, April 6, 1911; Peter Jefferson Smith Jr. to Emmett Jay Scott, April 18, 1911, ibid., 85, 106–108; Harlan, *Wizard,* 395–396.

25. Kellogg, *NAACP,* 80–83; Villard to Robert Russa Moton, April 5, 1911; BTW to Villard, April 19 and March 30, 1911, in *BTWP,* 11: 83, 109, 54–55; Harlan, *Wizard,* 392–393.

26. Addison Wimbs to BTW, November 8, 1911, in *BTWP,* 11: 363.

27. Lewis, *Du Bois,* 433–434; *Crisis,* June and July 1911.

17. THE MORNING COMETH

1. Karl R. Wallace, "Booker T. Washington," in *A History and Criticism of American Public Address,* ed. William Norwood Brigance (New York, 1943), 422.

2. "An Account of Washington's Tour of Louisiana in the Chicago *Herald,* April 25, 1915," in *BTWP,* 13: 281–283.

3. Harlan, *Wizard,* 338–358.

4. *Crisis,* August 1912, 181; Morton Sosna, "The South in the Saddle: Racial Politics during the Wilson Years," *Wisconsin Magazine of History* 54 (Autumn 1970): 31; Nancy J. Weiss, "The Negro and the New Freedom: Fighting Wilsonian Segregation," *Political Science Quarterly* 84 (March 1969): 61–79; Kathleen Long Wolgemuth, "Woodrow Wilson's Appointment Policy and the Negro," *Journal of Southern History* 24 (November 1958): 462–463; Harlan, *Wizard,* 410.

5. Harlan, *Wizard,* 414–417.

6. Pete Daniel, *The Shadow of Slavery: Peonage in the South, 1901–1969* (Urbana, 1990), 65–81.

7. *Atlantic Monthly,* June 1913.

8. BTW, "Is the Negro Having a Fair Chance?" *Century,* November 1912, in *BTWP,* 12: 64–82.

9. *Crisis,* December 1912.

10. Harlan, *Wizard,* 419.

11. "An Account of Washington's Louisiana Tour, June 19, 1915," in *BTWP,* 13: 325; BTW to William Malone Baskervill, February 12, 1913, in *BTWP,* 12: 115–117; BTW to editor of New York *World,* January 16, 1915, in *BTWP,* 13: 227–228.

12. Harlan, *Wizard,* 423–425.

13. Thomas Woofter Jr., ed., *Negro Problems in Cities: A Study* (New York, 1928), 26–33; *Crisis,* December 1910 and February 1912; BTW to George B, Ward, July 13, 1914, in *BTWP,* 13: 86.

14. BTW, "My View of the Segregation Laws," *New Republic,* December 4, 1915.

15. Al-Tony Gilmore, *Bad Nigger! The National Impact of Jack Johnson* (Port Washington, N.Y., 1975), 9–120; Gilchrist Stewart to BTW, December 16, 1912, in *BTWP,* 12: 89–90.

16. Thomas Cripps, *Slow Fade to Black: The Negro in American Film, 1900–1942* (New York, 1977), 41–69; Donald Bogle, *Toms, Coons, Mulattoes, Mammies, and Bucks: An Interpretive History of Blacks in American Films,* 3d ed. (New York, 1999), 3–10; Harlan, *Wizard,* 431–434; Emmett Jay Scott to BTW, October 28, 1915, in *BTWP,* 13: 416–417; Ed Guerrero, *Framing Blackness: The African American Image in Film* (Philadelphia, 1993), 12–15.

17. Harlan, *Wizard,* 427.

18. BTW to Oswald Garrison Villard, March 21, 1913; Villard to BTW, April 4, 1913; Seth Low to Villard, April 9, 1913, in *BTWP,* 12: 144–145, 159–161, 166–167.

19. BTW to Emmett Jay Scott, January 16, 1914, ibid., 417.

20. "Patient History of Booker T. Washington, Hospital of the Rockefeller Institute [November 1915]," document provided to author by Paulette Horton, Mobile, Alabama; George Perley Phenix to BTW, November 13, 1914; BTW to Phenix, November 16, 1914; Emmett Jay Scott to Henry Hugh Proctor, March 23, 1915; Scott to Robert Russa Moton, September 4, 1915; BTW to Fritz George Schmidt, September 17, 1915; George Washington Albert Johnston to BTW, October 4, 1915; BTW to George Cleveland Hall, October 16, 1915; Hall to Julius Rosenwald, October 25, 1915, in *BTWP,* 13: 171, 173–174, 258, 351–352, 365–366, 377–378, 387–388, 409–410. Paulette Horton is convinced that Washington's death was the result of poisoning. The evidence available to me does not support that conclusion but rather that kidney failure, arising from high blood pressure and perhaps diabetes, was the cause of death.

21. "Extracts from an Address at the Opening of the Mound Bayou Cotton-Oil

Mill, November 25, 1912," in *BTWP,* 12: 55, 59, 60; "A Memorandum on Washington's Itinerary, February 20, 1914," ibid., 448–450.

22. "An Address before the National Negro Business League, August 20, 1913," ibid., 264–265.

23. Harlan, *Wizard,* 451–452.

24. "An Account of Washington's Funeral by Isaac Fisher, November 18, 1915," in *BTWP,* 13: 453–458.

18. THE VEIL OF HISTORY

1. Madame C. J. Walker to Margaret James Murray Washington, November 15, 1915; Charles William Anderson to Emmett Jay Scott, November 16, 1915; "An Editorial in the *New Republic,* November 20, 1915," in *BTWP,* 13: 449–451, 462–464; *Crisis,* December 1915.

2. William G. Willcox to Julius Rosenwald, November 19, 1915; Emmett Jay Scott to Frederick Randolph Moore, November 24, 1915; James Carroll Napier to Rosenwald, November 30, 1915; Theodore Roosevelt to Julius Rosenwald, December 15, 1915; Rosenwald to Seth Low, December 16, 1915, in *BTWP,* 13: 459–461, 465, 471–472, 480–481, 482–484.

3. James Weldon Johnson, *Along This Way: The Autobiography of James Weldon Johnson* (New York, 1903).

4. Marcus Mosiah Garvey to BTW, September 8, 1914; April 12 and September 11 and 27, 1915; BTW to Garvey, September 17, 1914, and April 27 and October 2, 1915, in *BTWP,* 13: 126–127, 261, 354–355, 372—373, 133–134, 284, 376.

5. Ronald Court to author, July 24, 2007, in author's possession. Court heads the Booker T. Washington Society, an organization that promotes appreciation of Washington among students who attend schools named for him.

6. Horace M. Bond, "Negro Leadership since Washington," *South Atlantic Quarterly* 24 (April 1925): 116–117; Kelly Miller, "Washington's Policy," Boston *Evening Transcript,* September 18–19, 1903, quoted in Hugh Hawkins, *Booker T. Washington and His Critics: Black Leadership in Crisis* (Lexington, Mass., 1974), 89–90; Kelly Miller, *The Everlasting Stain* (1923; reprint, New York, 1968), 264; Woodson quoted in August Meier and Elliott Rudwick, *Black History and the Historical Profession 1915–1980* (Urbana, 1986), 11.

7. Charles S. Johnson, "The Social Philosophy of Booker T. Washington," *Opportunity* 6 (April 1928): 102–106, 115.

8. Sterling D. Spero and Abram L. Harris, *The Black Worker: The Negro and the Labor Movement* (New York, 1931), 49–52.

9. W. E. B. Du Bois, *Dusk of Dawn* (New York, 1940), 23, 72, 78–79.

10. Ibid., 76; Pete Daniel, "Black Power in the 1920s: The Case of Tuskegee Veterans Hospital," *Journal of Southern History* 36 (August 1970): 383.

11. Charles S. Johnson, *Shadow of the Plantation* (Chicago, 1934), 103–128.

12. New York *Times*, April 3, 1940, September 30, 1942, and July 16, 1946.

13. Robert J. Norrell, *Reaping the Whirlwind: The Civil Rights Movement in Tuskegee* (New York, 1985), 46–52.

14. Ibid., 41–127.

15. Ibid., 203–221.

16. J. L. Chestnut Jr. and Julia Cass, *Black in Selma: The Uncommon Life of J. L. Chestnut, Jr.* (New York, 1990), 49; Martin Luther King Jr., *Stride toward Freedom: The Montgomery Story* (1958; reprint, New York, 1964), 48, 87; Stephen B. Oates, *Let the Trumpet Sound: The Life of Martin Luther King, Jr.* (New York, 1982), 130; John Lewis with Michael D'Orso, *Walking with the Wind: A Memoir of the Movement* (New York, 1998), 18, 227; King, *Why We Can't Wait* (New York, 1964), 33; Eldridge Cleaver, *Soul on Ice* (New York, 1968), 81.

17. John Hope Franklin, *From Slavery to Freedom: A History of American Negroes* (New York, 1947), 386–391; Rayford W. Logan, *The Negro in American Life and Thought: The Nadir, 1877–1901* (New York, 1954), 280; August Meier, "Toward a Reinterpretation of Booker T. Washington," *Journal of Southern History* 23 (May 1957): 220–227; Meier, *Negro Thought in America, 1880–1915* (Ann Arbor, 1963). In 1955 Samuel R. Spencer Jr. offered what would be the last generally sympathetic treatment of Washington for a half-century in *Booker T. Washington and the Negro's Place in American Life* (Boston, 1955).

18. C. Vann Woodward, *Origins of the New South, 1877–1913* (Baton Rouge, 1951), 218, 323, 359, 366–367, 365.

19. Harlan, *Making*, vii–viii, 157, 160, 227, 228, 324; Louis R. Harlan, "Sympathy and Detachment: Dilemmas of a Biographer," in *Booker T. Washington in Perspective: Essays of Louis R. Harlan*, ed. Raymond W. Smock (Jackson, Miss., 1988), 187–188; Harlan and Raymond W. Smock, "The Booker T. Washington Papers," ibid., 183; Harlan, "Washington: The Labyrinth and the Thread," ibid, 199.

20. In the fourteen volumes of published Washington papers, Harlan included none of the documents demonstrating the white-nationalist assault on Booker. He did include a wealth of documents about the intensifying opposition to black education, but he hardly discussed them in the biography.

21. See Joel Williamson, *The Crucible of Race: Black-White Relations in the American South since Emancipation* (New York, 1984), 55–57; David Levering Lewis, *W. E. B. Du Bois: Biography of a Race* (New York, 1993), 265–342; Kevin K. Gaines, *Uplifting the Race: Black Leadership, Politics, and Culture in the Twentieth Century* (Chapel Hill, 1996); Houston A. Baker Jr., *Turning*

South Again: Re-thinking Modernism / Re-reading Booker T. (Durham, N.C., 2001), 56–78. In contrast to Harlan, who apparently was unsympathetic to his subject from start to finish, Baker offered a sympathetic view of Washington's strategy in *Modernism and the Harlem Renaissance* (Chicago, 1987), but his reinterpretation in *Turning South Again* almost outdoes Harlan in its condemnation of Washington. For examples of studies hostile to Tuskegee's educational approach, see Donald Spivey, *Schooling for the New Slavery: Black Industrial Education, 1868–1915* (Westport, Conn., 1978); and James Anderson, *The Education of the Blacks in the South, 1860–1935* (Chapel Hill, 1988).

Acknowledgments

The Social Philosophy and Policy Center at Bowling Green State University advanced the writing of this book by giving me a supportive and pleasant environment and research assistance during the summer of 2007. Fred Miller and especially Jeff Paul encouraged my thinking and significantly accelerated my writing. The Social Philosophy and Policy Center nurtures a broad community of scholars who are working on important problems, often from new and otherwise unappreciated angles, and I was fortunate to be included in its circle.

My largest personal debt in the writing of this book is to W. Fitzhugh Brundage of the University of North Carolina, who encouraged my interest in the subject by listening to my contrarian views, creating a venue for me to develop them, and then guiding my interpretation of Booker T. Washington. Jonathan Bean of Southern Illinois University took a keen early interest in my work and encouraged it in many different ways, including giving a close reading of the manuscript. James Cox, professor emeritus at Dartmouth College, provided shrewd insight into Washington's writing and much-appreciated enthusiasm for my efforts. Ernest Freeberg of the University of Tennessee brought his superb literary skill to a valuable critique of the manuscript. Waldo Martin of the University of California at Berkeley identified several shortcomings of interpretation and thus saved me from error. I benefited from the critical look at portions of this book by Lawrence Kohl of the University of Alabama and Dan Smith of the University of Kentucky. Three graduate students at the University of Tennessee—Paul

Coker, Neal Davidson, and John Kvach—provided valuable research assistance.

Three people interested in the life of Booker T. Washington have encouraged me in the development of this book, most notably Lee Walker of the New Coalition for Economic and Social Change in Chicago, who has done much in promoting the study of Booker Washington. Charles Thompson of Tuskegee and Ronald Court of the Booker T. Washington Society have bolstered me with their enthusiasm.

Various folks helped me in essential ways. While writing I benefited from the generous hospitality of Lynne Berry, Sandy Lubin, and Kay Anderson. The book might not have come into being without the intrepid help of Geri Thoma, friend through thick and thin. Joyce Seltzer of Harvard University Press reached out when Booker and I needed a helping hand. Ann Hawthorne's sharp editorial eye improved every page in this book. I am always able to count on the available ear of Lorri Glover, the constant concern of Jane Cooley, and the steady affection of Lissa Gay. My four children were adorable little kids and now are loving, admirable adults, and it is my honor to dedicate this book to them.

Index